THIS YEAR'S MODEL

This Year's Model

Fashion, Media, and the Making of Glamour

Elizabeth A. Wissinger

NEW YORK UNIVERSITY PRESS

New York and London

NEW YORK UNIVERSITY PRESS
New York and London
www.nyupress.org

References to Internet websites (URLs) were accurate at the time of writing.
Neither the author nor New York University Press is responsible for URLs
that may have expired or changed since the manuscript was prepared.

ISBN: 978-0-8147-9418-0 (hardback)
ISBN: 978-1-4798-6477-5 (paperback)

For Library of Congress Cataloging-in-Publication data, please contact the
Library of Congress.

New York University Press books are printed on acid-free paper,
and their binding materials are chosen for strength and durability.
We strive to use environmentally responsible suppliers and materials
to the greatest extent possible in publishing our books.

Manufactured in the United States of America

10 9 8 7 6 5 4 3 2 1

Also available as an ebook

This book is dedicated to Patrick and Cassielle Campi.

Patrick—thank you for making it possible.

Cassielle—thank you for keeping it real.

CONTENTS

"You should be a model." During my teenaged suburban youth, living on the outskirts of New York City, I heard it often enough to strongly consider it. Modeling represented a short-circuit escape from the stifling hell of adolescence into instant womanhood and an indisputable confirmation of one's beauty, legitimacy, and worth. I sincerely believed models had few self-doubts and were readily accepted by other people and that they were supremely self-confident and had high self-esteem, qualities I knew I sorely lacked.

I felt the first pull toward modeling when I was twelve. My junior high choral group's photo had appeared in the town newspaper, and a local photographer called my home to ask if I wanted to be a model. Would I! I could barely contain my excitement as I answered his questions. In my naiveté, I thought I had been discovered, that my chance for escape was at hand. Sensing something was up, my mother intervened, and through careful questioning of her own discovered that he wanted to shoot lingerie on little girls. I protested but eventually agreed that maybe this wasn't the break I'd been looking for.

Once awakened to the dream of modeling, I had to live with it. I carried it into high school; it seemed that every girl over 5'7" was hung up on the same idea. My friend Diane was not model pretty. She was blond and slim, however, and her height matched the magic number, so she felt the pull of modeling even more than I (at 5'6", I was beginning to wonder if I would ever be tall enough). We talked about it sometimes during freshman biology lab, when things were slow. We dissected frogs and discussed sending photos to agencies in nearby New York City. We drew amoebas and wondered whether we had it, whatever "it" was that won an agency contract. We diagramed ecosystems and dreamed of a different life.

Diane and I were acutely aware of one problem, however: our weight. We were both normal girls by medical standards, but everybody knew normal-weight girls are too fat to be models! When our dream came true for another girl in our class, our suspicions were confirmed. Sue Anne Kluge,[1] a very attractive girl who already looked like a model, had been picked up by an agency and was to appear in our monthly must-read, *Seventeen* magazine. Our anticipation was intense—a girl among us was to be immortalized! Yet when the story appeared, it sent shock waves through our small circle. There it was in black and white (with color photographs)! The experts had spoken: Gorgeous and skinny Sue Anne was too fat to be a model! Sue Anne's coveted modeling job turned out to be a story about how she needed to lose weight if she wanted to model again. I still remember pictures of the diet and exercise program prescribed: Sue Anne eating broccoli, Sue Anne swimming laps. Soon after the story appeared, Sue Anne had a new moniker that rhymed with her last name; she was stuck with "Sue Anne Huge" for the rest of her high school career.

Of course this meant the modeling prospects for the rest of us mere mortals were doomed. If Sue Anne was not up to their standards, we didn't stand a chance. By the age of seventeen, this realization was less momentous, as I'd begun to lose faith in my ability to grow any taller. Still one-half inch shy of the industry cutoff of 5′7″, I replaced my dream of escape via modeling with the reality of escape to college.

During those years, a career in modeling took a back seat to plans for becoming an attorney, a professor, an arts professional. There was the occasional pang of jealousy when the local photographer consistently chose my classmate Kelly as a subject. A small-timer with a big head, his greatest accomplishments were the yearly college calendar and an occasional show at the local bank. In retrospect, I realize his creative work with Kelly was amateurish at best, but during our years at a small New England college, Kelly's status as a model conferred a distinct aura; she was special, she was the one he chose. She seemed to live a charmed life: A photographer's muse had the objective status of "beautiful" conferred by a reputable source; what more could a girl want?

After college, I moved to the big city: New York. Not to become a model, although the thought still crossed my mind. By my early twenties, the pursuit of "cool" had become a full-time occupation. By the time I reached the age of twenty-three, New York's promise of the glamorous life had drawn me into a career in the arts and an effort to socialize on the New York scene. For the former, I had found a chic job at an arts institute on the Upper East Side. For the latter, I was aided and abetted by my boyfriend at the time, a fashion photographer whom I'd met shortly after my arrival in town. My life with him gave models another layer of meaning. I was in their world, if not of it; I shared the occasional banquette with an aspiring model and took inordinate pride in being mistaken for one—which I was, from time to time. I even got scouted a couple of times—a model agent tried to make my acquaintance in a Miami Beach restaurant; I met another at a party who told me to come by his agency the next day; a third stopped me in the street. I never had the courage to pursue those leads and knew that, at twenty-three, I was already too old to have any kind of career. My boyfriend's more intimate knowledge of the world I would have been entering sealed the deal, as he strongly cautioned me against it.

Eventually I did do some modeling jobs: When no funds were available to hire a real model, my boyfriend would toss me into the frame to get a shot of that one last outfit for whichever client he was currently shooting. I also donated my services to some of his friends. I modeled in exchange for products in his friend's magazine; a struggling photographer friend shot me to produce a catalog on a shoestring; and another put me in a group shot to sell sportswear. Even though I had this experience, hung out with models, and had gotten to know some of them, I knew I was an outsider with temporary insider status, someone who blended in with the crowd without being one with it. During those years, I got just enough exposure and experience to pique my interest in the world models inhabit. Without question it is a different world.

When I finally started graduate school, I left the world of glamour and fashion behind for my new role as graduate student. Or so I thought. I soon discovered, however, that when I brought up examples from that world in class or used it as the basis for a paper, I got positive feedback and piqued others' interest in this world as well. I pursued the topic and ultimately was able to turn this fascination into fieldwork. So, in the end, I *was* able to make more of myself, to realize my potential, and stretch myself beyond existing limits, but along a different path. It took a lot longer than a career in modeling may have, but I have to say, it was well worth the trip.

ACKNOWLEDGMENTS

Thanks are in order to so many, this abbreviated space will no doubt leave someone out, and for that I am sorry; you know who you are, and to you, I am also very grateful.

Many a research study begins with just one person, and this is no exception. Well, there are two. For the suggestion that started it all, I am grateful to Sharon Zukin, whose urban sociology class helped me see modeling as a research topic long before studying models became a "thing." The idea to investigate modeling sociologically would have been dead in the water, however, without my dear friend and associate Renée Torrière. Renée, I can't thank you enough for being my informant, inside track, and mega-conduit to the secret sacred world of modeling. You introduced me to some wonderful people, and I feel lucky to have met them. I am particularly grateful to the fashion stylist, whose name I've purposely forgotten, my first ever interview, in a sleek café where I felt completely out of place. No question was too dumb, and by admiring my lopsided attempt to style up my Jansen backpack with some rhinestone buttons, she gave me the jolt of confidence I needed to press on with my investigation. To all who took the time to meet with me or take me along, sharing the intimate details of your working lives, your generosity was amazing, and I thank you for it.

A project of this scope needs proper, consistent, and unstinting mentorship, and for that I am forever indebted to Patricia Clough—a tireless, uncompromising, inspirational, funny, kind, fantastic guiding light, who did not hesitate to remind me not to be stupid! Similarly, Stanley Aronowitz, thank you for being a brilliant interlocutor and lecturer. I had the pleasure of soaking up your ideas just about every single day for nine years, and I shall always be grateful for your courageous insistence on avoiding "scholarsh&t" by pushing us to return to the essential question, "What is at stake?"

I would have been lost at sea in the storm of ideas that was that thing called "graduate school" had it not been for my study group, sometimes known as the Women of Sociology. We helped each other through oral exams, dissertation distress, cheered each other on to marriages, babies, and tenure, and I hope we will continue to rally for one another through to our dotage! For their support of this project, acute commentary, and belief in me, I shall always be grateful to Ariel Ducey, Michelle Ronda, Lorna Mason, Ananya Mukherjea, Jeff Bussolini, and Gina Neff (more on her later). Most important, thank you for helping me see that I am not a frog!

Also in order are thanks to the intrepid readers in the craft of inquiry classes lead by the late, much beloved Bob Alford. I recently found drafts of my writing with detailed marginalia from Micki McGee, Jennifer Smith, Jean Halley, Mark Halling, Ariel Ducey, Lorna Mason, Kristin Lawler, Robin Isserles, and Veronica Manlow; your input was invaluable in making my ideas stronger and brighter.

Credit must go, as well, to the various forms of institutional support that helped me develop the backbone of this project. Early on, I was the fortunate recipient of the Monroe Carell Fellowship, which jumpstarted this work. Thank you to Hester Eisenstein and Lynn Chancer for being excellent readers, sounding boards, and also for being such good examples of feminist scholarship.

While writing this book, I enjoyed unbelievably great feedback from various City University of New York (CUNY)-supported writing seminars. The generous yet incisive commentary afforded by the members of the Faculty Fellowship Publication Program has been put to good use. I especially want to thank Stephen Steinberg for his gentle leadership. By putting me "on the block," he helped me see that history isn't bunk and that even sociologists can do it. The Andrew C. Mellon Foundation generously funded two years of writing and research, allowing me access (as a fellow) to a crucible of ideas in the form of my colleagues in the Emotions Seminar (through the Center for the Humanities) and the Science Studies Seminar (sponsored by the Committee for Interdisciplinary Science Studies). That year, especially, pushed my work in an amazing direction, exactly where it needed to go. For that I have to thank Victoria Pitts-Taylor and Jesse Prinz, not only for knowing that fashion models and science studies do not an oxymoron make but also for being so glamorous and smart in my general direction. Along the way, various grants from BMCC (Borough of Manhattan Community College) also supported the writing, including a faculty development grant and a Professional Staff Congress CUNY grant, which were both crucial to buying the kind of time needed to think clearly and deeply and then hone the writing to get to the pith.

For being the most amazing personal and professional ally a girl could want, Gina Sue Neff, I can't thank you enough. You are a shining light in my life; not a day goes by that I am not grateful to you for your mentorship, optimism, and deep, deep friendship. You are a superstar, and I thank you for helping me shine ever brighter. To my favorite and best collaborator, I have to say: Jo Entwistle, you inspire me in so many ways. Thank you for being my comrade at arms in forging a path for "model" scholarship and for being such a dear friend! Even though you are much, *much* younger than I am, you shall always be my fashion, work, and lifestyle role model. Speaking of role models, I also want to thank Eugenia Paulicelli for her unwavering enthusiasm, optimism, and can-do spirit! Thank you for believing in me. In that vein, thanks go to Veronica Manlow, as well, for her incredibly inspiring energy, and Agnes Rocamora for knowing quality writing when she sees it. I am indebted to Stephanie Sadre Orafei for sparking the idea that became the basis for theorizing glamour labor. I would also like to thank Ashley Mears for the inspiring conversations, for taking beauty seriously, and for being the best example of a "model" scholar I know. Thanks go also to Elizabeth P. Cutler, Rebecca Lifter, Amy Herzog, and Joe Rollins for seeing that I was a fashion scholar before I realized I actually was one.

I was inspired by my colleagues at BMCC, a convivial, jovial, and encouraging bunch, who finish books at an alarming rate despite the heaviest teaching load in the business. Special thanks go to Rifat Salam for being my shoulder to lean on, sounding board, and cheerleader throughout this process, and to the Deadline Fairy, Melissa Brown, without whose sprinkledust magic this project would never have gotten out the door. I am also grateful to my students for keeping my insights fresh and for asking to read my work even though it wasn't on the syllabus.

The work my students found appeared in several journals along the way, some of which is reproduced here. I am grateful to Sage

Publications for allowing me to include parts of the article "Modeling Consumption: Fashion Modeling Work in Contemporary Society," which appeared in the *Journal of Consumer Culture* 9, no. 2 (2009): 273–296, in Chapters 4 and 5. Parts of the following publications have also been reproduced in the following pages, and I thank these publishers for permission to do so: "Modelling a Way of Life: Immaterial and Affective Labour in the Fashion Modelling Industry," *ephemera: Theory and Politics in Organization* 7, no. 1 (2007): 250–269; "Fashion Modeling, Blink Technologies and New Imaging Regimes," in *Fashion Media: Past and Present*, ed. Djurdja Bartlett, Shaun Cole, and Agnes Rocamora, 133–143 (London: Bloomsbury, 2013); "Managing the Semiotics of Skin Tone: Race and Aesthetic Labor in the Fashion Modeling Industry," *Economic and Industrial Democracy* 33, no. 1 (2012): 125–143; and "Always on Display: Affective Production in the Fashion Modeling Industry," in *The Affective Turn: Theorizing the Social*, ed. Patricia Clough and Jean Halley (Durham, NC: Duke University Press, 2007), 231–260. Finally, I thank the Theorizing the Web conference organizers and editors of the resulting special issue of *Interface: A Journal for and about Social Movements* for helping me hash out a chunk of the writing that appears in Chapter 5.

A good book is a done book, and with Pam Donovan's supercompetent ultra-efficient editorial assistance, this book got both better and done. I am truly grateful as well to the consummately professional Brooke Duffy, whose generous comments and contagious clarity help me whip the public face of this book into shape.

Chapter 8, "Black-Black-Black: How Race Is Read," would not have been half as good were it not for the generous feedback and support from the faculty at the University of Sydney Business School. More important, however, I thank them for introducing me to Bondi Beach. As for the man who got me there, for his generous encouragement and excellent contributions to the literature (handily made in huge quantities with his co-author Dennis Nickson, among others), as well as for setting such a fine example of being scholarly yet cool, I thank Chris Warhurst. Speaking of cool, I want to thank Michael Hardt for helping me get the tenure I needed so that I could focus on finishing this thing!

As research assistants go, I won the lottery in the form of Kristin Miller. Years after being in my employ, I am still amazed at her competent, brilliant, diligent, organized, and sanity-saving assistance. I am sure she will be more famous than all of us when the time comes.

In addition to professional support, I thank the tireless friends and family who have seen me through the long haul of producing this project. I thank Daniel Kron for sharing his world with me, while keeping me out of the lion's jaws. Thanks also to Suzi Campbell for being my wingman in some crazy fashion settings and Robbie Campbell as well for helping me hook the big kahuna. To Crissy and Nigel Barker, thank you for corroborating what I had pretty much guessed already. To all the ladies in the group I shall not name (not safe for work, but you know who you are), thank you for listening to me sort through these ideas while also helping me sort through what the heck it meant to be a new mother. Thanks are due as well to Elaine (and Bob) and especially to Alan Z. for helping me see the donut, not the hole. Thanks especially to the Mama Crew and fellow working moms-at-arms Shirley Brady, Wendy Williams, and Jennifer Collins. They covered for me when footnotes needed tending, abstracts needed writing, and final drafts were due. From brainstorming during yard work (thank you, Sarah Maitland) to reminding me that brilliance comes in many forms, they generously shared insights, inspiration, and magic along the way, helping me know that anything is possible.

To Ilene Kalish and her editorial staff, a thousand thanks for your patience, your vision, and your faith in me. I have been happy to be your "model" scholar. Your on-the-spot support, cheerleading, and excellent editing advice have been central to helping this book reach its potential. To Managing Editor Dorothea Halliday, thanks for the eleventh-hour sanguinity while I was dealing with copyediting requests from the wonderfully exigent Jennifer Dropkin, for whose exactitude I am professionally grateful.

To my mom and dad—thank you for believing in this project, though at times you didn't really get it. I am especially grateful to my mother for her cheerful pep talks, and for providing the periodic writer's retreat when the time called for it. Thank you, Dad (wherever you are), for being our rock, our foundation, and for showing me that good writing is important, no matter what your profession. Thanks also to my sisters, Joanna and Cappi, for sharing the kind of unalloyed clarity that helps a writer write well. Both of you are excellent editors, and for that I am very grateful. Of course, any glimmers of brilliance in the manuscript are due to this collective input; any flaws are absolutely my own.

Last but not least, I have to thank my husband Patrick and my daughter Cassielle for understanding that love and passion take many forms, but one form does not exclude the other. For that, I am really really really really really really really grateful. That's *six* really's, and they know why.

Introduction

Glamour Labor

The excitement was palpable when the first model appeared on the catwalk of the DKNY show. With her vivid lips in a pout, her spindly legs in a blinding flash of cameras, she spiked the runway with definitive strokes, keeping time to the deep thrum of the blaring soundtrack. As she rounded the corner, the electricity sparking off of her was almost visible. Krista, a model who'd stomped many a runway in her day, described what it's like:

> There are thirty, forty cameras going off; there's a tension in the room. They're there, they're looking at you, making sure everything's just right, it's on their faces. It has an impact. I think wherever you are, you are having an interaction with it, and the moods blend. They set a mood, and there's paparazzi and champagne being drunk, and there's a fervor and this music going on. All that is a certain subtle tempest of energy. And models feed off of that. They get into it.[1]

What is this energy about? Frantically snapping my point-and-shoot camera as the models streamed by, I felt the zing of the crowd, the mood, the vibrations in the room. Hard to capture, or even define, it was the kind of dynamism that is both collective and singular, always moving, everywhere and nowhere at once. Spilling over boundaries, hooking us into our own vitality and interconnectedness, this is the energy fashion, for one, has sought to channel and market, and fashion models are among its most reliable conduits.

Fashion models as conduits? Aren't fashion models the people we love to hate, impossible icons whose inhuman proportions make the rest of us all too aware of our own inadequacies? The topic pushes buttons. When presenting my work, I confronted entrenched notions about the frivolity of the profession, feminist anger at its practices, and confirmed assumptions that make everyone an expert about the field. Sometimes, I found it difficult to get a word in edgewise. The sad spectacle of teen-aged girls dolled up to look like grown women, not to mention the unrealistic body types they parade as the norm, presents vital issues of concern that bear examining and combating. The attraction of model-ing for so many young girls and women calls out for demystification, by drawing back the curtain to reveal the magical workings of the glamour machine. The fact that so many are pulled in by its allure, skip college, or, worse, drop out of high school, only to be spat out by their "sell-by" date at the ripe old age of twenty-two, is worthy of real outrage.[2]

I understand these issues completely. I was exposed to them from a young age, when people started telling me "You should be a model." What did this admonition mean? I knew it was a compliment, but it also contained a challenge: Why didn't I make more of myself, try to realize my potential, stretch myself beyond existing limits? I was also deeply conflicted about it, having struggled with my own body issues and nascent feminist ire with regard to being valued only for my looks. The fact is, models are mostly women. Many of the images produced by the modeling industry can be interpreted as misogynist, at worst, and supportive of the status quo, at best. These issues were still with me as my graduate studies led me toward a deeper understanding of gender, bodies, technology, and society. Fascinated by discovering the fluidity between categories I had assumed were fixed, I found that looking to patriarchy or consumerism to explain why models look the way they do explained only part of the story. Although the "model" ideal reinforces sexual ideologies while prompting us to buy things, it also idealizes a way of being in the world that engages us with images and technology in rhythms that pass beyond bodily boundaries of sex, race, and class. My research on modeling revealed new insights into tendencies inherent in the Internet, social media, and biotechnology that facilitate the spread of neoliberal and biopolitical imperatives to fuzz the line between bod-ies and technologies in a manner that models make attractive. Taking this angle on modeling not only acknowledged the cultural construc-tion of gender, consumerism, and work but also highlighted the cul-tural construction of the body itself via a form of work I have dubbed "glamour labor."

Glamour labor works on both body and image—the bodywork to manage appearance in person and image work to create and maintain one's "cool" quotient—how hooked up, tuned in, and "in the know" one is. Glamour labor involves all aspects of one's image, from physical presentation, to personal connections, to friendships and fun. Its virtual mode involves the effort to keep up with the trends by reading fashion magazines, watching awards shows, and expending the energy to stay hooked into what's happening now in terms of styles, desirable brands, and how to get them. Its physical mode involves maintaining a fashionable hairstyle and working to achieve a body that fits the current ideal. Some scholars call these kinds of work on the body "aesthetic labor"— the work to look and behave like an image defined by one's employer.[3] Virtual manifestations of glamour labor have "immaterial labor echoes," in the work to foster networked connections and build a reputation within a community of workers for whom work and play are not clearly defined.[4] The endless possibilities for glamour labor also incite pressures similarly felt by cultural workers in fashion design, advertising, software production, photography, and other forms of cultural production, where scholars have noted the pressure to be available 24/7 for work.[5] The key difference is that glamour labor fuses both physical and virtual aspects of bodywork in pursuit of the fashionable ideal. When life, work, and body management bleed together, "glamour labor" is a better term for describing the work to achieve the overall image touted by fashion modeling as a means to the good life.[6]

The current era of live-streaming, geolocating, biosensing, taking selfies, and living online has intensified the pull for glamour labor. As we turn to the screen to find the information we need to achieve our new look, email, blog, or tweet about what we want to buy, be, or achieve, we intimately engage with technologies organizing bodies in time and space, with every click building an affective circuitry metering our engagement and potential, bringing it to market.[7] How have modeling and fashion attracted publics willing to expose their body's rhythms, connections, movements, and sensations through tracking "likes" and "dislikes," geolocating tweets, or mapping patterns of clicks? How has wearing a device that measures the body's vital signs and movements, engaging with new therapies, or ingesting experimental drugs, in hopes of possibly reaching optimal performance, become entangled with the pursuit of a model-perfect body? Models' glamour labor opens the way to optimization. Capitalizing on the body's susceptibility to enhancement, models glamorize offering the body's various modes of social and physical energy to be plugged in, worked out, and totally "made over" to fit today's ever-changing standard of the glamorous ideal.[8] By performing and promoting glamour labor, models are on the frontlines of selling a way of being in the world, which pulls bodies into productive matrixes in novel ways.

Models sell a way of life? Aren't they just clothes hangers used to display goods for sale? Krista, the model quoted above, was indeed modeling the DKNY clothes on the runway for the assembled glitterati in the room who might have a chance at buying them—or at least borrowing them. The fashion show's professed purpose of parading new styles to promote sales has recently morphed to promoting a brand, however. Now that images of shows instantly telegraph via the Internet to interested onlookers the world over, fashion weeks are big news, widely reported in newspapers and on television, with Internet and social media coverage of backstage shenanigans and gossip about front-row seating arrangements almost as important as the critique of what comes down the runway. Compared to the tiny fraction of audience actually in the room, the majority of onlookers couldn't possibly buy the fashions on display. It doesn't matter. Selling the products is only a small part of what the model does.

Of course, models do sell things, why else would a model still be required to pique our interest in this face cream, or that "it" bag, or whatever shade has become "the new black"? A larger part of the model's job, however, is to stir up energy, spark interest, and gain attention. By selling a brand, a logo, and a lifestyle, models invite varied publics into a web of matrixed attention and exposed vitality, systematizing responses and propensities, making them traceable, possibly controllable, and therefore profitable.

You, Inc.

The sociologist Kathleen Barry notes how flight attendants earned the "wages of glamour" by crafting their bodies and personalities to meet expectations of femininity.[9] In return, they garnered admiration and high status, but only if their work appeared effortless.[10] Similarly, the experiences of the models with whom I spoke resonate with the notion of work that is hidden or unrecognizable as such.

Blurring the line between work and play is an endemic feature of cultural production more generally, a trend that the communication scholar Mark Deuze dubs "liquid life."[11] "Cool" jobs entice young workers into Faustian bargains that sap their youth, potential, and financial resources in pursuit of glamorous work. Angela McRobbie describes this process as "the ruthless and tyrannical deployment of 'cool' as a disciplinary regime of work and leisure."[12] Models experience an extreme version this "deployment of cool," evident in the tone of advice given to them: You must be the CEO of you, it's your own responsibility for your success, you have to be adaptable, you have to be pliant, you have to be original, you have to bring something to the table, be professional, look the part, act "as if." You are responsible for your own destiny, and you'd better try to be a superstar. You have to be your best self not only physically but also emotionally, and personally.[13] As one informant pointed out, "Models are like mini corporations."

While flexible workers who treat themselves like mini corporations have been well documented,[14] the social theorist Emily Martin notes how these behaviors have taken on a manic tone, "pushing the limits of everything, and doing it all with an intense level of energy devoted to anticipating and investing in the future."[15] Stability and conformity are not valued in the current ideal worker; dynamism and change are. The individual is viewed as a set of "potentials to be realized and capacities to be fulfilled: self-maximization and self-optimization are the watchwords."[16] As such, fashion models, insofar as they traffic the volatile forces of affectivity and total self-maximization, are manic workers par excellence.

In the course of my research, I found that modeling work involves being "on" all the time, embodying the dream of a fully optimized life. As such, it contributes to the twenty-first-century trend toward making bodily potential and connectivity continuously available to metering and regulation. Glamour labor encourages an embodied entanglement with technology, as capital's constant expansion banks on possibilities inherent in both bodily vitality and the capacity for connection. A complex of technological mediations produces the model's body, from the minute they are first Polaroided (as they say in the business to refer to the first time they are photographed by a scout or potential manager) to the moment they are famous enough to be on the cover of a magazine and subject to the Photoshopping conventions now governing how fashion images appear.

Some scholars have separated these processes into the medicalization and mediatization of everyday life.[17] Glamour labor is physical, in terms of improving one's image by disciplining the body via diet, exercise, and medical intervention. It also encourages virtual forms of self-fashioning and self-surveillance made possible by Internet connectivity and social media.[18] Thus, while the social philosopher Nikolas Rose notes the rise of a "somatic ethic" in which "the maximization of lifestyle, potential, health, and quality of life has become almost obligatory,"[19] I would add that this ethic extends to the somatic presentation of self online as well. As this obligation to be all one could be both online and off has spread, pursuing glamour labor to optimize life has regulated those who engage with it, facilitating the exercise of power through a biopolitics of beauty, which governs decisions about organizing vital forces, speculating on the body's potential to gain or lose weight, grow stronger, mutate, transform, become more attractive, or connect.[20] The biopolitics of beauty organizes individuals not only as consumers with desires but also as populations ready for transformation, always already in need of a makeover.[21]

Consequently, glamour labor to look good or cool or "with it" is inseparable from the glamour labor aimed at extending the image far and wide, in the effort to put one's bodily potentials into the circuitry that make up your "presence" physically and virtually. Put succinctly, in the circuit of glamour labor, where the model/consumer/fashion/image/product nexus converges in the event of the model "look," models make the labor of physical and social enhancement attractive. Models glamorize encouraging a bodily variability that is not just about promoting diet pills or about getting you, the consumer, actively engaged in body projects but also encouraging investment in your engagement with others. Glamour labor varies, not just your wardrobe according to fashion, but also your body, your relationships, and your work styles, as you make your feelings, proclivities, and moods available to electronic calibration and measurement.

Those of us who exist in a manic state of constantly updating their Facebook statuses, getting shaves or new hairstyles to update their profile pictures, tweeting about their latest thoughts, checking in to identify their whereabouts, blogging about their interests, pinning images of their favorite things, tumblring their photos, or Instagramming to give them a nostalgic haze, are ideal glamour laborers. As such, we provide raw material to a system in which, as the communication scholar Alice Marwick points out, "online and offline behavior" is "combined, analyzed, and sold" by private data companies to "marketers, corporations, governments, and even criminals."[22]

In this climate, the tendency to look at, feel for, or be affected by a product becomes as important as buying what the model is ostensibly selling. The time and attention you spend engaging with fashion is a form of work, valuable in and of itself. Shop for a cardigan once, and those sweaters will haunt your screen margins for days because where you go online, where you look, with whom you communicate, and how you feel about it all is tracked by corporations that benefit from knowing your proclivities, constructing complex algorithms to decipher what you are talking about, where you are saying it, and how many clicks it took you to get there. It doesn't matter whether you buy Prada shoes but that you think about them and pay attention to when the new season's styles come out and know and use the Prada name. It matters that you are interested and are organized into a system of probability as a potential customer. Your virtual engagement opens pathways for connections to more luxury brands.

Some of your interest may stem in part from some model somewhere modeling Prada shoes on the runways or in a magazine. Whether you yourself have seen this photograph is irrelevant, however. Your engagement with fashion is far more complex than a simple one-to-one correspondence of exposure to images of fashionable products and the feeling of a need to purchase them. It is more complicated than desiring products of a certain brand, in part because brands are funny things, which aren't all that logical.[23] The indirect practices mobilizing brands have much to do glamour labor's broad terrain.[24] Every context of brands, fashion, and the social relations springing up around them pulls for glamour labor on some level. You do glamour labor when you participate in the fashion system, watch fashion television shows, post shots of street fashion, tweet about what you wore today, or chat with others about fashion or the latest model and celebrity exploits, whether tweeted or reported online. With these practices increasingly prevalent in twenty-first-century developed economies, glamour labor has become commonplace. Whether they are aware of it or not, those who live in the tripped-out blogosphere can no longer imagine a life outside the almost intravenous engagement with the logos or brands that now so frequently punctuate speech, experience, and daily life.

It is clear to see that glamour labor is not the exclusive terrain of fashion editors, models, or the fashion elite. Participation in the fashion scene ranges from the hardcore insider status of the designers and models who work with them, and the photographers who promote the designers' wares, to characters like Cecilia Dean, who has edited *Visionaire* magazine for the very select few fashion cognoscenti.[25] The scene includes the more mainstream, yet still quite elite, *Vogue* editor Anna Wintour and the editors who manage the various fashion magazines that dictate or drive tastes in fashion, such as *Harper's Bazaar*, *W*, or *Elle*. In the aughties, self-made fashion bloggers forced these elites to open their ranks, such as Tavi Gevinson, whose prescient observations and quirky style helped her blog her way to front-row status at many of the world's most preeminent fashion shows at just thirteen-years-old.[26] Elite meets street in the high school student whose onscreen ID is "topmodel212" and those who catch the eye of street fashion bloggers. One former model told me she couldn't walk through New York's Soho neighborhood without being stopped for a photograph, while a new recruit to the city felt that he achieved true "New Yorker" status when his look was snapped. In sum, no matter who is doing it, glamour labor involves work to be attractive, both physically and virtually, through managing one's physique, personality, and online presence to create an image of "cool," edginess, or relevance, an image that modeling and the fashion world has made hard to resist.

Why models, in particular? Don't movie stars, musicians, and other public figures also embody the glamorous life? Of all the forms of work that involve some aspect of glamour labor, modeling is one of the most direct examples for several reasons. First is the issue of accessibility. Unlike singing and acting, which in theory require a discernable talent, fashion modeling seems to require little more than a pretty face.

Second, modeling—whether by pop stars, film celebrities, or anyone in the public eye—is framed by a corporate culture that seduces many into engaging with images on a daily basis. Even those who steer clear of celebrity culture can't avoid fashion, since we all have to wear clothes.[27] Red-carpet fashion may be a fun spectator sport, but street fashion is a game available to everyone, bringing modeling and fashion closer to home than the aspirational world of Hollywood glamour. Third, while movie and pop stars, television personalities, and public figures often engage in glamour labor, fashion models *always* do.

Even those who don't officially work as models *are* models when they do glamour labor. When a movie star is asked on the red carpet, "Who are you wearing?" in that moment, she is no different from a fashion model, promoting the brand of the clothing she has on in an appealing lifestyle moment. Similarly, a celebrity in an advertisement becomes a model when she steps off the stage or the screen and into that branded world and works to maintain the right persona to keep that endorsement agreement. Garnering a magazine cover results either from successfully performing the kind of glamour work models always do (appearing on the cover of *Vogue*, for instance) or its failure (appearing on the cover of *People* magazine, being excoriated for letting herself go or engaging in activities that tarnish her image). What's more, while celebrities, pop stars, and the like might temporarily endorse a brand and then step back into their own personas, for which they have become famous, fashion models constantly brand themselves and in fact are prized for their ability to disappear into the brand, performing the glamour labor of personifying whatever it is the various brands for which they work need them to be at any given time.

In addition to being cool and on trend in one's habits and persona, modeling work, of course, entails looking the part. While not exclusive to modeling, looking "right" is frequently tangled up with a fashionable ideal. Even though current celebrity Kim Kardashian's eye-popping curves promote a desirable look, that look is frequently played off against a fashionable one. Celebrities of all types may or may not have the body that is "in" fashion, but models always do, and that fashionable body is often the measure of all bodies in the public eye, the norm from which bodies deviate. While actors and actresses famously rejected fashion during the 1980s in favor of being taken seriously as artists, now that celebrities have been pulled back into the fashion fold, celebrities perform glamour labor on a routine basis, both by maintaining themselves according to reigning attractiveness standards and by earning red-carpet raves for getting the look "right." With few exceptions, the rise to stardom inevitably smoothes and polishes aberrant bodies, toning flab, hardening muscle, and erasing perceived flaws (e.g., the disappearance of the comedian Tina Fey's scars, the pop star Carrie Underwood's transformation from rough farm girl to polished Barbie, and the voluptuous fashion model Sophie Dahl's apparent sellout to the forces of fashion when she dropped several dress sizes).

Embodying the fashionable ideal happens only some of the time for exotic dancers, flight attendants, and others whose image is a large part of their work, but for models it happens all of the time. Similarly, porn stars or sex workers call themselves models, but not vice versa. In each case, these workers embody the fashion model body, so in examining that ideal, it makes sense to go straight to the source to understand the glamour labor of embodying a fashionable look.

You've Got the Look I Want to Know Better

Embodying the fashionable "look" is a complex process. Much of models' glamour labor is caught up in struggling to produce the right look at the right time in the right place. Nobody knows, however, what "look" will sell at any given moment. The "look" is a volatile thing whose existence is distributed across social networks. It has meaning but is not merely an image to be read or interpreted. The model's look is both physically embodied by the model and represented by pictures in her book, and yet it is neither a person nor a representation. Not just an image or a series of images, the look emerges from a complex integration of objects, symbols, and activities, coalescing in this thing that is identifiable and calculable yet difficult to pin down.[28]

The "look" is elusive because the performance of glamour succeeds only when the work involved is deftly hidden from the audience.[29] This view runs counter to the assumption that "glamour" evokes over-the-top makeup, clothing, or hair, popular among drag queens or old-time movie stars. For my purposes, "glamour" refers to a "pre existing but previously inchoate yearning" a sense of "projection and longing," that the social commentator Virginia Postrel so eloquently described when parsing out what it is that glamour *is* and *does*.[30] In my argument, this yearning drives the calculated restraint demanded by editing a look to produce a saleable body and self in keeping with whatever is considered fashionable in the moment.

The fashionable "look" is more than the sum of its parts, lending it an ineffable quality. The sociologist Ashley Mears found that "bookers and clients often grapple for the right words," struggling to explain that a look is not just the "visible or an objectively identifiable quality inherent in a person" but, rather, "the 'whole package' of a model's being, including personality, reputation, on the job performance (including how one photographs) and appearance."[31] The sociologists Don Slater and Joanne Entwistle described the look as that "'certain something,' a magical quality that the old fashioned notion of 'charisma' or 'charm' goes some way to capturing."[32]

The look's volatile mix of energies is both bodily and mental, fluctuating and changing in different environments. The fashion model look includes the fashion production system, in which clothes are designed, made, and distributed; the techniques of making clothes and distributing them, but also of creating and disseminating interest in fashion; the skills, rules, and practices of fashionable expression, from the rhythms of the fashion shows, with the August issue of *Vogue* magazine marking the beginning of the new season; the seasonal obsolescence of clothing as dictated by the changes in fashion from year to year; the blogs and Internet sites that create constant turnover of fashionable images; interlocked systems and infrastructures (e.g., fabric manufacturing, distribution chains, retail distribution systems, cheap labor, and status hierarchies in which clothing plays part, with the Internet and social media providing access to fashion images and news about fashion insiders); and linguistic and visual codes. The look links photographers, agents, models, producers, consumers, and brands in circuits of exchange where the product is more of an event than a thing. Key to conceptualizing this system is the look's peculiar structure as both object and process.

Since the tangle of relations defining a model's "look" as a unit of sale includes "all of the images of a model,"[33] it must be managed in print and in the flesh. To that end, model agents edit the models' "book" of images, to ensure that the "right"—that is, the best or most prestigious—images go in. The book shows the history of the model's career, composed of clippings, or "tear sheets," from their appearances in magazines or other promotions, and the agent carefully chooses between those with "editorial" (high-fashion) impact and those with "commercial" (mass) appeal. This management also encompasses the models' physical appearance, as agents advise models when to cut their hair, go to the gym, wear high heels, or not to smile too much. Managers also scrutinize models' personal choices, from which airline to travel and where to socialize, down to what to wear, even when they are just popping out to the corner to pick up some groceries. In this process, the look is "constantly reconfigured" as it passes through a network of other mediators who affect it: stylists, photographers, designers, fashion editors, and consumers.[34] As such, when clients buy a model's "look," they pay for the model, her physical presence, and the resonance of that look within the broader networks of editors, designers, fashion professionals, and—importantly—fashion consumers.[35]

Kay, a makeup artist, explained that this is why models "have to go on 'go-sees' and be Polaroided in the raw, on the day of,"[36] to allow for the fluidity of the body's presence in the flesh, its very materiality and form affected by the networks into which it is placed. June, an agent who was a veteran of the industry, explained that "you can be gorgeous, but if there's no personality, dead in the camera, it's not happening, won't work." Similarly, Brian, a photographer who liked to do small, well-studied beauty shots, was of course attracted to a certain physical look, but he also valued a certain chemistry; as he pointed out, "It's just like anything, like meeting anybody, there's . . . I try to remain aware of whatever sort of chemistry there might be going on that I'd feel right away." In sum, the model "look" challenges given ideas of bodily integrity. The "magic" and ineffability of the look is that which is more, or in excess, of the picture, a quality that mixes with the changeability and force of the model's physical presence to make up what is best described as the model's *affectivity*. Models are links in a system through which energies flow. Their work imbues objects and circumstances with branded power to attract and organize action. Consequently, understanding their impact demands an examination of the ineffable and embodied force of affect.

The Superhighways of Suggestion

Any discussion of bodies and affect inevitably turns to the question of embodiment—that is, the body's physical role in apparently mental phenomena such as perception, cognition, and engagement with the world. How can looking at the work of fashion models inform our ever-changing understandings of embodiment? The force of affect in the space of encounter may go some way, for instance, in explaining why people still continue to gather in person for fashion shows, rather than simply look at pictures of the clothes. Over and above the struggle for status, there is something ineffable about being there in person. The ineffable and the embodied are key aspects of fashion's allure, with affective energy as its basis.

This notion of affective energy is useful for describing the indeterminate moments of potential—for instance, the potential to buy a new coat or to adopt a new fitness program, the potential for clothing to rustle when worn or for the body to beat in a pattern that is measurable—just at the moment when that potential exceeds what actually takes place when the action is taken, the thought expressed, the movement made. All material things have a level of animation. That spark, that life, exists as something not yet determined, a potential that, once realized, excludes other potentials clamoring for being alongside it. This excess of potential is part of the energy of the life force, the force of affect, and it explains what happens when a model moves her body in a way that sums up the exact mood of the moment, when she knows how to feel in a dress, or how the construction of the dress makes her move in a distinct manner and a certain look clicks, or feels right.

Modeling work glamorizes tapping into the bodily capacity to move, to act, to think, to be. The models I interviewed frequently described tuning into affective flow, going with a gut reaction, the viscerally felt impulses that guide actions whose causes, upon reflection, are hard to explain. The transmission of affect takes place physiologically, through the spoken, heard, seen, tasted or sensed. Sweaty palms make us realize we are nervous, a pulsing temple betrays our anger. Within affective flow, we "feel the atmosphere" in a room, producing a sense of belonging in a process that the psychologist Theresa Brennan claims is "social in origin but biological and physical in effect,"[37] in what the sociologist Deborah Gould calls "collective effervescence."[38] The communication scholar Brian Massumi, who argued that affect is most effectively whipped up and dampened by the media, quipped, "The skin is faster than the word."[39] In the same vein, the media scholar Anna Gibbs claims that media such as television and the Internet are "amplifiers of affect, heightening and intensifying affects." As such, they play a role in "affective contagion" in which bodies "catch feelings" as easily as they "catch fire," inflaming "nerves and muscles in a conflagration of every conceivable kind of passion."[40]

Attitudes can "catch fire" overnight in the fashion world. As an affective industry, fashion traffics in the moods, feelings, and predispositions that sweep everyone into their wake and then, just as suddenly, are gone. It is as mercurial and unpredictable as the weather. Sitting at her highly polished desk, Julie, a model agent at one of the largest agencies in New York, intoned in her Jamaican lilt, "You never know which way the breeze will be blowin' each day." Recent changes in technology have intensified the speed and range of these breezes into a perfect storm, recurring practically every fashion cycle. With the Internet now tracking reactions to events in real time, tracing geographical preferences in movie rentals, YouTube hits, and click-throughs on political websites, the flow of affect is more easily traced and, some argue, manipulated. These technologies help visualize the waves of affect that ripple through populations, leaving moods, feelings, and shifts in things as nebulous as, say, the consumer confidence index, in their wake.

There are, of course, regularities, otherwise no one could do business. In the face of ever-more volatile markets, however, the fashion cognoscenti struggle to navigate social conditions producing the elusive quality that makes a good photograph great, causes a dress to sell out in one day, or makes a model agent's phone ring off the hook for one particular face on his or her roster. While some of this arbitrariness stems from struggles for status and power in the highly uncertain markets of modeling, as the sociologist Ashley Mears has documented, even the highest level tastemakers whom everyone else follows are swayed by the affective energy flowing through the social networks where they engage in this struggle.[41] Waves of interest and desire for this or that product, model, or look bubble up from this social energy, energy that belongs to no one and everyone at once. It is a collective phenomenon existing only in transit, registered as a reaction that is hard to articulate.

When the sociologist Herbert Blumer found the collective nature of "incipient taste" hard to explain, for instance, he hinted at affect's ineffable nature. When fashion buyers said they chose one nearly identical dress over another because it was "stunning," Blumer mused that the relation between the forces of modernity to which fashion experts were trying to respond and the "incipient and inarticulate tastes of the fashion consuming public" was "obscure."[42] While he did not want to undertake analysis of it, Blumer claimed this relationship constituted one of the "most significant mechanisms in the shaping of our modern world."[43]

Blumer may have intuited it, but he did not want to tackle the impact of affective energy and its particular susceptibility to manipulation by the media.[44] Notably, he observed taste's "incipience" in 1969, around the same time television was becoming a full-blown social force reshaping modern life. Our attraction to and engagement with television, and ultimately to the proliferation of screens that now make up the fabric of most American lives, paved the way to a complex system of calibrating affective flow. Flying along the superhighways of suggestion and changeability, waves of bodily affect course through us every time we plug into the matrix of electronic relations that are now part of reality for so many. Fanning the flames of affective contagion, the affective circuitry of media technologies is reaching unforeseen levels of complexity. From the first moment an enterprising ad executive decided to put a person in the picture, to the myriad fashion images on offer today, models' glamour labor has been key to the unfolding drama of entanglement with the emotive/affective technology of the screen, making the modulation of affective energy not only possible but also profitable.

Notably, a surge of interest in affect and affect studies emerged in the mid-2000s, just as the Internet came to the fore as a social force. As television, film, and the Internet increasingly tap into and track these ebbs and flows, interrogating how technology manages affect has gained some urgency. These two phenomena are in fact inextricably linked. Affectivity and imaging are pivotal to understanding how the shift from three channels on a rabbit-eared rotary dialed television to the hundreds of channels, websites, and social connectivity making up the all-media-all-the-time lifestyle now the norm for so many brings with it new assumptions about what bodies are and what they are for. The glamour labor of modeling helped facilitate the organization of this bubbling energy within social relations, producing value in networks where images, attention, experiences, and attitudes are exchanged.

The effervescent value of a reaction, a mood, or a feeling is fleeting.[45] Affective energies rise and fall in the moments between sensation and sense making—that is, the moment when the glimpse of a color, flutter of movement, or fragment of tonality catch your interest before you know what you have perceived. As a result, advertising has moved away from telling a story toward focusing on making an impact. Text-heavy advertisements have given way to images that depict nothing but a small logo in a corner to let on what is being sold, as, for example, paragraphs extolling the virtues of this or that lipstick have shrunk to the single word, "Chanel," marking an ad.[46] The move to the sensed, rather than the meaningful, in advertising imagery points to attempts to tap into a pre-cognitive impact of images, an excess of consciousness stirred up in bodily interaction with images. As lines between work and play blur in our networked age, so do lines between bodies and technology, which raises an analogous question: How do various technological frames affect the value of the lived body's energy in the contemporary marketplace?

Life, in Pixels

Modeling work changed from a sleepy, backwater, insider industry to a globe-sprawling set of corporations that churn through bodies to produce new models and looks because media now play on the volatile and unpredictable forces of affect.[47] The rise of glamour labor in modeling tells the story of the changing role of affect and bodily vitality in contemporary markets. Why has bodily affectivity become such a valuable commodity? How does glamour labor work on and with that vitality? We live in a moment characterized both by speed and a veritable explosion in the availability of information, moving faster than the human ability to process it. Part of this speed comes from the fact that digitization transforms everything into a common language.[48] The unifying language of ones and zeroes brings everything that can be translated into it onto the same plane, smoothing out barriers that formerly slowed information's trajectory, speeding it up and compressing it.

The digital revolution of the 1990s infinitely expanded the possibility for image distribution, far in excess of the 1980s innovation of cable television's wildest dreams. Personal computing took on a new life with the birth of the World Wide Web. While it took some time to develop its potential (early users joked that the "www" acronym for the web stood more for "world wide wait" than for anything else), as the Internet grew in scope and power, images and information from all over the world and most points in history were soon just a click away. "Google" became a verb as search engines became more sophisticated. Everyone got an email address, and domain names became hot properties.[49] In a scant dozen years, the number of terabytes of information sent via the Internet increased from 1 terabyte per month in 1990 to between 80,000 and 140,000 in 2002. In the roughly same time frame, the percentage of adults in the United States with Internet access grew from 14 percent in 1995, to 46 percent in 2000, and to 79 percent in 2010, reaching 87 percent by 2014,[50] the year in which the number of Internet users was estimated to have grown to almost 3 billion worldwide.[51]

All manner of sports, news, and political information drew users as the print media hopped on board. On the burgeoning celebrity gossip and fashion infosphere, public exposure took on a whole new meaning as the introduction of YouTube sent many a celebrity faux pas—from Beyoncé and Madonna falling down onstage, to Naomi Campbell's famous runway wobble and fall off of her high heels—reverberating through endless playback loops instantly amplifying the humiliation for all to see.[52] In the late 2000s, social media such as Twitter and Facebook grew by leaps and bounds. Reportedly, Twitter had 255 million users, and Facebook 1.28 billion in 2014, not to mention the burgeoning crowds flocking to Pinterest, LinkedIn, Google+, and other services whose names will perhaps sound as quaint as the now defunct Friendster by the time of this book's printing.

The velocity and magnitude of the images flooding our lives has created what the sociologist Herbert Simon has called a "poverty of attention."[53] This epidemic of overwhelmed attention spans demanded a new "structure of attention," described by the social theorist Nigel Thrift as focusing on "those actions which go on in small spaces and times, actions which involve qualities like anticipation, improvisation, and intuition."[54] Photography, cinema, television, and the Internet shape these structures, altering the speed and quality of our perceptions, thereby creating different modes of visibility or imaging regimes.[55] Inspired by the journalist Malcolm Gladwell's turn of phrase, I've dubbed the current moment "the regime of the blink."

Leading up to the blink regime, photography enframed the body and gave its image new value, cinema offered the possibility of editing it to perfection for the camera's unblinking gaze, and television blurred the space between image and world as the glance usurped the gaze. In the fully mediatized age of the blink, a series of what Nigel Thrift calls "highways of imitation/suggestion" have proliferated as more data and images provide more distractions, links to click, or ideas to pursue, creating a suggestible crowd whose attention shifts as quickly as the silvery flashes of a school of fish.[56] This "networked jumpiness" causes us to flit from one image to the next with little time for conscious reflection and, at times, without our registering what we actually see.[57] Paradoxically, this new regime has also fostered an interactive engagement with images, pulling for closer "attunement" with imaging processes than ever before.[58] The value of this attunement has engendered a new interest in engineering the biological propensity to change, a key aspect of affectivity, making it become a target of corporate interest.

Glamour labor has emerged as a social force because of the rise of blink technologies' interaction with bodily affectivity, a change in technology that requires rethinking our understandings of what a body is and does. The rise of technologies embedded in our experience of embodiment has disturbed the formerly distinct boundaries of bodily integrity, forcing a new look at the meaning of the fashionable "ideal." At the same time, the biotech industry, facilitated by advances in the computational technology that gave rise to the regime of the blink, has worked on the notion that genetic codes are like computer codes and are therefore programmable. Once the metaphor for the programmable body spilled into the culture, the unprecedented levels of access to its functioning informed the trend toward manipulating smaller and smaller parts of the body. This trend showed up in several sectors of the modeling work I examined, including the intensified efforts to fine-tune the model's body through tighter management of every body part and the efforts to harness the unpredictable mutations that spread through populations in the bioprospecting practices of scouting. The following chapters will explore how the obligation to strive for the optimal body and self has become an imperative of glamour labor in the age of the blink.

In sum, glamour labor provides a basis for thinking how current levels of technological development inform notions of embodiment. Unpacking glamour labor delineates how the body's sensations and feelings are organized in space, regulated in time, and generally made available to tracking in movement and proclivities, entangling them with a system of enhancement, connection, and optimization. This system ranges from locating bodies in front of television sets and computer screens for the live broadcast of the Victoria's Secret fashion show, to producing the frenzied crush of bodies at the fashion designer Martin Margiela's release in H&M stores, to the daily effort of online tracking and sharing of one's intake and exercise levels to achieve a "model" body. Thinking this way situates the body within technologies that systematize our interactions with images, communal relations with others, and the life force coursing through us all.

In this environment, interrogating what images mean or how they shape subjectivities misses the complexity of the processes of entanglement with them. Meaning and subjectivity are the tip of the iceberg in examining how technical apparatuses—ranging from packaging and advertisements, to more diffuse means, such as Twitter and other social media—provide the mundane means for material and affective attachment to things.[59] It is not only the meaning of images but also our engagement and attachment to them through which corporations seek to resource the unpredictable and changeable energies of the body itself, not only in terms of its appearance or social connections but also in terms of its vital energies, drawn on by technologies that foster the tendency to perform in new and different ways.

You've Come a Long Way, Baby

If the regime of the blink facilitates behaviors harnessing the body as a productive resource, analyzing the ideal "model" body demands we look beyond the forces of patriarchal culture alone. Thinking about the body enmeshed in technology's boundary-troubling networks requires more than the usual feminist critique of modeling. Feminists tended to focus on the oppression of models who were forced to look borderline anorexic and on the women whose bodies could not live up to the industry's impossible standards. In the 1970s, Susie Orbach famously proclaimed, "Fat is a feminist issue!"[60] Sandra Bartky's much-anthologized 1988 essay linked Foucault's (newly translated) idea that modern forms of power created "docile bodies"[61] by the "disciplines that produce a modality of embodiment that is peculiarly feminine."[62] These feminine modalities included bodily practices that limit the size of women's bodies, their shape, how much space they take up, and how they are displayed.[63] Subsequently, the feminist scholar Susan Bordo incisively linked dieting to gender oppression, since keeping women slim and hungry distracted them from protesting their lack of power in other areas of social life.[64]

In the early 1990s, Susan Faludi and Naomi Wolf forcefully advanced this critique. They argued that each surge in power for women, such as winning the vote in the early 1900s or the new freedom wrought by the Pill after the 1960s, was met with a corresponding backlash of newly idealized images that got slimmer with every decade. They pointed for evidence to the boyish figure of the 1920s flapper, the gaunt glamour of angular mid-century models, or the famous model Twiggy's stick-thin limbs, which earned her that name in the 1960s.[65] Anne Bolin, an anthropologist who studied women bodybuilders, gave this argument another twist when she advanced an "interesting theory" that "during periods of liberation, like the 1920s, when women had just gotten the vote, and the 1960s, when the Pill became available, the ideal shape for women deemphasized their reproductive characteristics—the nourishing breasts, the wide, childbearing hips."[66]

The demand for a "model" body, of course, has powerful negative consequences for women. In the age of the blink, however, it is also important to explore how imaging and production technologies shape understandings and the physical appearance of the body, in all of its modalities.[67] Even the feminist scholar Laura Mulvey's famous analysis of the male gaze, which gave full attention to technology's influence on shaping gendered power relations, still failed to critically assess the origin of the ideals that were "cut to the measure of desire" in the first place.[68] That is to say, the feminist perspective on body ideals provides an important critique of gendered power relations. It misses, however, significant historic and culturally specific circumstances of this look's origins, as well as imaging and productive technologies' influence on producing these ideals.

Thus, while what Bartky called "the tyranny of slenderness"[69] may be forced on some women by patriarchal forces in developed countries, how have the various imaging technologies through which the body is viewed and depicted intensified or otherwise affected that patriarchally informed vision? If men are men and they want what they want, why hasn't the fashionable ideal been more constant over time? Bodies are shaped by gendered attitudes about what is desirable or considered ideal, but these ideals are also shaped and influenced by technology. From Twiggy's iconically minimalist proportions, to the "glamazonian" contours of the supermodels, to the hollowed-out silhouettes of the waifs, models "model" the body in fashion. This ideal body is forged in the nexus between productive and visual technologies, and delineating the "model body" traces the changing means of representing bodies, how they are put to work, and what they are thought to be for or should be.

Engaging with social media thus exposes our proclivities for various types of connections; in the same manner, the urge for enhancement, to be all that we can be, extends to bodily optimization in pursuit of an ideal as well. For example, you might troll the Internet to seek out that new therapy; submit your genetic information to a research study or biobank, in hopes of finding ways to reduce the effects of aging send away for that nutritional supplement that may be unproven but worked wonders on your sister-in-law's skin and hair; all while wearing a device that counts how many steps you took that day, making sure you let all of your friends know about your workouts, how long you slept, and your current skin temperature and heart rate. What's more, the glamour labor of models normalizes these practices, practices that regulate how individuals perceive and act in their bodies. This in turn regulates the overall health and enhancement of the population, optimizing its "state of life," as we manically strive to be our very best selves while corporate interests track our every move, banking on the value of our future potentials.

Plan of the Book

This book begins at a pivotal moment in the history of modeling, when Cindy Crawford became "Cindy, Inc.," a global corporation revolving around herself as a model, what she called "The Thing," and Christy Turlington and Linda Evangelista famously refused to wake up for less than $10,000. Chapter 1, "Supermodels of the World," describes how the increased effort to harness hard-to-manage forms of affective energy accelerated the demand for models to sell brands and how eventually, in the form of the supermodels, models became brands themselves. The inauguration of the supermodels brought the transition from a girl who models to the 24/7 supermodel icon and the supermodels who became the quintessential glamour laborers who were never off duty.

Facilitated by newly far flung webs of cable television and high-speed communications, the supermodels became household names. This transition laid the groundwork for the rise of mass fashion and the spread of glamour labor to the general populace. Prior to the regime of the blink, the fashion show, for instance, was nothing like the branded dazzle with which we are currently familiar. Chapter 2, "The Runway," explores how the fashion show changed as television and the Internet, systems for gridding affectivity for profit, spread. This chapter tracks these changes from designer Charles Frederick Worth's innovative use of live mannequins to the "disdainful beauties" of the 1950s, to Mary Quant's wild leap into the future when she recruited photographic models for the runway in the 1960s to, finally, the supermodels' celebrity and the ensuing everydayness of fashion.

Along the same lines, the regime of the blink changed the goals and methods of the fashion shoot. The value of what the model did changed from the 1900s discovery that a person's image could be owned by them and worth money to the carefully staged and scripted studio shots prevalent from the 1920s through the 1950s, to the far more intense and invasive practice of getting one's "soul sucked out" by the camera lens, as one model described it, to being given the puzzling direction to try to look like a rat (as the former supermodel Cindy Crawford reported).[70] Chapter 3, "The Photo Shoot," tracks shifts in photographic modeling, from using models as mere props to an intense experience in which the model is expected to reveal herself utterly to the camera. Models' stories about photographic sittings and shoots reveal how affective lability or mania became a valuable factor in modeling work for the camera in the age of the blink.

Chapter 4, "Cover Girl," documents how advertising's need to send a specific, meaningful message to an interested consumer shaped the work of model management in its early days. At that time, 1900s fashion designers, such as the incomparable Lucile, tightly controlled their mannequins, molding them into the "look" of their particular house. Mid-century models were given specific instruction in which expressions to wear and how to feel for a particular shoot, as photographer Richard Avedon directed models in the 1940s and 1950s. With the developing importance of capitalizing on the value of experiences and the body's changeability, however, modeling work evolved into the professional free-for-all that it is today, where it is anybody's guess what look clients will want from one moment to the next.

Similar changes surface in methods for obtaining and portraying the ideal body recommended to models in published manuals of modeling "advice." Chapter 4 also explores how the popular language of model management draws back the curtain on how we envisage the "ideal" worker as a culture, since changes in instructions given to models over the years interestingly have dovetailed with significant changes in productive technologies during the same timeframe. This connection becomes particularly evident when tracing the advice given to models in modeling manuals from the 1920s to the 1960s. Chapter 5, "The Fashionable Ideal," explores the significance of increasingly stringent and exigent dieting, exercise, and surgery advice from the 1970s onward, which reflected developing assumptions about the body's changeability and the imperative to engage with these kinds of changes through self-altering practices in order to be an acceptable member of society, as if the model were the ideal for the whole population and as if anyone who was willing to work hard enough at it could achieve this bodily ideal. Simultaneously , however, the body's vitality and mutability also came to be favored, as a biopolitics of beauty emerged, organizing and regulating publics at the level of population, as a standing reserve, always already in need of enhancement and optimization, ready for a close-up, in need of that makeover.[71]

In tandem with these developments, as more opportunities for exposure developed alongside the demand to make oneself more available in more ways, modeling work took on characteristics that prompted some of my respondents to refer to it as "the life," a state of working that felt to many like having to be "on" all the time, twenty-four hours a day, seven days a week. In the transition from day job to total lifestyle, playing the role of being a model—sashaying about in crinolines, carrying a hatbox containing waist cinchers and war paints (the badge of the model's trade), while ducking into movie theaters to make oneself scarce between calls—gave way to the casual street chic, "I only dress up on the runway" attitude of today, where models live the part, hiding the effort required to make looking glamourous seem banal but never boring.

While the general public engages in varying levels of it, the models and modeling professionals I spoke to for this study claimed they felt as though they were never off duty and were always at work to produce the right "look" in person, in photographs, and online. Model agents made it clear that it matters where models live, where they eat and shop, and on which airline they travel. As Chapter 6, "The Job," explores, some respondents reported being told explicitly by their agents they had to put on the show all the time, even if they were just running around the corner to do an errand, mindful of the impression they might make as they are out and about, conscious of their online image created by the photos snapped of them in fashionable neighborhoods or at social events and posted to blogs or websites dedicated to documenting the modeling world. It seems like a lot of work, but models who really want to "make it" report trying to make it look fun to be exposed in this way, to be "on" all the time, to be out there in the spotlight, as often as humanly possible.

Chapter 7, "Scouting," outlines how the turn toward affective branding has shaped a new image regime facilitating the model industry's rapid expansion into a global network, broadening the field for scouting of prospective models, intensifying competition and turnover as a result. Increasing interest in tapping into affect's vitality has intensified glamour labor as model managers have sought tighter control of their charges. This chapter tracks how the tightening of control over models was met with a widening field of scouting for new recruits to the industry. As the public's exposure to and interest in fashion has grown apace, fashion weeks have proliferated beyond the traditional fashion hubs, and scouting for new models has reached into ever-more remote regions. Consequently, modeling contests have grown in size and number, modeling agencies have opened offices in dozens of countries, and fashion has become "news" as television shows and websites treating fashion have became commonplace. Banking on the new value of mutability, model scouts have ranged farther afield in search of that precious combination of features that might make millions. The age of the blink has facilitated this expansion, converting more of the population into a standing reserve, made ready for their makeovers by a steady diet of reality television and twenty-four- hour access to the newest fashions, updated by the minute.

Scouting's rapid geographic expansion has done little, however, to broaden the racial parameters of the fashion aesthetic, as Chapter 8, "Black-Black-Black," documents. While models of color are more prevalent in high-fashion images today, historically the modeling industry has been closed off from taking the kinds of risks that involve troubling the idea of "fashion" as dictated by what the media studies scholar Alison Hearn has called the "corporate imaginary," that is to say, within the given signs and symbols that have evolved within the corporate world.[72] In the image economy of the regime of the blink, models strive to embody the values of their working environment, calculating their impact, self-regulating and commodifying in order to generate their own "persuasive packaging," their own "promotional skin."[73] For black models, however, the repertoire for creating a "promotional skin"[74] has traditionally been limited by stereotypes and cultural assumptions, which shape black models' glamour labor in specific ways. Their self-branding has demanded more intense forms of bodywork and self-commodifying, at times using their race as part of their brand, while at other times essentially erasing their racial characteristics by straightening their hair or pushing their bodies to fit a Euro-American standard. While my respondents experienced their race as something they created or dissimulated according to client's whims, at the same time they were keenly aware of how their work was shaped by prevailing expectations of what "race" should look like, indicating the power of pre-existing racial tensions into which they must fit the aesthetics of the look they build when doing glamour labor.

At the same time, as one model agent at a large agency put it, "The standards that people say about beauty, they're all malleable, they're always changing." He claimed this shift became particularly prominent after the 1980s, when the "standard of the blue-eyed blond was broken" and replaced by a "more global" ideal. Chapter 9, "Touch-Ups," explores how, in recent decades, modeling work has come to require embodying the ideal of a *malleable* body, especially since the 1980s and 1990s, when digital technologies facilitated the desire to manipulate appearances, since digitization enabled an infinite malleability of appearance down to the tiniest pixel. Modeling work increasingly became the work to always be ready for, or in the process of, transformation, and in so doing, models glamorized this practice for the general public. Finally, the Conclusion considers the theoretical ramifications of these phenomena, placing questions raised by looking at modeling work and its cultural impact within debates about affect, emotion, bodies, and technology in a digitized world.

Taking It to the Streets

Changes in the kinds of bodywork models are required to perform reflect changes in assumptions and practices with regard to affect's value, which shape the kinds of bodies models portray as an ideal to the general public. For this reason, I chose theories of affect and affect contagion, which serve to map the unsaid, unseen, emergent potentials efflorescing in the confluences of model-image-body-product, because they had far more explanatory potential than the usual "consumer reading an image" or "model selling a product" scenarios with which modeling is usually explored. Affective energy belongs to everyone and no one at once, however, which presented me with a dilemma. How could I examine the workings of affect, when it is a social energy that can only be detected in its effects? I knew the model "look" was constituted in part by affective energy, but I wanted to examine how affective energy got into the "look" in the first place. I knew that the model body was the "ideal" body, but I wanted to know more about what shapes that ideal and how our notions of what our bodies are for have changed over time. I suspected that models were showing us ways to be in the world that made our life energy and potential somehow available to be organized as a source of profit, but I needed to know more about exactly how that worked.

To explore this theory in the real world, I talked to models about the nature of their work to create their "look." I asked what they considered to be their job, what it was like to be in front of the camera or on the runway, how they experienced the industry as a whole, and how they got into modeling in the first place. Then I let those questions lead to further discussion. I also wanted to get a sense of the history of the lived experience of modeling and so turned to the records of expert advice in the field to see in what ways it meant to be a model, to be that ideal, has changed over time. I was trying to get a sense of what it's like to live in the camera's eye, to get at when, how, and why interpersonal energies are circulated by imaging technologies, and how that circulation is turning a profit in the circuits of value in which images, feelings, attitudes, and other forms of bodily energy are now being made productive.

How best to cut into the process, to investigate how imaging work draws us into a new level of engagement with technology? To get at this question, I hit on the idea of studying the history and practices of image production, and I zeroed in on those images that seemed a powerful influence in contemporary life—that is, fashion images. My interest in bodies and control led me to think about the most iconic bodies in the process of image making, that is, fashion models.

The choice made sense for a number of reasons. First, I had access. I live in New York City, and as anyone who lives or works in Manhattan can attest, it's hard to avoid contact with the fashion industry. Whether it's stumbling upon the lights and scurrying assistants of a fashion shoot as one turns down a side street or finding that your usual lunchtime spot has been temporarily transformed by the tents that used to mushroom overnight in Bryant Park, like any New Yorker, I couldn't help but be familiar with fashion.

Second, I spent my first few years in New York living with a fashion photographer and so was exposed to the modeling world through fly-on-the-wall access to photo shoots and industry events such as "model parties," where modeling agencies throw a party to promote their models to photographers and other potential clients. I was periodically "scouted" to be a model—that is, asked if I wanted to come to an agency and talk about possibly signing with them—but these casual offers never led to any real employment. Since I fit the part, however, and was living in that world, I did occasionally model. I posed in return for clothes or to do a friend a favor, but I never quit my day job. Once I decided to make modeling the topic of my research, I used my connections to the modeling world to start building a snowball sample, asking each person I interviewed to recommend one or two more. I was surprised at how easy it was to meet models, once I started asking. Contrary to conventional wisdom that models are self-centered, stuck-up, stupid, and snobbish, few of the models I interviewed fit the stereotypes; they were warm, friendly, and unusually forthcoming.

Finally, I didn't have to write a grant to get access to some of the most comprehensive collections of literature on fashion. They were right up the street in New York.[75] They included not only the few extant histories of the profession but also primary sources such as the model "annuals"—some of which survived from the 1920s and 1930s, showing pictures of the models on the roster in a given year for early model agents John Robert Powers and Harry Conover, for instance—and some of the remaining model "how-to" books or primers from the 1920s through to the present day, which provided insight into how dictates of fashion affected the bodily ideals to which most models sought to aspire, a piece of research crucial to understanding how these ideals have changed over time.

I did have assumptions about the modeling world, as many of us do. The dreams and allure depicted by fashion models flooded my adolescent years when, like many teenagers, I developed body image issues. I thought I was too fat when I compared myself to the menagerie of bone-thin models whose images I'd plucked from various magazines and taped up around my mirror. I both loved and hated those images. They taunted me with their inaccessibility combined with their promise that I, too, with a little work, could become like them. Fashion modeling seemed like a glamorous world, a one-way ticket to womanhood for an awkward fourteen-year-old, like stepping out of a constrictive skin into a world of freedom, excitement, and adventure.

This personal connection to models and modeling also resonated with the mood of the times when I entered graduate school in the mid-1990s. Models were everywhere. The reign of the supermodels was in full swing, and the public interest in models had reached a fever pitch, with the journalist Michael Gross's sensational pop history of modeling, provocatively titled *Model: The Ugly Business of Beautiful Women*, on the best-seller list. The world seemed to be on a first-name basis with Linda, Christy, Naomi, and Cindy. The transvestite singer RuPaul rose to fame admonishing the supermodels to "work it, girl." They could be seen cavorting in George Michael's "Freedom" music video, telling us about fashion on MTV's series *House of Style*, or on the arms of rock stars, prizefighters, and movie stars who were only too willing to be their escorts. This intense interest in models has become a facet of everyday life, a facet of the social world this book examines. The modeling world is anything but everyday, however, and gaining access to this rarified domain presented several challenges.

You Can't Sit with Us

How does one meet models, let alone get them to agree to an interview? Hang out in model bars? Follow them to their castings? Try to sneak backstage at a fashion show? For the average sociologist, these are not easy propositions. My life in the modeling world prior to graduate school helped, but my small circle of friends from that arena was hardly big enough to produce a research-worthy sample. I hit a gold mine when a friend sympathetic to my cause offered me an occasional day job as a casting assistant at the photo production company where she worked. In some ways, this break is just another New York story, since firms like my friend's production company tend to be clustered in fashion centers like New York (or Paris or London). As a casting assistant, I worked with models who were seeking jobs and took notes under the table, in between my regular duties of managing the flow of traffic coming in, getting the models ready to be photographed for their "tryout."

Sometimes we saw hundreds of models in a day, and I made use of this direct contact to make arrangements with anyone who was willing to meet me for research interviews. Sympathetic to my project, my friend sent models my way even when I wasn't in the office, and the collaboration proved to be quite fruitful. While this casting agency dealt only with commercial, not high-fashion, clients, I met a whole range of models, including those who had worked in high fashion. Even though I was not at castings for high-fashion magazines or other luxury-goods manufacturers such as Chanel or Dior, models who had worked for those clients often came through. What's more, journalistic and scholarly accounts of these types of castings describe situations similar to the ones I observed both as a casting assistant and in the field: a room full of models waiting to be seen, the client's desultory glance at the head shot or book, the quick dismissal with no indication of whether those few moments made a positive or a negative impression.[76]

The casting agency was a great resource but skewed my sample toward older models and, surprisingly, men, who, despite their minority status in the modeling industry, seemed to be easy to find. These men, or "boys" as they are referred to in the business, seemed to have no qualms about making arrangements to meet me in a coffee shop, or at their agency, or wherever. The ease with which I secured interviews with male models makes sense, given the gendered structure of power we live in. As indicated by their willingness to meet with me, and their willingness to give me the names of other models, I was a relatively unthreatening prospect for them. Perhaps the male models had less to lose as well—their schedules did not seem to fill up at quickly as those of the female models and, since they make less money than the women, perhaps less was at stake in taking time out of their day for an interview with a sociologist.

Getting access to the young female models who tend to do high fashion, however, was another story. The ones I got access to—at industry parties, for instance, or from other respondents—would say "no" outright when I called them for an interview or "yes" and then cancel. It was clear the female models demanded more drastic measures. I decided I needed to go to where the models were—the castings. When I managed to secure an interview with a female model who had walked runways and worked for trendy clients such as Abercrombie & Fitch, I took a risk and asked her to share her agenda with me. Typically, when they are looking for work, models get a list of castings each morning, and the day's work consists of trying to make it to each one of them, taking the subway or cabbing it all over town. I figured that I would go to these castings and pose as a model, if need be, in order to make the necessary contacts.

The first casting on the list was on lower Broadway, just north of Soho, in a relatively fashionable part of the city. I walked into the building with two other girls, both quite tall; one was very slender with long blond hair, and the other was more voluptuous with big eyes. They were unmistakably models and seemed to be looking for which floor to go to, so I asked, "Are you going to the casting? I think it's in Suite 903." They seemed grateful, and while waiting for the elevator, I made my move: "I'm a sociologist and I'm studying the modeling industry." I explained a bit of what I was doing, and they seemed receptive, so I followed them down the hall to a very big, open, and well-appointed office with sculpture on broad shelves, very large computer screens on desks perched at multiple levels, and a wall of windows looking out over lower Broadway.

We were asked to sign in, and the voluptuous one muttered under her breath, "You can be my friend." I didn't sign in; using my new identity, I went to sit and wait with them. The slender one was just starting out and had been in New York for only two weeks, up from Texas. My "friend," who seemed a bit older, had been at it for seven months. The first girl seemed nervous. She said she was trying out modeling on school break. I thought maybe she was on break from college, but later my new confidant said she was sure it was high school.

Eventually they called us into another room. We entered to see three people seated at a table. We lined up in front of them. Perhaps I appeared to be there for the job; one of the people behind the table gave me a quick once-over. It made me flinch to be looked at in such an appraising way—and it gave me a momentary insight into what models go through every day, as part of their job. After thanking us for coming, a woman who seemed in charge, dressed in all black with funky vintage shoes and glasses, dismissed us, and as we walked out, I invited my informant for coffee so we could talk more about her work as a model. She accepted, making it a very productive day.

Once I found how remarkably easy going to castings could be, I decided to try for more. One sweltering July afternoon found me out on the street in the blistering sun, staking out the entrance to a casting, accosting models as they came in or out. After receiving the brush-off from more than one model, I got lucky: A girl leaving the casting not only agreed to talk to me but invited me to meet her and her room-mates at her "model apartment," too. Agencies rent or own apartments and use them to put up girls who are trying out the industry or who are in town only for a few weeks and need accommodation. Usually these are regular apartments that have been fitted out like dorm rooms, with bunk beds and a chaperone, to look after the more-often-than-not teen-aged inhabitants. This particular apartment was in Tribeca and housed six models in what should have been a two-bedroom apartment. There was one bathroom for the six of them and a twenty-three-year old chap-erone. We did a group interview in their living room; miraculously, all six were home, my tape recorder worked, and I came away with new insights into how models get work (many of these girls were found at model search contests or scouted in the street) and how modeling can become a whole way of life.

By the time I did that interview, I was knee-deep in doing the research and getting bolder all the time. My sample was getting pretty well rounded, but I felt it needed more representation by top manage-ment. Calls to top agencies in New York had produced a few hits, but for the most part I'd been shunted to lower-level staff, and I wanted to talk to the head honchos. I decided to play the international card, and I cold-called modeling agencies in Paris, saying I was a researcher from New York, and would they take the time to meet with me? I secured five interviews with agencies in Paris this way, conducted in a whirlwind trip to Paris that included the coup of getting an appointment with the owner of the top modeling agency in the world at the time, who dis-cussed the modeling world with me in her beautifully appointed office overlooking a grand Parisian boulevard.

These interviews led to others, until eventually, I had spoken in depth to fifty-four industry professionals and models, some speaking with me for almost two hours. The population under consideration is not large. The reported twenty-two hundred modeling jobs in the United States are a relatively small group compared to the more than six hundred thousand jobs in advertising recorded for 2008.[77] Fashion models con-stitute an even smaller number within the population of models over-all.[78] I focused specifically on fashion models because they are subject to the strictest aesthetic criteria and therefore the pressures on them to perform glamour labor is easily identified.[79]

I asked respondents how they got into the modeling industry, what types of clients they worked with, how they felt about the opportunities available to them, and what their experience of the industry was more generally; the rest of the interview was open-ended. Taped with consent, transcribed, and manually coded, these interviews were conducted between 1999 and 2004 and between 2007 and 2012. The sample age ranged from sixteen to twenty-eight for the models. The other workers I interviewed tended to be slightly older, mostly in their thirties and forties. The sample's racial composition was predominantly white, with one female Asian model, four black female models, one black male model, one black female model agent, and two female Hispanic models, as well as one model agent of Hispanic origin, reflecting the white bias in fashion modeling my respondents described.

Models are not the only ones I talked to. Since modeling is an "art world," as the sociologist Howard Becker describes, made up of not only the front-stage players but also many supporting players, I also talked to photographers, stylists, casting directors, the occasional creative director, and model agents—or "bookers" as they are sometimes called.[80] Employing the ethnographic technique called "participant observation" when I wasn't interviewing, I read microfiched newspaper articles about modeling, thumbed old copies of books like *So You Want to Be a Model*, went on photo shoots, attended industry events, pretended to be a model at castings, staked out the lobbies of modeling agencies, and went to fashion shows.[81]

As I investigated the modeling world, people amazed me with what they were willing to share. It didn't hurt that I seemed to be part of their world, but I think it was also an advantage that I wasn't. Having that distance made me a safe stranger, what the sociologist Georg Simmel described as a person whose "distance and nearness, indifference and involvement" makes it possible to elicit sometimes the "most surprising openness—confidences which sometimes have the character of a confessional and which would be carefully withheld from a more closely related person."[82]

Working with these confidences, I hope to put these moments of sharing into context, to shed light on recent changes in technology that are tending toward engaging with affect to elicit a glamour labor aimed at revving up the body's potential to look and be its very best, to be fully enhanced and optimized. By analyzing how changes in imaging technology have made capitalizing on affective energy possible, I track how models glamorize this form of labor, which pulls publics into a form of entrainment, in which bodies, actions, and impulses are brought into alignment by the media technologies with which we so willingly engage, in part because models have made them so attractive. The value of directing affective energy, in the form of affection for a brand, or interest in looking at branded images, or participating in branded experiences, has skyrocketed in part because the rewards can be so great for hitting the right note with the buying public. Habituating that public to needing the new "it" bag each season and to "throwaway" fashion has become a huge part of fashion marketing, in which models play a pivotal role. Although we participate gladly, why are tracking and molding our pleasures and energies increasingly so important to the corporate bottom line? By investigating the glamour labor of fashion models, that is precisely what this book seeks to find out.

1

Supermodels of the World

Living the Life

Carolyn, a veteran model agent who had witnessed the profound transformation of the industry when models became "super," called it a "total freak-out" for the business, saying:

> It was '83–'84, and I'm a model agent at Elite at this time. So I'm on a board, with all of these girls starting at exactly the same time. Five minutes ago, there was no Stephanie Seymour, no Cindy Crawford, none of these girls, and five minutes later they're all there at the same time. It never happened again. Not in the last twenty years. That kind of sensationalism where all of these girls started to work at exactly the same time—it was mind-boggling, just a complete, total, freak-out to the business. The business was accustomed to maybe one or two girls of the moment. And now they've got like, ten girls of the moment who are trading off on *Vogue* covers and *Bazaar* covers, and *Mademoiselle* covers and working with Irving Penn, and working with Avedon, and it's just a crazy time in the industry. And from there, this terminology, "supermodel" came up.

The "elite clique known as supermodels" included five or six women: Naomi Campbell, Linda Evangelista, Cindy Crawford, Christy Turlington, Claudia Schiffer and, as NY Times journalist Alex Kuczynski once quipped, "depending on your mood, Kate Moss."[1] The modeling stars of the 1950s and 1960s may have been muses to famous fashion photographers, but supermodels in the 1980s and 1990s were celebrities in their own right.

After Linda, Christy, and Naomi started working consistently with the bad-boy photographer Steven Meisel, famous almost as much for his rabbit fur hats and kohl-lined eyes as for his photographs, they were soon known as "The Trinity. " The three worked together, doing the fashion scene in Paris, London, New York, and Milan, telling *People* magazine in June 1990, "We're an Oreo cookie in reverse. We're only a third without each other."[2] In the space of a few short years, they had become so famous, bodyguards pushed them through the mobs of fans waiting for them outside of shows.[3] They dated rock stars (Seymour had a volatile affair with Guns N' Roses lead singer Axl Rose that ended in allegations of violence on both sides), prizefighters (Campbell dated Mike Tyson), associated with royalty (Schiffer was linked to Prince Albert of Monaco), and married movie stars (Crawford married Richard Gere in Las Vegas). Whole issues of the various *Vogue* magazines seemed devoted to them.[4] They posed nude for *Rolling Stone*, appeared on celebrity television shows such as *Entertainment Tonight* and MTV news, and starred as themselves in a rock video, lip-synching the words to George Michael's song "Freedom."[5] With the growing interest in models and modeling, and the growing paychecks, even some men got into the game. Although Marcus Schenkenberg and Mark Vanderloo garnered nowhere near as much attention or money, the frenzied interest in models and fashion made "supermodels" of them as well.

After their meteoric rise in the mid- to late 1980s, by the 1990s, the supermodels' place in the celebrity pantheon was secure. Cindy Crawford's *Shape Your Body Workout* video hit the shelves in 1992. In 1994, both Naomi Campbell's novel about the industry, *Swan*, and Robert Altman's film about the fashion world, *Ready to Wear* (*Prêt-à-Porter*), were released. *Unzipped*, designer Isaac Mizrahi's documentary prominently featuring the supermodels, came to theaters less than a year later.[6] The year 1996 immortalized models Karen Mulder, Naomi Campbell, and Claudia Schiffer as action figure dolls.[7] A restaurant featuring celebrity models, the Fashion Café in New York City, temporarily became the epicenter of the public interest in supermodels.[8] The year 1997–1998 could have been dubbed "The Year of the Model": Supermodels Marcus Schenkenberg and Veronica Webb each published an autobiography,[9] two well-known authors published novels about models: *Model Behavior* by Jay McInerney and *Glamorama* by Bret Easton Ellis, and a series of teen novels appeared sporting catchy titles like *Model Flirt* and *Picture Me Famous*.[10] Cable shows like CNN's *Style* series, hosted by Elsa

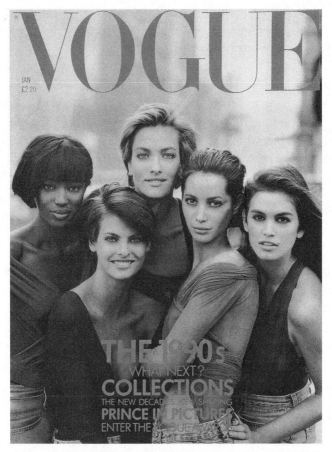

Figure 1.1. Supermodels circa 1990, in *Vogue* UK: Naomi Campbell, Linda Evangelista, Tatjana Patitz, Christy Turlington, and Cindy Crawford. Photo by Peter Lindbergh.

Klench, *Behind the Velvet Ropes,* with Lauren Ezersky, and MTV's *House of Style,* hosted by the supermodel Cindy Crawford, brought fashion and modeling into everyone's living rooms. As Ezersky pointed out in a phone interview,

> Before the 1980s, the collections were small. Once they [were] televised, they were seen by hundreds of people. The shows themselves got bigger, too. Now five hundred, eight hundred people might attend a show. In

the 1970s, when it was smaller, people still cared about it, but there were fewer outlets. There used to be just a few pictures released after a fashion show, but it's more accessible now.

Interest in fashion was so high by the end of the 1990s, network television took the plunge and produced two network shows, *Veronica's Closet*, about a lingerie designer, and *Just Shoot Me*, a sitcom about a fashion magazine, which, at the time, represented a large portion of the primetime market.

The transition to fashion as entertainment made the lives of the supermodels fodder for the entertainment mill. Anything models did became worthy of exposure, from the fabulousness of walking the runway or going out on the party circuit, to the mundane rituals of shopping or going to get a facial. Models became household names, a turning point in the industry, key to organizing the development of glamour labor as a widespread practice. Nicholas, a fashion public relations (PR) agent, pointed out that

> there's a hunger for content because there are more outlets. The number of magazine titles in the past ten years has something like tripled. So you need more content, so you search for more subject matter. And in that search, the media writes about the lives of models, which I don't think twenty years ago anyone would have given a damn about.

Only about twenty himself, Nicholas may be forgiven his ignorance of the models Dorian Leigh and her sister Suzy Parker's famous exploits, chronicled in the gossip sheets of the 1940s and 1950s, the 1960s media's complete captivation by all things Twiggy, or the *New York Post*'s and *Daily News*'s relentless coverage of Cheryl Tiegs's marital woes in the 1970s.

Clearly, people did "give a damn" about models' personal lives, but the number and importance of scandal or gossip items related to models in the past couldn't compare to the explosive growth of media images of models and modeling in the 1980s and 1990s. The fashion historian Harriet Quick described how in this era, "Fashion entered every facet of life":

Everything got bigger in the eighties. Fashion was fashionable; the elite sport blossomed into a global consumer industry. Designers licensed their names into perfume, accessories, chocolate, cosmetics. Brand names became so lucrative, Yves Saint Laurent was able to float his business on the stock market. Fashion entered every facet of life. Nothing was quite as grand or indeed pretentious as the biannual *prêt a porter* collections; broadcast through satellite and TV stations world-wide, the collections turned into a media spectacular. In 1986, the Paris shows were attended by 1,875 journalists and around 150 photographers: nearly a four-fold increase on the figures recorded for 1976. Front rows were studded with celebrities, backstage awash with champagne.[11]

The 1980s and 1990s saw huge leaps in modeling's visibility, globalization, and profitability. In the proliferation of cameras backstage at runway shows and in media following models' lives, documenting their antics, boyfriends, and tantrums in ever closer detail, fashion—the perfect filler for the newly created expanses of hundreds of channels—reached more audiences and began to infiltrate daily life. Fashion became entertainment, and models became superstars. Fashion's elite circle increasingly entangled average consumers, drawing them into fashion's rhythms.

The story of the supermodels is the story of fashion's encroachment on the everyday, entraining publics to its whims. By the 1980s, fashion consolidated into global mega-brands, and cable and satellite technology sent carefully crafted, globally appealing images zipping around the globe. These new networks honed crude forms of branding and mass fashion, originating in the 1960s and 1970s, into a sophisticated machinery of appeal, enabling models to become "super" and laying the building blocks for glamour labor. The transition from selling products to selling brands profoundly changed the face of modeling, linking models, images, and consumers in novel ways. The regime of the blink refigured the world into publics willing to brand themselves and those unwilling or unable to do so, as the regularizing forces of the biopolitics of beauty became more firmly entrenched. During this seismic shift in the 1980s and 1990s, the supermodels were a "total freak-out" for the business, as my respondent Carolyn put it, because they didn't just represent products, they lived the life of the luxury brands to which they lent their "look," inhabiting that fantasy world so convincingly that we all started to believe.

Pierre Cardin Frying Pans

The transition to a world of designer kitchen appliances and brand-scapes shaped by lifestyle-consumption choices has its roots in the early 1970s. As communication became a key element of production, the ability to do it well became highly prized. As the dominant Fordist mass production, distribution, and consumption structures fell into decline, post-Fordist structures of flexible labor and just-in-time production emerged.[12] The 1970s transition to a post-industrial economy, combined with advertising's efforts to reach "niche" markets, made signs and symbols, such as Pierre Cardin's designer cachet, rather than product durability or performance, into important selling points. The question was less *how* something was made than *who* made it, a powerful draw for designers who slapped their names onto everything from blue jeans to frying pans.

The emerging preeminence of brands over products shook the fashion world to its roots. Models and designers played the branding game with consumers and the paparazzi at the Studio 54 nightclub, as the new cable and satellite technology inaugurated a veritable blitz of visual images that irrevocably changed the quality of everyday life, intensifying the competition for attention. While Twiggy was mobbed on her first visit to New York and Cheryl Tiegs and her compatriots often made headlines, their fame was qualitatively different from that of the supermodels. The supermodel moment emerged from a rare confluence of factors. Cable television flipped television imaging into overdrive, laying the groundwork for the regime of the blink, with images moving faster than conscious human perception could process them. This imaging speedup in the 1980s relied on technologies that also broadened markets, expanding fashion's purview, as sending a message halfway around the globe in a manner of minutes and receiving shipments overnight from another continent became routine. Global mega-brands emerged, born of a scuffle in which corporate behemoths gobbled up smaller labels, consolidating the fashion land-scape into a newly global business.

The "Wolf in Cashmere" and the Consolidation of Fashion

Business has always been a part of fashion, but prior to the rise of the fashion mega-brands of today, individual fashion houses had retained at least the aura of artistry. The newly international fashion world's growing emphasis on brands blurred the line between high fashion and high finance in modeling, commercializing fashion design in unprec-edented ways. Seeing the opportunity to generate customer attachment in an increasingly cutthroat field, multinational conglomerates bought up individual fashion names, plying them as brands. The *Wall Street Journal* fashion journalist Teri Agins reported that LVMH, the luxury-goods conglomerate, after acquiring top fashion house Dior, and later Louis Vuitton, Céline, Givenchy, Loewe, and Kenzo, began aggressively shopping for American and Italian fashion brands in the mid-nineties. Bernard Arnault, the head of LVMH, dubbed the "Wolf in Cashmere" by many, explained this strategy:

> It isn't a question of country, but a question of power of the brand and its capacity to be developed on a worldwide scale. Fashion is very different in today's world. It is very important to link up with each other.[13]

After scooping up a 34 percent stake in Gucci, Arnault hired the Amer-ican Michael Kors to revive the Céline brand, an increasingly typical move. Designers hopped between continents and clothing lines as their new multinational owners sought to revive dying design houses. Once parent companies called the shots, the tolerance for creative foibles diminished. In some cases, one bad collection could spell the end of a career, or designers, balking at taking orders from outsiders, quit, as was the case when designer Jil Sander "quit her eponymous house after only five months under Prada" or when "menswear designer Hedi Slimane resigned his post at Saint Laurent."[14]

In the volatile climate of pitched battles for the better names, it seemed all the old rules were suspended. Arnault's archrival, the French billionaire François Pinault, challenged LVMH's grab at Gucci by securing a 40 percent stake in the company and combined it with Sanofi's newly acquired existing beauty products division in a play to create a "multi-brand luxury brand group" to rival LVMH. The battle for Gucci was seen by a *Wall Street Journal* fashion reporter as "emblematic of the New Europe that is taking shape with the launch of the common currency and the globalization of the industry: two Frenchmen squaring off for control of a Dutch-based Italian company, run by a U.S.-educated lawyer and an American designer advised by London-based American investment bankers."[15]

While LVMH was busy building an empire, other major players like Calvin Klein, Ralph Lauren, Giorgio Armani, and Prada sought an increasingly international pool of consumers. Paris's grip on centrality of power began to slip, and other fashion cities in the London–New York–Milan–Tokyo circuit began grabbing for it. Attempting to maintain stylistic dominance, the Chambre Syndicale trade group took Paris runway shows to far-flung places like Belarus, Beijing, Shanghai, and Budapest. Despite these efforts to re-establish Paris's centrality, the globalization of fashion was already too far along. Soon Paris was no longer its sole arbiter but, rather, one voice among many in an increasingly crowded field.[16]

Intensifying branding practices broadened advertising's goal toward framing lifestyles, rather than just selling individual products. The need to transmit a feeling about a brand, to whip up that "feeling-cum-behavior" of affective response, profoundly affected the advertising industry and, by extension, the fashion and modeling industries. In the new branded world, supermodels commanded high prices, lived a glamorous lifestyle, and became media darlings, packaging and selling "living in fashion" as something everybody couldn't help but want.

The trend toward insinuating brands into the minutest corners of everyday life brought a new kind of model to preeminence, a precursor to the highly paid, globally visible supermodel. As the curators Harold Koda and Kohle Yohannan observed, "Blurring the line between high fashion and high finance, the commercial model became the most expensive, most sought-after means of inspiring envy, desire—and product sales—known to the world," while their mass appeal made them "widely influential upon popular culture."[17] While the 1960s model Twiggy had been a prototype for commercial models, "the first fashion superstars" included Cybill Shepherd, Cheryl Tiegs, and Christie Brinkley.[18]

Starting in the 1970s and into the 1980s, these celebrity models capitalized on the brand power of their image, selling their likenesses and names to jeanswear, exercise videos, and beauty products. Cheryl Tiegs's signature appeared on the back pocket of thousands of pairs of jeans in a telling shift from function to form: the rise of designer denim. Nothing could come between the very young model Brooke Shields and her Calvins in an era when American designers, who had formerly been backroom workers—on a par with "the help" as Bill Blass put it—"came into their own" and became branded celebrities as well.[19] They attached their names to handbags, belts, wristwatches, and sheets—even bidets and frying pans got the "designer" imprimatur, making designers into household names.[20] To make their names known, and so boost the sale of licensed goods, designers began publicizing their "lifestyle" as part of their image. Calvin Klein boosted his notoriety by regularly socializing with other fashion designers and celebrities at local nightclubs, such as Studio 54.[21] Fashion designer Halston, always impeccably turned out, never went anywhere without the Halstonettes, "the famously leggy entourage who accompanied the couturier to the chicest parties and night spots," draped on his arms.[22]

The model herself as brand became so valuable that Lauren Hutton's milestone $500,000 contract with Revlon, for a national cosmetics campaign, suddenly made sense. Shortly thereafter, Margaux Hemingway broke that record, with a million dollars from Fabergé to become the face of their "Babe" fragrance, further augmenting the value of a model's face and modeling's celebrity.[23] Cheryl Tiegs became so famous, she appeared on the cover of *Time* magazine twice in the same year. The week the second cover appeared, *Time*'s competitor, *Newsweek* had a feature on her as well. In her meteoric rise to fame, she reportedly signed a deal to write a book on beauty and a two-million-dollar contract to appear on a major network, ABC-TV, all while achieving the dubious honor of knocking "Farrah Fawcett-Majors off the walls of the rooms of several million adolescent American boys" with a poster of herself in a pink bikini.[24]

In the new worldwide frontier of global marketing, the supermodel "brand" could command outrageous figures. Recently formed conglomerates launching "worldwide cross-platform campaigns to reach their newly expanded consumer base" and emblazoning, for the first time, the model's image "simultaneously across the pages of magazines, on billboards, and on bus placards" had to pay for that much exposure.[25] Even as pay went up for the select few, as the burgeoning mediasphere laid more affective pathways, diminishing levels of attention called for more and newer models. In response, the model agencies restructured, expanded their recruitment techniques, and incorporated the glamour labor of selling a lifestyle into the model "look." In this transition, the model industry went from a mom-and-pop operation to a world-girding set of corporations that sucked in and used up bodies according to ever-shorter "sell-by" dates. All bets were off, it seemed. Fights over models and jacked-up pay rates re-branded modeling as a rock 'n' roll, fast-paced, early burn-out lifestyle, where the stakes were high and the rewards were many—but the spoils only went to an anointed few.

The "Model Wars"

Until the 1980s the modeling world was essentially "a sleepy backwater business run by a dowager empress."[26] The globalization of fashion in the regime of the blink spurred a profound change the structure of the industry, shaking it to its core.[27] Carolyn, the boutique model agent, described how, until the 1970s, there were Ford Models, Wilhelmina Models, another agency called Stewart Models, "and that was *it*. They were really the only agencies with any kind of clout. There weren't the thirty-five, forty different agencies, there was just them." Modeling was nothing like the cutthroat, globally networked industry with which we are familiar today.

Where the fashion world may once have moved at a fairly predictable pace, the new demands of transcultural imaging markets raised the stakes for success both for models and agencies. Being the most powerful player in Paris no longer cut it; now the contest was for top modeling agency in the world. Among upsets and takeovers, model's pay rates jumped by leaps and bounds, and the desire to control the model body, to manage its minutest details, intensified.

The model agent John Casablancas was among the first to ride the globalization wave, making his Elite agency a very powerful player within a very short time. While fashion modeling has involved travel abroad since the French fashion designer Paul Poiret brought his mannequins to America in the 1920s, model agencies had tended to be local, using loose affiliations with agencies in other markets to manage their models when they went abroad. In the 1970s, the few agencies in business were based in Paris, London, or New York, and informal partnerships managed models in foreign markets. This arrangement made "model poaching" an occupational hazard, however. A model would be sent to Paris to get photographs and modeling experience to bring back to New York, and the Paris agency would end up stealing her.

By opening a branch of his agency in New York and poaching several of Ford's top models in the process, Casablancas became a major player in two cities on the fashion axis while neatly sidestepping the poaching problem himself. In this new method for managing models, he could offer them twice as many markets, fashion seasons, and photographers or editors to go see, all within his own agency. If a model wasn't working in Paris, he could send her to New York but still keep her under his control. Utilizing his powerful cross-continental marketing abilities, he made the most of a trend toward global modeling markets.

Casablancas understood the primacy of branding better than his predecessors. Marketing modeling as a "lifestyle," he created an image of his girls that was more sex and drugs and rock 'n' roll than the proper behavior and professionalism that had always been Eileen Ford's rule of thumb. The boutique agent, Carolyn, a denizen of the New York modeling scene, as she had been an agent in the business for twenty years, described Casablancas as a sort of lothario who was "hot—so sexy! He was sleeping with the girls, and his command of the language and his charisma brought in the clients." Sitting on a leather chair in her office, beside a bouquet of orchids, she told me the story:

> John Casablancas had the most famous agency in Paris, in the late seventies, early eighties, but he was only known in Europe. Until that time, there was really only Wilhelmina, who was alive then, and had just opened up her agency, in the early eighties, there was another modeling agency called Stewart Models, and then there was Ford.

John Casablancas comes to town, steals the head booker from Ford models, a woman named Monique Pillard—she has since been one of the presidents of Elite for a long time—and he finds a very savvy woman named Lisa Herzog. Finds her in a club. She's like twenty-something years old. And with Lisa and Monique, and by stealing Ford's big models, which included at the time Christie Brinkley, Janice Dickenson, and Grace Jones, the black singer, and a bunch of others, he opened up Elite New York in the early eighties.

Stealing models, sleeping with them, taking them abroad—these antics made Casablancas hard to ignore. He understood the innate sexual appeal of the business and glamorized it in ways that others had either ignored or wanted nothing to do with.

The *Vogue* fashion editor Polly Mellen told the journalist Michael Gross that Casablancas "was a ruthless womanizer, and the girls loved it"; he took a tame little business and "turned it into Hollywood." As a result, Gross reported, "People started to get interested. They wanted to know, 'who is this guy?' Everyone was talking."[28] Modeling's new notoriety generated mountains of publicity, with Casablancas often appearing center stage. His public affair with then fifteen-year-old model Stephanie Seymour shocked many, and his behavior around his models earned him a *New York* magazine feature entitled "Girl Crazy" that painted him as a "champagne guzzling pasha of pleasure, ogling the breasts of his charges."[29]

Yet despite his faults, Casablancas was a shrewd player who shook up the modeling business by taking advantage of trends that older adversaries such as Ford seemed to have missed and made more money more quickly than others who had been at it for years. While increasing the value and visibility of glamour labor, his goal to build a global network of agencies was prescient, hooking into a trend toward the globalization of image networks in the regime of the blink barely nascent in the 1980s. By the early 1990s, this change had had such profound effects, all the major modeling agencies began opening offices in Europe and beyond.

Ford Models did not open in either Paris or Milan until 1990, years after Elite started blazing the path in global expansion in 1986.[30] Elite and Ford battled for domination in America until the mid-1990s when, in another shake-up, Mark McCormack, the head of the modeling division of IMG, a privately held sports marketing and management firm, hired new staff at his modeling divisions in London and New York, opened a new modeling division in Paris, and lured away another ten of Ford's top-earning models. The firm offered models unprecedented access to IMG events and television divisions, with a global presence and diversity of services that positioned IMG well ahead of the pack when competing for new earnings possibilities opening up for models, such as endorsement deals or licensing contracts, as well as television and publishing deals.

Like Casablancas before him, McCormack understood the "model as brand" strategy quite well, banking on associating his agency with the big-name models he lured away from other agencies, using their star power to encourage up-and-coming models to try IMG.[31] The strategy worked, and IMG clawed its way to almost instant market domination with only a few strategically positioned model agencies within their larger network. Diane, a high-level agent, sitting petite and blond on a brocade divan at IMG's Paris office, smugly told me:

> We're the number one modeling agency now in the world, and we're the smallest. Think about just having three offices compared to other places that have huge numbers. Elite is huge. They have modeling schools, they have dozens of offices. We only have three offices, but we have a system that works for us.

That system worked in part because IMG saw the writing on the wall. Anticipating the growing public interest in fashion fomented by the supermodels, the growing number of fashion weeks, and the symbiotic relations between fashion's rhythms and the needs of cable TV, IMG's McCormack sought to use his company's events and television divisions to "act as the agent for fashion and modeling industries in America in their attempt to sell the exclusive right to film their twice yearly catwalk shows."[32] As models became brands in themselves, they not only modeled products to sell that brand to consumers but also joined the force of their "look" with products hoping to be associated with their personal brand.

In the pitched battle for our dwindling attention, the supermodels became the go-to girls for linking one's brand to the model "look," such that all the associations of fame, fashion, and fortune associated with that "look" might stick to the brand. Calvin Klein's effort to "own" Christy Turlington's look in the late 1980s was a telling moment in this process. Seeking to merge her brand with that of his new fragrance, Klein offered Turlington a multiyear deal in exchange for a lump sum: $3 million for eighty days' work a year over four years. The arrangement included contract clauses forbidding her from doing interviews, editorial spreads, or other advertising. Although his attempt ultimately failed, with Turlington renegotiating her contract a few months later, Klein's attempt to brand Turlington's face as his own echoed a growing desire in fashion to attach one's name or product to a memorable face and blur the lines between a model's look and one's brand as thoroughly as possible. From exercise tapes to international brands of soda, fashion became associated with whole new areas of everyday life. Once we were on a first-name basis with Cindy, Naomi, Linda, and Christy, this familiarity brought with it the astronomical paychecks for which the supermodels have become known.

While branding was an influence, paychecks would not have been quite so astronomical had it not been for "model wars" of the 1980s. After Casablancas took New York by storm, in the ensuing bidding war, he pushed up the price tags for all models' work. A female model I interviewed in a midtown coffee shop who had worked with him during this time explained:

> There just wasn't this super stardom yet. And John had a lot to do with that. He was asking a lot of money, and then was like fine, you don't want her, I'll take her elsewhere. He did this with Cindy [Crawford], he upped the ante. He tried to do it with other girls, but they were less dependable. He made Cindy a star.

Casablancas understood that modeling could be about celebrity, the fast lane, the gossip pages, and big money. While Ford's models dutifully listed their rates on their cards, by removing the prices from his promotional materials, Casblancas made the rates negotiable, paving the way for a new high of $1,500 a day for his top earners.[33]

Over and above the model wars, the 1980s witnessed a new kind of celebrity for models, and a winner-take-all market in modeling, which skewed the industry's pay scale in favor of a select few at the vast majority's expense. In the early 1980s, the industry still had a "parochial" feel, as one model agency owner put it; markets were local, smaller, and "nearly everybody on our books was working and making a good living."[34] Models were not yet celebrities in the sense they would become. The supermodels' high price tags and immense fame were due to several factors. First, they emerged into a power vacuum in Hollywood created by a sudden need of the time. While nowadays it may be hard to remember a time when every fashion magazine did *not* have an actress on its cover, this practice was nonexistent in the 1980s, since, as Katie Ford told *Vanity Fair* correspondent Bob Colacello, "politically minded Hollywood stars 'wouldn't do advertisements or be associated with fashion. So models took the place of actresses as icons of glamour.'"[35] As actresses started to hide themselves from this kind of work, people "needed something else in their mouths," that is, something to talk about, so, in the "next story came the models," as Parisian model agent Gerard Marie observed.[36]

Second, the lucky few who became supermodels benefited from a moment when the winner-take-all tendencies of the market combined with the evolution of models from mannequins or clothes horses to the personification of brands. Citing concrete limits on human attention, such as the difficulty people have processing lists that contain more than seven items, the economists Robert Frank and Philip Cook explained that "people do not possess sufficient time and energy—enough 'shelf space' to focus on any but the top competitors" in any field.[37] The upsurge in the number of images of models reduced the number of opportunities for stardom owing to this small problem with the human capacity for attention, whose limitations became starkly evident in the regime of the blink. As Frank and Cook observed,

Although our ability to generate and process information electronically has grown rapidly, our capacity as human beings to absorb and make sense of information has changed relatively little. The amount of information we can actually use is thus a declining fraction of the total information available.[38]

As information availability exploded, this fraction became miniscule. In the narrowed field caused by the widening image array bombarding our senses in the regime of the blink, only a few images could stand out, and those who succeeded in making such an image garnered the winner's spoils.

Many saw this as a winning strategy. According to one model agent, "In the days of the supermodel, you could open up a magazine and see them in several different advertisements or editorials because clients *wanted* familiar faces."[39] This ubiquity bred familiarity, and the "sheer amount of exposure brought almost immediate international name recognition and global celebrity status to models."[40] Seeking to leverage models' new branding power, even small companies jumped on the bandwagon; as the Milanese model agent Marcella Galdi told the journalist Michael Gross, "It's like buying a Gucci bag. . . . You show the world you have the money. Especially for an unknown company, you show the world that small as you are, you have twenty thousand dollars."[41] The transition from hiring a model to walk your runway, to hiring a brand to mark your product was clearly in evidence when designer Gianni Versace decided it was worth it to pay double or even triple to be the only designer any one of these models worked for during his March 1991 couture show. As the *Vanity Fair* correspondent Colacello explained, "Versace was the designer who pushed that concept [of the supermodels as a group] the furthest—reportedly he would outbid the competition to ensure that he got all the biggest stars for the same show, in the process inflating their rates from $10,000 to $50,000 for a half-hour appearance."[42] Gross observed that, once Versace started paying extra for exclusive bookings, "then all the other designers said, I'll match that. I'll pay you the same thing and you don't have to be exclusive." He noted Christy Turlington's recollection:

> It got bigger and bigger because they were outbidding themselves. Every year I thought, I can't make more than this, but every year I almost doubled my income. It's supply and demand, like sports. The best of the sports people will be paid any amount.[43]

At that time, in 1992, her estimated income had reached $1.7 million, which was, as she said herself, "a ridiculous amount of money."[44]

The fees grew so great, Linda Evangelista's quip that she and Christy Turlington liked to say "We won't wake up for less than $10,000" was not far off base.[45] In comparison to model rates in the past, supermodels commanded staggering sums. While superstar models in the 1960s, such as Penelope Tree, made $12 an hour and $60 a commercial, by the late 1990s, models of that caliber could make $50,000 in a single day.[46] Carolyn, the model agent from the boutique agency, explained:

> In the mid eighties into the early nineties it just kept snowballing and got bigger and bigger, and that's when you may have heard Linda Evangelista or Christy Turlington say "I won't get out of bed for anything less than $10,000 a day"—and they were right, they didn't have to. It was a true statement: These girls were making from $10 to $25,000 to $50 to $150,000 dollars a *day* for certain jobs.

After appearing on over 300 magazine covers, Cindy Crawford won a contract with Revlon cosmetics and also became the all-American face of Pepsi. In 1994, her gross earnings were estimated at $6.5 million.[47] By 1998, her earnings reportedly reached $8 million, and that same year, Claudia Schiffer topped out at $10.5 million.[48] Other sources estimate even higher amounts, reporting that Crawford, Turlington, Evangelista, and Campbell were all earning between $20 million and 30 million by this time.[49] Even for those who were not supermodels, the huge sums earned at the top trickled down. By 1999, the potential value of a model's image had increased so much that even an untried fourteen-year-old might start out earning $70,000 and within a few years be able to command as much as $100,000 to half a million dollars.[50]

With these astronomical paychecks, their lives took on the trappings of power and privilege. The fashion historian Harriet Quick described how, at the peak of their fame, the supermodels "traveled in limousines, wearing dark glasses. Bodyguards protected them, assistants opened fan mail, accountants invested their earnings, publicists protected their image, and consultants advised their careers."[51] The supermodels were living a moment in which modeling moved from representing brands to being a brand, and their glamour labor became glamorous indeed, popularized through their fame and the swirls of publicity that had become a part of their everyday lives.

Figure 1.2. Claudia Schiffer in the *Guess* perfume ad campaign, 1992.

Nicholas, a PR agent, argued that, just as Michael Jordan changed the rules of the game in sports, the supermodels changed the modeling business irrevocably:

Lightning does not strike twice. But it affects what happens now. [The supermodels] made it possible for girls to earn that much money. Even though the "quote" supermodels *now* aren't super in the way those girls were, they make just as much money. Look at what Michael Jordan did for athletes; it's the same thing. He paved the way for them to get a lot of money for endorsement deals, way more than anybody before that. He was the first athlete brand.

By becoming the Michael Jordans of fashion, the supermodels reaped newly stratospheric rewards, profiting from the way the brave new world of too many images to process made a recognizable face worth millions in the winner-take-all market of modeling, as success bred success for a very fortunate few.[52]

Not surprisingly, the idea of winner-take-all markets was recognized and named in the mid-1990s just when the regime of the blink was coming into full force. Models, more in demand than ever, filled the content vacuum created by cable and satellite technology's explosive growth, gave a recognizable face to expanding brands, and fanned the newly insatiable mainstream appetite for all things fashion. Awash in a rising tide of images, with little more time than the space of a blink to take them in, advertisers and imagemakers bet on the familiar face proven to sell well. The supermodels also became "super" because cable imaging shrank the world and suddenly everyone wanted their MTV.

Wallpaper TV

Within the newly dominant imaging mode, attention spans shrank as the sheer volume of images increased, forcing marketers and advertisers to find new ways to attract eyeballs. Ted Turner's 1980 inauguration of CNN made him the first to bring us all news all the time. In 1981, rock 'n' roll icons such as Pat Benatar and Mick Jagger appeared in television ads declaring, "I want my MTV," a sentiment apparently echoed by millions of teenagers, which helped launch a new era of music television. Cable technology spread like wildfire. Between 1975 and 1981, "The number of subscribers doubled, then jumped another 50 percent by 1985. By 1990, almost 60 percent of the American homes with television sets subscribed to a cable service, and industry revenue had reached $19 billion."[53] The cable revolution inundated viewers with images that came at them faster than ever. New satellites that "could transmit to earth all of the *Encyclopedia Britannica* in less than a minute," accelerated the global circulation of images, bringing events live from one part of the world to another for the first time.[54] The precipitous drop in prices for reaching cable markets facilitated this acceleration. By the 1980s, satellite images could be "picked up and placed before the viewer by a cable relay station whose cost in 1975 had been $125,000, but in 1980 was less than $4,000" because of quick technological advances.[55]

With this speedup in the flow and frequency of cable images, following fashion became a global pastime. Fashion images, with their appeal and relative ease of production, increasingly became part of the new electronic ambience of daily life. In the open-air loft offices of a world-renowned agency based in Soho, New York, Cameron, a young model agent, explained that suddenly "there were large channels of information looking for content, and models were a great thing to fill empty hours on the television." In a cable-televised world, shifts in styles that had taken weeks to communicate were transmitted instantaneously, accelerating the velocity of change and piquing the public hunger for knowledge about the fashion industry. Throughout the 1990s, the interest in fashion seemed to be growing unabated.[56] Fashion's iterations of slightly different themes and its constant stream of young and beautiful people inspired a Paris-based firm to launch a fashion channel in 1998, Fashion Television, devoted solely to depicting models pacing up and down the runway.[57] The managing director François Thiellet described it as "'wallpaper TV"; absent commentary, it presented "just music and fashion."[58] Fashion Television's wordless broadcasts obviated the need for translation or subtitles and eventually spread across the globe, reaching audiences from Milan to Mumbai.[59]

The bombardment of wildly different images on offer twenty-four hours a day made it impossible to indoctrinate the masses with a clear-cut ad campaign spelling out the advantages of one's product. Fleeting audience attention left little room for impressing on them with the idea that your product fulfilled a need they didn't know they had. Rather than the targeted mass campaign for a particular product, advertisers took a generalized approach, fostering a feeling about one's brand. The image's impact or contact became more important than its meaning.

According to media theorists, owing to its endless flow, viewers do not necessarily need narratives or stories to be attracted to or attached to watching television. Some scholars refer to this shift in the mode of imaging as the difference between the cinematic *gaze*[60] and the televisual *glance*.[61] The cinematic gaze is conceived as long and continuous, taking in an unfolding storyline, suturing together a series of images. The televisual glance takes in the transmission of disconnected images characteristic of television without needing to make sense of them or to turn them into a specific story or narrative.[62] Those stories that do exist on television are discontinuous, interrupted regularly by commercial breaks, changing channels, or the intervening time between weekly installments.

On fashion television, there was no story line, no narrative, just an endless series of models walking runways, producing the "wallpaper" effect its creator described. Starting in the 1980s, the new norm of surfing the constant stream of images, zapping from one channel to the next, had advertisers struggling to reach an increasingly distracted viewer. The VCR's time-shifting ability allowed viewers the freedom to watch what they wanted when they wanted to, destabilizing advertising's grip on specific markets at specific times even further.[63] Competition in media markets intensified as advertisers chased increasingly elusive attention, fractured by the new ability to zap away from advertisements or to slip in a tape and avoid them entirely. In the ensuing turmoil, media outlets consolidated, and marketers tried to pinpoint their appeals by segmenting markets into niches, through programming and advertising catering to viewers' market-researched needs and to their "consumption defined 'life-styles,'" operationalized by newly advanced methods for opinion surveys and other forms of testing markets.[64]

By the 1980s, new cable technologies made television's ever-present "now" into a twenty-four-hour show. Narrative content still had its place on television, but to fill all the available airtime would have been prohibitively expensive. Evolving from its organization into separate channels watched at specific times, television's continuous flow became what the media theorist Nigel Thrift describes as a "continuously diffracting spatial montage" in which channels run into each other as the viewer continuously surfs along. In this montage, rather than the "temporality and spatiality of the narrative, playing out once and for all," we find a "progression based on a shuffling between loops."[65] With the rise of the twenty-four-hour news circuit, the fashionable life became grist for the entertainment mill, and models its subject of choice. Instead of stories with a clear narrative arc, or installments that progress in a particular direction, continuous loops of news, weather, talk, shopping, sports, and fashion soon filled the void created by the wild new twenty-four-hour frontier.[66]

Fashion since the 1960s, with its sampling of all eras preceding, seems to epitomize this logic, with all of the past poised and ready to appear at any given moment in the present. The decline of narrative reconfigured the dominant circuits of attention to focus on the semi-conscious "feeling-cum-behavior" of affect, the energy that fires the volley of nerves and synapses, enabling the body to act before the conscious self is aware of its intentions.[67] Television's networked flow skipped over subjective narrative identification, instead creating a direct attachment to images that did not necessarily have to pass through meaning; rather, it was achieved through habit or exposure.[68] One is reminded of the proverbial "couch potato," one who watches without really seeing, absently clicking from one channel to the next without engaging with a particular storyline in any focused way.[69] With no need for a viewer to slow down watching for the time of subjective perception, the instantaneous impact of selling brands became a new way to create and maintain relationships with consumers. This was a radical shift, in which modeling became a life-encompassing endeavor, not something one could do part-time. One no longer worked as a model, one *was* a model, a shift that represented a whole new understanding of what modeling was and what constituted the modeling life.

The Biopower of Beauty

Before modeling clients realized how to play the odds in their favor, the supermodel moment elevated modeling to the highest levels of glamour, placing a new value on modeling's ability to generate and cement public engagement with its practices. With the expansion of television and, subsequently, computer networks, branding techniques and the globalization of fashion created a new environment in which interacting with fashion was normalized, expanding its ability to bind consumers to the rhythms of fashion weeks, the need to follow trends and fashion seasons, and the increasing attraction to interacting with and via brands. The supermodels were the star performers in this expansion, making the fashionable lifestyle and the concomitant glamour labor needed to achieve it seem like something nobody could do without.

The supermodels glamorized beauty as a "form of right living," as the fashion theorist Mimi Nguyen aptly puts it.[70] As such, following beauty's "promise"—by entering into efforts to be "beautiful" through proper self-monitoring and branding in the manner the supermodels employed to become "super"—engages beauty in a way that enlivens within a biopolitics that separates those who adhere to the norms and forms of beauty from those who do not, and valuing them accordingly. By mixing the allure of power, femininity, beauty, glamour, and fun, the supermodels "modeled" a form of empowerment that, as Nguyen observes, is "increasingly inseparable from deployments of structural and other forms of dominance."[71] This is the crux of the issue surrounding glamour labor as I've conceived it. Sold to us as a program of empowerment, by engaging in glamour labor, we implicitly sign onto a program that promotes forms of dominance the effects of which we remain only dimly aware.

When beauty is a biopower, the management of life according to its terms requires that those who do not subscribe to its techniques for maximizing life will not be valued within the system that values beauty. While Nguyen is concerned with Afghan women and the use of Western beauty norms to construct them as either good citizens who subscribe to beauty's precepts or cultural others who may serve as collateral damage in the pursuit of a more just and true world,[72] I am interested in how the same mechanisms within the biopower of beauty mark some bodies as fashionable while others are viewed as expendable in the processes that produce fashion. In other words, optimization is seen, in the biopolitics of beauty, as a pathway to becoming valuable, and the cultural trends originating in the supermodel era have elevated glamour labor as a means for achieving that value.

The right to engage in glamour labor is recognized only selectively, however. In fact, one of the functions of the glamour in "glamour labor" is to hide its connections to its biopolitical effects. Only the fashionable body is valued, the body that is engaged with technology and the rhythms of obsolescence. Those cut off from those engagements are used up in the production of the means to those engagements— producers of technologies such as silicon chips under toxic conditions, sweatshop workers worked beyond their capacities, through weariness, close to death, in order to make those objects of desire that draw others into the fashion system. The following chapters tell the story of how publics have been seduced by fashion, increasingly entrained with its rhythms. The biopower of beauty organizes the population into those who are willing to seek to enliven and optimize themselves by engaging with technologies and those who do not have access to this chance. Discourses of beauty as maximization link it to futurity, to its future promise of engaging with the world in an acceptable way.

The story of modeling reflects the story of how we exist in and through technologies of optimization that enframe us. The technologies we use are of our own creation, but once we set them forth into the world, they reflect back on us, showing us who we think we are and whom we aspire to be. More than a mere reflection, we live in and through the technologies we create and, in turn, are shaped by them, and telling the story of glamour labor within the biopolitics of beauty goes some way toward making sense of this complexity.

The supermodels became household names during the process of fashion's normalization, with its new ubiquity entering every facet of modern life, from what to wear to the office to what kind of toaster to buy. This significant transition in fashion's role in everyday life made living in the regime of the blink quite different from what came before. When the supermodels became brands, they made modeling a brand, which came to represent a way of being in the world that was about being "on" all the time, connected to all things fashion, where the personal and public became irrevocably mixed. This transition forged new pathways for affective branding and laid the foundations for the selling of glamour labor. Modeling work changed within each successive imaging regime: From the photographic frame, to the cinematic gaze, to the televisual glance, and on to the networked blink, the actual work of modeling evolved in ways that indicate ever-more encompassing forms of glamour labor, which not only intensified the demands of the modeling life but also engaged us with seeking to meet similar demands in seeking the fashionable life.

2

The Runway

Step into the Room Like It's a Catwalk

The air outside the tents at New York City's fashion week crackles with energy. I am on a research mission, milling around in the crowd outside the tents. Paparazzi, fashion students, film crews, fashion reporters, and curious onlookers jumble together as fashionistas and their acolytes in sky-high heels totter by. Still in their wild hair and makeup from the runway, models stop amid calls of "Over here!" "Just one more!" to pose obligingly for the battery of flashing cameras before disappearing into the black cars waiting to whisk them off to their next show. The excitement is palpable, filled with an energy that has taken on new significance since the Internet and social media have become a part of our daily lives.

A car pulls up and two young women emerge. The clutch of photographers bristles with lenses, shutters clicking in hopes of catching a newsworthy item or look as the women passed by. Who were they? No one seemed to know, but just by heading into the tents, they were fashion news. In the regime of the blink, the fashion show is no longer confined to the runways. Once designed to sell dresses to a hand-picked clientele, it is now a celebrity-studded spectacle, showcasing luxury brands and lifestyles through fashion coverage that no longer distinguishes between front of house, the runway, the flurry of activity backstage, and the crowd in the street waiting for a glimpse of a designer, editor, or the latest fashion trend. The attendees, the models, the preparation for the shows, the backstage, the parties—all are fodder for the fashion and style mill, churned out by newspapers, magazines, television, and the Internet. This chapter illustrates three key moments when the work of modeling reflected significant shifts in economic structures and imaging environments, changes highlighted when the form and function of the fashion show changed.

clothes need a body [handwritten margin note]

The Mannequin Parade

A mannequin is not that wooden instrument, unprovided with head or heart, on which robes are hung as on a clothes hanger. [That] the living mannequin . . . was invented . . . proves that the wooden mannequin did not fulfill the need.

—Paul Poiret

In contrast to the leisurely stroll for which "mannequins" were once known, brevity and impact are now the goals on the runway, a brief flash of excitement in a packed fashion week, one of many in a frenetically crowded fashion calendar. For Elena, a top model who has been the "face" of an international cosmetics brand, walking in the rarified air of couture fashion shows is a moment of breathless tension, over so quickly, she cannot think of anything at all:

> For me the most tense moment is when you are lined up backstage and they kind of literally have to like push you out. They have to push me out, I should say. And then once I'm on the runway, and once I take the first ten steps and I haven't broken my heel, or fell into the crowd or something like that, I just kind of focus on one photographer, and walk straight towards them, and don't think about anything, really. I don't think about anything. It's this one moment where you're just totally . . . silence; my mind just goes totally blank and then I turn around and walk back downstage, and then I go backstage and then I realize how fast my heart is pumping, and *then* sweat will come . . . [*she trails off, laughing*].

erratic changeableness [handwritten margin note]

Pinning her tension on the moment's brevity, she explained: "It's such a fleeting moment because the attention is on you, but the fashion industry is notoriously fickle, right, so you walk out, people stare at you for ten seconds, size you up, and then the next girl comes out, so you know you only have ten seconds to be in that limelight."

This crucial ten seconds speaks to the mechanisms of affectivity and speed that characterize the regime of the blink. The model's brief moment in the limelight typifies the imaging structure in which that limelight flashes more like a strobe light than a steady beam. In today's twenty-four-hour news cycle, there is a fashion week somewhere in the world practically every week, and images of couture are a click away. In the regime of the blink, the fashion show is the much anticipated flash of excitement, briefly dazzling the crowd.

The delirium of the fashion world has not always spun at such a frenetic pace. From the 1850s to the 1910s, showing fashion amounted to not much more than a leisurely stroll through the couturier's salon by salesgirls pressed into service from the shop floor to show how a dress looked in motion. Less frequently, there were elaborate presentations, shaped by storylines with evocative titles like "Gowns of Emotion" and "The Seven Ages of Woman."[1] After the early 1900s, as cinema bloomed into an economic and cultural juggernaut in the United States and consumer culture organized social life, movies played a pivotal role in making fashion accessible to a wider audience and extending its influence. In this confluence of spectacle and salesmanship, the first fashion runways presented a series of models walking in a line, idealizing images of identical bodies making identical movements on the assembly line. By the 1940s and 1950s, the doyennes of fashion elaborated these trends into an art form as they sashayed elegantly, epitomizing the pinnacle of glamour.

Even as the cinema and the burgeoning magazine industry aided fashion's spread into mid-century American lives and minds, fashion still moved relatively slowly, from shows, to career arcs, to the news of fashion itself. Prior to the advent of television, fashion news took months to arrive from Paris, the center of the fashion world at the time. While news of fashion weeks from Shanghai to Sao Paulo are instantly available today, "fashion week" traditionally happened only in the big three cities of the fashion nexus—Paris, London, and New York. It wasn't until March 1953 that *Vogue* magazine, owing to the new availability of jet travel, could publish its first international issue, reporting "for the first time in one issue . . . on couture collections in five countries."[2]

Prior to the 1960s—the speedup of travel and fashion on so many fronts—fashion shows were a lazy affair sometimes lasting as long as three hours. For the first several decades of its existence, the fashion show, or "parade" as it was called at the time, was an exercise in regal glamour, a sober affair in which models struck dramatic poses and walked sedately, reflecting the social status of their clientele. Models

person with unique skill as a result of long experience

coming into being

sometimes held a small card denoting the model number of the gown they wore, for ease of ordering. While there were some exceptions to this rule, such as the designer Lucile's first Parisian presentation, in which her mannequins tangoed wildly to an orchestra at a sort of thé dansant,[3] from these early origins until the 1960s, the fashion show was about buying the fashions wafting by.

What accounts for the evolution of the fashion show from a periodic stroll by models through a couturier's salon to the highly sought after, intensely focused, widely publicized events of today? The fashion scholar Caroline Evans marked the origins of this change in the 1960s, when the decline of haute couture and the rise of ready-to-wear clothing made "much of the couture side of the business" into "a loss leader, generating the publicity and prestige necessary for the licensing deals, perfumes and cosmetics that brought profits in."[4] Obviously, methods of fashion production, international relations surrounding couture, links between fashion and art, gender norms, and the demands of capitalism all came into play. This change also occurred, however, during the advent of television imaging. Television moved away from what the visual theorists Laura Mulvey and Kaja Silverman deem the *cinematic* norm, where seamlessly edited images construct a narrative with which the viewer identifies[5] and objects on display had ample time to coalesce into a meaningful set of images. The new dominant norm shunned narrative, favoring instantaneous impact instead.[6]

While scholars have noted imaging methods' influence on fashion show formats, few examine the dominant imaging regime's effect on how bodies are valued. The fashion historians Caroline Evans and Elizabeth Wilson have both linked styles of runway presentation to developments in productive technology, aesthetic concerns, and political movements.[7] Evans and the media studies scholar Charlotte Herzog, among others, also note relations between cinema and the catwalk.[8] Evans, in particular, clearly shows dominant productive technologies' influence on fashionable "ideals" presented by popular cinema in the early twentieth century. Extending this analysis, however, reveals how presenting not only fashion but the model's body itself symptomatizes media technologies' role in organizing bodies, making them more efficiently available to work. In this transition, photographic and cinematic technology's heavy influence on the format and timing of the fashion *politics concerning environmental influence*

show gave way to television's new conventions, employing structures later accelerated by the 1980s cable revolution and tripped into hyperdrive by the advancement of the Internet.

Within a biopolitical context of branding and affective connections built through the glamour labor of paying attention, television's emergence as a full-fledged force in the 1960s and 1970s shattered the discreet restraint so valued in mid-century couture models. Time-consuming and carefully crafted glamour seemed outmoded. Immediacy and "realness" became favored ideals, mimicking the intimacy and, soon, the ubiquity of the television image. Breaking with the smooth continuity of presentation consonant with the cinematic regime, models no longer walked slowly, turning to show a garment to full effect. Breaking from the cinematic norm, models ran, jumped, and struck instant poses, creating a barrage of disconnected images registered as snapshots of a brand. Photographic models took to the runways. Pushing aside the traditional runway models' faithful replication of a walking style or body stance designated by the designer, the model's own "look" became an important component of the fashion show. The 1980s took this immediacy and primacy of the "look" into overdrive, as the supermodels became household names. Fashion shows became elaborate spectacles designed for the camera, paving the way for the whirlwind of fashion weeks beamed immediately worldwide. The story of modeling from fashion show, to photo shoot, to scouting the world for the next profitable face illustrates key moments in the development of glamour labor. Informed by changing notions of the working body and affective connections facilitated by new technologies, models' glamour labor is a prime resource for analyzing the biopolitical regulation of bodies in twenty-first-century capitalism.

One of the first living mannequins was not employed as such. Married to the Parisian couturier Charles Frederick Worth, he dressed her in his creations and sent her to the horseraces at Longchamps, where "the newest fashions and most striking examples of the dressmakers' art were displayed"[9] during the mid- to late 1800s. Marie Worth, dutiful wife and mannequin, was not a member of society. She appeared at so many fashionable gatherings, however, her husband's clients eventually befriended her, inviting her "to weddings and sometimes to fashionable balls."[10] This collaboration with his wife led naturally to Worth's idea of putting dresses on live models, keeping them ready at hand "to put on new dresses for the inspection of a client."[11] Accordingly, this "use of living models to show his dresses" was Worth's "chief contribution to the Haute Couture."[12]

Worth's first live mannequins weren't expected to do much more than walk back and forth in the salon, allowing prospective clients to inspect the garments and see how they looked in motion.[13] A model's personality, her movements, her bone structure, and presence were not yet the sites of investment and the bases of various economies they would become. In those early days, "Models were chosen more for their availability than for anything else."[14] Modeling was not glamorous—a model only had to look pleasant and walk in a straight line. With recruits drawn from "the workshop floor, or found among the demimondaine," modeling gained a shady reputation. Not only did it employ women of questionable origins, it required them to display their bodies for a living.[15] As the fashion historian Diana de Marly described it, the "model" girl eventually began to "replace the seamstress and the shop girl in the imagination of the predatory male as the sort of girl who was ripe for seduction but not for marriage."[16] This assumption that models were easy prey stemmed from an ambiguity surrounding "what, exactly, was for sale: the dress, or the woman modeling it."[17]

The blurred boundaries between model and product, body and image, point to the peculiar aspects of modeling work informing my analysis of media systems, illustrating how they don't just entertain but also make optimizing bodily resources for corporate profit seem like a good idea. The model—both person and thing, image and body—is institutionalized within ideas and practices shaping fashion, gender, class, hierarchy, and, most important, what a body is and what it is good for. Seen from this angle, the early stages of modeling in the late 1800s to its organization as a profession in the 1920s and 1930s and on to its first cultural heyday in the 1940s and 1950s not only tells the story of changes in the world of fashion but also reflects the systematization and standardization of bodies at work idealized by the fashion show. Further cultural, technological, and economic trends originating in the 1960s and kicked into overdrive in the 1980s then shifted the emphasis from standardization toward optimization, significantly changing fashion image production, the kinds of activities models performed, and model recruiting and employment. Like canaries in the coalmine, models' glamour labor is symptomatic of changing ideas of what bodies are good for and what they are worth.

A model's "look" was not always a commodity. The interlocked institutions and practices that made the "look" into a saleable thing were not yet in place at the onset of modeling. In the early days, the idea that one's individual style of walking or unique demeanor, appearance, or personality could be something from which a model herself could profit, was not part of the modeling transaction. While today's models try hard to make an impression, models showing clothes in late nineteenth-century Paris fashion salons were not allowed to talk or even make eye contact with the clients.[18] As the social theorist Nick Lee observed, the term "mannequin" captured the ambiguous role of these early fashion models "quite neatly," referring to both the inanimate dummies used to show clothes as well as to the model herself. Highlighting the model's need for effacement, he explained:

> When modeling clothes, the mannequin had to be present and absent at the same time. She was required to lend the support of her body to the clothes on display, and depending on cut, fabric and type of clothing, she was also required to lend animacy to the clothes, to display how they would look in real life. However, as a temporary surrogate for the client, dressed only to give an impression of how another might look in those clothes, the mannequin was also obliged to efface herself. The likelihood is that the former seamstresses or shop-girls doing the modeling already had plenty of experience of pretending 'not to be there' when in the presence of wealthier women. As was the case in other service roles, the models' visible presence and movement was absolutely necessary, but any articulate presence was not.[19]

The fashion designer Paul Poiret once told an interviewer, "No, mademoiselle . . . do not speak to the girls; they are not there." Although they were standing right next to him, he meant they were not there "socially."[20] Similarly, in London, the models showing gowns "barely smiled and never spoke, their working class origins as ambiguously veiled as the beautiful bodies they paraded to an audience of middle- and upper-class men and women."[21]

Figure 2.1. Paul Poiret and his matched set of models, 1926.

This uniformity in silence characterized the standardized performance expected of fashion models from the early days in the 1850s
through the 1910s and 1920s. Unlike the "floating norms" described
by the sociologist Ashley Mears, where it is anybody's guess what will
be required of a model from client to client and day to day,[22] models
working for the salons and fashion houses of Charles Frederick Worth
or Poiret in Paris, and for Lucile in New York and London, learned to
present themselves in a style exclusively designed by their employers. In
contrast to the personally developed or signature "walk" contemporary
models cultivate as part of their unique image or "look," in the 1890s,
designers imprinted how the model used her face or moved her body
for display, especially when she walked or interacted with others, creating a uniform image for that designer's salon. Similarly, the model's
carefully hidden personality created a blank surface on which the client
could project her desires.

Consequently, individuality and uniqueness were solely qualities of
the designer, and early models articulated only the designer's presence.
For the French couturier Poiret's six-week tour of Europe in 1911, his
nine mannequins' traveling uniform consisted of identical blue serge

dresses and beige plaid cloaks.[23] Each model, similar in height and carriage, presented a graphic figure, amplifying the effect of the Poiret image nine times over. The British designer Lucile, "the supreme dictator of elegance during World War I,"[24] created her "goddesses" by training girls mainly drawn from working-class London suburbs in specific types of "carriage and deportment."[25] She "groomed the girls she hired, gave them exotic names and refused to allow them to wear the black satin maillots," the modest all-over body covering commonly used in dress salons to hide from clients any of the model's exposed skin.[26] By exploiting "a frosty and detached snobbishness in her models,"[27] her mannequins achieved a level of glamorous carriage that made them the darlings of the British press, "renowned for their regal manner and unsmiling hauteur."[28] In this nascent form, glamour labor was tightly scripted, defined by the designers, and trained into the models in order to create the standard image of the house.

Origins of the Catwalk

In the early 1900s newly minted practices of mass production and circulation, a simple fad could become all the rage. During this period, it was not uncommon to find more than half a million people on the beach in Coney Island, "the most giant amusement outlet of Greater New York," which, according to a *New York Times* article in 1909, catered to "the crude imagination of the masses."[29] Luring the mass desires toward profitable ends became the favorite pastime of this era's brand-new public relations experts, in whose hands advertising became a powerful tool of mass persuasion.[30] This creation of mass entertainments did not amount to total pacification, however; realizing the strength of their numbers, unrest bubbled up among the ranks as well. The new immiseration of production-line fashion workers that was becoming the industry norm met with strident protests, such as the 1909 walkout by twenty thousand shirtwaist makers from nearly five hundred garment shops in New York City after a mass meeting in the Great Hall of the Cooper Union.[31] Built on the backs of these struggling workers, the garment industry rapaciously prospered. By 1915 the textile and garment industries had grown to great proportions, becoming the third-largest industry in the United States, behind only steel and oil.[32]

Mass fashion

moving image, moving body of the model!

The creation of mass taste and the rise of mass fashion went hand in hand. Following fashion became a new pastime in the United States. Fashion edicts from Paris elicited mass conformity to a certain skirt length or hairstyle. Starting in 1910, newsreels included footage of Paris fashion, and short films depicting forthcoming styles became popular.[33] Film was an especially potent medium. Its availability to a mass audience usurped photography as the dominant mode of imaging. The still image remained important yet held nowhere near the allure of the moving one. By the mid-1920s, going to the movies was a United States national obsession. There were eight big film companies controlling distribution in theater chains via companies commanding five hundred to one thousand theaters each.[34] The movies, deemed by the media scholar Stuart Ewen "the most powerful agency of mass impression," began to play a role in the rise of mass fashion.[35] Consumer culture emerged in full force, selling images of fashion as paths to modernity.

Cinema's automation of imaging and fashion's standardization and wide distribution represented a new productive ideal. Technology that would enable the first feature film was just around the corner in 1914, when Henry Ford introduced the eight-hour, five-dollar day. A fan of scientific techniques of Taylorization, Ford organized his plants for maximum efficiency, dictating workers' movements in assembly lines moving with mechanic precision. A series of bodies, working as one, epitomized the image of the mechanical body, or body as machine. Standardization began to overpower the craft of the artisan, replacing the handmade one-off with industrially produced identical objects. As the historian Elspeth Brown has convincingly argued, photography played a key role in the development of an idealized efficiency and standardization of movement. Owners such as Ford used motion studies that mimicked cinema, inspired by Eadweard Muybridge's series of photographs studying locomotion from thirty years prior. Using Muybridge's techniques, corporate managers in the 1920s dissected individual worker movements in the factory to edit out waste according to what the theorist Jean-Louis Comolli called a technique of "visible mechanics."[36]

The "visible mechanics" of bodies moving with syncopated efficiency on the assembly line became a cultural talisman. This pattern reverberated through the chorus lines of the "Tiller girls in Berlin in the 1920s,

8hr/
$5
day

farmer

and then the Rockettes in New York's Radio City Music Hall in the 1930s," as well as the "abstract patterns made by the repetition of female bodies in the films of Busby Berkeley," in which identical girls kicked in unison, gaily greeting the modern age.[37] Linking the chorus line to modern industrial mass production, the German film writer Siegfried Kracauer argues that it symbolized the capitalist system, subsuming the identity of each chorus girl into a "mass ornament,"[38] echoed by the a parade of models' bodies evident in the first American fashion show.[39] With proceeds earmarked for European war relief, this *Vogue* magazine–sponsored event took place in New York in 1914,[40] the same year a catwalk was constructed at a Chicago trade exhibition, for the first time extending into the audience to afford a good view of the clothes.[41]

In the burgeoning culture of consumer capitalism, department stores increased in size and number. As stores proliferated, so did the competition between them. Each store tried to outdo the other as "fashion spectacles" (what shows were called at the time) became more elaborate and common. By 1915, fashion shows could be found in every sizable city in the United States. As a result, as the journalist Michael Gross observes, "Mannequins became an important factor in the American fashion scene."[42] Models glamorized the dominant mode of work at the time, presenting as a thing of beauty and allure bodies moving in precision, organized by industrial rhythms. The story of the fashion show is the story of the "social and economic rationalization of the body in the early twentieth century," as the fashion scholar Caroline Evans puts it, by industrial technologies such as mass production.[43] Models led the way into a consumption-defined lifestyle by showing goods as a way to become part of the consuming community and, perhaps, win a chance to share the limelight.

Foreshadowing the mimicry glamour labor elicits, the historian Marlis Schweitzer describes how models, "walking in procession along a conveyer-belt like runway," represented a promise that "with the appropriate consumption of goods one might find membership within a larger community and perhaps even win a moment in the spotlight."[44] Following the prototype in fashion shows depicted in film, the fashion show was an exercise in modeling glamour labor. As the media studies scholar Charlotte Herzog claims, fashion shows in films showed

to teach publicly

young women how to act like models. As such, 1930s cinema promul-
gated glamour labor in terms of displaying and making desirable certain
forms of comportment and dress.[45] The film studies scholar Charles
Eckert calls these practices of display and comportment toward fashion
a "potent acculturation provided by Hollywood." [46] This process made
audiences receptive to subtle cues and associations, fueling consumerism through exposure to Hollywood depictions of luxury and glamour,
expressed by objects made desirable by how they were portrayed in film.

The understated elegance of 1930s models soared to new heights in
the form of the elegant swans of the 1940s and 1950s. Hollywood's influence was still strong, and movies such as *Cover Girl* (1944) and *Funny
Face* (1957) depicted modeling as a world of glamour, fun, and romance
while fanning interest in fashion via providing tools and information
useful for engaging in fashion practices. *Funny Face*, in particular, dra-
matized glamour labor's promise, showing how anyone could imitate
the fashionable practices the film depicted, thereby turning their "funny
face" into a fashionable one.

Disdainful Beauties

the ideal example

The acculturation to glamour by Hollywood created a mystique around
the runway model, an apotheosis incarnate in the elegant runway
models of the 1940s and 1950s. Elaborating a tradition of embodying
the New Woman, the fashion historian Caroline Evans argues, early
twentieth-century models sought to appear "cold, unavailable, detached,
at work."[47] This prized hauteur became definitive of modeling work.
Mid-century models paid strict attention to carriage and formalized
presentation. Dutifully maintaining the specific "look" associated with
the couture house for which they worked, they cultivated a controlled
uniformity of walk and style of self-presentation consonant with the
"aesthetic of the designer" in charge of the house.[48]

In an early precursor to branding, there was a recognizable Dior walk.
Chanel's models struck the famous Chanel pose, "one foot forward, flat
belly, head held high, chin up and one hand in the pocket of her skirt."[49]
The scripted performances elicited by each designer reflected the cinematic ideal of telling a story. The fashion show audience had time to

detached —

Figure 2.2. A typical Chanel pose. *Vogue*, November 1926.

see and absorb what was on display, along with information about the
fashions modeled and how to buy them. In the strict order of presentation common at the time, the story almost always ended its predictable
arc with the wedding gown as the finale of the show.

By the 1940s and 50s, the model "look," shaped by the demands of
each fashion house, became formalized into the structure of the *cabine*,
a group of roughly seven to twelve models who worked exclusively for

one couturier for the duration of the construction of the collection. The fashion historian Jean Noel Liaut defines a *cabine* as

a word with a dual meaning: in the literal sense the *cabine* (studio) was a room, usually narrow, shaped like a corridor, in which each model had her own appointed place, in front of a table with a mirror above it.[50]

Figuratively, however, the word referred to a group of models working primarily for one couturier.[51] *Cabine* models generally did only runway work.

Up until the 1960s, with a few exceptions, runway and print models were two very different types of model, one shaped by the desires of the camera, and the other by the needs of the live audience. Before television technology fused these needs into one, very few models could cross the border between the two. For the runway models of this era, the demands of the camera did not shape their ability to project energy and capture attention. Having the right skin to reflect light photographically was not yet a job requirement, but embodying the right carriage and attitude was.

As Liaut paints it, the "height of elegance" in this period was "a disdainful beauty and an air of distinguished boredom."[52] To project that ideal to an audience, the typical runway mannequin's "demeanor was unsmiling, glacial and immobile."[53] Shows had an intimate, exclusive feel. Only ladies of a certain level of society were invited, along with select members of the fashion press. Models did not jump or sashay. As Evans observed, "in the 1950s, models slithered along the catwalk, at most pulling on or off a glove."[54] Runway models were not necessarily good looking. Shows were not yet media events, and the qualities necessary to produce an attractive "close-up" were not required. Consequently, the faces of show models were "not of paramount importance." The model historian Brigid Keenan observes that a show model

need not be pretty; some of the stars have been downright plain . . . Christine Tidmarsh, who worked for Yves Saint Laurent when he first started, had an enormous mouth and bad skin, but no one noticed. She would bound into the *salon* with such verve and energy, that when she

[handwritten margin note:] to think unworthy of notice, to consider something beneath oneself

spun round the hem of her skirt would catch all the front row journalists' notebooks and send them flying off their knees.[55]

One historian deemed Bronwen Pugh, a famous runway model at the time, "an untidy, sulky-looking girl" who made an "overnight reputation for herself when she first modeled for Balmain in Paris. A reporter described her as 'that Welsh girl who drags a fur along the runway as if she had just killed it and was taking it home to her mate.'"[56]

Figure 2.3. Christine Tidmarsh had such energy that when she spun round, the hem of her skirt would flick all the front row journalists' notebooks off their knees. From Brigid Keenan, *The Women We Wanted to Look Like* (New York: St. Martin's Press, 1977), 111.

Figure 2.4. Bronwen Pugh, "that Welsh girl who drags a fur along the runway as if she had just killed it and was taking it home to her mate," circa 1957. From Brigid Keenan, *The Women We Wanted to Look Like* (New York: St. Martin's Press, 1977), 109.

difference between runway and photographed models

Great in action, typical runway models were "seldom photogenic"; Pugh, for instance, was "rarely photographed. Whilst she was supreme on the catwalk, photographers found her doe-eyed looks and angular proportions too exaggerated for readers of *Vogue* and *Harper's Bazaar*."[57]

The success of models like Pugh depended on their skill at manipulating their facial expression and body movements to produce a subtle, controlled, and direct modulation of audience response aimed at stimulating desire for the dress on display. Popular during the cinematic regime's golden age, this presentation style resonated with the narrative pace of image production, allowing time for the viewer to absorb meaning and for the overall effect of an image to produce a specific emotional quality or attachment. While many of the *cabines* survived into the 1970s, their dominance receded as the converging forces of cybernetic and television technologies in the regime of the glance gave runway modeling a wholly different feel.

Enter the Gamine — [handwritten: slim, often boyish elegant young woman who is percieved to be mischievous / sexually appealing]

It was 1964, and Mary Quant's fashion show was about to begin. Suddenly, the models burst onto the runway, all smiles as they kicked, danced, and ran. This style of presentation, like nothing anyone had seen before, projected a wild energy that shocked and fascinated the fashion public. Dressed in cowboy boots, tweed knickerbockers, and Norfolk jackets, the models bounding down the runway employed props to eye-popping effect. As Quant told it,

> One girl carried an enormous shotgun; another swung a dead pheasant [handwritten: bird] triumphantly round her head. Perhaps too triumphantly because the poor thing, which we had bought from Harrods across the road, thawed out in the heat of the place and blood began spurting out all over the newly painted walls; even over some of the journalists.[58]

Seeking a "greater sense of speed and movement," Quant sped up the proceedings to a breakneck pace, showing forty garments in fourteen minutes, producing a show whose format all fashion shows would eventually adopt.[59] Apparently nobody minded either the breakneck pace or being splattered with blood. At the end, "the place just exploded" with applause.[60] [handwritten: skip about in play]

That same year André Courrèges's beaming models gamboled down the runway in the Mod look that would come to define a generation. This revolutionary fashion moment showed clothes on what the fashion historian Caroline Evans called "a new kind of girl in a new kind of salon."[61] This "new kind of girl" was a photographic rather than a

Figure 2.5. One of Mary Quant's rock 'n' roll dancing mannequins, 1965. Note the electric guitar in the foreground. From "The Mary Quant Show at Best's," September 1, 1965, *New York Herald Tribune*, September 2, 1965, 10. Courtesy of the Queen's County Library, New York.

runway model. Quant, for one, liked the photographic models' ability to "hold a graphic pose."[62] She explained:

> We managed to persuade nine of the top photographic girls to model the clothes for us. We did this because I wanted to show the clothes moving, not parading, and these girls move beautifully and naturally. They walk swingingly and when they are still for a moment, they stand arrogantly.[63]

Quant categorically rejected the "mincing up and down, stop and start, stylized movements of the usual fashion model."[64] Many designers followed suit, and the stately parade of fashions in the daily ready-to-wear show, held for private customers during a luncheon or tea, became a thing of the past. Fashion designers like Courrèges and Quant understood the climate change and embraced the idea of making an impact. Amid the clamor of the youth quake, the struggle for new rights, and upheavals in the centuries-old traditions of couture, television brought with it a turning point in which the instantaneous impact of a designer's overall image became all that mattered.

From the 1960s forward, the fashion show's goal shifted to presenting the designer's signature "look," sometimes at the expense of actually showing the clothes. Going for impact, rather than information,

Figure 2.6. A barefoot model with a Vidal Sassoon–style bob models a Paco Rabanne shift, 1966. *New York Herald Tribune*, March 29, 1966. Courtesy of the Queens County Library, New York.

demanded reconfiguring the fashion show into a media event. What's more, print models' invasion of the runway brought photography's demands for appearance and presentation in their wake. On the waves of images continuously projected by television, models ascended to the status of pop icons, popularizing imperatives for slimming, dieting, and pursuing youth that would soon become a way of life.

No longer presented as identical cogs in a machine, slithering as haughty ice queens in a formalized conceit stamped uniformly by their couture house, runway models were increasingly chosen for their ability to "bubble over and clown."[65] Improvisation on the runway was highly sought after, analogous to the shift away from the obedient, conformist, ideal worker toward the emotionally labile, self-creating, sometimes manic worker that would become highly valued in the coming decades. Subsequently, the live fashion show became show business, and the models were its stars. Starting in the 1970s, the pay for models with personality and a sense of humor that would bring in the press bounded to a new high, and soon "the top ten models could command more than $1,000 for an hour show."[66]

As television's glance was flooded with the influence of blink technologies, Theirry Mugler's 1984 ready-to-wear show marked the beginning of a new era, the fashion show as mass entertainment.[67] It was the first time "the general public was ever present at a live Paris show."[68] As the regime of the blink came into full swing, Mugler captured audience attention with "light displays, epic soundtracks, and models on six-inch stilettos in rhinestone corsets."[69] No longer the buyers' or special clients' exclusive domain, fashion shows became rock 'n' roll spectacles with audiences of thousands. Elaborate effects staged by promoters and producers included dry ice fog, suds, fur runways, and light displays.

As the trend toward the globalization, popularization, and branding of fashion progressed, the number and scale of "fashion weeks" increased. By the 1990s, "there were a staggering 1,500 major showings on the calendar" of the London–Paris–Milan–New York circuit. When the "television cameras joined the parade" to capture runway footage for fashion news programs, "high fashion turned into high entertainment" in which designers tried to outdo one another, with "seminude costumes, strange hair and makeup, and gimmicky staging." The fashion

fashion became more of a vision rather than the exchange of clothing

magazines "just couldn't seem to get enough of the wild and crazy images" from the catwalks.[70] More opportunities opened for models to work globally, walking catwalks in not only Paris but also Singapore, São Paulo, and Madrid, and getting tear sheets not just from one of the *Vogue* magazines (American, British, Italian, or French), but also non-mainstream publications like *I-D*, the *Face*, and *Paper*.

In 1991, in Versace's spectacle of money, excess, and over-the-top promotion, Naomi, Christy, Linda, and Cindy burst onto the runway together, "miming to George Michael's *Freedom*" the rock video in which all four had starred,[71] looking like rock stars in their own right. As Evans puts it, the fashion show was becoming a "showcase for the designer's mind." Referencing Walter Benjamin, Evans notes that the "'aura' . . . ascribed to the artwork had become detached from the goods and associated with the designer's vision."[72] As runway photographs appeared in more magazines and newspapers and were broadcast through satellite networks worldwide, showing the aura of the designer's vision became far more important than selling this or that dress. Shifts in the role of haute couture in fashion also shaped the fashion show, as well as changing notions of femininity and gendered consumption, but these influences do not fully account for why the fashion show changed so dramatically. While Evans also stipulates that the "altered role of the image as a promotional and marketing tool from the 1960s on" changed runway modeling, she is less interested in seeing in these events evidence of growing affective connections, where the fashion show plays a role in establishing affection for a brand, the feel of a brand's look, and stimulating interest in fashion as a way of life.

The fashion show's changing form and practice became fertile ground for the glamour labor of optimization and enhancement as we know it today. After Quant and Courrèges mobilized their innovations, models soon had to be all one package, with the right walk for the runway, the right face for the camera, the right verve to stand out, making it look natural and easy all the while. Models with personality were sought after and revered. No longer a "pin-money job," modeling became all-encompassing work.[73] One did it as a career, a career so absorbing it grew into a lifestyle, packaged and sold as a commodity itself.

modeling & media sought the lively attitude of models rather than the subordinate "cabine girls" because designers wanted to bring attention to the shows

- tap into the model's affectivity to make the shoot unique
* commodification of "the look" (84)
* ownership of images (83)
* "Age of the Face" (1950's (95)
* the image as a whole rather than just posing (87)
↳ theatrical photography

The Photo Shoot

Strike a Pose—There's Nothing to It

In her supermodel heyday, Cindy Crawford described how an up-and-coming fashion photographer asked her to act like a small rodent in order for him to get the shot he was looking for:

> The first time I worked with him, he'd want you to do things like, you know, like can you be a rat? And then he would take pictures. This was in my big cover heyday, and I was like, oh my god, what if he runs this picture? I'm still not sure why he made us do that. I think it was just to break the . . . so he got something different out of you. Because when you went from doing this (she mimicked being a rat by wriggling her nose and baring her teeth), at least you've broken the mood and when you went back to your more normal modeling, it kind of worked itself out.[1]

While the runway may be the public face of modeling work, the photo shoot exerts its own behind-the-scenes iconic allure. Rather than the solo runway turn, here teams of professionals working with the model to produce just the right effect to be captured on camera. The history of the fashion shoot, much like that of the fashion show, illustrates a gradual shift away from a highly scripted performances elicited by tight control of the model toward a more free-form exchange prompting the model to bring the unexpected to the transaction.

Directing a supermodel to try to look like a rat stands in stark contrast to the carefully arranged scenarios of the cinematic age. Arguably, the photographer above hoped to elicit something unpredictable from this supermodel, pushing her out of her comfort zone to do something unexpected. Going for the nonsensical, he was playing on the model's affectivity, tapping an energy flow that might make a good photograph great.

prime peak
causing emotion / feeling — fashion shoot = more free exchange of acting
* inwardness of the model's look, she learned to feel and express the clothes (105)

80

rationing in WWII → end of model photography (88)
Dior's "New Look" (89)
Pop culture (youth) > sophistication (94)

This energy was not always valuable, however. Prior to the 1900s, one's personal image was not one's own. A stroke of a judge's pen made the image personal property and photographic modeling into a job. For the workaday mannequins from the 1920s to the 1930s, however, it wasn't much of one. Personalities were less important than pose, as they usually constituted just one element in a carefully constructed scene. While models gained importance in crafting the finely honed formalism of 1940s and 1950s haute couture fashion photographs, it wasn't until the 1960s' immediacy and exposure of the model in the image—in which she worked to appear to be caught off guard or in an intimate moment—that modeling resembled anything like it is in the current stage. Now fashion imagery's affective economics depend on what the social theorist Nigel Thrift describes as "loopholes through which the new and quirky can make their way,"[2] a source of the unpredictable, made newly valuable by the digital age.

In the age of the blink, glamour labor's new dimensions called for deeper investments from the model. Modeling work evolved from telling us and showing us to hinting at something fleeting, something hard to grasp, as working with affectivity and affective flow became centrally important for producing the desired 'look." The transition from artifice to authenticity, no matter how contrived, made the model's glamour a central player in the drama of enticing publics to become glamour laborers themselves. Modeling work shifted from something one did during the working day to living "the life," a life that made total exposure, being "on" all the time, in the know, and *in* fashion, irresistibly attractive.

The Photographic Frame: Modeling Becomes a Job

In the 1890s, the idea that a model would have the right to profit from the use of her image was absurd. The glamour labor of constructing one's "look" to control one's overall image in print and in person was confined to a very few who regularly appeared in the public eye. Owning the rights to one's personal image is a modern-day conceit. Even Minnie Clark, a sought-after model for the iconic Gibson Girl image, popular in magazine illustrations, was paid just a one-time fee for the sitting and had no claim on how the images were used or the money they made thereafter.[3] In fact, when photography became a viable alternative to

Figure 3.1. A Gibson Girl illustration by Charles Dana Gibson: Evelyn Nesbit, her head and hair forming a question mark in the illustration "Women: The Eternal Question." From *Gibson Girl Illustrations*, selected and arranged by Carol Belanger Graft (Mineola, NY: Dover Publications, 2006).

commercial illustration, "models in the 1890s hiked their fees if photos were taken, for the camera bilked them out of hours of income from posing."[4] In the shift to photography as a mass-distributed medium, the time required to create an image mattered less than its place in a broader system, where the context of production and the network of affective connections through which that image circulated determined its value.

The market for photographs picked up considerably when the half-tone press, patented in 1881, made it possible to print photographs on the same page as type. In 1892, *La Mode Practique* used halftones to show fashion for the first time.[5] Photographs became a cheap alternative to illustrations, which had become an overly expensive indulgence,[6] increasingly reserved for creating the idealized images on magazine covers.[7] In 1895, slightly more than 90 percent of newspaper and magazine advertisements used pen-and-ink illustrations. A mere twenty years later, this number had dropped to 20 percent.[8] The burgeoning market for photography prompted the Western Camera Publishing Company of Minneapolis to run a "Photographs Wanted" ad in 1904. The accompanying copy "signaled the dawn of a new profession: 'There is a large demand for photographs suitable for use in connection with *Modern Advertising*. We are in a position to know what is acceptable work and to place it where it will command the highest price.'"[9] Where models once were paid for their patience, stamina, and ability to hold a pose, photography brought with it a different kind of work. After a legal tussle about the status of one's personal image, photographs took on a new value, making photographic modeling into a paying job.

In the age of rampant selfies, and an almost ubiquitous desire for exposure, it is hard to imagine the shame eighteen-year-old Abigail Roberson felt when, with the distribution of twenty-five thousand lithographs of her likeness, she became the "(unknowing) poster girl for Franklin Mills Flour."[10] When she sat for a portrait in a photographer's studio and innocently granted permission for a lithograph to be made from them, this was not her plan. When her image appeared on thousands of posters and magazine advertisements to sell flour, she was not flattered, she was angry. Not only had the milling company used her image without consulting her or paying her, modeling for advertisements was not something ladies of polite society did. A "plucky" young woman, she sued the company, claiming she had become an object of derision, with jeering neighbors causing her such mental distress, she demanded $15,000 in damages and an injunction.[11] Her 1902 lawsuit broached the idea that a photograph might violate a person's right to privacy, starting a chain reaction that changed the terrain of commercial photography, kick-starting modeling as a paid job. Her original claim was dismissed, because "no 'so-called' right of privacy existed in

Figure 3.2. The likeness of Abigail Roberson that appeared in *Profitable Advertising* (August 1902). From the *Historical Society of the Courts of the State of New York Newsletter*, no. 4 (2006). Reproduced with the permission of the Public Library of Cincinnati and Hamilton County, OH.

New York" at the time; however, after much public outcry, the New York state legislature changed the law, allowing legal action if a "plaintiff's name or likeness has been used for advertising purposes or for purposes of trade without written consent."[12] This ruling placed a new value on a person's appearance, body, and demeanor, and a person's "look" became a thing that could be bought and sold.

The commodification of the "look" made consent an important variable in the production of commercial photography.[13] In that moment, "property and personhood met at that crossroads, the body," giving birth to the idea that there was a legal right to profits made through the production and distribution of one's image.[14] With this new value of the image came a new era in modeling.

In a prototypical form of glamour labor, models became workers who sold their likeness for profit. While artists once recruited their friends as models, or sought out a particularly inspiring face to sit for them, mass distribution of photography changed the rules of the game. By the early 1900s, the sale of images proceeded briskly with fashion magazines a major factor in the dissemination of fashion information and the organization of consumption into a predictable, and perhaps controllable, practice. The new telegraphs, steamships, and passenger liners sped up the transmission of ideas and designs and shrank the time gap between the fashion center of Paris and customers in New York, thus "intensifying the tempo of fashion."[15] This newly available information about fashion's vagaries whetted the public's appetite for not only fashionable clothes but also fashion images. While in 1865 there were about seven hundred magazine titles with a combined circulation of about four million, by 1905 there were approximately six thousand magazines with a total audience of sixty-four million. At the same time, technical advances brought color to the high-quality mass reproduction of images on magazine covers.[16]

The Franklin Mills Flour girl lawsuit was one of several early 1900s rulings regarding ownership of images. They marked a transitional point in dominant forms of imaging. As photography surpassed illustration and painting, it became the image of the "new." Photography's rise to dominance fomented what Paris-based filmmaker Jean-Louis Comolli called a "frenzy of the visible." In the second half of the nineteenth century, this "frenzy" was whipped up by the "social multiplication of images" in the "ever-wider distribution of illustrated papers, waves of prints, caricatures, etc."[17] On the crest of these waves of images, fashion became a popular subject in photography. The idea that only illustration could properly "interpret . . . designers' latest creations" fell by the wayside. [18] By 1913, Condé Nast's *Vogue* magazine hired Adolph Gayne de Meyer (also known as Baron de Meyer) as its first official fashion photographer, pioneering fashion photography as a serious profession and thereby creating new markets for models.[19] As the curator and historian Harold Koda observes:

Suddenly, a market developed for photogenic young women whose elegant poses and gestures evoked the attitudes of the day while convincingly portraying the lifestyles and aspirations of the magazine or advertiser's target market.[20]

Up until the 1920s, there had been very little need for models. Magazines deemed socialites most suitable for their forays into fashion photography. What Gertrude Vanderbilt Whitney and Mrs. Howard G. Cushing wore was fashion news, with images of these well-bred and well-kept ladies much sought after by fashion periodicals such as *Vogue* and *Vanity Fair*.[21] When the demand for fashionable images began to exceed the supply of rich young ladies, the burgeoning film industry provided a fresh crop of photogenic women more than willing to pose. At the other end of the social spectrum, these were chorus girls and other women of colorful reputation. As a model who worked in 1920s Paris observed, "Modeling was considered very fast and loose and no model girl was received in polite society."[22] Models were adventurous women who viewed their posing more in terms of art than of commerce. As one of Man Ray's models said, "Half the photos that were made of me were done for nothing . . . modeling was for camaraderie, you know, for pleasure more than anything else."[23] As photography's popularity valued modeling work in new ways, new demands for a standardized body, stimulated by the professionalization of fashion image making, took on industrial-sized proportions in the dawn of the cinematic age.

"Hold It!" Creating Drama without Moving a Muscle

While the photographic frame remained highly visible as an imaging norm, the cinematic rose to dominance. In this period, as the media theorists William Leiss, Stephen Kline, and Sut Jhally explain, "The explicit depiction of the relationship between people and products became central," increasing the desire to use images of people in advertisements.[24] Consequently, advertising's goals shifted: "Emphasis on what the product *did* diminished, while the visual increasingly explored what the product could *mean* for consumers."[25]

While once aimed at capturing an essence and framing the soul, cinematic influences nudged photographic practice toward creating a scenario and layering it with dramatic flair. The models of this age posed in settings that were like theater sets. The model historian Brigid Keenan observed that

> less effort went into preparing the girls for the pictures, than into perfecting the backgrounds. Photographers scoured around for witty and appropriate props and would paint the most elaborate scenery for their pictures. Cecil Beaton was a past master at this. He used mirrors to give infinite reflections. Paper hoops through which his subjects burst like circus dogs, fake snow, painted landscapes, plaster busts and miles of tulle.[26]

Top 1930s photographers, such as Adolph de Meyer, Cecil Beaton, Horst P. Horst, Edward Steichen, George Hoyningen-Huene, and the indomitable Man Ray, used stylized, theatrical photography, which instilled an architectural, graphic quality into the fashion image. The advent of the "talkie" in Hollywood's golden age fostered a "symbiotic relationship between Hollywood studios and consumer product industries in the 1930s."[27] Hollywood's pervasive cinematic norms invaded print advertising in the form of motion picture frames used to illustrate action or multiple points of view.[28] Top fashion photographers infused their images with Hollywood glamour via dramatic studio lighting and theatrical studio sets. The model became a "polished, untouchable goddess" in sculptural images starring the clothes, with the model a mere backdrop of mood or attitude.[29] The quest for Hollywood drama in still images elevated "the classical siren of the 1930s" in fashion images where composition, gesture, and lighting became centrally important.[30]

Models had to project this drama under rather trying circumstances. One did not just go with the flow. The unexpected, openness, and vulnerability to the camera are products of the current regime. In contrast, the cinematic mode of imaging demanded strict discipline and endless amounts of patience: "This was the time of 'the most enormous sort of camera with three slides that went through, and you had to keep still the entire time,' recalled an English model, Iris Lockwood, who had worked in London in the thirties."[31] For holding the requisite pose in motionless splendor, models in this period sometimes depended on a device that held them up and kept them still for the appropriate amount of time. Lockwood reflected, "Often we had what was called a 'model stand.' It

[handwritten margin notes: "cannot be subdued / overcome"; "survival"]

was a stand with a bar across which was shaped so that it went into our waist, and as long as you had it there, you knew whether you were still or not."[32] The American model Joan Clement pointed out how just how exhausting keeping still can be. In a 1930 interview, she explained:

> Color photography requires so much care with light and slow exposure that it's a terrible strain on the model. Try to keep still for two and a half minutes at a time. You'll want to be paid for it.[33]

Apparently, she "charged double, and cabbed it" to her last color shoot and felt even this was not sufficient recompense for the strain.

Holding still for two and a half minutes is a far cry from jumping, running, or the fluid motion so prized today. Models did not have to look real or accessible; in fact, the desired look was quite the opposite. As the model historian Charles Castle points out, runway models "could certainly walk and show clothes superbly, but . . . they lacked the stillness and camera technique required of this demanding craft."[34] During show weeks, photographers brought along their own freelance models to photograph the collections in the studio, where they could manufacture the requisite drama of the haute couture style of the day.[35] The cinematic mode of imaging orchestrated everything toward a particular goal, a picture with a defined look. The model, propped on her model stand, did her best to strike a pose, to project drama along clearly prescribed paths.

World War II brought an end to fashion photography's Hollywood "glamour of the thirties."[36] The shift in mood was to be the end of an era. The "1930s high fashion model had no place in this world of austerity," a world wrought by the rationing and shortages prevalent during the war. As the model historian Brigid Keenan observed, "Not only were materials and embellishments impossible to obtain, but they were also forbidden by law after the war."[37]

Absent during the war years, fashion and consumerism returned to the United States in the late 1940s with a vengeance. In 1946 more than two hundred mass-oriented magazines were launched in the United States.[38] Magazines developed a new slick look using high-quality color photography to tell a story through pictures, and fashion was a big story to tell. Back from a virtual standstill, fashion emerged as a central focus in social life in 1947, emblemized by the moment when "Christian Dior opened his new couture house in Paris with a collection of the prettiest clothes that had been seen for eight years."[39] The change was such a shock that, during a photographic session in a Montmartre market, the extravagance of the look scandalized the impoverished crowd, who attacked the model and tore her clothes.[40] Regardless of this public approbation, Dior's New Look took the fashion world by storm. According to one report, cheers broke out and some of the audience wept when the models at the Dior fashion show strode in,

> arrogantly swinging their vast skirts, the soft shoulders, the tight bodices, the wasp-waists, the tiny hats bound on by veils under the chin. They swirled on, contemptuously bowling over the ashtray stands like ninepins.[41] *↳ scornful/disrespectful*

The swish of vast petticoats was "positively voluptuous," like a "new love affair, the first sight of Venice, in fact a whole new look at life."[42] According to another report, the New Look was so "wildly extravagant and so utterly unlike the plain practical clothes" women had been wearing, that, after Dior revealed the New Look on the runway, "John Fairchild of *Women's Wear Daily* said that 'it was enough to say "Dior" anywhere in the world. Women got hysterical. Cash registers rang.'"[43]

Fashion, photography, and consumerism surged to a new crescendo in the post-war economic boom. Magazines not only distributed ideas and information aimed at selling fashion, they also created audiences for it. An advertising creative director pegged this as a critical time, saying in an interview, "The ability to produce a high-quality print product that people wanted to buy and consume was the most critical development in the print medium at this time, since it allowed advertisers to cost-effectively reach much more narrowly defined targets than traditional broadcast media, such as television and radio." During the late 1940s, magazines segmented to target-specific populations, such as teens and African Americans. The "high-quality print" fashion magazines offered new avenues for image distribution that cemented fashion photography as a genre in its own right.

Figure 3.3. A model wears Christian Dior's New Look in 1947. From Nigel Cawthorne, *The New Look: The Dior Revolution* (Edison, NJ: Wellfleet Press, 1996).

This mid-century consumer culture idealized conformity in the form of the "company man," strictly enforced gender roles, and "keeping up with the Joneses." The power of persuasion seemed limitless to the burgeoning advertising industry. The sociologist Liz Moor theorized brand advertising as the "paradigmatic mechanism" for suturing citizens into a capitalist system.[44] The glamorous images found in *Vogue, Harper's bound to capitalism—▷ sold ideas*

Bazaar, Life, and *Look* magazines linked the public to the system with seductive promises that true love and happiness might be possible if one just made the right purchases or that hope could perhaps be found in a jar. As the labor force constructing this iconography of desire, models "modeled" this promise. In their hands, glamour labor—paying attention, following the trends, shaping one's body to the current style, and consuming in just the right way—seemed a small price to pay in exchange for the promised beauty, popularity, or success (sexual or otherwise) embodied by models.

Thus, borne on the crest of a new wave of mass-produced goods and the mass distribution of images to sell them, the models who "dominated the fashion modeling scene in New York in the fifties"[45] became iconic figures of glamour and affluence. No longer the denizens of the demimonde, occupying a class only slightly better than a chorus girl, fashion models became the apotheosis of high class and style, embodying "an aspirational model who could appeal across national and class boundaries—a woman of the world."[46] With this new artistic value and glamour in fashion photography, the curator and fashion historian Harold Koda noted that models such as Dorian Leigh were prized for their "forbidding haughtiness that inevitably invested photographs with a sense of narrative, status, and grandeur."[47] Youth and novelty mattered less than grace and hauteur. The iconic models Dovima and Dorian Leigh were well into their thirties at the peak of their careers, where they projected a womanly, sophisticated image.[48] Experience counted, and long-term collaborations, often spanning decades, were the norm. As Richard Avedon's muse throughout the 1950s, Suzy Parker became "one of the first fashion models of the twentieth century to become a household name."[49] High-powered photographers such as Avedon, or Irving Penn, blended art and commerce in iconic photos, such as "Dovima and the Elephants," which is "now regarded as a masterwork of mid century photography."[50] These collaborations made Parker and Dovima international photographic stars, as well as Lisa Fonssagrives, Dorian Leigh, Carmen Dell'Orefice, Jean Patchett, Dolores Hawkins, and Sunny Harnett. Within with the slow build of the cinematic regime, it was a given that crafting photographs, and careers, took time.

a person who regularly frequents a place

highest point

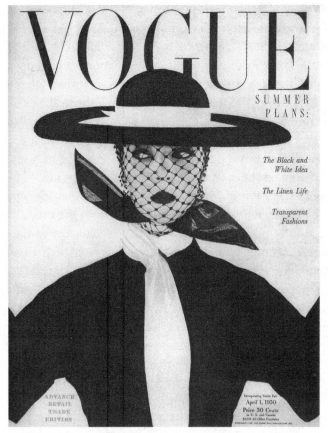

Figure 3.4. *Vogue* cover, Irving Penn's "Black and White Idea" photograph, 1950. From *Vogue*, April 1, 1950. Photo by Irving Penn.

Chasing a Bluebird

While runway models worked in broad strokes, using the cant of a leg or the swing of a hip to telegraph style, work for photographic models was far more subtle. The graphic pose still dominated, as it had throughout the 1930s, but the importance of expressing a certain feeling or projecting an aura had grown. This new pull for models to dip into the unpredictable and hard-to-control domain of affective engagement was still highly scripted, however. Jean Patchett, one of Irving Penn's favorite models, recalled:

I'd get into an outfit and stand on the white paper in the studio, and he would tell me a story . . . he would say . . . "it's at the opera, and I'm looking for this lovely man I'm madly in love with. It's intermission, and I can't find him. Suddenly, I see him in the distance and I'm trying to catch his eye over everybody's heads." Another time I would have to pretend to be on the street looking for a taxicab, or at Cartier's looking at a jewel.[51]

Photographs told a story, models were the characters, and the pictures were about showing or representing the clothes. Gayle, a Ford model who had worked with Richard Avedon and other well-known fashion photographers explained that,

if you look at pictures from the fifties, they showed the clothes, you wanted to see them. If you look at the pictures, they could have a whole background, but basically, you could see the outfit, more or less.

The revolution of digital photography was a long way in the future; film was expensive, and shooting a large number of frames for one

Figure 3.5. Models on haughty display. *New York Herald Tribune*, October 14, 1959. Photo by Ted Kell. Courtesy of the Queens Borough Library, New York.

shot was an investment. Photographers like Penn and Avedon were well aware of the possible reward, however, and often went to extremes to get it. According to Patchett, "At one sitting, we would easily take five hundred pictures for one outfit. [Penn] called it chasing a bluebird."[52] To capture that "bluebird" would mean getting a shot that could became an iconic image, one that sold not only clothes but the image of fashion itself.

As the glamour era of the 1950s drew to a close in the dawn of the television age, however, the fashionableness of fashion flipped into overdrive, as images became available in more places at more times than ever before. The vulnerability projected by young, fresh "girls" was in demand. Models no longer had time to create a carefully constructed image, they had to appear to *be* the image, without artifice. Rather than use makeup to create the illusion of youthfully translucent skin, they had to *be* young. Without corsets to nip in their waists, or bras to project their bosoms, they had to embody the ideal in the flesh. Wide-eyed gamines soon jostled aside the carefully painted and powdered "disdainful ladies" of high fashion. Youth and vulnerability, the hallmark of a new age, launched key trends in glamour labor, valuing exposure and new scrutiny by the camera, seemingly down to one's very pores.

The Age of the Face

In the "flurry of instants" characterizing this new imaging norm, a memorable image called for a whole new kind of modeling work. With the increased emphasis on small gestures, facial details, and surfaces, the "static poses, ethereal models, and theatrical gestures" that typified the 1950s' "bias toward sophistication" seemed overwrought, out of sync with the needs of the time. The new "realness," personified by the "sexy, friendly, and relaxed disposition," was the hallmark of models such as Jean Shrimpton and Penelope Tree.[53] As Shrimpton said herself, "I embodied ordinariness—which is, of course a hugely marketable quality."[54] Coupled with the youth movement, jet travel, and cybernetics, the revolutionary nature of television resulted in an upheaval of social norms that is highly contested to this day. The power of pop culture replaced the urge for urban sophistication as novelty, youth, and freedom became the new cultural ideals.

Television's new aesthetic of the surface demanded a different kind of labor from the model. While cinema worked in the "territoriality of the spatial," framing a space into which the viewer is drawn, television works in the space of the depthless surface, whose characteristic framing is that of the close-up.[55] Daniel Harris, a scholar of consumption and style, has observed that until photography finally supplanted illustration as the "primary means of advertising clothing" in the 1950s, glamour inhered less in the face of the drawing, which was by necessity schematic and generalized, than in the sketch's attitude, posture, and gestures, especially in the strangely dainty positions of the hands. Glamour once resided so emphatically in the stance of the model that the faces in the illustrations cannot really be said to have expressions at all, but angles or tilts.[56] Facial expression was not the focus; tilting the head at just the right glamorous angle was.[57]

In the 1960s, as attention shifted away from the body, the size of the face in fashion images grew. As Harris explains:

> Throughout the 1940s and 1950s, the face grew incrementally in size until, by the 1960s, it frequently filled an entire page . . . unlike the aesthetic of exclusion, which deliberately fosters a relation of inequality between the viewer and the model, the aesthetic developed in the Age of the Face emphasizes communication and directness.[58]

In the television age, this blankness became a sign of visual intimacy, as it signaled a total lack of awareness of being seen, as if the viewer were privy to the models' most inner, intimate, moments. The photographer David Bailey, the real-life prototype for the sex-crazed photographer in the iconic film *Blow Up* (1966), claimed that the 1960s was the moment when the "art and artifice of ladies, . . . was replaced by the gamine."[59] Fresh-faced girls such as Jean Shrimpton, Twiggy, and Penelope Tree became the world's newest models, usurping their older predecessors with the flip of a mini skirt. Up to and especially in the 1950s, the model was powdered to perfection, her body cinched and shaped by girdles, her breasts cantilevered to just the right angle by the latest technology. The artifice was, as one photographer at the time described it, a "full thing" that could transform even the plainest girl into something else entirely. As he saw it, Simone, a well-known model in Paris and

Figure 3.6. The cover model in an elegant pose, shown as a full body with her head-turned profile, preventing her face from being the focus of the image. *Vogue* UK, March 1945. Photo by John Rawlings.

London in the 1950s, was a master at this technique; "Her face without make-up; zero. But when she had the full thing on, the shading, the make-up, the hair, the eye lashes, she was dazzling."[60]

Jeremy Gilbert-Rolfe, a philosopher who ventured to contemplate the sublime in terms of the contemporary fashion model, identified this process of covering and uncovering first in clothes:

Fashion has proceeded smoothly from the Victorian presentation of the body through layering to one of presenting the body not so much

Figure 3.7 A model interacting with the design of the magazine title. She's anonymous, as her face only shows in a half-profile. "Summer Beauty Issue." *Vogue*, May 15, 1941. Image by Horst P. Horst.

through revealing as through intensifying it: a general principle of display as uncovering has replaced one of covering as display.[61]

He argued that in this process, display as uncovering became the norm not only for the body but also the face. By the 1960s, the surface of the skin especially became a space of intense focus:

During the same period, cosmetics have replaced the idea of layering as enhancement through obliteration—powder—with that of intensification as clarification . . . the powdered face gives way to the moisturized one, matte to gloss, a complexion obscured by white opacity to one enhanced by a flesh colored glaze.[62]

Television's mobile images are made of light, which elevated the skin's translucence in the growing dominance of the video image, lit from within.

With such close attention paid to the surfaces of skin, hair, and body, soon each part required its own expert, in the form of hairstylists, makeup artists, clothing stylists, nutritionists, managers, and personal trainers who worked on, or sometimes with, the model to achieve the desired look. Given the fact that models now routinely spend four to five hours in hair and makeup before they are deemed ready to appear for the camera or the runway, looking as if they just "are" that way, it is hard to imagine a time when every surface of a model's body was not scrutinized and manipulated. Prior to the dawn of photographic modeling, the look of a model's skin, the value of its changeability, or the

Figure 3.8. *Vogue* cover featuring Marisa Berenson, her face and eye standing in for the whole model, her clothes—irrelevant. *Vogue*, January 15, 1966.

Figure 3.9. A 1966 Vogue cover, "A Feast for the Eye," illustrating the new importance of the head and the face in the 1960s. *Vogue,* December 1, 1966.

angles her body could produce in a photograph were not issues. In a non-photographic world, "paint," the word for cosmetics at the time, was not a necessity. The desire to create a surface for the play of light was not yet a factor in the construction of a model's persona. Neither was the push toward presenting a perfected image that could withstand the brutal honesty of the camera.[63]

Up until the 1950s, fashion models did their own makeup and supplied their own shoes, jewelry, and hairstyle. The creation of the hair and makeup for the fashion image was simply not a site of investment. The models' self-styling made valuable contributions to the work process but was not yet the source of the economies eventually mobilized by the model's body, with teams of workers devoted to creating the look of each part. The emergence of these teams of stylists represented an expansion both of the model's work to submit to bodily manipulation and to the economics of producing the model "look."

In fact, when Cover Girl began a campaign in 1961 to find a perfect face to launch its cosmetics, it was clear that the model's "chief attraction" had become her face.[64] Reportedly, by the late 1990s, Cover Girl was investing millions of dollars per year to find just the right faces, "a laborious, international treasure hunt that one industry analyst estimates costs as much as $119 per facial pore of each of the seven models finally chosen to advertise only four of the company's products."[65] With this major investment in model's faces to represent a corporate image, faces became a "priceless commodity."[66]

As the opaque, powdered face gave way to the glossy moisturized one, the youthful face that exuded a dewy freshness became the face of "fashion," and the digital age exacerbated this tendency. The number of dots per inch in digital images became denser, rendering every detail naked to the camera's searching eye, arguably inflaming new forms of anxiety about appearance, as evidenced in the emergence of "High Def" or "HD" products, designed specifically for the "high definition video cameras that capture every pore."[67] While originally intended for on-camera professionals, products named "Photo Op" and "Camera Ready" were soon marketed more broadly. As one makeup professional put it, "It started out with HD, but it's not really about stars anymore."[68]

Once set in motion, this emphasis on the flawless surface brought with it an increased emphasis on youth, which only became more extreme in the regime of the blink. As one modeling manual put it, among the qualifications required for high-fashion modeling, "First on the list is youth!"[69] By the nineties, some models were starting out as young as thirteen-years-old, at a much younger age than in decades past.[70] Prior to the 1960s, if a model did start young, her youthful looks were often covered over, to conform to the popular look of worldly sophistication. Although Carmen Dell'Orefice started at thirteen, as the youngest model ever to appear on the cover of *Vogue* in 1947, her makeup and coiffed hair resembled a worldly thirty-six, with a dark lipsticked smile crowned by a carefully smoothed bun. After the 1960s' youth quake branded the youth ideal as fashionable, however, the demand to look young and fresh was not met by using makeup but by using young girls such as Twiggy and Penelope Tree, both sixteen at the peak of their careers. In the 1970s, models also started out in their teens (Rene Russo and Lisa Taylor were discovered at seventeen and nineteen, respectively). While Brooke Shields's youth scandalized 1980s audiences, by the 1990s supermodels such as Christy Turlington, Cindy Crawford, and Naomi Campbell started around fourteen or fifteen without raising an eyebrow. Kate Moss was discovered at fourteen, and Gisele Bündchen, the ubermodel of the 2000s, was just thirteen at the time she was discovered eating a Big Mac at a MacDonald's in São Paulo.[71]

Youth's value has led to earlier retirement ages, as well. With the speedup and desire for the "new" in the regime of the blink, a model's "sell-by" date, as the sociologist Ashley Mears has termed it, comes much sooner.[72] While the great models of the 1940s and 1950s worked well into their late thirties, by the 1990s, if you were a "really great high fashion model" you might be able to stretch your career into your "middle to late twenties" if you were "very lucky," as one 1990s model agent explained, admonishing that a career of this length is "truly an unusual phenomenon . . . so the earlier you start, the better your chances are at making a career in this field."[73] She concluded, bluntly, that "the Eileen Ford Agency is not interested in seeing anyone over 22, and, for some girls, even that is too late."[74]

The new aesthetic in fashion photography of the 1960s valued surfaces and how they created shapes, textures, or moods. The desire to convey a moment or instant, rather than a whole narrative, valued the affectivity of the face and the body in motion. This emphasized the "purely visual" aspects of the image, creating different demands on models. Odd juxtapositions and puzzling scenarios that could even seem offensive became popular. A New York photographer whom *Harper's Bazaar* editors accused of making a "rude comment" by including an egg or a rubber band in his photographs protested that his interest was visual, not narrative, and so should not be interpreted so literally:

> That wasn't what I was trying to say . . . it was purely because the shape interested me, and I was working in a purely visual level; there was no message I was trying to put over.[75]

In place of staged scenarios and spending hours to "chase a bluebird," this photographer demanded models be "prepared to show you something of themselves; the aspects of how they think or feel."[76]

Consequently, the kind of direction models were given went from painting a specific scenario to elicit a scripted reaction, such as looking for one's fiancé at the opera or admiring a jewel, to a more atmospheric call to be in the moment, with instructions like "Divine, divine . . . hold it . . . hold it . . . HOLD IT . . . wet your lips, fantastic, marvelous, don't move . . . say Friday . . . say Thursday . . . great . . . great . . . lick your lips again . . . that's GREAT."[77] Vague instruction of this type reached more for unscripted vulnerability than a calculated facial expression or reaction.

Top sixties model Tania Mallet aptly described this new mode's intensity of emotion, facial expression, bodily attitude, and other means of revealing as "having your soul sucked out through your eye sockets."[78] Similarly, Jean Shrimpton, a very famous model at the time, related how "when a session goes right . . . 'suddenly it all happens. You feel the mood of the clothes, you feel irresistibly attractive, you give the whole essence of yourself to the camera.'"[79] The fashion scholar Jennifer Craik, in her cultural studies treatment of modeling, describes how the photographer John French "recognized the importance of capturing the 'personal projection' of a model," saying that

> he likened the great models to alchemists: "their personality suddenly bubbles and bubbles and you realize that they react and make that fantastic rapport between the photographer and the model that makes for a lively and exciting picture."[80]

The ability to project energy became one of the key qualifications for modeling work in the coming era. From then on, no model, no matter how pretty, was able to succeed without it.

She Wore a Short Skirt and a Long Jacket

A diminutive girl with large eyes and a relatively pretty face, Twiggy had the right look, but her success was not just about her looks. Not only did she have the right look at the right time, she also embodied

Figure 3.10. Twiggy, photographed by Barry Lategan in 1966.

qualities that became highly lucrative for those models who would become "super" in the coming decades. It was more than just posing: "When Twiggy sat in front of the camera, her awareness of what she was doing was extraordinary," Barry Lategan, a photographer who took some of the most iconic images of her, mused. "Being photogenic is never a question of features alone," he continued, "It's a sense of projection: and Twiggy had that."[81] Twiggy's success also indicated a trend in the televisual regime that emphasized being an all-around personality. As Diana Vreeland opined in her autobiography *D.V.*, "The sixties were about personalities. It was the first time when mannequins *became* personalities . . . these girls invented *themselves*. Naturally, as an editor, I was there to help them along."[82]

Once television inaugurated the era of the face, the model's ability to transmit or amplify affect came into focus. The model's glamour labor connected viewer and viewed via forms of identification and mimesis that, as the theater studies scholar Maurya Wickstrom has pointed out, are a common feature of the brandscapes in which we now live.[83] Rather than play a pre-scripted part, models tuned into the atmosphere of the studio to pick up on what might be appropriate for the shoot in settings where it was anyone's guess what the outcome would be, and the happy accident was sometimes more lucrative than the most carefully thought-out scenario.

Seen from this angle, prompting Cindy Crawford to "be a rat" is less surprising. Models told me similar stories about their collaborative work, which belied the notion of models as the clay shaped by the photographer's directives. When no direction was given, they channeled the mood and energy in the room, opening themselves to the possibilities of the moment, collaborating with the photographic and styling team assembled in the hope of capturing something unexpected, something that moved beyond the norm, toward the unknown.

According to the models I interviewed, this lack of direction has become quite common. Bitou, a young model who had worked on several high-fashion shoots, explained:

> Sometimes they just want to let you do it. The photographers and clients aren't always so directive, they want to let you be yourself. So you have to be able to define your own way that you look better. You learn from seeing pictures of yourself. . . . Because often you have to smile and you have to find the right smile that is not too fake, and not too much at the same time. For me it's a feeling. I cannot put it on.

This experience was most common among the models I interviewed who had begun working in the 1980s or later, after the dawn of the blink regime and its emphasis on affect.

This regime valued models who could "go with the flow," as Kay, a makeup artist, described it:

[handwritten margin notes: "the range of brands available on the market" and "imitation/mimesis"]

Some girls will get on the set, and they'll just have a fabulous flow and variety and movement, and they get it, and they look at the outfit before, and they look at the hair and the makeup before, and they'll get on the set, and they'll just . . . it's almost like watching an actress where there's no direction required, they're just flowing with it, they get it, and they've paid attention, and the photographer can take pictures for over an hour and not have to say one word because everything is just wonderful.

In this instance, affective energy informed the model's movements, channeling the energy between her and the photographer, tinged with the team's excitement.

Sometimes working with affect is more tactile, however. Several models I spoke to referred to knowing how to feel in a dress, almost as if the sensation of the fabric on their skin or the form of the styling on their body could be translated into the mood they projected for the photograph. When this came up with a couture model, I asked whether she had to think about her body or her face as an object, as other models had mentioned to me they had done. She adamantly concurred:

Oh yeah, you are a thing. The thing. That's what Cindy Crawford called herself. Absolutely. I read that somewhere and was like, that's a perfect way of putting it. But it's true. You transform and you have to look at it, you have to observe it. Like, okay, what do I feel like now, is this appropriate with what I'm wearing? You know you are not going to look like a grunge thing when you are wearing an evening gown. I wouldn't. I'd be like, Oh, this is an evening gown, it makes me feel this way.

Knowing how to feel in the clothes depends on opening to sensations that others might ignore, in picking up on feelings informing the look of the model's stance and expression, based on a the smoothness or constriction produced by the garment/body interaction.

A model who had done many couture shoots, including shooting with top fashion photographer Patrick Demarchelier, spoke of this inwardness. She found things worked best when she went into her own world, explaining:

For me I'd go into my own little world, like, Okay what does this person want? They might describe it, but if they don't, and they let you do what you want, it's a funny dynamic between you. Especially, like, Patrick, sometimes, Demarchelier, wouldn't say anything, just put you there and be like . . . and you'd be like, Oh, okay, and it's all on you, everybody is standing there, you know, like watching you. Perform, basically. I'd go in my own little world.

Demarchelier's silence contrasts quite clearly with the scenarios Avedon painted for his models about being at the opera or trying on a new hat. As these quotes indicate, the style of work in modeling for the camera during the regime of the blink moved quite clearly toward the affective, toward trying to capture the unsaid, barely felt sense of a feeling or mood for a photograph.

This opening up to the mood of the moment, even to the point of opening up to the sensitivity of one's skin, denotes a form of affective labor. The model exploits the body's tendency to exceed its boundaries, putting herself and feelings into relation to the technology of the camera, the fabric of the garment, and the networked relationships of her collaborators in the room. She must also be fully aware of the collective mood and reactions, channeling the energy of those assembled, sensitive to its flow. This chapter has described how the glamour labor of modeling for the camera, to present an appropriate "look" for the lens, evolved from the straightforward, highly scripted manipulation of emotion, pose, and facial expression to a much more free-form, sensation-oriented practice. In the age of the blink, the model and her bodily sensitivity to affective flow became paramount for producing the sought after "look." The openness to technology and collaboration evolved not only in creating studio images. With the onslaught of the all-media-all-the-time lifestyle of the Internet age, modeling work expanded imaging via social media, such as blogs and Twitter feeds about models, or as models began to post and share images of themselves backstage at shows, attending social events that promoted a brand, and other forms of self-promotion.

The management of affectivity in the regime of the blink extended to both models' work in the studio and on set for a fashion shoot and in terms of how invasive or personal agents' directives became with regard to models' social lives, eating habits, and overall image online. These practices in turn glamourized micromanaging the body and social world of models, selling it to the general public as a means to success, glamour, and cool. As the following chapter illustrates, after the 1980s, the work of modeling transformed from something a girl might do for fun to a highly professionalized corporate-driven enterprise in which only the tallest, the leanest, and 100 percent committed would survive.

Demarchelier ▷ ~~tot~~ didn't give direction
Avedon → "look at a window of
Cartier" to affect emotion
Lo "the regime of the "blink" to
try and capture an emotion

*slim bodies are ready for the movement of the ~~fa~~ industrial/modern world (114)

*~~f~~fashion/thin body was used by politics to create "a national female look" (115)

*↑ of advertising in fashion (117)

Managing the Model Body

*models had to maintain a persona outside of work (118)

*"The Power's Girl" (120)

*engineering a body to manipulate consumer behavior (124)

*shift in body image engendered by models

In the mid 1990s, journalist Michael Gross's observations echoed the popular sentiment that the supermodels were breaking new ground in modeling. He argues that they were so powerful, they 1940's

> even remade the idea of perfection. No longer was it necessary to have a belly like a washboard, or skin as white as snow. While [models] Irwin, Patitz, and Mulder all are classic blondes, more than half the super-models, including Turlington, had dark hair. Some even had dark skin. Crawford has a mole near her lips; Campbell, a scar on her nose. Evange-lista is scrawny; Schiffer is strapping.[1]

They may have broken the stranglehold blue-eyed blonds had had on the fashion industry, but with regard to body size, the supermodels did not stray very far from a very slender body ideal. Although somewhat more voluptuous than the flat-chested models popular in the 1970s, such as Cheryl Tiegs and Lisa Taylor, these models were by no means large. Christy Turlington, 5'10" and weighing 119 pounds at the peak of her career, had a twenty-three-inch waist, with breast and hips measuring only thirty-four inches. Cindy Crawford, famously known as a "cow" in the industry because of her curves, measured 34-26-35, a size very close to the model standard in the mid 1990s epitomized by Linda Evan-gelista's classic 34-24-34 shape. Naomi Campbell's 5'9" muscular frame may look solid, but at 34-22-34, her proportions are much closer to those of the average fashion model, who is by most accounts 5'9"–6' tall, weighing in at 110–118 pounds.[2] Despite their reputation for being more womanly, the supermodels' slender proportions were far from average.[3]

The supermodels' billing as trendsetters moving fashion toward a new voluptuous silhouette came of efforts to differentiate their look

108

*guide for ideal body (Powers) p.134)
↳ disseminate "healthy body" image to the public/manage health

from previous bodily fashions. Thus, while Twiggy's 32-23-32 inch frame was considerably smaller than the amazonian bodies of the super-models, she was also small all over, at a height of 5'6". Further, while 1970s models were, as one New York magazine editor put it, "skinny skinny skinny,"[4] the supermodels' supposedly womanly figures none-theless still adhered quite strictly to the dominant modeling norm of slenderness.

Why *are* models so skinny? Have they always been that way? How was this ideal a reflection of the "model" worker at the time? As the haute glamour age of modeling in the cinematic regime morphed into the translucent appeal of the television age, how did model's glamour labor feed into biopolitical efforts to regulate the population's health in a war against fat—with models as its soldiers on the front line?

From Lax to Lean: Standardizing the Model "Look"

When thinking of contemporary fashion models, "plump" and "ele-gantly rolled" do not come to mind. Yet in modeling's early days, the French couturier Paul Poiret fondly described his favorite model as just that : "Paulette was for a long time the one I preferred. . . . With round arms and rounded shoulders, she was plump and elegantly rolled as a cigarette. How comely, how French!"[5] This description sharply con-trasts with contemporary modeling manuals, which state clearly that "in order to work the collections, female models must be 5'9" or taller, with a maximum hip measurement of 34 inches."[6] Although models in the early days may have been naturally slender, and taller girls were sought after, the first models to work in the various dressmaker's shops and couturier's salons that adopted the practice were not subject to the strict standards for a "model" body.

Much has been made about the differences between French and American models of this period, as exemplified by the photographer Horst P. Horst's complaint about French models: Although he found them "ravishingly beautiful, and very smart," he lamented that they had "short legs and large behinds." He preferred the American girls because they had "this beautiful long line."[7] His statement echoes a common sentiment of the day, in which American models were believed to be more useful for showing fashion owing to their rangy physiques. In

Figure 4.1. The Poiret model Yvonne Deslandres, similar in
build to the beloved Paulette, 1920. From Yvonne Deslandres, *Poiret: Paul Poiret, 1879–1944* (New York: Rizzoli, 1987).

modeling's early days, however, this American look was one among
many. Models' bodies were by no means as uniform as they are today,
and entry into the field was rather lax.

This laxity stemmed from several causes. Modeling was not yet a
profession; it was more of a sideline for girls recruited from the shop
floor when the occasion demanded it. Models often went unpaid, or
earnings were meager at best. Most notably, models were not yet a cultural ideal but, rather, exotic creatures working in a questionable world

where bodily variability was overlooked in favor of the willingness and ability to show a dress to its full advantage.

With the standardization of ready-to-wear garments, however, all this would change. The French designer Charles Worth was among the first to introduce the idea in couture that "one pattern piece could be utilized for innumerable designs."[8] The labor historian Nancy Green describes the 1800s as a period in which "measurement was separated from the individual body" for the first time, thus allowing the division into piecework and automation of clothing construction.[9] The military was the source of this innovation:

> The mass measurement of soldiers in the nineteenth century helped support a notion that most tailors already intuitively understood: that the human form, for all its amazing diversity, could be categorized.[10]

At this key juncture, the standardization of garments eventually helped fuel a desire to standardize, through management, the bodies they were intended to clothe.

Prior to this paradigm shift, however, early models' bodies were corseted into the shape that was in fashion to produce a uniform appearance and silhouette. In stark contrast to the total exposure of every inch of skin, and of every aspect of one's life, with the concomitant demands for high-level grooming and self-branding, early models did very little glamour labor. The need to polish one's skin or physique was obviated by the "uncomfortable boned corsets, often reaching from bosom to knee" worn by most models.[11] They did not speak to the clients, so did not need to project a unique personality. If they modeled evening dresses, "they had to put them, for decency's sake, over black satin undergarments that covered all exposed flesh," a covering sometimes referred to as a "*maillot*."[12] The fashion historian Caroline Evans describes the *maillot* as "a V-necked, tight fitting black satin garment worn over the corset and under the dress, which was briefly replaced by a flesh-colored stockinette," a practice that persisted until around 1907. In Charles Worth's salon, the models' dresses may have been the height of fashion, but they "were invariably made in black with long sleeves and high necks,"[13] hiding, rather showing, the model's body.

In an important chapter in the story of glamour labor's development, the photographic regime was absorbed into the cinematic, as photography's pull for beautifully crafted, clean-lined silhouettes intensified into the need for a taut body in motion. In this transition, the practice of covering, compressing, and molding the body into a uniform shape and size from without was gradually internalized, as the fashion historian Valerie Steele's seminal history of corsetry points out. Over time, Steele argues, as the steel and bones of the corset, and then the tight panels of the girdle, were absorbed into the body and became muscle, external forms of bodily control gave way to efforts to create a lean line from within.[14] The result? As the fashion historian Caroline Evans quips, "The outer discipline of the corset" gave way to "the inner disciplines of diet and exercise."[15] In a move from a mechanized ideal to a biopolitical one, the waist-cinched delicacy of mid-century mannequins gave way to the gangly proportions popular in the 1960s, while the combined forces of medicine, finance, and fashion popularized the notion that everyone should strive for the fashionable line. As the cinematic regime gradually gave way to the age of television, the art and artifice of creating the fashionable look was usurped by demands to appear to be the ideal in the flesh, pressuring models, and those who sought to look like them, to become increasingly slim, echoing a 1920s paradigm.

Thin and Mobile: The Flapper Ideal

In the roaring twenties, the fashion aesthetic circulated by the new genre of fashion photography undeniably imprinted the fashionable body as the thin body in the popular imagination, a sentiment that the historian Lois Banner suggests became "canonical" after fashion photography's professionalization. To this day, the notion that "clothes are best displayed on lean bodies which do not compete for viewer attention with the model's attire"[16] has become the unquestioned rule within the industry. As the slender ideal linked up with the productive ideal within the rationalizing workplace, favoring young and lithe bodies promoted the slender body as the healthy body. This tendency in turn fed into new notions about reducing mortality rates and maintaining a healthy (and productive) population, adding a further complication to the usual explanations for why, to this day, the slender body is still so closely linked to the fashionable body, representative of a modern silhouette.

During the transition from external bodily control to the internalized girdle of the modern line, the trussed and corseted angels of the house were left behind in the parlor, and the cigarette-smoking, bob-haired flapper became the icon of the modern age. Within eddying cultural and economic forces, the flapper's slender line not only reflected changing notions of womanhood but also epitomized bodily ideals of modernity and productivity, which eventually became synonymous with fashion. This transition was by no means smooth, however. The flapper did not simply shed her corset and pick up a tennis racket. She danced her way toward modernity through the rise of fashion photography as a genre, the burgeoning power of the cinematic regime, and a swirl of new freedoms, aesthetics, and work styles. The complexity of these influences speaks to the tangled web of bodies, images, and technology that has wrought the fashionable ideal we know today.

There are many debates about the flapper's lean lines, some of which are patently false. While most assume the flapper was free to breathe in her body skimming garments, in fact, as the curator and fashion historian Harold Koda points out,

> The couturier Paul Poiret, with his designs inspired by the Orient and the Directoire, was said to have liberated women, at least those fashionably svelte, from their corsets. Poiret's columnar silhouette supplanted the wasp-waist. However, since an overall slimming of the body was required, a more encompassing, though more supple, corset was introduced. In a curious paradox, this torso-wrapping corset persisted through the 1920s.[17]

Similarly, some claim the newly visible practices of dieting and slimming common in the flapper age represented a political backlash, instigating new forms of private control in response to the surge in women's public power.[18] For the fashion historian Elizabeth Wilson, however, the idea of dieting as modern anti-woman discourse completely missed the fact that, "at least since the seventeenth century," dieting has been a *severe self-discipline*

instilled by persistent instruction

Western preoccupation "as part of medical regimes, as well as religious asceticism."[19] Wilson numbers women's oppression as one among many catalysts for the inculcation of the slender ideal. Among these, she cites the industrial revolution's formative influence on a culture newly concerned with regimentation, which "assisted the work ethic and obsessional time-keeping of the industrial world."[20]

Whether as a symbol of new freedom or a backlash against it, in the popular imagery of the time, not only did the flapper, with her lean lines and lithe form, represent a depiction of sexuality within the complex evolution of the disciplining of femininity, she also embodied a new ideology of bodily management that encouraged productivity. While women's new-found freedom from body-destroying corsets may have resulted in part from new thinking about women's rights and place in the world, this influence does not adequately explain this new look's parallels with industrialist ideals. More than simple patriarchal backlash, the slim aesthetic was also informed by a modernizing world whose ideals were spread by the growing power of fashion and cinema.

As the media studies researchers Stuart and Elizabeth Ewen observe, connecting the chorus lines of the Rockettes, or Tiller's girls, with Busby Berkeley's spectacular films depicting lines of identical women performing movements in sequence, film and entertainment "were not only vehicles of fashion ideals in the public consciousness, they were also ideals of mobile industrialism and efficiency."[21] As they point out:

> By the 1920s fashion had begun to emulate the logic of industrialism. The fashion ideal for women increasingly became that of the "young, agile, long limbed girl, whose naturally shaped body is well suited to the working requirements and mobility of the modern world. Her well-proportioned figure is easily clothed by a standardized manufactured garment."[22]

Claiming that this imagery was that of the "mobile, engaged woman of the industrial age," once this new ideal emerged, they argue that "the cushioned, parlorbound woman of the past was now described in metallic and mechanical terms."[23] Seen in this way, the 1920s flapper embodied industrial age notions of mechanical power achieved through standardization and scientific management.

This mechanized ideal, characterized by clean lines, smooth surfaces, and mechanical force, dovetailed with the modernist aesthetic taking hold in Europe. In her thoroughgoing treatment of fashion under fascism, the fashion studies scholar Eugenia Paulicelli observes that fascist attempts to create a unified national identity relied heavily on displaying similarly dressed women whose youthful, clean-lined bodies epitomized a sport-toned dynamic modernism. Analyzing fascist propaganda documenting public displays of womanhood, Paulicelli notes the regime's exaltation of a national body via the toned bodies of the "modern" women marchers occupying "perfectly symmetrical and geometric space."[24] Paulicelli carefully notes the complexity underlying this apparent simplicity, since the same footage also displays the "disorganized and scattered space occupied by the women in regional costumes" who marched alongside the much younger and leaner women representing the future, a juxtaposition that attempted to include "every single woman of the Italian peninsula in its purview."[25] While one group seemed diametrically opposed to the other, in fact, Paulicelli argues, these opposite figures "turn out to be two sides of the same coin, two products of the same ideology that aimed at controlling women in the same breath as it put their differences on display."[26] In the nationalist intent to create *the* Italian body, marching toward modernity, economic strength, and power, standardization was key.

The idea of sport-toned vigor, signifying modernism, also echoed through French fashion in the 1920s, as the fashion historian Valerie Steele points out. The "new idea of sports for women"[27] informed many designs, even though some sniffed at "*le menace yankee*,"[28] in which American women supposedly swarmed Paris, bringing their modern tastes, perverting the refined sensibilities of French fashion. The new, sporty, and lean lines of the modern woman, dubbed "*la garconne*" (the female boy), made many uneasy about the future of French womanhood. Steele quotes a 1925 Parisian law student who lamented the appearance of "*la jeune fille moderne*" (the modern young girl) "without breasts, without hips, without 'underwear,'" who engaged in mightily unfeminine activities such as smoking, working, arguing, and "fighting exactly like boys."[29] Regardless of critics who saw in it the downfall of French womanhood, during the 1920s and 1930s, Steele observes, "To look *sportif* was rapidly becoming a fashionable obsession," along with the lean, clean-lined body the look demanded.

Whether mechanical ideal or modernist aesthetic, both suggest that standardization to produce uniform goods was an ideal not only of industrial production but of modern life more generally. In an age enthralled with, as historian Elspeth Brown puts it, "efficiency and the utopian promises of the machine,"[30] bodily control aimed at producing uniformity and lean lines idealized a serially repeatable form. Fluid or fat bodies signified not only excess but also nonlinear proportions. While fat may layer onto a human frame in uniquely shaped ways, skeletal bodies have a uniform look, providing straight lines more easily replicated than a baroque curve.

For the fashion historian Elizabeth Wilson, this industrial technology of vision was integral to shaping the fashionably thin ideal, as the technical demands advanced by fashion photography's emergence as a genre in its own right demanded the lean lines of the fashionable silhouette. In the medium of black-and-white photography, images readable only as planes of light and shadow "intensified the importance of line, contrast, and abstract, architectural forms"[31] more easily portrayed by a slender silhouette. Citing the fashion historian Anne Hollander's assertion that "photography accentuates width,"[32] Wilson also notes the modernist aesthetic's heavy influence, in which fashion "imitated aspects of modernism in featuring abstract designs and in rendering the body as two-dimensional and flat as possible."[33] As such, the "love of form suggestive of movement and speed," along with the "rejection of the 'natural,'" called for a slender body, one of straight lines, rather than fluid, hard-to-manage curves.[34]

"Modern" became a catchword for all that is desirable in the fashion image, forging the first real links between the optimum type of working body and its glamorization by fashion models as an ideal. As this cultural ideal of thinness began to take precedence in the United States, a bootstrapping entrepreneur who styled himself a "broker in beauty" began organizing and managing models like so many cogs in a machine, elevating his slender and standardized Powers Girls to new heights of admiration and influence.

Cinema, the Powers Girls, and Engineering the Model Image

In 1923, John Robert Powers irrevocably changed the world of fashion *in a way that can't be changed* modeling by conceiving of the idea of a "professional" model. A photographic model himself, Powers worked at a time when print advertising was catching on and the demand for models kept pace. During the 1920s and 1930s, "advertising grew to the dimensions of a major industry. . . . In the period 1900–1930, national advertising revenues multiplied thirteen fold."[35] Advertisements for "women's" products did especially well. Expenditures for cosmetics, for instance, "in the thirty largest mass-circulation magazines mushroomed from $1.3 million in 1915 to $16 million fifteen years later."[36] Using photographs to promote products was powerfully attractive, catching the eye of PR and advertising executives tasked with creating alluring images to excite and, above all, capture the public's attention.[37]

Photographing all of these ads required models, but they were not all that easy to find. As Powers tells it, when he started his agency, modeling "was a completely unregulated business. In fact, it was scarcely recognized as a business at all. When an artist or a photographer needed a model, he generally stuck an advertisement in a newspaper and waited to see what would turn up."[38] Noticing the high volume of classified ads placed by commercial photographers looking for models, Powers's wife had a striking idea:

> "You know," [she] remarked thoughtfully, "there must be lots of commercial photographers looking for models. And we know dozens of actors and actresses out of work who would like jobs like that. Why can't we find a way of bringing them together?" And that was the beginning of the first agency for models.[39]

Powers's New York City agency quickly came to dominate a growing market.[40] While he may have been the only game in town in the early 1920s, by 1935, eight modeling agencies had already sprung up, and the number increased each year.[41]

Powers, one of the first to understand the intangible value of the model "look," sought to control and manage the model's body and image both on and off camera, in the studio and in the street. No longer hidden by the body-covering *maillot*, the model left the designer's salon, stretching her repertoire beyond the targeted training in the specific style of each design house. With the bulk of the modeling work now in advertising, rather than on the shop floor, models had to present a more complete persona. The closely edited image of a standardized and easily distributed ideal echoed techniques made newly valuable in the transition from the photographic to the cinematic regime. The desire to closely manage the model "product" stemmed in part from the new value found in engineering an image, thus creating a specific impression and uniform "look" as a commodity, framed by a carefully scripted narrative. As Powers notably observed, "models are a commodity, a commercial product which must meet certain requirements."[42] During the coming decades, as the fashion aesthetic solidified into a single dominant form, the notion that ideal bodies were not only desirable for women in fashion but for the population more generally began to take hold.

influence

Engineering the Image

In its early days, modeling had nowhere near the cultural clout it has today. In fact, it had an image problem. A popular magazine, *Collier's*, reported in 1930 that, in the not too distant past, it was "generally conceded" that girls, who were essentially hostesses, went by the name of "models," and their "daytime work was supplanted by labor after office hours."[43] Apparently, "beauty and spare time amiability" were the only job requirements.[44] In contrast, this profile of three top models' virtue, aptly entitled "Model Maids," explained that,

before

after

> now, beauty is less important than brains. The girls have finesse, technique, savoir-faire and an abiding sense of personal dignity.[45]

lustful

Exploiting the overtones of modeling's salacious past to full effect, the author of the article described his subjects as modern mannequins who had "better form—both ways—than their predecessors. They are very, very nice, but not very naughty."[46]

While he did not pull it off single-handedly, this shift in attitude represented many years of hard work on Powers's part. According to

Figure 4.2. Powers's Long Stemmed American Beauties. *Top*: "A dozen Powers beauties in Miami, after an eight-hour flight from New York City. Eastern Airlines' Capt. Dick Merrill in the middle." Courtesy of Eastern Airlines. *Bottom*: "Orange Bowl Festival, L. to R.: Sandy Rice, Suzanne Sommers, Jane Davis, Marion Whitney, Jeane Black, Doris Gibson and Florence Dornin." Courtesy of Eastern Airlines.

a popular historian of the modeling industry, Michael Gross, Powers hated the word "model," lamenting that "women with no means of visible support called themselves models. People thought of them as empty-headed floozies."[47] In fact, "to be a model, was usually to reap a harvest of lifted eyebrows."[48] To counteract these forces, Powers made sure his "all-American girls" were not naughty at all by strictly managing their professional and personal lives.

In particular, Powers separated his models from the usual "association with loose, off-color theatrical living" by carefully narrating a new story to suture the image of modeling to "naturalness" and the "all-American way." To avoid association with the word "model" altogether, Powers hit on the moniker "Long Stemmed American Beauty." In his self-appointed role as a "broker in beauty,"[49] he tutored his models into the "Powers Girl" brand: Under this concerted tutelage, the "Powers Girl" emerged as the "most charming girl in the world."[50] To cement this brand, Powers described his "girls" to news reporters and in press releases—in fact, to just about anyone who would listen—as "typical American girls, pretty, healthy, vivacious, and self-reliant."[51] The Powers type was a

> natural girl, without excessive make-up, without the mincing artificial walk associated in the popular imagination with models. Instead, she is poised, charming, graceful, a model for any woman to follow.[52]

Powers strongly believed that this natural image would sell products more readily than the glamorous and sexy chorus girl image. As he put it, the Powers Girl was an all-American girl who would sell to "the average woman" who did "most of the nation's purchasing" and "shied away from the product displayed by the model who, though she might be very pretty, did not represent qualities which the buyer admired."[53]

Powers used every weapon at his disposal to construct the myth of his models and to create their brand. With "a showman's flair," he invented a symbol to differentiate his models from the rest:

> When a Powers girl broke the handle of a satchel in which she lugged around the tools of her trade—her pumps, her waist cinch, her war paints and brushes—Powers replaced the bag with a strong round

[handwritten margin notes: "woman who has a reputation for promiscuity"; "stitch together"; "dainty"]

Figure 4.3. Powers Girls on the move. *Top*: "Just before the Powers girls left for Orange Bowl Festival at Miami Beach and a show at Burdines, MacClelland Barclay, well known illustrator, painted the Long Stemmed American Beauty Doris Gibson on the Plane." Courtesy of Eastern Airlines. *Bottom*: "Dick Merrill, pilot, shows Babs Beckwith the latest weather report during the flight from New York to Miami Beach." Courtesy of Eastern Airlines.

cardboard hatbox from John Cavanagh, where he bought his headgear. The boxes sold for fifty cents apiece and became the badge of honor for the Powers model.[54]

In producing this uniformity of presentation, the Powers walk became as much a signature as the hatbox. Powers enjoyed describing how, in his office, the girls waiting in the lobby to be interviewed for a chance to model were intimidated by the swan-like elegance of his working models, who passed "in and out with their long, lovely walk."[55] Each, of course, had the "hat-box, the badge of their profession, hanging from their arm," presenting a uniformity of movement and silhouette constituting a total "look," which became Powers's stock in trade.[56]

As the sociologists Don Slater and Joanne Entwistle have observed, the model "look" behaves like a brand.[57] Brand names, resulting from revolutionary innovations in packaging, marketing and distribution, eventually developed into various forms of "brand identity." During this revolution, goods were transformed—from undifferentiated sacks of sugar, for instance, to small packages of "Domino." In the same manner, by packaging them and giving them standardized prices, Powers packaged his "girls" and standardized their rates. Slater and Entwistle remind us that attaching an "identifying mark" to a good is a key step in the branding process, a logo whose credibility depends not on some abstract series of signs and meanings but, rather, on the broad range of practices linking goods and signs, relations within which experiences loop back onto the sign, giving it stability. Thus the Powers Girls's signature hatbox, while a de facto means of carrying their modeling supplies, came to represent the dependable quality and high standard to which the Powers Girls were kept, through a series of practices and relations that attached to the hatbox as a "sign" of a professional model "look."

Professionalizing the model "brand" especially entailed professionalizing behavior. Before there were model agencies, models had been notoriously unpredictable. According to the model chronicler Charles Castle, it was a good day when the model showed up, since "fashion houses and photographers . . . were never sure whether the model would actually appear at the appointed time."[58] Under Powers's control, models showed up on time and ready to work, and they soon attained new levels of status and pay. The average model made $35 per week in 1923; by 1930, some models made $100 per week, and exceptional models could command that amount or more for a single photo session or fashion show.[59] In demanding professionalism from his models, Powers produced a predictable and malleable product (e.g., the model) that could produce according to industry standards. *commitment*

As the demand for adherence to particular standards of appearance and behavior became more common, model agents and photographers followed Powers's lead, dictating the story of modeling, scripting roles for models to play. The models followed suit, working with the suggested costumes and characters, styling their makeup and hair, and donning the model uniform of hatbox, dress, and gloves, to create the highly polished and glamorous persona of the fashion model. In a key departure from the design house–crafted image of the past, however, one was no longer a Dior model or a lady by Lucile. The Powers Girls were capable of showing any brand to best advantage, satisfaction guaranteed, no matter what look or style the client required. These practices of control and standardization of bodies and images, aimed at editing the model "look" to produce a desired result, represent the first glimmerings of glamour labor practices aimed at managing both the physical and the social aspects of the body. In the cinematic mode of image production, those who excelled at engineering images began to reap sizeable rewards, not the least of whom was Powers; "in the course of 20 years," he observed, his "little agency" became the "largest of its kind in the world."[60]

Mechanization and Modernity: The New Silhouette

formed / arranged for a particular purpose

In organizing what was essentially an ad hoc occupation, Powers inaugurated radical changes in how models conducted themselves. In the complex interplay between products, industry, advertising images, and ideals, the Powers Girl became the gold standard. Implicit in the idea of engineering these images—the notion of engineering a response, building an infrastructure for accessing and shaping bodily energies to desire particular products and lifestyles—was the organization of bodies in space and time to be resourced not only as individuals but as tendencies or population-wide trends. Advertising imagery was the first step toward this industrialization of feeling; soon the looming Goliath of Hollywood took over on a grand scale as the cinematic regime came into full force.

As the burgeoning film industry standardized into a studio system, studio lots, like image factories, churned out movie images on a mass scale, in a process that some theorists claimed created an "industrialization" of vision.[61] Similar to Henry Ford's Taylorization of automobile production according to scientific principles of standardization and control in the 1920s, cinema Taylorized image production, organizing images and their consumption in unprecedented ways. According to the film theorist and experimental filmmaker Dziga Vertov, the machine effect of the camera and film projector, products themselves of a mass industrial age, regulated and syncopated the movements of the eye, and the images available to it, into what Vertov calls the "kino-eye," or "film eye."[62] The notion of automated vision, or machine vision, was, for Vertov, an ideal type of vision that could perhaps see more truly than the human eye, giving it new capacities.

The new corporeality demanded by industrialized perception pulled for serially interchangeable models, with identical proportions portraying this attenuated ideal. Those who did not fit the standard were eventually winnowed out, with Powers leading the charge. As a result, from the 1920s into the 1940s, the fairly relaxed atmosphere in modeling, with room for a variety of body types and sizes, moved toward a reliance on a uniformity of type, with more strictly enforced measurements. Taking his efforts to reign in the body's variability and affectivity to new levels, Powers was among the first to require that his models adhere to strict norms for height and weight, a bodily script to follow. In the face of considerable opposition, he became a staunch defender of the slender type, observing that

> the tall, slight figure complements the lines of clothes and makes them more effective; because it has a fluid quality which enables it to assume graceful and dramatic positions. A short girl has a stubby effect in photography and cannot display clothes to the best advantage. . . . In other words, they must be tall and slim, well proportioned and able to handle their bodies with perfect control and a maximum of grace.[63]

The new, body-focused requirements came as a surprise to some. A "refined magazine editor" who had witnessed this transformation in the industry told the tale of "how shocked she had been when agencies became more orientated towards photography and spoke openly about girls' measurements, 'as though they were prize cattle.'"[64]

This new form of control, treating models as so much prize livestock, represented the first real surge in glamour labor in the modeling industry resulting from changing imaging and productive norms. Archival data reveal that, from the 1930s into the 1940s and 1950s, bodily requirements for modeling became standardized (see Chart 4.1). These new requirements were discussed in the media, were reflected in modeling "how-to" books, and were particularly evident in records about models' bodies published in "annuals" from each agency, picturing all the models on their rosters, with their clothing sizes, height, and weight statistics helpfully listed beneath each picture.

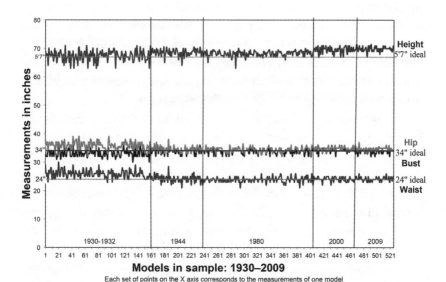

Chart 4.1. The standardization of model measurements over time ($N = 521$), 1930–2009. Models in the sample are assigned numbers 1–521 and are arranged along the x-axis by the date of the model annual in which they appeared. Their measurements are plotted by height, hip, bust, and waist in inches along the y-axis. The right-hand axis gives the baseline "ideal" model measurements, which are depicted as lines through which the fluctuating model measurements pass.

Producing a models' "annual" was common practice in the field for decades. According to Jamie, a contemporary model I interviewed, an "agency book," or annual, is "a big promotional piece with fun art direction," featuring pictures of all the agency's models to promote the agency. Until recently, agencies put them out every year, but now "with the Internet, they have become obsolete."[65] Early annuals are particularly helpful for seeing how the model body changed as the space and time for crafting the look for the camera was eventually squeezed out by the demands of the moving image. Within this shift, a uniform standard emerged, the variety of sizes dropped out, and model proportions became extremely slim.

Powers's efforts to edit his models' bodies in keeping with his overarching narrative of "slender, tender, and tall,"[66] was clearly evident in his agency books. While Powers may have published annuals in the 1920s, none have survived on public record. During the 1930s these books came out reliably every year, and a few examples remain extant. Looking through a sample of these annuals reveals the standardization of the model body with particular clarity. In the space of just two years, for instance, the models on Powers's books grew both thinner and taller. The variety of his models' shapes and sizes available in 1930 was no longer evident in the models pictured in 1932 and, according to other archival evidence, completely disappeared by the 1940s.

In 1930, at least ten of Powers's models had thirty-nine-inch hips, a hip measurement two to three inches larger than the maximum standard of today. Several of them were 5'5" and under, two inches shorter than today's minimum standard. Betty Maar, for instance, was certainly tall enough by today's standards, at 5'9", but she weighed 135 pounds and measured 35-29-38, a size that would currently be considered unacceptable for modeling. Even her contemporary, Kay Ross, who weighed a somewhat lighter 128 pounds and measured 35-27-37, would probably be politely shown the door if she were to seek high-fashion modeling work now, as her body stats are two to three inches larger than the minimum standard of today.

By 1932, however, all who did not fit the "slender, tender, and tall" standard had mostly disappeared from Powers's books.[67] That year's annual still included models in the 5'3"–5'5" range, but the majority were over 5'8". On the whole, the group was thinner. Many models weighed

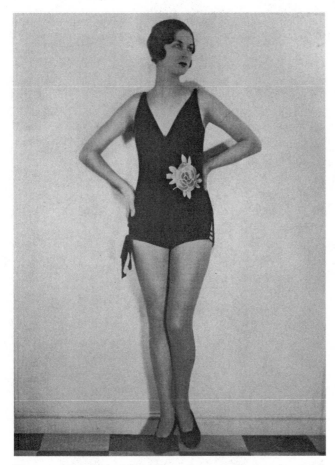

Figure 4.4. Powers model Kay Ross, who was taller than the typical model of the era at 5'9", had non-standard proportions 35-27-37 in 1930.

under 120 pounds, and new models were added—such as Babs Shanton, at 5'7", 110 pounds, and 32-24-35, and Stella Bayliss, at 5'7", 115 pounds, and 34-24-36—who fit today's ultra slender standards. Only one or two had a hip measurement of larger than thirty-six inches, despite the fact that many of them were over 5'8". In a set of ten pages picked at random, more than half of the fifteen models pictured were 5'7" or taller, true to Powers's standard. True to his word, it seems Powers would allow only the longest-stemmed and slenderest American Beauties onto his books.

Figure 4.5. Powers model Stella Bayliss was closesr in 1930 to today's proportions at 5'7" and 34-24-36, but she still had a much softer look than any model working today.

Powers's ideal was not yet dominant, however. Powers's own Joan Clement, for instance, a "Model Maid" profiled as a top model in *Collier's*,[68] was highly successful and certainly tall enough by today's standards, at 5'10.5". She weighed 135 pounds, however, and measured 34-27-39, measurements that are now unheard of in modeling, unless it is for specialized work, such as the celebrated curves of Sophie Dahl, famous in the early 2000s for breaking the ultra slim norm on the runways. Similarly, a famous English model of the 1930s, Elsa Whittaker, was quite well known and worked frequently, "even though, like all

English women, she was pear shaped," with narrow shoulders and wide hips.[69] Her American contemporary, Anita Counihan, dubbed "The Face," due to her perfect features, appeared on fifteen magazine covers in a single month, in spite of having "heavy legs and a thick figure."[70]

The success of these models speaks to the tendency during the 1930s and into the 1940s toward anxieties about shoring up a healthy body, possibly borne of the privations of war, evidenced by the desire to "build up" the body, to achieve "a chubby, well-groomed figure."[71] This obsession with healthy curves competed, at the same time, with an obsession

Figure 4.6. "The Face," Anita Counihan (Colby), 1936 RKO Pictures headshot. Image courtesy of the New York Public Library Bill Rose Theatre Collection.

[handwritten: joined togeth]

with slenderness as a sign of health. Additionally, while norms of imaging in the photographic regime that valued crafting a look dovetailed
with the cinematic practice of close editing to produce a narrative
sweep, paradoxically, the cinematically engineered image also contained
the means of destroying its own narratives. The moving image, first on
the silver screen and then in the everyday of television, demanded a
fashionable body that was not contrived to look as slender as the ideal,
but actually was.

[handwritten left margin: just coming into existence]

Once again, the two cultural ideals of womanhood, curvy and voluptuous, or lean and long, were the subject of public debate. The spread
of standard sizing within the democratization of fashion's long history
of lean, coupled with nascent biopolitical forces organizing publics
into potentially lucrative makeovers-in-the-making, proved too much
for the womanly figure to bear, as breasts and hips were deemed even
more unfashionable than ever. This ideal did not go out without a fight,
however. In well-publicized exchanges, proponents of womanly curves
dueled with Powers for cultural dominance, with the leanest and longest
emerging triumphant.

The historian Elizabeth Matelski documented Powers's competitor
Walter Thornton's public rejection of the "tall, willowy woman, built
along the lines of a window dummy." While Thornton admitted such
a figure may prevent "fitting problems" when showing clothes, it was a
figure he found universally unappealing.[72] Competitor Harry Conover
was of similar mind. He specialized in Cover Girls, prized for their
beauty and photo-friendly faces, rather than their lithe silhouettes.[73]
In a very public competitive exchange, "when John Powers turned
down the model application of the reigning Miss America (he claimed
she was built too much like a football player), Conover signed her to
a contract."[74] This move epitomized Conover's efforts to differentiate
his girls by decrying the "cardboard silhouette" standard that had been
popularized by Powers and later picked up by Eileen Ford.[75] In a magazine article entitled "I'm Fed Up with Thin Girls," Conover claimed
his agency steered clear of "the girl who has starved herself into looking like an Adam's apple mounted on a pogo stick." He liked his girls
"healthy and round."[76] Driving the point home, he explained, "The sur-
est way to a man's ulcer is through a woman's empty stomach. Frankly, I
made up my mind long ago that life was too short for me to kowtow to

[handwritten bottom: act in a subservient manner]

Figure 4.7. Conover model, Elaine Bassett, 1945.

these melba-toast prima donnas whose waspish figures are matched by equally waspish temperaments."[77]

Conover's annual "agency book," a self-published title called *Who Is She?*[78] tells a slightly different story, however. It pictures Jean Bowen, whose towering 5'8.5" inch form weighed in at only 112 pounds and sported the magical 34-24-34 ratio that has become a golden mean in the industry. The majority of Conover models listed had similar proportions. Elaine Bassett was among the highest paid, at $15 per hour. At 5'10.5", she weighed a heavier, by modeling standards, 128 pounds, but her body measured a relatively slim 35-24-35. More in keeping with

Conover's publicized preferences, Bernice Fisher's 5'10.5" frame measured a decidedly large 36-29-37 and weighed 139 pounds. These exceptions to the rule were few and far between, however. Compared to the ten or so nonstandard models in Powers's 1930 annual, Conover's 1945 *Who Is She?* included only two "round" girls, evidence belying his professed love of that type. *[contradicting]*

In fact, by the late 1940s and into the 1950s, the wasp-waisted fashion mannequin came to dominate the popular consciousness as the fashionable ideal. Despite the 1950s popularity of voluptuous women such as movie stars Jayne Mansfield and Marilyn Monroe, after a brief moment of shunning the too-skinny figure,[79] slimming became a national obsession. The idealized slender form emerged within overlapping tendencies reflective of transitioning imaging norms. Haute couture, body-crafting practices that created the illusion of slimness for static photographic images, on the one hand, vied for attention alongside diet and exercise advice from Hollywood "flesh sculptors" that aimed at producing slimness in the flesh, on the other.[80] This body sculpting set out as an aspirational goal by glamorous Hollywood personalities and fashion models began to trickle down to the general public when key developments in fashion and media technologies, coupled with changing cultural attitudes, pushed ideal bodies into a calculus of risk and profit maximization that helped extend the slim aesthetic to larger portions of the population.

[shift to thinness compete]

In this transition, models who could produce the illusion of slimness eventually gave way to those who actually were slim. As the field professionalized, the variety of shapes and sizes gradually disappeared. As Chart 4.1 illustrates, the size of oscillation between large and small measurements gradually becomes more uniform and starts to approach the "ideal" much more closely. Measurements that were all over the map straighten out into almost a flat line. It is clear that the models' heights also trend upward as time progresses. Presumably, in mechanistic body practices consonant with the static demands of photography, a basic figure could be waist-cinched and bullet-bra'd into submission.[81] Information available in model how-to books from the same period similarly indicates that the model look was achieved as much by shaping the body from the outside, through corsetry—or waist cinchers, as they were known at the time—as through diet and exercise.

In contrast, film stars had no room for such artifice. They had to have the right look in the flesh, and gymnasium directors at Warner Bros., Metro-Goldwyn-Mayer, and Paramount admonished their movie-stars-in-the-making to skip rope and pull weights to build muscle, to produce an image "so explosively healthy, that vitality just naturally bursts out all over the screen."[82] The Left Coast body culture linking slenderness and health was, not surprisingly, at the cutting edge of a coming trend dictated by the demands of the moving image, which was taken into overdrive in the television age. During this period, both haute couture models and starlets modeled fashions, with fashion plates and double features disseminating fashion in equal force. The cinematic mode demanded physical embodiment of fashionably lean lines that fashion models, within pockets of haute couture still dominated by photographic ideals, had the luxury to create. Thus, even as late as 1954, the

Figure 4.8 Engineered for projection: foundation garments for Dior's "New Look," 1947. From Nigel Cawthorne, *The New Look: The Dior Revolution* (Edison, NJ: Wellfleet Press, 1996).

modeling kingpin John Robert Powers's modeling guide, *The Secrets of Charm*, may have suggested diet moderation in passing, but corsetry still figured strongly in creating the ideal: "Four factors always add up to the ideal figure. In order there are: proper diet, exercise, posture, and corsetry."[83]

The transition was not completely smooth, but the bodily diversity in modeling that my data indicate seemed to be on its way out as early as the mid-1940s. Corroboratively, while a 1944 human-interest piece nodded to the fact that various body types had traditionally been acceptable in modeling, saying, "It is difficult to generalize about the 'typical' model, because each agency tries to build up a diversified roster of feminine faces and figures,"[84] it concluded, somewhat definitively, that the "really successful models . . . don't have voluptuous curves nor sensual faces. They have skinny bodies and hollow gaunt faces with prominent cheekbones,"[85] the norm to this day. Whatever room for variety there may have been, by the mid- to late 1940s the "skinny body" and "hollow, gaunt face" became the dominant ideal, in a shift arguably linked to biopolitical concerns about the health of the populace, disseminated by "ideal body" charts in fashion magazines, which in turn converted that populace into a market for weight control and management, a market organized and regulated by messages conveyed by fashion models' glamour labor.

While it has been attributed to various causes, such as the push to get women back into the kitchen after their temporary foray onto the factory floor during the war years, the spread of body-sculpting practices by Hollywood, and, ultimately, fashion modeling, reflected concerns wrought by the burgeoning science of bodies that underscored the new need to control their shape and size in order to ensure a healthy and available workforce, while making profits for the life insurance industry.[86] Thus, the rise of the wasp-waisted 1940s and 50s fashion model reflected not only a bid by patriarchal forces to reassert themselves but also biopolitically inflected changes in attitudes about appearance that solidified the fashion aesthetic into a single, dominant norm by drawing the line between healthy bodies and those that were at risk. The notion that ideal bodies were not only desirable for women in fashion but for the population more generally began to take hold, aided and abetted by two significant changes in the fashion industry.

First, in fashion, the mass-produced ready-to-wear market experienced its second most significant expansion since the late-nineteenth-century adoption of the sewing machine.[87] As a result, the mass market for fashion spread its purview beyond elite society circles to encompass everyday women. In this era, for the first time, "high-fashion pictures were appearing in mass circulation newspapers" and "not just in the glossies like *Vogue* and *Harper's*" as fashion model historian Brigid Keenan has pointed out.[88] As fashionable ideas became available to more people, the market for mass-produced fashionable clothes strengthened, and the need for models who could conform to ready-made patterns created a stronger pull for a homogenous body type.

This type, however, may have been based on data skewed toward a figure that is unusually thin. As the historian Elizabeth Matelski found in examining the origins of standard sizing, when the National Bureau of Home Economics in the Department of Agriculture compiled "the measurements of more than 15,000 white women to help clothing manufacturers develop their ready-to-wear clothing,"[89] their results may have been a little off. The participants were offered a small fee for volunteering, and, as Matelski points out, since the country had not shaken off the ill effects of the Great Depression, the participants could have

originated from the most impoverished populations, using the token compensation towards food for their families. This complicated the representative figure of the "average woman," as social conditions may have skewed data toward underweight body types.[90]

These flawed data about the "average woman" may have in turn reinforced the fashionable ideal toward the extremely thin.

Once the standardization of clothing sizes according to these data was in place, newly created actuary tables put forth by the Metropolitan Life Insurance Company in 1942 and 1943 that mapped healthy frame sizes and their corresponding ideal weights advanced this ideal. These charts suggested that being overweight for one's frame size was "unhealthy as well as undesirable," feeding the notion of body size and weight into the matrix of risk and profit maximization.[91] These biopolitically inflected "ideal body" charts drew the line between healthy (insurable) bodies and those that were at risk, while shifting the burden of risk for the population's health onto the individual. In popularizing these tables, ostensibly to help their readers set weight goals, fashion magazines took matters into their own hands, and the insurance companies' originally neutral language of small, medium, and large frame sizes and their recommended weights and heights morphed into "slim, ideal, and stocky," as one magazine put it.[92]

Starting in the 1950s, fashion models' glamour labor enticed many Americans to incorporate these market logics into their flesh by modeling an ideal body determined by market imperatives.[93] In this subtle shift, the notion of the ideal body got further mixed in the public consciousness with slenderness, dovetailing with the idea that the slender body is the healthy body, a desirable body, one that falls on the correct side of those who adhere to reigning beauty norms, as opposed to those who can't or won't. This trend was compounded by another development in the determination of "ideal bodies," the demonization of fat as unhealthy, which contributed to the emergence of a nationwide set of anxieties about body shape and size, pushing these standards beyond mere aesthetics, raising the stakes of avoiding fat to a matter of life and death.[94] As fashion modeling entered a golden age, the model's body became the symbol of a kind of disciplined glamour for which everyone was encouraged to strive. Instrumental in creating this goal were the innovations of a scrappy entrepreneur whose practices of strict management and hard-core negotiation authored one of the most highly edited and soigné images of modeling, an image born in a "tiny, grubby office ... with six telephones on a card table."[95]

A Cover Girl Looks Every Bit the Part

In 1946, the indomitable Eileen Ford set up Ford Models.[96] Her management style diverged strongly from her (mostly male) predecessors. Harry Conover reportedly had five hundred girls but "didn't pay attention to any of them." In contrast, Ford's more intimate approach represented a level of involvement that few others had attempted.[97] In so doing, Ford's practices fostered an intensification of models' glamour labor while also making the practice attractive to the general public.

cannot be subdued/overcome

With the rise ~~of the golden age of~~ couture, glossy magazines, ~~pow-ered by influential photographers and admen, taught an image-hungry public what their hearts should desire.~~[98] For the first time, what models did became what everyone should do. In 1948, the model agent Clyde Dessner—who, incidentally, coined the word "supermodel"—likened modeling to the "art of being a woman," saying,

> ~~Professional modeling is the art of being a woman brought~~ to a high ~~degree of perfection. . . . For this reason the essence and mechanics~~ of ~~modeling are of unusual value and significance to every woman.~~[99]

In this atmosphere, fashion models emerged as icons of right living, as Ford's close engineering made them into a "model" of desirable behavior, impeccable from every angle, at every moment of the day. Ford's exaggeration of the notion of packaging models, managing their image as well as their labor, picked up the trend originated by John Robert Powers. Through protective coddling of her models, feeding them, clothing them, inviting them into her home, Ford's close vigilance over personality, bodywork, and conduct set newly intense standards for models' glamour labor.

When it came to managing her model's bodies, Ford was not one to mince words. Creating a model who was worth her high price tag demanded close supervision and an iron hand. Apparently, when she first met would-be model Jean Patchett, who eventually became quite famous over a long career, Ford bellowed, "You're as big as a horse! You'll have to lose weight." Already slim at 5'9" and 127 pounds, Patchett burst into tears, but then, as she told reporter Michael Gross, "I lost weight. Eileen made appointments. I was working—immediately!"[100]

~~Ford's iron-fisted management extended to her models' public personae, as well, training her models not only in appearance and comportment with clients when they were on the job but also for any time they appeared in public.~~ While the majority of models at the time "wore hats and gloves and pearls and dressed as elegantly off the set as on," carrying hatboxes filled with their professional accoutrements as they shuttled between fittings, shoots, and shows,[101] Ford took this practice to a new level, adhering to strict standards of grooming and presentation, as Gayle, who worked with Ford in the early days, explained. Still slim and attractive in her early sixties, she spoke to me in her Upper East Side apartment, surrounded by exotic objects reflective of her world travels, recalling that

> we always had our make-up on; we wore high heels, and there was a time when we wore white blouses and full black skirts with crinolines underneath it, and you had your little black hatbox, and you looked the part.

Looking the part became part of the job of engineering the Ford Model image to produce an idea of propriety and exclusivity, and this demand became a founding notion in the expansion of glamour labor in fashion modeling in the ensuing decades.

Looking the part entailed playing the part as well. Being a model all of the time, never letting the image slip, required producing the illusion of being "on" all the time, a requirement that eventually ceased to be an illusion and became a lived reality of the modeling life. Creating the image of exclusivity involved controlling models' time to support the notion that they were worth a lot of money per hour. When she worked in New York City from the 1940s into the 1950s, Gayle recalls being told:

> Your time is too valuable; we can't say that you are worth so much an hour, if you drop in and you are doing nothing. So girls used to go into a lot of movies—to be scarce—to not be seen just wandering around.

When interviewed late in her career, the model Jean Patchett was similarly described as being "wise enough not to overexpose herself, believing that the more you are seen, the less you are wanted. 'When you're in demand, they can't get you, they want you all the more.'"[102]

This technique of limiting access to models' time represented a new intensity of image management that seeped into the model's off-camera life, blurring the line between work and life. Once Ford set the precedent, her competitors followed suit. A perennial fixture in the industry, John Robert Powers ramped up his publicity machine, publishing an autobiography in which he claimed "Girls Are Always News," hosting a radio show, and writing a syndicated newspaper column called *The Secrets of Charm*,[103] all instrumental in helping the "model girl" to capture the popular imagination in the United States. He denied, perhaps a bit disingenuously, doing any kind of promotional activity or tie-in for his models, however:

> Curiously enough, I myself have never sent out promotional material on the Powers girls. The enormous amount of publicity releases which they are constantly getting is unsolicited, a spontaneous indication of the public interest in them. Their presence stimulates interest in almost every type of public event.[104]

He went on to point out that "if Mrs. Smith cooks and keeps house for her husband it is of interest to no one but Mrs. Smith. But when a model has domestic tastes, she is photographed buying groceries, basting a roast, taking her baby out in his carriage."[105]

The fact that models were becoming the "darlings of the newspapers"[106] signified a significant extension of work time into domains that were previously considered personal, glamorizing a level of exposure that would serve as a building block for the kinds of glamour labor prevalent today. The need to manage one's image for the camera in the studio, or for the runway, or even on the street to "look the part," as the Ford model Gayle had described it, was expanding beyond the time spent on the job, seeping into a model's personal life, so that what she did when she was not "on duty" also had to be managed or engineered to keep it in line with the overall image her management sought to project. The trend toward having to be camera ready at all times had begun and brought with it new requirements for models' looks and demeanor.

Prior to the 1960s arrival of television, however, modeling had not yet become what sociologists call a "master status," that is, a status that supersedes all others. Models did not have to worry about their photo being snapped by chance while emptying the garbage or on a toilet paper run, as is the case today. If such a "chance" event were to occur, it would have been a planned accident, a publicity event tied to the notion of promoting the glamorous life of modeling. The national engagement with all things fashion was not yet as obsessive and all encompassing as it would become. The 1960s saw a blurring of the lines formerly separating the haughty couture model and the more accessible movie star, as models themselves became celebrities. With the dawn of the television age, creating the illusion of slenderness or height was out; actually embodying the increasingly strict standards for modeling work was in.

The 1960s emergence of the regime of television pulled the power of the moving image from the sanctified darkness of the movie house into the everyday, leaving no room for artifice as the body in motion came under close scrutiny, characteristic of television's intimate and instantaneous nature. The "natural" look and willingness to be exposed from all angles was in. In this transition, modeling work became all encompassing, and the model had to reach deeper within herself to produce a productive "look." At the same time, new restrictions on model bodies were met with a new emphasis on the power of projection, which opened up the ideal to the unpredictable as its constantly receding goal.

A new kind of pub (models & must be ready @ all times "DIGITAL UNREAL" (156)
* transition from "glance to blink" (143)
* Twiggy's "glamour labor" (144) — importance of projection (145)
* height requirements (154)
* idea that everybody could be a model if they tried
* camera charisma (155)
* inflexible requirements & tremendous body work (152)
* affective labour (161)
the body increasingly becomes a space for intervention / investment (159)

5

The Fashionable Ideal

Looking Like a Model

When Mary Quant took her "Look" to Amsterdam in the early 1960s, her visit made the kind of splash typical of the "glance" regime. There for only one day, Quant made every minute count. Describing the tour in a 1966 autobiography, she gushed, "My models spent practically the whole time being photographed," so much so, the next morning they "made the front page of every single newspaper in Holland," and "every single one of their magazines as well."[1] At a pace in keeping with the times, a subsequent trip to New York City allotted only four days to "launch the . . . collection to the Press, do some radio work, make some television, particularly the Merv Griffin show," and return to London.[2]

This type of media blitz represented a new form of promotion and a different kind of exposure for modeling. In another shrewd publicity move that worked wonders for her reputation, Quant managed to get an eight-and-half-minute film of her models wearing the "Look" to "fifty television stations" across the United States. Quant mused, "It is estimated that, one way or another, something like fifty million people have seen it."[3] Going for maximum coverage clearly paid off. On a twenty-one-day tour of the United States involving "thirty different planes" and "god knows how many thousands of miles to cover on deadline timing," it was not unusual for nearly "two thousand kids" to show up to see the ten-minute fashion show of the short skirts and youthful attire that became Quant's claim to fame.[4]

Producing this kind of publicity demanded a different kind of work from the models; they had to be camera ready at all times, practically sleeping in their makeup. They may have been "up since five in the morning and traveling in the milk plane since six"; nonetheless, they had to arrive "immaculately turned out and ready for the photographers."[5] The pace was grueling, as was the atmosphere. Throughout the tour, the models "worked non-stop for ten days being bawled and screamed and shouted at all the time. They were brutally overworked. There was not even a let up for a coffee and a sandwich at any time during the day."[6] As if producing the "Look" for the cameras while they were on public display weren't enough, Quant recalled that at the end of the tour, the *New York Herald Tribune* photographers even "jostled into the girls' dressing room" and "found them lying flat on the floor absolutely out." The "terrific pace and impact and fantastic effort these girls have to make to translate the mood into visual fact" had finally taken its toll; "this was the picture the photographers took. It appeared the next morning."[7] Photographing models in seemingly private moments of openness or vulnerability to the camera brought new bodily ideals to the general public. The 1960s bad-boy photographer David Bailey saw in this publicity surge a need for models to become a

three dimensional entity. . . . As opposed to just stills photography, the sixties girl had exposure on the catwalk, television, and film. She became a more rounded, and more accessible, public figure.[8]

Accessibility drove out artifice, valuing new qualities in modeling. Without the time to construct a haughty persona for the camera, the white-hot exposure of the flashing cameras everywhere brought a newly intense scrutiny of the face and the body. New demands for translucence, transparency, and a "natural" look emphasized vulnerability. Not only did these imperatives of the regime of the glance come to the fore during the 1960s youth quake and new thinking about women's role in society, they were also the product of evolving image regimes and shifting productive metaphors for the ideal body. The pressure to be "model" thin stemmed more from volatile fluctuations in affectivity emerging in the glance of television, exacerbated by the blink of the Internet than it did from the needs of a partriarchal or consumerist society.

Male sexual desire and the constant creation of artificial needs offer little analytic insight into how, for instance, after remaining relatively stagnant for decades, starting in the 1960s, the model ideal rapidly attenuated, becoming extremely lean and long. In addition, looking to patriarchal and consumerist forces does little to explain the growing emphasis in modeling on projecting a strong personality or quirky

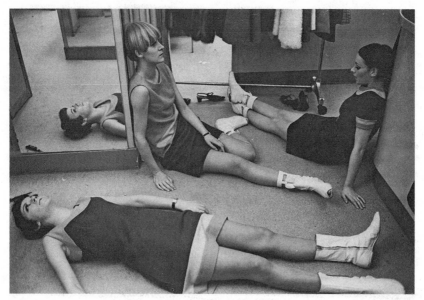

Figure 5.1. Quant models collapsed in their dressing room after a breakneck dancing show, 1965. *New York Herald Tribune*, September 2, 1965. Courtesy of the Queens Borough Library, New York.

edginess that became almost, if not more, important than appearance after the 1980s. Exploring the contours of affective economics in the transition from glance to blink technologies, however, elucidates how micromanaging the body while also fostering its volatile unpredictability and pushing it to extremes became newly valuable glamour labor practices in the age of the blink, deeply affecting the model "ideal."

Twiggy and the Power of Projection

to be a sign/ indicate

Twiggy's wide-eyed, bare-legged gangliness denoted a kind of immediacy typical of the "glance" regime. Her youth was eminently photographable with the lit-from-within technology of the cathode ray. Of course Twiggy's youth flew in the face of the sophisticated drama of the soignée mid-century mannequin, the glamorous "woman of about 36, dressed in black satin with a string of pearls."[9] On the wings of the new jet travel and the increasingly inclusive scope and scale of television, Twiggy became an international celebrity. Twiggy also rocketed to stardom, however, because she epitomized the antithesis of the cinematic regime. Similar to Quant's fast-forward timing, the speed of Twiggy's rise typified the new staccato pace of imaging. Crowned the next "it" girl on the strength of a single set of photos, a fashion editor at the *Daily Express* in London dubbed the sixteen-year-old "the Face of 66 ... The Cockney kid with the face to launch a thousand shapes."[10] That first shoot spawned bookings in *Elle* and *Vogue* almost immediately. Unlike the decade-long careers of the 1950s swans, in the space of three short years, Twiggy became an international celebrity, made a splash on two continents, sold her image to countless periodicals, licensed her name and face to many buyers, and then all but disappeared.[11]

Twiggy's coltish figure was the total opposite of the former ideal, the wasp-waisted hourglass, trussed up with bullet bras and waist cinchers. Twiggy's diminutive proportions only added to the weight of her impact. At just 91 pounds and measuring just 31-22-32 and 5'6", Twiggy's ultra-slim figure became the focus of a desire that dovetailed with a growing obsession with diet and weight loss across U.S. culture.[12] This shift represented a era in which the model's body became a link in the chain of health and weight concerns that pulled people into habits and behaviors focused on bodily management, such as buying diet books, specialized food, or gym memberships. Coupled with its roots in the 1960s sexual freedom that revealed the body in unprecedented ways, the diet culture bloomed in the 1970s. The fact that Twiggy's image was able to mobilize bodily economies of dieting and hair styles, as well as the speed at which she reached the top of the profession, suggested that newly dominant forms of television imaging were shaping habits and behaviors around the body's ability to be manipulated and changed, paving more avenues for capitalizing on the body's potential for transformation.

Just when the rise of robotics coupled with human labor broke out as a new productive paradigm, Twiggy shocked the fashion system. Her boyish, anti-model, lean lines opened new pathways for inciting glamour labor, as women everywhere sought to copy her coltish charms, heedless of the fact that they were almost impossible to replicate. Unlike the haughty dames who preceded her, Twiggy was everyone's model, whose popularity spread far beyond fashion magazines. Within a year of those first photos, according to the model historian Brigid Keenan's account, Twiggy was everywhere:

Car stickers said FORGET OXFAM FEED TWIGGY, there were Twiggy clothes, Twiggy eyelashes, Twiggy dummies in shop windows and in Madame Tussaud's. Twiggy was taken to Paris to comment on the collections, and her ingenuous remarks—"most of Balmain's clothes were a bit of a giggle"—were quoted by reporters who took care to reproduce her cockney accent in print.[13]

Children carried Twiggy lunchboxes and played with Twiggy paper dolls. British teens imitated her hairdo and makeup style, while adults went on starvation diets to achieve a "Twig"-like figure, engaging in not-so-subtle forms of glamour labor emerging along new pathways to communing with the glamour and excitement of international air travel, fast-paced fashion, and youth, associated with the promise of Twiggy's "look."

Twiggy was part of a trend toward pulling as much of the population as possible into the rhythms of fashion, into subscribing to the modeling ideal of being ready to be photographed, while boosting the importance of *projection*. Richard Avedon summed up this moment by saying that Twiggy was one of the women who moved in ways that "convey the air of the time they live in," thereby "bringing her generation in front of the camera."[14]

Thus, having the wrong look at the right time was, as it so often is, the ticket to toppling what had come before. In the transition from the cinematic gaze to the intimacy of the televisual glance, however, it was not only Twiggy's appearance but also her power of projection that made her the new face of fashion overnight. Her success pointed to the fact that in the regime of television, being an all-around personality became as, if not more, important than fitting the bill for modeling's "standards," elevating projection to a new importance in any model's bag of tricks.

Starting in this era, practices surrounding the ideal body evolved from treating it as a mechanized system of predictable outputs to one of a body open to technological manipulation, through the use of diet pills, exercise machines, mood enhancers, or plastic surgery. While bodies have been manipulated throughout history, the new inclusiveness of these methods, coupled with their particularly high-tech, scientifically oriented approach, was a break from what had come before. The idea that any body that does not meet the standards can be fixed, in tandem with tightening requirements for entry into the field, caused a strange thing to happen in modeling. In the 1970s and 1980s, within changing discourses of women's rights, acceptance of bodily display, and relaxing sexual mores, modeling became more popular, widening the pool of aspirants. At the same time, management grew pickier. While the boundaries for entry became ever-more narrow, with only the most lithe—and increasingly the youngest—given a chance, this tighter surveillance over the model's body was met with the idea that looks mattered less than energy in the growing dominance of the power of projection, spark, and attitude, typical of the affective economics of the age of the blink. Over the next few decades, advice given to models paradoxically encompassed increasingly strict *and* inclusive language. The 1990s blink technologies brought this paradox into sharp relief, as the chance one's image would "read" as fashionable shrank to a narrow window, while predicting which look would be a hit in the newly volatile image landscape became anyone's guess.

Be a Model . . . or Just Look Like One

To track the evolution of the "model" ideal, where best to look? Are photographic representations the only resource available? These representations can be retouched and reflect more of the fantasy of what could be than the reality of the lived body. Further, photographic representations reveal little of the work that went into their production. To see the evolution of glamour labor within changing imaging technologies, what better place to look than the advice from the top, penned by gurus counseling all those seeking to enter the inner sanctums of bodily perfection represented by the fashion model?

A shift from seeing modeling as a rarified domain to seeing fashionable beauty as something to which everyone should aspire was clear in the modeling "how-to" books I consulted. At the same time, gradually in the 1970s and more intensely after the 1980s, they exhibited an increased emphasis on surveying the body to bring it within ever-tightening standards. The level of attention to diet and exercise tips provided by modeling manuals from the 1940s and 1950s I looked at was nowhere near the urgency of the later manuals. While John Robert Powers was recommending corsetry as the key to a "model" figure well into the 1950s, after the 1960s and into the 1970s the art and artifice of ladies represented by waist cinchers and girdles was gone, internalized as a muscular corset created through diet and exercise.[15]

Consequently, hints at the difficulty of achieving the model figure through proper foundation garments were crowded out by pages detailing just how much work it was to *be* that figure. Whereas early discussions of weight and exercise were presented as an either/or proposition (either you had—or could fake—the right proportions or not), the implication gradually grew that everyone should and could try to achieve them. Thus, while would-be models in 1964 were told, "if you are a size 14 and always will be, don't make yourself sick by dieting. Think about another career,"[16] by the 1970s, model manuals advocated for behavior modification to "take off the excess weight, by going on a diet," or "exercising it away."[17] The type of exercise recommended grew progressively more intense. While Eileen Ford recommended some light stretches and book balancing in the 1970s, one mid-1980s manual recommended balancing oneself between two chairs to build the biceps (see Figs. 5.2 and 5.3). By 1987 one manual went so far as to say "Plastic or cosmetic surgery can be a very useful adjunct to a model's career" and went on the tout the benefits of breast implants or nose reductions.[18] Also in the 1980s and into the 1990s, the idea began to take hold that *everyone* should "be a model or just look like one."[19] This idea came into full force when the outbreak of the Internet saw invitation-only fashion shows live streaming to the general public, and supermodels became household names.

As the affective economics of fashion heated up in the age of the blink, the ensuing uncertainty pushed contemporary modeling professionals toward adhering more tightly than ever to "model" standards, even as they kept an eye out for the unusual or quirky look that might be the next big thing. The growing value of the unpredictable and quirky pulled for new thinking that everybody could and should try to model, expanding the pool of potential models. At the same time, to read as "fashionable" to a fickle public, all those who weighed more than 110 pounds and stood less than 5'9" tall were admonished to think twice about modeling. Thus, while one book from the late 1990s claimed that "there is no prescription for becoming a model, and the 'in' looks change from season to season . . . sometimes they want more full-bodied girls

A FEW MORE EXERCISES:

1. Get on your hands and knees. Drop your head and hump
   up your back. Pull in your stomach and hold for a
   minute. Next, drop your back in a deep sway, bringing
   your head way up. Hold this position for a minute.
   (This one is great for problem backs.)

Figure 5.2. Eileen Ford's proper modeling exercises in 1970, mostly
stretching and book balancing.

and sometimes the 'waif' look is considered chic,"[20] another claimed
that, if you were not young, tall, and as "lean as the proverbial race-
horse," you'd have to be "very lucky to make it in modeling."[21]

In this confusing extension of glamour labor to the general public,
these later-era modeling manuals gradually blurred the line between
requirements for models and the rest of us. In 1968, for example, Eileen
Ford's discussion of desirable proportions claimed, "No one weight is
right for everyone of the same height, age, or sex." Drawing the line

between models and regular people however, she exclaimed, "In our business, of course, the weight problem is much more crucial. Just a few pounds in the wrong place can ruin . . . a career!"[22] In her 1970s direct address to aspiring models, her advice was completely unforgiving. Beneath a chart explicitly laying out the height and weight requirements for becoming a model, she wrote, "Anyone seriously thinking about photographic modeling must realize that if she doesn't fit these requirements she had better forget it. The competition is tremendous and the requirements inflexible."[23]

Figure 5.3. Exercises for models in the 1980s, showing a model with actual muscle definition doing arm raises using two chairs. These are just the traveling exercises! From Kyle Roderick, *The Model's Handbook : For Every Woman Who Wants to Be a Model or Look Like One* (New York: Morrow, 1984).

Similarly, Candy Jones, a mannequin who rose to fame in the 1950s, penned a 1969 how-to book that claimed that a model's "vital statistics" were key.[24] Any applicant in the field had to be certain of her measurements "and be able to rattle them off with the sureness with which she can recite her address, zip code, and phone number."[25] Slimness was paramount—"I've never heard of a waistline too small"—and for "high fashion work," the model "should have no fanny to speak of," and her hips "should be sort of nonexistent."[26] From Jones's point of view, modeling clearly wasn't for everyone, but if a girl had the right proportions and the courage to try to make it in a very difficult, discriminating world, then more power to her, because "there's a lot of work involved."[27]

In contrast, the model manuals of the 1970s in the sample were encouraging to various types, as long as the aspirants were willing to diet or exercise. Former model Viju Krem shared her secrets of success in the aptly titled 1975 book, *How to Become a Successful Model*, explaining, "There are certain basic physical requirements for modeling that you should meet although there is a wide range within those requirements."[28] At the same time, she went on to point out that, "if you are too heavy, you will want to take off the excess weight, by going on a diet. If

Figure 5.4. Chart showing the industry standards for model height and measurements, as set out by Ford Models, 1970.

JUNIORS:
Height: 5' 7" to 5' 8" in stocking feet
Bust: 32–34 inches
Waist: 20–23 inches
Hips: 32–34 inches
      Average weight: 105–116 pounds

MISSES:
Height: 5' 7" to 5' 8" in stocking feet
Bust: 33–33½ inches
Waist: 20–23 inches
Hips: 33–34 inches
      Average weight: 106–116 pounds

HIGH FASHION:
Height: 5' 8" to 5' 9½" in stocking feet
Bust: 33–34 inches
Waist: 22–24 inches
Hips: 33–35 inches
      Average weight: 115–120 pounds

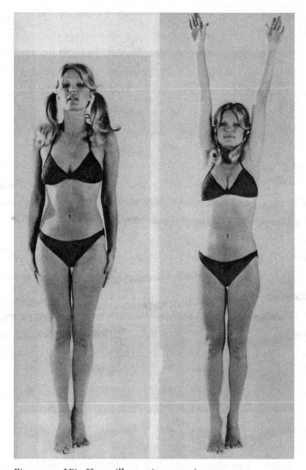

Figure 5.5. Viju Krem illustrating exercises.

there is excess fat on places such as your midriff, hips or thighs, you will have to think about exercising it away."[29] To that end, later in the book, she included a chapter called "Keeping Trim," illustrated with photos of her bikini-clad form fetchingly demonstrating "some . . . of the most effective exercises I know."[30]

The ideal of the manipulated body, achieved by controlling inputs and outputs to manage the system, made its appearance in the form of increased emphasis on the necessity of strict diet and exercise, coupled with encouraging words that everyone could and should try to adhere to these regimes. One 1975 manual claimed to be encouraging to all comers while also advancing the holy grail of the "model" figure: "Models can be short and fat. Tall and skinny. Pleasingly plump. Round and pinch-able," yet at the same time, high-fashion models had to be "tall" and "ultra thin."[31] To achieve this trim line, the 1970s fashion model's body was coming under intense surveillance, as evidenced by this comment, pages later:

> It may come as a surprise to you, but your agency will be constantly watching your weight, keeping after you about dieting, so that the straight vertical lines of the manikin figure won't be disturbed. With the camera adding from about 10 to 15 pounds, any untoward bulges created by the relaxing of your diet, could be disastrous to your career.[32]

Similarly, Viju Krem, who claimed that there was a "wide range" accepted within the physical requirements for modeling, later admitted that, for fashion work, there was only room for models who were "tall (five-feet-seven and up) and willowy, with a very slim figure."[33]

The "tremendous" competition and "inflexible requirements" mentioned by Eileen Ford empowered management to try new, intensified forms of bodily control to ensure their "product," the model, met industry standards. This was the era in which managers could afford to be so inflexible because, why bother with a girl who didn't fit the bill exactly? There were hundreds more clamoring at the door, and with luck, one of them would be the one who hits the jackpot.

In the 1980s, tightened control took the form of daily or weekly weigh-ins and measurements. The 1980s manuals put the ideal requirements front and center, using very narrowly defined statistics: "Women should be between 5'7" and 5'9" and wear a perfect size 6, 8, or 9."[34] Accordingly, "curves are not assets in fashion modeling."[35] The variety of body shapes and types evident in the 1930s models' bodies had fallen away, and by the mid-eighties, a set of very narrowly defined statistics had solidified into a "classic female fashion type." A 1984 manual was succinct; the girl who could model was between "5ft 7in to 5ft 11in, with well-defined bone structure, wide set eyes, long legs, and a perfectly proportioned" body.[36] This narrowing of the acceptable range for models' body size is clearly reflected in the model measurement statistics I gathered. Chart 4.1 demonstrates a flattening out of the oscillating variations in size, showing measurements zeroing in on a standard ideal for all.

As the 1990s approached, the reigning standards grew even narrower: "Are you 5ft8 in or taller? Do you weigh 110–120lb? Do you measure 34B-24-34? Do you wear a size 6–8?" Apparently, if you answered yes to these questions, "perhaps you could become a print fashion and/or runway model."[37] The desired frame was growing taller and leaner, and fitting the standard became increasingly necessary; "excess weight" could "turn an agent off immediately."[38]

By this time, the regime of the blink was in full swing, and the rising tide of images flooded our visual field. To transmit "fashion" in the split second conferred by our distracted attention, model agents and the experts who advised them claimed that successful models not only had to be leaner but taller, too. While 1950s top model Dorian Leigh was only 5'4", by the 1990s, height requirements were set at lofty proportions. One of the main requirements for high-fashion modeling was, as one manual trumpeted, "height!"

> Your height must be somewhere between five feet ten inches and six feet four. A really stunning beauty at five feet eight and a half inches could get by.[39]

This new emphasis on height is reflected in the model size chart as well. Starting in the 1980s, the models' heights in my sample zeroed in on 5'7" and above with almost no exceptions.

This desire for longer and taller models became more pronounced after the 1980s when cable television and the nascent computing industry changed our experience of the image. Prior to this shift, some would-be models were deemed too tall, such as the sister of one of my respondents. She got her start in the 1970s, when she and her sister ventured from their suburban Long Island home to try out to be models. The agency liked her, but,

> yeah, she was 6'2". Back then that was too tall. It was in the seventies. I didn't start until 1979, but we went into [the modeling agency] Wilhelmina in 1978. My sister was too tall. The right height was between 5'8" and 5'10". That was before the six-foot tall girls we see now. Ashley was

the first girl to be six-feet tall in the 1980s, and then Rachel Williams, and all these girls over six feet. I'm 5'9.5"–5'10." So we went in, and to me, they said, "Oh, you're too young, go back to school," and to my sister, "You're too tall, thank you very much."

Throughout the 1980s and into the 1990s, the fact that models were reaching new heights did not produce a corresponding increase in the ideal model's body size, however.

Lest an aspiring beauty get the idea that it was okay to be big-boned, this 1999 guide was quite stern: "Weight is critical. You cannot weigh more than 115 pounds, and that should be on the tallest frame. Most of the models weigh around 110 to 115. Your weight has to stay consistent."[40] Proportions were also mentioned explicitly; "You must not have any bulges or even any visible bumps. Long and slender is the guide. Arms, legs, torso, and neck should be as lean as the proverbial race horse."[41] At the same time, this guide also pointed out "the more projection a model has, the better the look of that person will be remembered, and that's what will make the hourly rate skyrocket."[42]

This mention of projection highlights an apparent paradox, which emerged in the model manuals from the 1980s onward. While emphasizing the importance of strict diet, constant vigilance, and the struggle for weight loss, they also emphasized a new quality that grew in importance during subsequent years. In her 1978 model guide, for instance, model agent Nina Blanchard cautioned that you can't train to become a model: "A girl either has the qualifications to start with or she doesn't."[43] Yet a few pages later, Blanchard extemporized that while "certain basics must exist," more important is "attitude." The model

must be all things to all people, a canvas for the makeup artist, a mannequin for the editor, a robot for the whims of the photographer, and the projection of the fantasies of the reader.

A model must be beautiful, of course, but only a few have the right "projection, vitality, and intelligence, assets easy to recognize, but impossible to describe."[44] The notion that the model must be a robot for whims is particularly notable, as it connotes the model's role as a kind of conduit for affect the next chapter will describe.

what a model should be for the public

Projection was also high on the list for this 1983 guide, claiming any aspiring model must of course "satisfy the same physical requirements as the fashion-show model . . . considerably slimmer than the average female—since the camera adds about ten pounds."[45] In a new twist, she also must have "camera charisma," which is "the ability to project her personality through the camera."[46] Similarly, a mid-eighties manual admonished aspirants to the field that "you must be trim" and if "you are overweight, the pounds must come off."[47] On top of the physique, however, the author noted that models sell both their looks and energy, so they need to strike a balance between dieting and staying energetic. This new emphasis on energy's role in a model's attractiveness was clear throughout. A model agent gushed that the best models "just RADIATE personality that comes through the camera and is imprinted indelibly on film."[48] In other testimony, professionals looked for "personality, you look for projection,"[49] a theme that appeared in later manuals as well.

"Being overweight is not just another problem; it is a disaster!"[50] proclaimed one 1992 manual. At the same time, calls for "great energy," personality, and projection peppered its pages.[51] In keeping with this new mantra, a 1998 manual explained that regardless of which looks might succeed, "chemistry" and "spark" were paramount.[52] Foreshadowing how the emphasis on projection rather than prettiness would bring wider fluctuations in acceptable looks, this author observed how the "'in' looks change from season to season"; sometimes it is "ethnic girls; sometimes they tend toward the blonds with blue eyes. Sometimes they want more full-bodied girls, and sometimes the 'waif' look is considered chic."[53] While she made it seem as though anyone could be a model, the author acknowledged the norm of rigorous control emerging in post-1990s modeling, pointing out that "some scouts and agents will actually measure a model on a weekly or monthly basis to keep track of their size and watch for any severe fluctuations."[54] Somewhat presciently, however, she also foresaw the mercurial changes emerging in the affective economics of the blink regime, saying, "I do not want to dwell on the physical requirements, because industry standards change all the time and there always seem to be exceptions to every rule."[55]

This paradoxical mix between an anything-goes market with room for all types and an increasingly rigid limit on points of entry was clear in the manuals from the 2000s, when it seemed that the bottom limit of model sizing had been reached. In the *Complete Guide for Models*, published in 2004, the ideal size for a female model went all the way down to zero.[56] While the guide claimed the best models ranged in dress sizes "0–6," it went on to point out how the demand for even smaller models had come about rather suddenly. The authors explained, "Less than ten years ago, the ideal model was a size 6," but size 0 to size 2 was becoming the new norm. A model agent interviewed in 2004 noted the change, saying, "During most recent seasons, all my designers want size 0 to size 2 models. . . . The girls were still just as tall, but they were tiny. They had to fit in the sample clothes, and they had to look good."[57] At the same time, this same primer also asserted that "personality might be your most important business skill in the modeling industry" and went on to point out that models who will "make" it not only have the right look but have the right sense of "energy" about them, as well.[58]

Image makers' efforts to get noticed absolutely had to hit the mark, but the mark was a much more swiftly moving target. As the public's networked jumpiness increased, the measures taken to ensure the marketability of a model's image in the face of this affective volatility became somewhat draconian. Affective volatility became newly valuable in the digitized age of the blink, not only in the form of projection but also in terms of the body's physical potential to change. It is in the very nature of pixilation to afford itself to changeability. The digital image is the fully manipulatable image; its growing precedence over other imaging techniques not only valued projection in new ways but also fanned a long-standing desire to manipulate appearances.

While photo retouching has always been a given in fashion photography, after the 1990s, the popularity of the image-editing computer program Photoshop took off, and pixilated thighs were shaved thinner, splotches were erased, and pores, under-eye-circles, and wayward hairs magically disappeared. Despite the fact that fashionable images of extreme slenderness and poreless perfection could only be achieved through technological manipulation, this new "digital unreal" created a tension between the fashion images in circulation and the real people they supposedly represented, resulting in an even stronger push for models to seek to embody an increasingly impossible "look." As one model agent told then–top model of the aughties Coco Rocha when she weighed just 108 pounds, "You need to lose more weight. The look this year is anorexic. We don't want you to be anorexic, we just want you to look it."[59]

state of being strong / active

Digitization pulled body size and vitality into a calculus that considered, as sociologist Tiziana Terranova argues, "everything that amplifies or dampens an individual productive power as an economic factor, while defining such economic factors as vital forces."[60] Arguably, disseminating information linking the healthy body to the slender body defined the slender body as more economically valuable. At the same time, the new value of projection pulled the body's social vitality into the mix, determining the value of bodies according to potentials to be healthy or potentials to connect, indexing them to the "dynamics of economic growth" such that the public emerged as a market whose productive power was measured not in labor time but in lifetime.[61]

In this shift, the healthy (qua slender) body took on a new meaning, as a goal to strive for, whose productivity is tied not only to capacities to work but also to the affective capacity to change, to become, to maximize potential. Whether that potential was reached was irrelevant; what mattered was the body's susceptibility to change, its openness to optimization, whatever the optimum standard may have been at any given time. The metaphor for the programmable body has spilled into the culture and informed the trend toward manipulating smaller and smaller parts of the body, allowing unprecedented levels of access to its functioning. Several sectors of modeling work I examined evidenced this trend, including the intensified efforts to fine-tune the model's body through tighter management of every body part and the efforts to harness the unpredictable mutations that spread through populations in the bioprospecting practices of scouting. This move toward seeing the body as a series of parts to be treated, with specific activities and products and anxieties attached to each body part, reflects an even more detailed focus on the body in modeling and on the potential markets that could be created surrounding its management. In the trend toward separating out body parts for scrutiny and management, one guide added breasts to the list, saying, "Surprisingly, there is also a bra size requirement. Most agencies are looking for women with cup sizes no larger than B."[62]

Another handbook contained the usual sections on deciding whether one has "what it takes" to break into modeling and details on the logistics

the Body's susceptibility to manipulation

of managing a modeling career, but it also included a more intensified focus on bodily economies of dieting, weight loss, and grooming. A section called "Looking Good" broke the body down into areas of concentration. Apparently, advice on improving just one's face was no longer sufficient. Each body part had to have its own section, in turn, with whole segments devoted individually to one's skin, eyes, lips, hair, body, teeth, hands, and feet, each full of detailed advice on how to optimize their appearance and performance.[63]

Models strive (and therefore suggest to the public that it should also strive) to follow the trends in bodily fashions that fixate on working on or modifying one body part or another in a constant modulation of bodily capacities. Although there have always been fashions in bodies and a changing focus on this or that body part, the idea, for example, of spot reducing or building up one's eyebrows has been a more recent conceit. Jenna, a veteran model who had worked through several decades of designer fads, saw breasts go in and out of fashion, alternately taping hers down and letting them out:

> Well there was a whole rage [of plastic surgery] at one point. All these girls were getting boobs. I was going to work and was like, Oh my god. You know, and I remember strapping mine down, and nobody wanted to see them, and then all of a sudden, boom, they're in. And I was like, Wow, I can breathe again! But then they went away again.

Stephanie, another female model who has witnessed body parts coming in and out of vogue, noted variations on several levels at once:

> Well ... it doesn't matter—I've seen flat girls who are totally no hips with short hair—and then next season it's really curvy girls with hips.

Fixations on this or that body part are not new (women's ankles used to be erotic zones, for instance). It seems, however, in the age of the blink's tendency toward ever finer splicing of the parts of the image, fixations are growing more detailed.

After the 1990s, glamour labor increasingly focused on specialization, as each body part from toenails to eyebrows became economically valuable in their own right. While 1950s models did their own hair and makeup, the highly paid supermodel had whole teams of professionals assigned to work on every detail of the model's appearance, investing time and energy into the model's hair, her skin, her fitness, her nutrition, her personality, her style, and her overall image.

The models were (and still are) also expected to invest in their appearance in a similar manner themselves, as Kay, a makeup artist, explained:

> I say this is your product, and you are going to invest in it (and it *is* an investment), or you're not. Either you are going to find the right dermatologist, a good facialist if that's what you need, or you're not going to apply yourself. Either you're going to go to a gym and you're going to tone your body the right way—you may be as skinny as a pole, but that doesn't mean that you're in the right shape. Or, you might not. . . . I'll ask if they are eating right. I'll talk to them about going to a nutritionist. Finding out what works well with their body. What they should and shouldn't be eating, and that's going to react to their energy level how they feel emotionally, their hair and skin quality as well as their weight.

This intense level of specialization has resulted in a veritable army of stylists in the industry. Refinements are so detailed, it is not uncommon for photo shoots to employ not only clothing and hair stylists but nail stylists, brow stylists, and even lash stylists, such as Christian Zamora, who claimed on his website to have done lash styling for fashion layouts and photo shoots for *WWD* and *Vogue*, among others.[64]

This new focus represented an investment in bodily capacities, body parts. This trend makes the body modular, such that the body is treated as an assemblage, with parts that are dissectible, replaceable, duplicable, or generally manageable.[65] The modularization of the body importantly links with Elizabeth Grosz's formulation in which the processes of removal or addition via medical technological intervention and the process of inscribing the body with cultural object/signs applies to the surface of the body.[66] This conceptual link between medical intervention with the body and the idea of cultural intervention dovetails with the idea that glamour labor works with the body's capacities, through all kinds of interactions with various technologies, as the body increasingly becomes a space of intervention and investment.

just coming into existence

This trend toward the digital unreal flowed from the nascent bio-political forces within the rising regime of the glance that organized publics into potentially lucrative makeovers-in-the-making. When would-be models are encouraged to think of their bodies in parts to be addressed individually and managed in turn, women, most certainly (although recently, at least some men also), feel the pressure to seek to resemble those models by going to the gym, getting plastic surgery, and buying makeup that leaves them "pixel protected."

Important here also is the movement from the notion that anyone could do glamour labor (of bodily improvement, for instance) to the idea that everyone should do it. Glamour labor's emergence as a form of right living entangled market imperatives to manage the physical body in a socially acceptable manner, further mixing the body's biological and social powers into the effort required to achieve the right "look" for modern living. In this new climate, images of worked-on, worked-out, "working-it" models' bodies idealized embodiment of a new type, in which the body was inserted into the productive matrix, not as just a worker that runs the machines, but as a productive machine itself.

Thinking of the body as units of information informed not only the productive networks of bioscientific technologies but also the new media technologies of television and the Internet, technologies that make it possible to "grasp and manipulate" the "imperceptible dynamism of affect," as the social theorist Patricia Clough points out.[67] Affect's new role in the structures of capitalism and the pixelation of visual technology drew on the body's changeability, its tendency to exceed its boundaries. The pressure to achieve digital perfection in the flesh did not stem solely from the growing ubiquity or intense definition of images, however. The lure of using a technological interface to tamper with images of bodies, creating polished perfection pixel by pixel, extended to interfering with the physical body as well.

From Twiggy's era onward, the pull on populations to enter the rhythms of fashion has amplified, as has the idea that everyone should work toward being ready to be photographed while marshalling one's energy to project the right image at all times. From these subtle beginnings, the idea that everyone had a duty to try to fit the model norm soon came into full flower. The shift in attitude from thinking that there are various types of bodies and there isn't much to be done about it to the thought that anyone can be beautiful or fashionable if they just work hard enough emerged in the language of model manuals between the mid-1960s (just prior to the fitness boom) to the 1980s. Correspondingly, the new attention to personality, energy, and projection evidenced a new emphasis on ineffable qualities demanded by the newly competitive world of imaging, inaugurated by the regime of the blink.

While advice from the 1970s onward given to would-be models is shot through with this theme of tightening control, it wasn't until the 1990s and 2000s that it was joined by an equal but opposite trend toward encouraging the models to bring something of their own to the modeling transaction. While the working models I interviewed in the 1990s and 2000s continued to experience the kind of tight discipline and surveillance evidenced here, they also described instances that indicated an emerging form of "un-control," in which the model was asked to bring a certain *"je ne sais quoi"*[68] to the equation, with little guidance as to how to produce the look of attitude that would help them get or keep a job. The change in modeling's atmosphere, toward being both more tightly scrutinized and yet less tightly scripted, reflected two kinds of shifts in modeling work and in image production, more generally. The first indicated the changing goals of advertising, from dictation to suggestion that characterized the move toward branding and lifestyles as promotional modes. The second pointed toward the new productivity of the unexpected, chaotic, and unpredictable in creating the "moods, desires, impulses, pleasures, and attentions" that the social theorists Patricia Clough and Craig Willse argue have become increasingly valuable in recent decades.[69] The emphasis in imaging was transitioning from meaning making to sheer impact, from a need for continuity to the ephemeral goals of contact or contiguity. Dominated by new forces, modeling work leaned more toward the unsaid, the barely felt, the channeled-under-the-surface kinds of understandings and reactions that moved the work toward the realm of affective labor.

6

The Job

Nice Work If You Can Get It

Looking in from the outside, the job of modeling seems fairly simple: Basically it's just smiling for the camera, right? In reality the work is a bit more involved than that. According to Title 2, Section 511 (i, ii), of the New York Labor and Compensation Law, a professional model is someone who

> performs modeling services for; or consents in writing to the transfer of his or her exclusive legal right to the use of his or her name, portrait, picture or image, for advertising purposes or for the purposes of trade.[1]

He or she will transfer the right to their image "directly to a retail store, manufacturer, an advertising agency, a photographer, or a publishing company" who will dictate the models' "assignments, hours of work or performance locations." The model is compensated in return for a "waiver of his or her privacy rights."[2]

This last item is especially interesting to consider. After the explosion of pathways for image distribution brought on by the age of the blink, models basically lost all rights to privacy. Prior to the onset of blink technologies, the model's life or image off the runway was legally her own. The job description specifically delineated the "services" in question as "the appearance by a professional model in photographic sessions or the engagement of such model in live, filmed or taped modeling performance for remuneration."[3] As the Internet and social media became major players in social life, however, compensation demanded waiving privacy rights, which broke the job wide open, a crucial point that speaks to the development of glamour labor into the kind of all-encompassing immaterial and affective work it has become in the digital age.

A young blond model, whose fresh face belied her seasoned sensibility, put it succinctly:

> You're always on display; you have to put on that show twenty-four hours a day. It's not as though you can go to the office and then go home and relax. You're always watching what you eat. You're always worrying about how you're coming across, always worried about being seen at the right places at the right times. It's just never ending.

Many of my respondents spoke of the "never-ending" "24/7" nature of the job. As such, fashion models are an excellent case study of larger societal trends. Modeling work is so absorbing, many of my respondents referred to it as "the life."[4] As a nineteen-year-old female model put it, "It takes over your life. It's not like when you go work at the Gap and then can come home and be normal." As one young woman pointed out to me in a West Village café in New York City, where, in doing our interview, we were the perfect picture of work as play, "First you have to distinguish what my job entails, which is keeping myself in shape. I consider going to the gym as part of my job, going to the manicurist and pedicurist."

The constant demand for self-maintenance, while always a theme in modeling work, reached a new high within the increasingly stringent bodily requirements borne of the digital age. In a dual push to achieve both the physical and fashionable ideal, both physical and virtual upkeep rose to prominence, as new mediations of the social via Twitter feeds and online life exponentially intensified the demand for "being seen at the right places at the right times."

These respondents' observations, and the following examples, speak to ways in which modeling work, in the age of the blink, took on immaterial overtones as it began to encompass activities that were normally coded as leisure pursuits, such as shopping, getting a manicure, or getting one's hair done. To look at modeling as affective and immaterial labor is to understand how it can feel "never ending" and require a twenty-four-hour commitment. The term "immaterial labor" refers to the way that work has changed in developed economies after the information revolution created the kinds of networked production found, for example, in the creative sectors of today's economy.

The Italian *operaismo* theorist Maurizio Lazzarato defined "immaterial labor" as work that "produces the informational and cultural content of the commodity."[5] Rather than produce a material object, immaterial labor produces the ineffable qualities that make a fashion photograph glamorous or make a model's "look" the one to have. This kind of work involves a

> series of activities that are not normally recognized as "work"—in other words, the kinds of activities involved in defining and fixing cultural and artistic standards, fashions, tastes, consumer norms, and, more strategically, public opinion.[6]

As the following examples illustrate, modeling work involves many activities that are not normally recognized as work, including going to the gym, shopping, and going to parties, yet these activities are integral in "defining and fixing" cultural standards, such as fashion. Models sell fashion not only by walking runways and appearing in fashion advertisements but also when photographed on the street or at parties. Living the "life" of modeling guides consumer norms by representing a lifestyle grounded in luxury consumption, making it "aspirational," as some of my respondents deemed it.

Not only has modeling become "endless," in terms of higher demands for physical upkeep and for maintaining a fashionable image, but the nature of posing has also moved away from producing carefully calculated emotion toward calling on bodily sensitivities that channel deeply felt but hard-to-express surges of feeling in energetic exchanges that are difficult to process or control. While photographers and model managers once had shaped models into standard formats of dress and behavior, post-1960s models worked in an environment where allowing their "soul" to be "sucked out" through their eye sockets was the new ideal.[7] When my respondents talked about knowing how to feel in a dress or trying to give themselves up to what was going on in the studio or on the runway, their experiences were quite unlike the models from previous decades, who were often cast in precisely designed scenarios with a clearly defined role. This change from conforming to a preset norm or ideal to seeking to engage the unexpected and unpredictable reflects a significant shift in the structure of production and consumption systems between which fashion images mediate.

Moving from gaze, to glance, to blink transitioned the importance of individually embodied, meaningful, emotion toward an affective free-for-all in which unpredictable energies were set loose to produce in unexpected ways. As such, the work became "never ending," but at the same time, its glamour and attraction was undeniable. Constructing the model "look" involves not only work on the body but also shapes lifestyle choices in a calculated endeavor aimed at elevating visibility while making it look as though the model just "is" glamorous, fashionable, and in all the right places at the right times.

Within this amorphous space of living the "life" of modeling, lines between being a model and just working as one blurred. This transition had three effects. First, posing or display work became less scripted and more open-ended as affective flow increasingly figured in image production. Second, as affect's tendency to spill over boundaries animated manic work practices in contemporary capitalism, being a model increasingly required living a lifestyle premised on the idea that you are "always on display" in a work/lifestyle that is "never ending." Finally, as "model consumers," models glamorized this "boundaryless" work within a complex interplay of brands, urban spaces, and the concatenations of cool.[8]

The regime of the blink brought with it a new aesthetic value that the journalist Virginia Postrel quips "shows rather than tells, delights rather than instructs."[9] Postrel's take typifies thoughts about style within the rise of what some scholars term an "affect economy," in which the circulation of bodily, interpersonal, emotional, and affective energies is being calibrated for profit.[10] The affect economy rose to prominence in the shift from a product-based economy to an experience-based one. The sociologist of brands Liz Moor described this shift as a change of frame, in which advertising morphed from dictating consumer reactions toward attempting "to frame everyday life and provide pathways for certain types of behavior and not others."[11] Nigel Thrift argues that, rather then sell products directly, this free-form, goalless reading of the body positioned it as a "mine of potentiality" from which to "generate and harness unpredictable interactions as a source of value."[12] Engaging rather than controlling consumers, however, "does two rather contradictory things simultaneously," as the communication scholar Sarah Banet-Weiser notes.[13] The "loosening of control from the corporation as far as determining the final product" both "tightens the hold of the corporation over the consumer" by getting uncompensated labor from them, in the form of "likes" or testimonials or other aspects of participatory consumer culture, and loosens the corporation's hold over what exactly the consumer will bring to the transaction of producing the brand.[14]

This relaxed grip is particularly significant to understanding the immaterial aspects of models' glamour labor. While Banet-Weiser is concerned with consumers' uncompensated work in building brand value, in their role as "model" consumers models attract publics to participatory practices that set the bar high for working hard at giving it away for free in the competition for status or cool. This loosening of control also affects the physical act of modeling for the camera. As branding became a cultural phenomenon, affect took center stage, prompting a desire to generate and harness unpredictable sources of value by tossing out the script and calling on the model to just "be" in hopes of capturing something unplanned, unthought, but perhaps, in the end, unbelievably great.

"Do You Want Some Chocolate?" Modeling Work as Affective Labor

"More energy!" "Give it to me!" "I've got to see the fire in your eyes!" Models are often admonished to produce energy in this way. Their work is more physically expressive than verbal; successful models can be exquisite communicators without saying a word. In the regime of the blink, in order to succeed, most models have to develop a kind of sixth sense about the kind of energy they work with—termed a "funny dynamic" by one model respondent, referred to by others as a "flow" they have to get into in order to do the job well. In contrast to the highly orchestrated production of selling common in mid-century modeling, contemporary models open themselves up to the sense of their own affectivity, working to feel the atmosphere in the room. They let waves of affective energy flow through their bodies to get a feel for how to move in the clothes or how to become whatever the situation demands in the moment. In so doing, they channel these waves into a demeanor, appearance, or attitude in a practice the sociologist Emma Dowling has termed "affective reconnaissance."[15]

Particularly at the high end of the fashion hierarchy, where the work veers closer to aesthetics than commerce,[16] models find themselves in situations in which they are not given direction. Mining the body for unpredictable interactions as a source of value, models might be prompted to "be a rat" or "just flow" with no articulate goal in mind but with a definite openness to capturing the accidental, spontaneous, and momentary. In contrast to the sociologist Arlie Hochschild's flight attendants, whose emotional labor carefully cultivated desired emotions in both themselves and the passenger,[17] contemporary fashion models are valued for their ability to unleash a wide range of responses that might shift or be modulated faster than they can be subjectively recognized as emotions. Getting into the flow has become the model's job in the affective labor of opening up to the mood and environment of image production.

This "getting into the flow" is a very different task from the mid-century modeling job. Instead of following a specific script to shape one's face into a desired expression for the camera, contemporary models try to tune into affective forces that animate posture or expression, to transmit energy. Contemporary models strive to be as open as possible to that flow, to keep it moving without capping it off and defining it as any particular way. As Carol Alt, a model who came to prominence in the early stages of the age of the blink, put it, "I [also] go with the flow when I model, I feel a dress, I don't think about it . . . I try to keep my mind *off* when I'm shooting."[18] Cameron, a young model agent put it bluntly: Models are "just conduits most of the time."

Revving up affective energy is collaborative work. Pounding music, lavish food, or staged scenarios can produce sensory overload, or "affect contagion,"[19] in which affect flashes through bodies, creating a mood that a model channels to get into in the feel of the moment. If the model fails to get with it, the members of the creative team will try to help things along. Assistants at shoots use food and words of encouragement to elicit that ineffable "something" so many of my respondents described as the goal of fashion photography today. Sometimes it just takes a little coaxing; sometimes more drastic techniques are required. As Kay, a makeup artist put it:

> Once you've invested in the day, you do have to try to make it work. So sometimes it's about coddling the models, sometimes it's a lot about coaxing them, the hairstylist and I tend to be a little more of the support system for the model, help her through the day emotionally, help her feel cared about and cared for. If it's cold, to bring her a cup of tea, or if her energy is sagging, or if she's not feeling like a good connection with the photographer, I might go over to her and say, You know, do you want some chocolate? In a devilish tone. Whatever it takes. You know, stand on the side of the set and talk to them, so that their face looks a little bit more animated. Maybe they want me to get them to laugh, when the model can't do it themselves, because some people can't laugh on a dime; you need to talk to them to keep them awake looking.

Whether proffering chocolate, telling jokes, or even using the element of surprise to shock the model out of her comfort zone to get an unstudied look, these efforts to amplify and modulate the flow of affect use physical proximity and bodily stimulus to channel shifts in energy just below the surface of awareness. Rather than concentrating on producing a particular expression, "feeling a dress" calls on the body's receptivity and its power to be affected, its openness to manipulation, to act and be acted upon. In this sense, a model's affective labor exploits the body's tendency to exceed its boundaries, putting the body in relation to technologies that can measure and organize this excess, amplifying the body's affect, its potential "power to act," to use Spinoza's definition.[20]

Thinking of production from this angle demands thinking about how energies formerly thought of as natural and individual are increasingly networked so that life's uncontainable force, its ability to produce something in excess, becomes profitable. As the science studies scholar Richard Doyle puts it, in recent decades, "life's habit of refusing containment" has become interesting for capital.[21] Although he is more interested in developments in biology that have determined sources of profit in living tissue's potential to mutate and change, for instance, I see a continuum among the resourcing of a cell line's potential, the body's unpredictability, and a quirky or edgy image going viral in the rise of buzz created by glamour labor.

As modeling work began to demand exposing more of oneself to the camera, the drive to channel bodily mutability's uncontainable energies spread to social interactions as well. Living "the life" of modeling idealized ways of living that funneled one's social world, one's private moments, one's bodily presence, into productive networks seeking profit in physical and social volatility. Through glamour labor qua affective labor, models, and those working with them, tap into a sense of commonality and shared capacity, striving to get on the same wavelength of shared social energy emanating from the excitement and proximity that the studio, set, or runway may generate.[22] The new emphasis on affective labor in modeling within the brand culture of the 1980s onward pushed the purview of modeling beyond its traditional limits to areas of life not recognized as work. In the age of the blink, models not only sell products but the model lifestyle as well, through managing looks and social relations in forms of immaterial production that add up to making living "in" fashion attractive to the general public.

Always on Display: Glamour Labor and Immaterial Production

In contrast to the complex machinations behind it, the typical image of a fashion model is deceptively simple. Models often appear as if in a solitary moment of fashionable repose. This iconic stance (think of Kate Moss, clutching a purse to her naked breast, or Karlie Kloss's intimate stare) belies the teams of workers surrounding the model at any given photo shoot. Outside the seemingly intimate frame, we find the photographer and her or his assistants, the stylist(s) and their assistants, the makeup artist, the hairstylist, the client whose product is being advertised, advertising agency personnel, the shoot's producer and assistants, possibly a set designer, a manicurist, a prop stylist, and personnel from the venue where the shoot is taking place—and these are just the people *in* the room.

The network extends to each creative's agency that manages their career, helping them to find work. Management agencies contract out these stylists, photographers, set designers, and the like, a process constituting a significant portion of the work of assembling the team for a particular project. At times, the photographer, client, or advertising firm might contract a casting agency to search for the model appropriate for a particular picture or campaign. Getting an agent is paramount, as it is the gateway to other relationships that can be career defining. An agent functions to manage a model's status by fostering continued interaction with professionals whose status can augment the model's.[23] Reputation determines the value of a person's work, but not only monetarily—a job's value lies just as much in the relationships produced by doing it as it does in the final paycheck.[24] A model develops these relationships both on and off the clock, during both paid and leisure time. Within these networks of agencies and firms, reputation is the coin of the realm, built and maintained through careful relationship management, within the affectively volatile social networks that have become valuable in contemporary capitalism.

Managing these relationships is key aspect of the immaterial mode of glamour labor. In the course of a normal working day, the model has a very short time (sometimes just a few hours) to make a favorable (e.g., re-hirable) impression on the photographer, the stylist, the makeup artist, the client, the assistants, and/or the other models. This impression is crucial to future employment. Kay, a makeup artist, emphasized the importance of forming a strong relationship with the photographer, for instance, in order to build a team:

> A lot of photographers have a lot of control as far as recommending their own team: people they have worked with, who they are comfortable with, and know what they'll get from them.

Models, acutely aware that they are expendable, constantly "work the room" to keep things copacetic. It is not unheard of for a model to be fired from a job before the contracted time is up. One model respondent who was working her way through graduate school described being kicked off a shoot for not being "fun" enough, since she was reading her book between takes instead of chatting up the other members of the team.[25] This model's experience resonated with many of my respondents' descriptions of having to be "on" at all times, open to the flow of energy to forge affective connections that cement their position within the networks of production in which immaterial relations of "status," "reputation," and the "look" are treated as objects that can be bought and sold.

Often schmoozing is aimed at shoring up productive relationships that are frequently in danger of slipping away. Within these fragile networks, easily disrupted by the wrong look or a careless word, modeling is precarious work. Veronica Webb, a successful black model who worked cheek by jowl with the supermodels, summed it up:

> The problem is that you don't own it. You can never own it, and it can be taken away from you at any moment. Someone could throw hot coffee in my face. Some designer can say he doesn't like the way I look. Some magazine can decide that's horrible. Every four years a new generation comes up. And another generation is getting ready to happen right now. It's just very, very, very fragile. There's no sense of security.[26]

Modeling work is chancy at best, organized on a short-term basis, with no guarantee of future jobs. As one model explained, "Whatever you did yesterday is what matters. Not last year, not two weeks ago, nobody cares. It's just like the entertainment industry." Another explained, "I always thought my last job was going to be my last job. Ever." This feast-or-famine mindset can lead to "bulimic" working conditions.[27] Since model agencies "sell" the model to clients by the hour or the day, work is short-term, contractual, uncertain, precarious, and subject to high turnover. Coupled with the low levels of education and the experience required, once the glitz and glam are peeled away, modeling is in some respects like a secondary labor market, albeit with atypical racial characteristics.[28]

Unlike most contingent jobs, however, modeling is not a bad job. Like other "winner-take-all" markets in the arts, sports, and entertainment, the possibility of high rewards outweighs the high risk, and the high status of the job outweighs its "bad job" qualities.[29] To claim that modeling is precarious work is not to say that modeling is truly contingent labor, superexploited and barely surviving. I am not arguing that elite fashion models have the same problems as those on the lowest rung of care workers, as the cultural labor scholar Angela McRobbie has suggested.[30] Of course models are of a much higher class than those in occupations normally deemed as precarious work. The point in calling modeling "precarious" is not to make a case for their plight as exploited workers but, rather, to highlight the hidden precarity in the kinds of work that models glamorize and sell as fun and desirable, particularly to young girls and women.

The question becomes then not, Can modeling can be claimed as precarious work? but, rather, How does modeling work fit into an overall cultural attitude in which precarity has become so appealing? Rather than gloss over feminist concerns regarding the plight of precarious workers, this stance highlights how these concerns must be brought to the fore as more of the population begins to come under similar constraints.[31] Glamour work is often gendered female, and women are at the forefront of the glamour laboring ranks, but at the same time, the kinds of insecurity driving this labor is now extending to parts of the population who were formerly insulated from these concerns by their race and gender. Within modeling's overwhelming appeal to girls and women lie the seeds of a more general popularization of ideas pumping up the appeal of jobs that offer little security as well as link employability to visibility and having the right image. In other words, fashion modeling in the age of the blink has contributed to the appeal of work that normalizes calling on affective resources of loving one's job, living your work as your life, embodying your work identity as yourself, in informal work environments with ill-defined rules, that blend work and play in a manner that engenders anxiety about when the work will be for pay and when it will be for fun and whether one will get work at all if one has not been keeping up with a rapidly changing field.[32]

Part of the reason so many are willing to take on the risks associated with the "bad" job of modeling is that, for some, it has worked out pretty well. As the sociologist Ashley Mears has explained, many stay in the game because it is like a crapshoot: The promise of the chance to "hit the jackpot" glitters just around the corner, and you might have another chance at it if you can hang in long enough.[33] The dense connections made possible by the Internet and social media have sped up the pace of change in fashion, raising the stakes in the game. As supermodel Heidi Klum put it, "In fashion, you are either in, or you're out."[34] The crazy promise luring the gambler's mindset stems in part from the difficulty in quantifying value in an affective economy. Modeling's "products" can be wildly overvalued (as in the case of the supermodels in the 1980s and 1990s) or lose value almost instantly (as was the case, temporarily at least, with supermodel Kate Moss, when her reputation was threatened by a drug scandal).[35] To engage in modeling is to submit oneself as a conduit for affective energies that are volatile, unpredictable, and difficult to control.

When glamour laborers embody an optimized image and a full-on fashionably "fashion-able" lifestyle, they work in an extreme manner on both body and soul. They are always on, always available, always up to the minute with the latest trends. This optimized body and lifestyle creates an image within a complex web of relations connecting workers, consumers, and products. An agent put it succinctly: "The image is the commodity," and models must engage in specific consumption practices in order to create the right image for their look, which they then sell to clients.

Working to produce the "look" constitutes a significant aspect of a model's glamour labor. Megan, a booker I spoke to, has new models look at magazines and then sends them shopping so they will be dressed "right" for clients. They are also sent to an agency-approved salon for a haircut and color and are required to buy makeup and get a manicure and pedicure. A casting agent noted: "Models actually wear the fashions they model—to get the job, they have to look like they know about fashion." A model who was near the top of the profession for several years remarked:

> You have to look a certain level, you have to go shopping (so there are certain rules of appearance in terms of your clothes). . . . It's hard to describe what professionalism is.

Another model linked this attention to appearance, to the goal of projecting an image of being in demand, saying, "You have to look like you are making money, you must look like you are working." She found getting the varied and subtle looks called for by the job demanded frequent shopping; she "forever" found herself "running into stores at 7 a.m." on the way to castings to get what she needed to project the right look for that day.

In this respect, the model's glamour labor of bodywork, in terms of physical upkeep, makes these practices attractive by embodying an image that is polished, groomed, and constantly maintained in settings in which this look is interpreted as a cultural ideal—that is, in the pages of magazines, on the runway, or in leisure spaces of luxury consumption. The body is treated as material, but the glamorous body has immaterial overtones. It echoes or emanates immaterial qualities that exude "glamour" in an apparently ineffable way, with the decided calculation and effort that went into constructing this fashionable look carefully edited out.

She Works Hard for the Money

For a top supermodel like Kate Moss, embodying her signature look involves not only maintaining a body that has famously stayed "model" thin and fashionably appropriate, despite the fact that she has had a child, it also requires dressing the part at all times, which, as she has reported, is not always easy. During her tenure as designer for the British retail clothing chain TopShop, she was well aware that "any pictures of her help promote her own products" and that, "when I am going out at night, I know I am going to be photographed." The constant pressure to appear effortless came at a cost, however: "If you're going on the school run and you have to think about looks for the world's paparazzi, it's not so great."[36]

This need to be ready for public scrutiny whenever one goes out is not only a problem for celebrities but in fact also affects lesser-known models who are also called on to live as if they *are* the look they sell, as this model discovered when she pinned up her new bangs for a quick trip to her modeling agency. Her agent came running from across the room yelling at her:

> "Ahhhh! Bangs, bangs!" gesturing toward his forehead saying, "You can't wear them like that!" and I was really surprised. He didn't like it pinned back because it was uncool, it wasn't stylish. It was so annoying. If they see you in the street, they say "You can't do this! You have to blah blah blah," you know? Like you are supposed to be on your job 100 percent of the time!

This model was learning that modeling entails not only promoting commodities via paid work but also calls for promoting oneself as a commodity "100% of the time" by engaging in practices aimed at producing a look that exemplifies the kind of lifestyle choices models' paid work promotes.

Producing the carefully edited self is a fact of life in contemporary economies that the sociologist Alice Marwick argues fetishize "entrepreneurialism, self promotion, and careful self editing" as a means to success.[37] The self-branding Marwick described is driven by a neoliberal need for subjects only too willing to embrace status-seeking behaviors consonant with the practices my model respondents described. Producing the aura of glamour is part and parcel of the self-commodifying work common in the trade, part of creating the "look" that will sell on the model market.

This self-commodification seems to extend to all aspects of the model's life. Just as the street becomes a place that demands professionalism and attention to the minutest details of self-presentation at all times, models' glamour labor in the immaterial mode also makes one's nightlife into a workplace.[38] Although the paparazzi didn't capture this incident, a young female model I spoke to in a sleek café/lounge, told me how her agency knew immediately when she had been out in the public eye behaving in a manner that was not in keeping with the look they had been working with her to construct. This incident clearly illustrated the 24/7 feeling of the job:

> When you are out, you can't be trashed, you can't be totally stoned. You have to do your job, basically, when you are in your off hours. I did that once two years ago, my boyfriend was like, Oh let's go to this bar, and I was like, No, I don't feel like it, and he was like, Just go in the clothes you are wearing right now. I was wearing, like, watching TV clothes [*she laughed*]. We walked down to a bar, and we got into this big fight. Like me and these four guys. I don't know why. We were yelling at each other, and I looked like shit, I totally didn't want to go out in the first place. My agency calls me up the next day saying, This photographer called this morning saying that if you are going to be like this they're never going to book you ever again. The photographer was in the bar, saw me, recognized me, called up my agency, and said, If she's going to be like this, we

are not going to work with her. And after that day, I was like, I'm never going to go out again!

This pressure to behave in keeping with the look can translate into never letting one's guard down, always feeling as though one is "on display," and getting the sense one works 24/7 at the job.

In other words, models produce their image not only in the pictures in which they appear or how they appear in the street, going shopping, or en route to a photo shoot or fashion show but also via the energy generated in the various social networks that are a key element of production in the industry. After hours, models and modeling professionals perform glamour labor, investing time and energy socializing with others in the industry with an eye toward making possibly profitable associations through building networks. In this blurring of the work/life boundaries, models often work for free, on "spec," so to speak.[39] This unpaid time devoted to getting work takes place within what one freelance fashion editor called the "circuit of scenes." These scenes are composed of the many dinners, parties, and other social gatherings that are a major part of modeling work's constant schmoozing to build productive relationships, blurring the line between life and work, so much so it becomes what one model, Kate, called "the life."

Gilt by Association—Branding and the Fashionable Life

When models and their acolytes live "the life," they generate energy, hype, or buzz wherever they congregate. The practice of appearing to live a fashionable life is attractive to urban nightlife venues, which try to exploit the modeling industry's social scene as a means for creating a potentially profitable image for themselves. Brands try to associate themselves with this glimmering social life in hopes that some of the glamour and attractiveness of the "scene" will rub off on their product. The "model" lifestyle consequently enlists consumers in the production of its value, engaging them with the fashionable life as a branded experience, spending their free time watching television shows, building websites, and fostering a community along pre-programmed lines that shape and guide their apparently autonomous behavior.

In one such practice, modeling agencies, photo studios, bars, clubs, and restaurants throw "model parties," a term used that describes a party ostensibly for models and other workers in the industry. Agencies spend money to get their models and potential clients into one place, and the agency and the venue for the party benefit from the kinds of interaction enabled by such a setting. At a model party, a photographer, for example, may meet the "it" girl (or boy), befriend her, and so get a chance to photograph her on her next job. The models, an agent explained, get exposure in the right sort of setting; "their names get out there, they make contacts." If the press comes, "all the better"; the agencies' and the models' notoriety is built, which produces publicity for all involved.

This subtle form of branding has the side effect of blurring a perceived reality with what David Grazian refers to as the "synthetic excitement" generated by the "pseudo event"[40] in urban nightlife. Grazian describes the process as "reality marketing,"[41] in which "public relations firms . . . recruit actresses, models, and pop stars to make seemingly casual appearances at their clients' most fashionable hot spots, for a price,"[42] a practice that infuses their "branded image with a shot of nocturnal cool" to "legitimate the venue among an even broader crowd of wannabes and hangers-on while attracting the paparazzi and entertainment news media."[43] A freelance fashion editor I talked to saw this legitimation process as "a circuit of 'scenes' or power centers; it's very organic, and sometimes it makes a place or a company." She cited Balthazar, a hot restaurant in New York at the time, as an example of how becoming popular with the fashion crowd can confer a white-hot status on a restaurant. Trying to attract this scene sometimes has its drawbacks, however. As Grazian points out, this crowd's insularity "drastically limits" the "ability to reach more heterogeneous, wider webs of consumers who make up the bulk of the city's nightlife market."[44] When these consumption practices do make it into the public eye, however, they glamorize a lifestyle, making it attractive in ways that influence far more lifestyle choices than merely whether or not to go out at night.

Clubs and bars want to host these parties to associate themselves with fashion, glamour, and beautiful people, an association that might then attract a clientele of a certain caliber. According to a young female booker, model parties enhance the bar or club's image, as well as having an immediate effect on the bottom line, since, in her experience at least,

> female models attract men with money, which brings in a higher bar tab.
> They'll use any excuse—a model's birthday, a stupid holiday. . . . Deals
> go down in bars frequently. . . . Brands of alcohol throw these parties too
> . . . to get the "right" people there, drinking their product to create the
> right image.

In one example of the value of attracting the "right" people to patron-ize one's business, a nightclub venue in New York City hired a hand-some twenty-one-year-old Englishman as "image director," paying him a weekly stipend to "create relationships with agents, designers, model agencies, and with the celebs." Essentially working as what is known in the business as a "model wrangler," he was sent to "Milan, Paris, and London during their fashion weeks and to the Cannes Film Festival," an investment the club made because "he could be our connection between the A-list and our venue," thereby cementing its market value in the cur-rency of image.[45] The sociologist Ashley Mears's current research docu-ments this ongoing phenomenon, tracking club promoters who are paid hefty fees by nightclub venues to bring models to their clubs to party and "dress the room," as the saying goes.[46]

A young model backstage at a New York fashion show was explicit about it: "Fashion parties are about meeting people, not about having fun." Another model at the same show explained, "I get jobs when I go out into the nightlife. It's unbelievable who you can meet." When she first started, this model went out seven nights a week because she found she made "so many connections," but after having achieved some measure of success, she became more "moderate—I go out about two to three nights per week." A model who had worked in both Europe and New York said she has gotten jobs from going to parties because it builds familiarity:

> I've met a lot of people through that. And then you meet them again, and
> you're like, Oh, it's like old friends, instead of meeting them for the first
> time at a casting. So a lot of times they book you because they know you.

Going out is usually a model's choice, but a young girl from Slovenia who had been in the industry for about a year said: "Sometimes even the bookers tell you, you have to go out, this night, because this photographer might be there. Certain parties at a studio you'll have to go to, too." When a voluntary activity becomes compulsory, it is no longer play, but work.

This not-so-subtle message that they must "play the game" on the nightlife scene engages models and those with whom they work in what Elizabeth Currid has called the "economics of a dance floor,"[47] where workers in creative industries ranging from models to photographers, art directors, designers, and merchandisers meet and inspire one another, forming contacts for potential collaborations or production teams in "social interactions" that are "essential to the overall production system"[48] in the creative industries. While Currid celebrated this use of urban nightlife spaces by creative people "as ways to advance their own careers and the cultural economy more broadly,"[49] she missed how for models, and for other aspirants to the "hot" jobs in "cool" industries,[50] there is a downside to this form of production. Namely, Currid's interviews with the highly successful participants in the creative economy underplayed what the sociologist David Grazian has called "the darker side of these adventures in compulsory networking and self-promotion," given how

> the growing instability of the flexible creative economy requires workers to take on the burdens of entrepreneurial labor . . . by shouldering more of the risks and overhead costs of developing artistic careers in the first place.[51]

While Currid herself points out that Dior's fashion designer Hedi Slimane has said that he "plug[s] into the nightlife scene to become inspired" for his collections, she fails to acknowledge that the "unknown girl on the dance floor" who sparks his creative process is most likely an aspiring model who goes out night after night with the hope of making a connection that will be her big break, with no guarantee of a return on her efforts.[52] These processes of compulsory networking and a blurred work/life divide have also been compellingly documented by the sociologist Gina Neff in the new media industries in a form of work she calls "venture labor," which, like venture capital, involves taking on large amounts of risk, by working for free, in return for delayed rewards, which more often than not do not pan out.

While going out every night may seem like mere fun, I am interested in how the willingness to engage with this lifestyle in the pursuit of "cool" feeds into marketing strategies that are capturing social energy generated by glamour labor for productive ends. By creating a scene that appears glamorous or fashionable and thereby generates publicity, workers in the modeling industry help produce a common framework in which goods have value, where getting into the hot nightclub or restaurant, or having the "it" bag or shoes, or reading and blogging about these practices will be a meaningful experience, creating a sense of belonging to, or being a part of, a fashionable life. Arguably, modeling creates frameworks for tapping into common areas of social life as a source of value. This organizational structure presents the possibility for pulling consumers into creating their own market-driven experiences, experiences that promote patterns of consumption that increase the value of brands.

Marketing commodities in this scenario shifts the emphasis away from a Fordist form of advertising—in which "what to do with the object," or how precisely the brand was "supposed to enter social relations," was spelled out—toward a "very abstract level of 'mood' and 'feeling'" to provide "an environment, an ambience, which anticipates and programs the agency of consumers," as the brand theorist Adam Arvidsson reminds us.[53] In this kind of environment, the goal is not to compel consumers to buy but to nudge them to interact with the brand in a guided way. In the post-Fordist paradigm of promotion, it's all about suggestion. The directive is not "'You Must!'" Rather, it suggests "'You May!'"[54] The changes in modeling work I have described here echo this formulation, in the shift from gaze to glance to blink, from careful posing, to projecting personality, to being in the moment in a controlled form of letting it all hang out.

The modeling world produces an ambience for brands by playing on the layered associations between models and the products their work advertises, the fashionable and attractive ideal they seek to embody, and the lifestyle they strive to create the impression of having. By "'farming out' the diffusion of a branded good, or the construction of a sign value, to a particularly influential or attractive group,"[55] brand managers cede control of how the process will work and instead trust that the productive social networks that typify this crowd will produce some valuable associations for their brand. This ceding of control is typical of the glamour labor of models in the regime of the blink. Just like the supermodel who was prompted to "be a rat," the very unpredictability of the scenario in this setting adds value and energy to the product, denoting an openness to the unexpected that is an integral part of the production of value in this type of economy.

Models' glamour labor makes the kinds of compulsory self-commodification I have described attractive by promoting a lifestyle and a particular pattern of consumption in which being in the know or part of "fashion" becomes a good in and of itself. The "circuit of scenes" makes up part of the model mystique, an image of a lifestyle that is then packaged and sold in the form of television shows, websites, ringtones, and other branded products that consumers use to create a sense of community around the idea of fashion in a form of pre-programmed, yet nonetheless open-ended, agency that is profitable for marketers. As Arvidsson contends, this new form of brand management capitalizes on the energies and meanings consumers themselves bring to branded experiences and, as I have illustrated here, models, as "model" consumers, bring into the production of scenes, the ambience of the model life, and the fashionable lifestyle. Marketing commodities in this scenario is achieved through biopolitical control, which Arvidsson argues is a form of governance that "works from below by shaping the context in which freedom is exercised, and by providing the raw materials it employs."[56] From this perspective, what to do with the object is not spelled out; rather, "brands work as platforms for action that enable the production of particular immaterial use-values: an experience, a shared emotion, a sense of community. This way, brands work as a kind of ubiquitous means of production that are inserted within the socialized production process that consumers engage in."[57]

Models, and those who work with them, seem to be living a dream, a dream in which glamour labor disguises work, setting the stage for increasing levels of immaterial labor. In this process, model consumers pave the way toward pulling consumers' social networks toward productive ends. Socializing, making work "fun," promotes a sense of community, which is in turn sold as a commodity within the system of fashion as a lifestyle brand. As such, models seem to be freely pursuing what interests them, or creating something that matters to them, while in fact they are creating value for a brand and providing a crucial platform for that brand to realize it, as more consumers are pulled into the promise of "You May!"

The desire stirred by the image of the modeling world seems particularly acute among the thousands of young people who turn out to audition for contests such as the Ford modeling agency's Supermodel of the World or the *America's Next Top Model* television reality show. Reportedly, the Ford Supermodel of the World contest has selected its finalists from thousands of aspirants in fifty different countries.[58] In 2008, for the first time ever, one finalist was selected from some twenty thousand hopefuls who submitted their photographs for consideration via the Ford Supermodel of the World Myspace page.[59] On a typical thirty-eight-city tour of the United States, the auditions for the television show *America's Next Top Model* drew fifteen hundred young women in one day, all hoping to win a spot on the show.[60] Contestants flock to all of the *Top Model* franchises throughout the world, which at its peak had spread to over a hundred markets internationally, including not only England and Canada but also China, Ghana, Nigeria, and Honduras.[61]

As the physical spaces of the "model life" made the jump to the virtual world of television and the Internet, numerous "reality" television shows and websites about the modeling industry cropped up. Television has treated modeling on shows such as *The Agency, Make Me a Supermodel, America's Next Top Model, The Janice Dickenson Modeling Agency,* and *A Model Life* in the United States. The modeling world, as occupied by workers in the industry, or as depicted in these mediated settings, creates a framework of self-expression shaped by modeling and fashion. Consumers contribute to the value of this framework by spending their free time watching the television shows about modeling or actively participating in online communities associated with them, downloading the "smize yourself" (meaning "smile with your eyes") app from Tyra.com,[62] sending each other phone messages "from Tyra Banks" via the *America's Next Top Model* website,[63] commenting on the blogs, voting to elect the "model of the week," buying *Top Model* T-shirts and other merchandise, or joining the Facebook group "Addicted to *America's Next Top Model*," which had more than thirty thousand members in 2009, while the show's Facebook fan page had more than seven million "likes" as of 2013. Various sites cover the model life in detail, such as *The Modeling Industry Online* (www.modelnetwork.com) and *Models.com* (www.models.com), where participants can pick their favorite model, rate runway looks and models' online portfolios, or follow blogs about the "hottest newcomer" or about fashion weeks around the world. Models and modeling also attract publics to fashion and modeling websites such as *Style.com* (www.style.com) and *Fashionista* (www.fashionista.com), as well as to the discussion of all things fashion at *New York Magazine*'s "The Cut" (http://nymag.com/thecut) and YouTube's endless loops of models walking runways.

This level of intimacy with the modeling world shapes consumer agency and glamour labor in both direct and indirect ways. An American fashion publicist pointed out to me, in a trendy Soho coffee shop, that "people who watch reality television shows about models used to just aspire to be glamorous. Now they aspire to have that specific model look. . . . They have a new familiarity with models and what they are and how they look." Less directly, the familiarity with models and fashion that these television shows and websites promote doesn't sell particular products; it provides a platform for brands to become part of the modeling world, and in so doing, enter ours. The propensity for glamour labor is increased each time you enter these networks, watch these shows, buy into the idea of being fashionable, or seek to emulate the kinds of images models promote. Glamour labor shapes and guides consumer agency, precisely by giving the impression that it is autonomous. In fact, however, it is directed in ways that increase the value of brands by feeding likes and proclivities into a system of biopolitical regulation, which seeks to track and profit from the shifting moods and dispositions on a mass, rather than an individual, level. This process divides the world into those who get with the glamour labor program and those who can't or won't.

In short, models play a social role in which they "model" a form of life. In doing so they mediate our experiences with commodities not only when they pose for the camera or walk down the runway but also when they are walk down the street, attend a party, or have coffee at a local café. The structure of modeling work demands that models produce the appearance of living a certain kind of life, thereby making it attractive, as something consumers would want to participate in or know about. Marketers play on this attraction to the fashionable life, providing it as the raw material that consumers then use to build communities of fans or of people who are "with it" or in the know about fashion. As desire for community is directed toward pre-determined ends, consumers produce themselves as attentive audiences, delivering themselves for free as marketable units of attention to be bought and sold in the commercial marketplace. The means offered for belonging in this world are the commodities with which this world is associated, not only via the pictures in advertisements in which models appear but also in the form of the "model life," which those in the modeling world work so hard via glamour labor to produce the image of living. By engaging with this system, models allow their leisure time to become worktime, bleeding the edges of their working days to expose and produce more links, affiliations, and networks, which not only optimize connectedness but also their availability to be tracked as measurable units of energy brought to the marketplace. The model lifestyle, packaged and sold as a commodity, becomes an experience that can be had for the price of our attention, the payment of which makes us glamour laborers par excellence.

In the growing affective economics of fashion, the body becomes a resource in these ways. At the same time, as populations train to self-commodify, they, too, become a productive resource, as the following chapter will illustrate. The scouting system in the modeling industry, for instance, plays a part, not only in recruiting new models but also in organizing the population with which it engages into a market, as a standing reserve, always already making themselves ready to be discovered, learning the steps, training in the rhythms of fashion. As supermodel Paulina Porizkova observed of the irresistible allure of modeling, "I don't think there's any fifteen year old girl that will turn down the chance to be called beautiful."[64] This undeniable attraction, combined with the winner-take-all aspects of an industry that promises huge rewards for very little effort and with the mounting pressures for glamour labor, kindled the explosive growth of the scouting system, spurring a newly voracious hunger for new faces.

7

Scouting

The Hunger for New Faces

Sitting in her Park Avenue apartment on the Upper East Side of Manhattan, Gail, a model of a certain age, served me tea, as I sat on a white couch. She was a regal-looking woman with pronounced cheekbones and a lovely complexion. There was some speculation at the casting agency that put me in touch with her that she had a tendency to wear a wig. Wig or no, her elegance was undeniable, as was the wealth of her experience in the industry.

I asked her how she got into the business. When she started out, unlike teenagers of today, she didn't know much about models or modeling and didn't care much for it until she met one face to face. She related her first encounter with a model, as a goggle-eyed fourteen-year-old:

> An apparition came into the house, with her cousin. They were both models, and they were the most gorgeous things I'd ever seen. It made a huge impression on me.

Bitten by the bug, although introverted by nature, at fifteen she went to the big city:

> I was supposed to see about a trip to Europe, but instead I checked on Robert Powers. I came down [to New York City] and stayed at the Y. I went to his office. I knew nothing about it, and I walked into this gigantic office, and the man was at this desk, and I leaned over and grabbed the desk and said, "I want to be a model, but I *don't* want to go to your modeling school." And he laughed and had me walk up and down and looked at the pictures I'd brought and sent me upstairs to learn about makeup. I went home and told my mother, I'm going to be a model! And she said okay, but don't tell anybody.

"Don't tell anybody." . . . Model recruiting has certainly changed since the early fifties.

Modeling once was a buyer's business, in which the girls came to the agencies, not vice versa. When Jean Patou placed a call for models in the *New York Times* in 1924, five hundred young women showed up; similarly, in the 1940s, John Robert Powers, in a typical boast, said that about one hundred fifty thousand women applied to be models every year.[1] With this apparently steady supply of model aspirants, it would seem unnecessary to lift a finger to find more, and many in the industry were perfectly happy with the status quo. Yet the scope and scale of scouting has grown to mammoth proportions since this shy but elegant teenager grabbed the corner of John Robert Powers's desk. What drove the intensification of the scouting industry? What prompted the nets to be cast ever wider? In particular, what happened in the 1980s that made this casual, ad hoc affair into the highly disciplined, wide-ranging occupation it is today?

Prospecting for the Fashionable Face

A model "scout" searches for people who seem to possess model potential. Exercising a "license to approach the physically advantaged," a scout asks "attractive strangers" personal questions about their plans for the future and looks literally anywhere for new talent: in the street, at the airport, at a club, or, more recently, on YouTube.[2] In contrast to the coordinated behemoth it has become today, casual street scouting was common practice for many years. When the boutique model agent Carolyn began her career in the early 1980s, the organized scouting system was not a big part of the business:

> I started in 1983. Prior to that, I believe the scouting was done through the European agencies. And they would find girls through their scouts, but it was just people standing on the corner, seeing pretty girls walk by.

It was nowhere near as sophisticated and far-flung as it would become.

As the regime of the blink came into full swing in the mid- to late eighties and early nineties, attention spans were snapped to the breaking point by the huge upswing in the availability and accessibility of fashion images. As the supermodels' lock on the top spots gradually gave way, a model's *newness* became a huge factor in her marketability. By the midaughties, as one model "how-to" book put it, "Models have become more disposable because new faces are currently so desirable. . . . Today, they want unique faces—this means a constant turnover of new talent."[3]

In the blink's expansion of the image world, new faces were needed. A young New York model agent, Cameron, observed:

> There's more media so there's more advertising, there's more advertising so you need more models. If you need more models you've got to scout more. If you scout more, you go to more places.

This relatively simple explanation for the scouting explosion misses some crucial economic and cultural dynamics that came into play during the blink regime, dynamics that profoundly affected relations between screens, images, and bodies and their value, distribution, and use.

A funny thing happened in 1980. In a significant confluence of events, the U.S. Supreme Court made the landmark decision to patent a genetically modified life form, developed by imaging DNA, thereby launching the biotech industry.[4] Also in 1980, Ted Turner inaugurated his Cable News Network (CNN), making global audiences for real-time images a reality. Not insignificantly, that same year, Ford Model Management held their first model search contest, attracting aspirants from all over the world. While Big Pharma imaged countless genomes in search of the cure-all gene, and the cable networks searched out new forms of attention, the nascent scouting industry routinized scanning for a winning combination of attributes. Screening publics became big business, in a form of bioprospecting that banked on the unpredictable nature of mutability. Both biotech and new forms of media operated on the emerging notion of the body as a series of potentials, of probabilities of more or less vitality, seeking to profit from what can be best conceptualized as the biomediated body.[5] While bioprospecting refers literally to the search for "biological, chemical, and genetic material (in the form of plants, microbes, insects, etc.) that may prove to be effective for future pharmaceutical products,"[6] it speaks more broadly of relations between local communities and large and wealthy organizations who benefit unequally from the structures of exchange around these materials. It is an easy jump from the idea of genetic material contained in plants and microbes to the "genetic accident that can make millions" contained in a person, the holy grail for most of the scouts to whom I spoke. Like biologists combing the Amazon for populations with unusually resilient genes, model scouts ventured into towns barely on the map, and young hopefuls traveled hundreds of miles, hoping to find or be that face that would spark a new trend.

As such, the burgeoning number of model search contests mined the population ever more finely to discover that accident or freak of nature that might make large sums of money for those who could exploit that potential. Within this logic, the expansion of the scouting industry organized publics into potentials to capture a chance mutation that might become the next big thing in a market made volatile by shimmering waves of affectivity. Since the 1980s, the scouting system's structure and function have grown to manic proportions into what Tony, a seasoned agent and scout, described amid the Old World décor of his Parisian office as a "worldwide net cast in the most disparate and unexpected places to find what will sell, to mine the human variety for the genetic accident that could make millions."

As scouting spread, changes in the cultural meaning of work in the information age gave rise to pressures shaping decisions made by young people the world over. The number and reach of images expanded, and so did the desire to be made visible by them.[7] How do young people, especially young women, become interested and willing to be sucked up into the scouting machine? How do they learn to want to subscribe to the values of fashion and beauty, particularly by entering contests of this type? Did they willingly seek scrutiny by modeling experts because of a lack of work opportunities or the influence of the gendered division of power that tells girls their looks are their only source of validation? Partly, yes. The eagerness to participate, however, also points to the growing influence of beauty as a biopower, which works by billing beauty as a "universal human need." As the fashion studies scholar Mimi Nguyen has cogently asserted, conflating the pursuit of beauty and that of freedom serves to instrumentalize "beauty" as an index of employability, legitimacy, validity, humanity, and modernity.[8]

To leave home in pursuit of a modeling career is to be thoroughly modern and free, a pursuit that has become terribly attractive. Arguably, an image-obsessed society sees achieving the brand of "beautiful" from a fashionable point of view as the only way to autonomy and personhood. Since the inauguration of the regime of the blink, the glittering dream of reaping the rewards of success in exchange for honing one's skill at becoming someone who is seen as fashionably beautiful has never seemed more real to more people, in more places.

Diving for Pearls

As bioprospecting's speculation on the biomediated body gridded the planet for new markets, the scouting industry spread its tendrils farther, wider, and deeper. Starting in the 1980s, whole companies rose up solely to scout for new talent. In 1987, the International Model and Talent Association, or IMTA, was created, with its own schools, website,[9] and nationwide search contests. Another large scouting agency, ProScout, started in 1993, specialized in bringing scouts to secondary markets, for example, the potential models in Arizona, Alabama, or Ohio, rather than the major model markets of New York, Paris, London, or Milan. Their stated mission was to "match exciting people with exciting top agencies. We make it easy by holding free scout sessions in over 300 cities across America."[10] A more recent addition, started in 2001, Model Scouts, guaranteed that "all photos submitted and uploaded into ModelScouts.com member accounts will be carefully reviewed and evaluated by legitimate and experienced model scouts and agents representing over 100 top international modeling agencies."[11]

Cameron noted the marked increase in the amount of scouting since he started in 1995, saying:

> The scouting structure has changed in the world. And grown. In the past seven years, all of these scouting companies in America appeared. When I started, they were just getting going. There used to be two, and now there's like six.

In the glittering promise of the valuable new face, the scouting companies incessantly stage model search events, thereby creating a glut of models, as Cameron noted: "It's a relentless scouting network in America, especially, and it has created more models than there ever needed to be. More than we would like." With this oversupply at home, why do model agents from Western countries look so far and wide for new models? Why do they scout in Africa, for instance?

It is not unusual for agents from the United States or Europe to go into the rural areas of Kenya in search of the new Alek Wek or Iman (both of whom are African supermodels who were discovered by scouts). According to one account, an enterprising scout held up a Coca-Cola advertisement, asking village elders if they wanted their daughters to be the girl in the picture and bring back a lot of money to the village.[12] Tony, the agent I spoke to in Paris, spoke of "training" his eye to recognize that one special look that has dollar potential. Once he proved he had a good eye, he was sent around the world to scout for models:

> I was taking a chance, and the girls became stars, so I proved myself. So I started to travel because of this. They gave me the opportunity to travel the world and scout for girls.

While it sounds like a lot of fun, in fact scouting is deadly serious. Cameron, based in New York, referred to scouts who travel internationally as "mining" the world for new girls to feed the "hunger for new faces:"

> One of the biggest costs for the agencies is overhead for scouting trips. You've got constant hunger for new faces, and you've got to go farther and farther to find them. They mine different areas of the world.

Going "farther and farther" includes fostering relationships with agencies in other countries, to create a conduit for girls who are discovered in China or Russia to come to the markets for them in New York, tossing these fresh young faces into the fashionable pool to see who would sink or swim:

> We have a partnership with agency in Moscow called Red Stars. We had an agency before the wall came down, and then the structure changed after it came down, but we still have an arrangement there. I mean you have to, that's an important market for scouting. That's the kind of place that's so closed, it's so insular, I mean you can't just go and appear in

Moscow and scout the streets for a lot of reasons, so it's important to have relationships in those kinds of countries.

Money and time are the great facilitators in this process. With enough of both, even areas such as Cuba, formerly closed off from the United States, could be opened. As Cameron elaborated:

> If you find a great girl anywhere in the world, you can get them out. I've had models come from Cuba, you just pay enough money, enough times, to the government to get the model out. Of course, it's trickier, if they're from Cuba, they can't, they have to seek asylum, and they can't go back to Cuba, and they can't leave the U.S. for a while. But if someone is worth enough trouble, you can make it happen.

Why take the trouble? If the girl makes it, the scout collects a finder's fee for the rest of her career. Just like in baseball, there is a "farm system" in modeling, in which the best players are consistently transferred to the most lucrative and powerful markets. If, for example, a girl is "discovered" in Illinois by a local model scout, rather than send her out for work in Chicago, the "mother agency" system provides an incentive to send the girl's pictures to New York, to get her signed there. A "mother agency" is the one that discovers the model and will have the right to 5 percent of her future earnings. While Dallas, Phoenix, or Chicago will send their "best" models to New York, agents and scouts in Berlin and Madrid will send their best girls to Paris. Megan, a New York model agent, explained that

> New York is the top in terms of billing; that is where the publishers of images are, where all the magazines are, advertisers, designers, photographers. LA may be chic, and Miami might be busy, but the regional markets are generally less lucrative, as they deal in lower-end catalog work, department store modeling, and the like.

As Renata, a Brazilian model from São Paulo, put it: "New York is the money stop." Teri, a model who moved to New York from Virginia, explained, "Chicago, Atlanta, L.A., Dallas, Miami, Phoenix, may have modeling agencies, but New York is the place to make dollars, so agencies in those areas will scout and 'sell' the girls to the big agencies in the city for a finder's fee." For New York model agent Megan, these regional markets are full of "Podunk agencies" that have little incentive to keep a "good" girl in such a small market—"Why not send her to bigger markets and get 5 percent off of her fees for the rest of her career?"

What, however, makes agents decide to send models to larger markets? How do agents know when a model has *it* and will be "worth enough trouble" to become the "pearl" that will emerge from a sea of mostly identical faces? In fact, they don't. Time and again, my respondents couldn't tell me what *it* was but claimed that "you know it when you see it." Many of the agents I spoke to liken the experience of finding a model they think will do well to a gut feeling, a visceral reaction, which they can't quite explain. Model scouts may claim to be looking for a specific set of characteristics, but what makes those characteristics valuable in any given moment is subject to fashion's whims and depends on a scout's ability to pick up on and channel the inchoate and hard-to-identify flows of affect that animate the buzz, the gossip, and the collective sense that *this* is the look of the moment.

Obviously there are standards; the tall and thin bodies of models, so often blamed for presenting unrealistic standards of women's appearance, were cited frequently. Generally, it seems a given that models must be tall (over 5'9"), have unblemished skin, interesting features, and a good personality, but when pushed a little further, few were willing to say these requirements were written in stone. One agent, June, couldn't really put her finger on what qualities she looks for in a model:

> It's hard to say—it's like fallin' in love, you don't know when it's gonna happen, but it happens. Of course there are the rules of thumb: nice face, clean skin, unblemished, you know, expressive eyes, personality. Everything goes hand in hand.

Cameron referred to these as the "elements." When he first talked about it, he was quite sure of what he looked for in a model:

> Everyone knows what type of model makes it. It's very clear. That's what we scout for. It's not in anyone's interest to find a short basketball player.

Yet when pressed to spell out how he knows when it's worth the trouble, he was more equivocal:

> You know, it's a guessing game; in this business, there's not that much logic. But you try and look for the elements, if someone has the right body to do shows, or they have the right body to do fashion . . . like a size 4, a size 2 to 4, really skinny, you know, that's what the designers want, 5'10" to 5'11", those are the girls that do well on the runway, so they have to have that body, and a face that isn't boring.

In a business where there is just "not that much logic," however, what does it mean to say a face "isn't boring"? How does one assign a value or a standard to that?

It seems that having a face that "isn't boring" is the unquantifiable idea that produces the gut reaction scouts value so highly. For the Parisian agent Tony, if you have the "eye," you will be more adept at finding the "pearl":

> You are born with the eye. If you've got the eye to get a girl. Sometimes you see people and you can't see it, but they have a fantastic eye. It's something you are born with. Or you can train, but it's different. You train your eye to recognize which is the pearl.

Tony described how he looks for that quality at a casting:

> What you do when you arrive in the office, and you have girls sitting down waiting on the couches, you look at them. They don't know you are looking, and they don't know who you are. When you are going to a casting in Prague, for instance. They know they are waiting for someone. Do they know it's me? If you have ten girls waiting for you, you look. Normally what happens is, if you have someone like a future star, you will see it from the way she moves the hands, the way she looks at you, it is different. It is just different. If you have the eye, she appears, and the rest of the room recedes.

Is Tony's "eye" really all that different from the rest of us? What can he see that we sometimes cannot?

For the sociologist Ashley Mears, "The booker's eye is fundamentally a relational skill, and it sees not beauty or talent, but a field of positions in a prestige contest."[13] Accordingly, the "hot" look of the moment reflects little about the actual appearance of the models. Similarly, one of my respondents, Diane, prided herself on her sense of intuition and her refusal to be guided by such conventions as "beauty." Head of a top agency at one of the most powerful agencies in the world at the time of our interview, she was high enough in the hierarchy to claim not to be influenced by other trendsetters, rather making her own trends, determining what is beautiful herself. Amid the gold and baroque detail of her impeccably appointed Paris office, she explained:

> I don't follow trends. I can't be concerned with them. I go on intuition and what, if it's well marketed, will sell. . . . Who gives who the right to make a trend? I don't think it's a risk. If you find something and you are smart about it, how can you go wrong? A trendsetter is someone I don't know telling me what's in, what kind of faith could I have in that?

From her perspective, she is one of the few who can tell who will be a winner, and she does not need to depend on others to point her toward which look would be a success. At the same time, she was keenly aware of others' tendencies to be swayed by trends:

> They're always talking about the new this or the new that, like, [*she takes on a sarcastic tone*] the new wave of ugly models! I'm like, wait a minute. When Lauren Hutton was modeling, they thought she was ugly! And when Twiggy was modeling they thought she was ugly. . . . There's always gonna be—it goes around and comes around, again and again. They try to make it seem like it's so new, and the same trends have always been prevalent. There are classically beautiful women, we all know what they look like, and then there are women who are tangential to that. Whether they are called *jolie laide*[14] or they are called atypical or anorexic, or I don't know, I never move in trends, I don't believe in putting a square peg in a round hole. It's insulting. There is no such thing as ideal beauty.

Similarly to my respondents, the agents interviewed by the sociologist Ashley Mears felt strongly when judging potential models—either "you have it or you don't." When Mears asked what "it" is, the "it" that makes them pick one girl over 699 other teenagers with exactly the same qualifications, one booker claimed, "Whatever *it* is at the moment."[15] Whether affective agitation or arbitrations of taste, the structural influence on their decisions was largely hidden to them.

Hidden or no, the struggle for industry dominance deeply influences the qualities that are considered *the* "look" at any given moment. In Mears's analysis, unstable expectations and market uncertainty prompted professionals to rely on conventions and look to each other for cues as to which look is the one to want.[16] These pressures created a remarkable convergence with regard to what looks are sought after each season.

Mears's findings indicated that "top" agent Jordan Banes's choices, for instance, resonate throughout the system. If he says a girl has "it," she becomes a standard of "beauty"—that is, her look contributes to defining the desirable look of the season. Owing to his position in the hierarchy, Banes's choices dictate what the "whatever" look will be, and the rest of the industry struggles to get in line. Once the top few tastemakers have made their choices, so goes the rest of the pack, booking either those same girls or girls with similar qualities.

Interestingly, however, even the top casting agent in the industry could not put his finger on what prompted his decision. In the early to mid-2000s, when Banes told Mears of "discovering" a model and casting her to open the Prada show, the top designer in the world at the time, he rehearsed a line a heard again and again in my own interviews. He exclaimed that when he sees the "right" look it "does something very physical," and then he "just knows!" she is the one.[17]

Banes himself cannot explain his own decision because having the eye is partly a function of being a creative person, who is sensitive to aesthetic qualities that bubble up or effervesce. Yet these ineffable qualities are nonetheless made quantifiable in "aesthetic markets," as the sociologist Joanne Entwistle points out.[18] The link between the ability to define "beauty" and one's position in the network touches on the arbitrary nature, and the fluctuating value, of what constitutes a good "look." Whatever an agent's place in the hierarchy, learning to have the "eye" results from being sensitive to trends affecting the definitive look for any given season. Good bookers train themselves to pick up on the moods of the moment.

As Mears herself points out, "The very fact that bookers, clients, and even models cannot articulate just what this special quality is means that it does not exist as a physical property."[19] The "it" look, in fact, exists in the "vibrant exchanges" between players in the field who hang out together and form a community online, trading gossip and inside scoops, while jockeying for position in a constantly evolving landscape in which "nobody knows" what look will be the next "hit."[20] Recall the sociologist Herbert Blumer's 1969 observation that "incipient taste," or a feeling in the air, is a collectively produced notion that this or that look is "stunning" and causes buyers to converge on one dress as the look of the season.[21] Choices that bookers attributed to personal taste more often than not resulted from collective urges fomented by the vibrant exchanges that make up their highly networked and interpersonally connected worlds. With the "it" look more ephemeral, the chance to dictate who or what will be the next big thing came more frequently. While Mears was less interested in a detailed exploration of the particular historical moment in which she made her study, in fact, as technical means for expanding scouting networks became more available, so did the frequency of opportunities to jockey for position within them and the intensity of the networked urge for this or that look. This speedup raised the stakes for scouting as digital technologies whipped up waves of affectivity, amplifying the cacophony of buzz in recent years.

Tastemaking, as the French sociologist Pierre Bourdieu reminds us, is directly related to power.[22] Bourdieu resonated through Mears's interest in dissecting how "chasing the future direction of fashionableness" plays into the construction of status hierarchies that dictate the power and value of a given "look" at any given time.[23] The chase, however, informs not only status hierarchies. With the spread of blink technologies, chasing the "future direction of fashionableness" becomes a first world problem that seeks to insinuate itself into every world's value system, organizing populations into markets to be tapped for future sources of value. Buying into the buzz, the dream of modeling engages publics in actions that feed the system, educating themselves about fashion, holding themselves to its dictates, attuning to its rhythms. While so many clamor to become models, at the same time, publics tire more quickly of those who do. In the age of the blink, shortened attention spans have forced a kind of strip mining that demands more frequent returns, cutting more deeply and widely to supply the relentless need for the new. Not only has the "pearl" become harder to find, the ones that are found become dull so quickly, the demand for newer and brighter jewels has grown insatiable.

Have You Got the Look of the Year?

Models once were valued for their level of experience, their age, and their skill at styling their own look and for providing their own wardrobe, makeup, and hair to project an air of sophistication. In this regime's fragmentation of attention, however, the value of the new began to trump all else. Skill became less important than the potential to be the next big thing. Since the inauguration of the regime of the blink, scouting has focused on getting as large a pool as possible to maximize the chances of discovering the one who becomes a star. How to get everyone to jump in? Since the 1980s, the industry's much-vaunted model search contests have fueled the dream of either finding or being just the right face. In 1983, Elite inaugurated its Look of the Year, holding contests in no less than fifty countries. In 2013, three hundred fifty thousand contestants from sixty countries paid a fee to compete for highly contested employment contracts with Elite.[24] Through 2012, Ford's Supermodel of the World regularly attracted contestants worldwide before morphing into the *V Magazine* model search contest. Promising the winner a photo shoot in this trendy magazine, the tagline read "Thousands will enter. One will win."[25]

Ford's model search contests are a well-orchestrated publicity stunt aimed at boosting Ford's brand. The year I attended, the contest was a fully produced show with lights and costumes, attended by fashion insiders and professionals who work with them. Hosted by fashion's favorite bearded lady drag queen, André J., and model darling of the moment, Chanel Iman, the show had contestants dutifully parade out and strike a pose in Ziegfeld Follies–esque tableaux, as backdrop to some witty banter from the hosts, and, after a quick change, paraded out again. The

Figure 7.1. Ford Supermodel of the World contest, 2008.

still-gorgeous octogenarian model Carmen Dell'Orefice made a short speech to the girls. There was a full catwalk, with space to do a twirl for the photographer's pit at the end, just like in a real fashion show.

While the event was called a "contest," the girls had competed during the week prior, receiving walking training, getting fitted, and doing photoshoots, snippets of which were available on Ford's website. When I later asked a Ford model agent about its potential as a public event, perhaps as good television at least, the agent intoned, "Oh no, we want it to remain an insider thing, we don't want to show it to everybody. It's not that kind of thing." In fact, the outcome was decided behind closed doors, before the "contest" actually took place.[26]

In stark contrast to Ford's glamorous, well-rehearsed pageant, *Girl Model*,[27] a 2012 film documenting international scouting practices, depicted somewhat harrowing images of model agents inspecting young hopefuls in a hotel ballroom in Siberia. One of the more memorable scenes showed a mirrored room full of moon-faced girls stripped to their skivvies, bikini bathing suits stretched over gaunt, pale flesh. Like paper cutouts, they stood in awkward rows, waiting to be viewed by the assembled "experts." The film made the strong case that scouting in modeling capitalizes on young girls' desires, promising much and delivering little. It also painted a picture of a growing pool of aspirants, willing to put up with what seemed like humiliation just to get a chance to step into modeling's glittering world.

What drives these and increasing numbers of young people to seek out this treatment? The possibility of being discovered, like Lana Turner at the soda fountain, plays no small part, and, in fact, some models *do* get discovered this way. While it happens to these lucky few, for the vast majority the model contest, or convention, is an exercise in futility. Carolyn, an agent at a boutique agency specializing in high-fashion models, had a very dim view of these contests. The tiny number of participants who ultimately are selected bothered her the most:

> The scouting process is very diverse. There are scouts all over the world who are going to these model schools that are basically scams. Here's the bad part. They've got these schools all over the country that charge models thousands of dollars, promising them that they can work in New York or Paris or whatever. Maybe one out of a thousand of those girls is going to make it. Your parents' entire life's savings could go down the drain.

For many in the business, model conventions represent the dark underbelly of model recruitment, schemes that profit from the notion that every young person has the potential to be a model, that in fact bank on the idea that everyone should try.

One jaded model compared the model searches to "dragnets" used in deep-sea fishing, which pull in everything in their path:

> There's maybe 1 percent of the population who's got the right height, the right bone structure, and can maintain the right weight. They do the searches because there's always the chance. They go fishing with a dragnet in the deep sea with these forty-mile-long nets because they know they're gonna pull in a tuna somehow.

Just like tuna fishing, however, there is a tremendous amount of waste involved. The "model search" pulls in all types, including those who never should have been netted in the first place. While contests held by industry leaders such as Ford and Elite are for insiders by insiders, the dragnets cast by ProScout or Model Scouts will take all comers and seem designed more for collecting the participants' cash than for actually finding models who will find work in the business.

The model search contest may seem not all that different from Hollywood talent searches from days of yore, such as the Fame and Fortune contests run by *Motion Picture Classic* and *Motion Picture* magazine in the nineteen teens and twenties.[28] A key difference, however, is the number and frequency of these events and the steep entry fees. ProScout competitions happen so frequently, one booker claimed that "I've been to Dallas *twenty-five* times" to attend these competitions. Another distinguishing factor is the sheer number of participants. Some industry insiders referred to the conventions as "cattle calls," in which hundreds, sometimes thousands, of young people presented themselves to be "discovered." A booker from a well-established modeling agency in New York City, who has been to contests all over the country, recently made a trip for "this one scouting agency that flies in agents from New York to see an *arena* full of people."

Banking on the dream is certainly lucrative for the companies involved. As the New York model agent Megan pointed out:

> Scouts go to cities, run advertisements for an open call—they screen whoever shows up, after they've *all* paid a fee of $275–$500! And then they send them to this big sort of go-see, in which thousands of people parade by so the agents can have a look.

This practice angered Carolyn, the boutique model agent, who exclaimed,

> Most of these girls will never—these are girls are ones who'd be walking down the street and you wouldn't even turn your head. Unfortunately. Less than average. It's just so dirty and so scammy, these conventions. . . . There's no hope! You've got five thousand girls coming to meet New York model agents. Five thousand young girls, coming to a model convention and maybe out of that five thousand, *maybe*, three of them might get an offer from a New York modeling agency. So 4,997 of them are going

home, having spent their parents' savings, and all they are left with is this portfolio that isn't worth anything.

This type of profit making is no secret. Model "how-to" sites warn against it. A website devoted to information about modeling, *Model-news.com*, included a "Scam Watch" section in which one contestant posted in a forum highlighted the irresponsible manner in which contestants were signed up, claiming that

> of the close to 700–900 hopefuls only about 1% might have truly had real potential, of course I realize I am probably not qualified to make such a judgment but, we all watch fashion shows and study the print models look, to get a sense of what sells, so my question for ProScout is, who signed all these people up who, clearly had not the smallest, most remote chance of making it as a model?[29]

With all these terrible prospects, why do bookers still attend the conventions, and why, given their slim chances, do so many pay the fee and show up?

Several of the agents I spoke felt they didn't have the option not to, as it would have been difficult to explain missing a contest at which their competitors discovered the next supermodel. The high-end agent, Carolyn, pointed to the stacks of money to be made when they find that one in a thousand:

> I've had to go on these things. Model conventions. And the money that these conventions make is not only from enticing these young girls that they can become a New York model and make thousands of dollars, but then, let's say they *do* have that one in a thousand, they send the girl to New York, and they get a commission on that model. . . . So there's a lot of money to be made in these so-called schools and conventions. Lots and lots of it.

In Megan's experience, the one or two with potential *are* actually considered seriously. In practice,

> There is the runway component and then a picture review, in which they parade by, showing their picture. Then the agents give them a call back,

and then maybe even a second one for a few of them. Then they take Polaroids which go back to New York with the agent. The division head decides whether or not they will want the boy or the girl.

This sliver of real possibility has been stretched into a tangible reality for a disproportionate number, as blink technologies have magnified the allure of the fashionable lifestyle as a "not-to-be-missed" opportunity for more of the population. As Carolyn mused,

> The other side of the coin is that they got to fulfill some kind of dream within themselves. They got the chance. Maybe that means more to these little kids than the rejection.

A 2006 book entitled *Under Investigation: The Inside Story of the Florida Attorney General's Investigation of Wilhelmina Scouting Network, the Largest Model and Talent Scam in America* estimated that between 2000 and 2003, close to 2.7 million young people

> were approached by representatives of an Orlando-based outfit and propositioned as potential models. After the "excuse-me-are-you-a-model?" routine, over 150,000 prospects were hooked and reeled in, paying an amount ranging from $395 to $995 each to have their dreams of being a model fulfilled.[30]

In this case, those taken in by the scam got nothing at all, not even a chance to compete in a model contest.

As Megan pointed out, these scouting contests are "selling hopes and dreams" and not much else. Yet they have become moneymakers because participants—both would-be models and agents—feel like they are doing something important, engaging in something they have to try, whether or not, or maybe because, the chance of success are so tiny.

In other words, the search contests function to sell glamour labor's imperative, to "be your best self,"[31] to be the "CEO of me," to take the risk and try to "put yourself out there." Many of the models I spoke to who had competed in a modeling contest mouthed the rhetoric of "venture labor" to explain their motivations. The communication scholar Gina Neff's "venture labor" describes risk-taking behavior among tech-sector workers, fostered by entrepreneurial trends that have appeared as a defining characteristic of work in developed economies from the 1980s onward. Just as venture capitalists bet on high-risk concerns, knowing most will fail while one might produce spectacular returns, venture laborers speculate with their time, commitment, and sometimes their own money (since one can't use stock options in a fictional company to buy groceries) to seek big payoffs. The hope is that, if their company finally hits it big, their invested time and labor will more than make up for the sacrifice. As Neff so aptly points out, structural shifts in modern economies have made it nigh impossible to avoid pressures to buy into a system where the risks are great and the rewards few.[32]

By paying out of pocket for a hefty entry fee and travel expenses to a contest, a young person may think she is investing in her possible future as a model, which, if she were to succeed, would afford a return on her investment in spades. Several of the models I met who made it into the industry because of a search contest referred specifically to the need to take a risk. Stuart, a male model who was just starting out, won a model search in Atlanta prior to being signed by an agency in New York City:

> I went to a modeling convention. I was just like, whatever, it's worth a try, you know, to see what will happen. But, you know, it's an experience, you have to take risks in life, I guess. It's a waste of money, maybe, maybe not, you've got to see what happens.

When I pointed out that the contests can cost a lot and that some people see them as scams, he agreed that they aren't always a positive experience for people:

> Yeah, I think mine was about $400, but some of them cost up to $3,000. And some of the kids, nothing happens for them, and it's really bad.

Stuart's experience with model contests was extremely positive, however. In the contest he entered, sixteen of the eighteen agencies there wanted to sign him.

Similarly, the spirit of "nothing ventured, nothing gained" animates quitting one's paying job to go to a new city to speculate on trying to be a model. Brittany, a freckle-faced young woman with auburn hair, with whom I spoke at the Union Square Starbucks between her casting appointments, did just that. Her story reflected the strands of venture labor that so often thread through the glamour labor of "putting oneself out there" in the drive for visibility recently so prevalent among young people in the age of the blink.

Coming of age in Minnesota, far from the fashion centers to which she was drawn, Brittany took it upon herself to shoulder the risk of seeking a new life. Working as an office assistant at the time, she used the then-innovative technology of the fax machine, a development that many of my respondents said proved revolutionary in the globalization of the modeling industry during the 1980s and 1990s.

Taking a local photographer's advice, she made comp cards,[33] "wrote up a letter," and "sent it to all the agencies":

> Thinking back to this, it was kind of crazy, but I don't know, I didn't have a boyfriend, and I wanted to do something else. So I sent my comp card in this letter introducing myself, "I'm 5'9", and I'm interested in relocating," etc. I sent it everywhere. Even to Australia, Paris, you know, everywhere. I was working as a secretary at the time, and I gave them my fax number and my home telephone number, and out of fifty things I sent out, I got about forty responses. I would just keep getting faxes. It was like whoa! So I was like, I've gotta do this, I was so brave. I kept talking to the Pommier [agency] in Florida. It's kind of a good starting market, it's not as hard as Paris and New York, and it wasn't that far from home, and I really got along with the bookers, so I just packed myself up and I left. I don't know what I was thinking.

Taking the risk and being brave, saying "I gotta do this," made perfect sense within the venture labor logic that spurs glamour labor. When Brittany paid her way to travel to the big city, found an agency that was willing to represent her, and got an advance for startup expenses, she took a risk that her efforts would pay off, working for free, by going to go-sees, socializing, and posing for various photographers to build up her book in order to perhaps win a paying job. If she did not succeed in making an income by modeling, she still would have owed the agency those startup expenses, a situation several of those I interviewed said was not uncommon. She shouldered the risk that her efforts to break into modeling might not succeed. Whatever the risk, of course, Brittany should pack up her bags and go, of course she should take the chance, she had it all to win, and only herself to blame if she didn't take the risk and just do it.

Even though model aspirants claim they might have been a little "crazy" to try, since the chances of being discovered and becoming a highly paid fashion model are slim, the glamour labor system makes the rags-to-riches possibilities seem tantalizingly real, especially in terms of the well-publicized "discovery" story. This story feeds a particular dream, one made popular by various media, in which merely walking down the right street, at the right time, with the right "look" can change your life. It also makes modeling attractive, insofar as it promises the possibility of success to any and all who care to engage with glamour labor's precepts of self-care, willing exposure, and adherence to constantly vacillating standards of fashion and beauty. With the promise of a modeling career putting stars in their eyes, young people eager to commodify themselves work hard to produce a fashionable look and engage in activities that models' glamour labor makes look easy and fun. Part of this dream's power stems from the various scouting success stories made famous by supermodels like Kate Moss (found in an airport), or Gisele Bündchen (found eating hamburgers in São Paulo), or Natalia Vodianova (plucked from obscurity while selling fruit to help her family out of poverty in small-town Russia).

While these life-changing moments are well known, do ordinary models—that is, those who do not become celebrities but do model for a living—actually find work in this way? From what my respondents told me, the possibility of being discovered while stopping at the proverbial soda fountain (or airport or disco, as the case may be) does have some basis in reality. Nea, a Eurasian model from Germany, was discovered selling croissants, for instance:

> I was in a bakery selling croissants, and someone asked me if I wanted to do it. It was a photographer. He got me a cover. I tried to go back to my normal life in between. But then a month later I did a little bit more. So I did it part-time. I was eighteen.

Success came quickly. By the time she was nineteen, she had moved to New York and was modeling full-time.

Similarly, a Christmas photo was the golden ticket for one model. Stephanie explained: "My mom took some Christmas photos of my brother and me, and there was this competition, and she sent my pictures in, and I won." She subsequently traveled to New York from Europe, where she had been modeling successfully for three years when I met her.

Close to a third of the models I interviewed were discovered in this way,[34] like the one who said simply that she was "found on the street in the city." A friend emailed me a story detailing a typical scenario: She told how a friend was walking down the street in Soho and a booker approached his fifteen-year-old, 5'11.5" daughter, who was "drop-dead gorgeous," according to his description. This booker introduced them to an agency that does not have open calls; "There is no way to access them, they come to you." Upon meeting her, the agents offered this young woman a contract on the spot.

Rachel, a model I met at a casting in the Soho neighborhood of New York City, told me over coffee at a nearby Dean & Deluca that she was discovered at dinner. She happened to find herself at a downtown New York restaurant's "model night" (at which models are given 20 percent off their meals). A freelance agent, friends with the restaurant's owner, approached her, saying,

> You know, you have a great look, you should do modeling, and I was like, Alright, if you think so. . . . She explained that she's an independent scout, she hooks girls up with agencies, I really think you should be doing modeling, give me a call. And so I called her, and she said, Why don't you meet me at Next at 11 a.m. So I met her there, and the people at Next were really into me, and she was like, Okay, don't make any decisions yet, and we went up to Elite.

She became a model that day and had been working steadily since.

While the cutthroat business of finding new models to feed the constant demand for them may drive scouts to be aggressive, at the same time, modeling's glamorous mystique is an attraction that translates into a subtle but constant pressure on young people who seem to fit the standards, which pushes them toward modeling whether or not it interests them. The success of the few who make it drives a dream that creates a reserve army into which young people willingly draft themselves. Socialized into wanting the fashionable life at a young age, young people are only too ready to say yes if the opportunity should arise, which it often does for anyone who seems to fit the part. As my personal experience can attest, a walk to the gym, a dinner out, or having fun at a party all provide opportunities for being scouted, and the pressures of the fear of missing out and the drive for visibility make it seem as though, if a professional is saying you have a chance, you have to try. Glamour's promise has become an imperative, a primary way to achieve legitimate being in the world.

Rachel, the model picked up by the independent scout, had been recruited to be a model periodically from the age of fifteen on:

It's one of those things that, if you have a certain look about you, your whole life people will be like, You should model. I've had it so many times, people asking me, Do you model? You should model. I lived in Boston where there's not so much fashion taking place, and so I never really pursued it that much. I thought maybe I should be, but what are you going to do? I was in school, and I had to work every summer, so I couldn't just come up to New York.

Similarly, Nicholas, a PR agent for a modeling agency whose girlfriend is "model pretty" but tried the business and didn't like it, reported that she was approached by scouts weekly:

Take, my girlfriend, for example—she walked away from it. She got scouted when she was fifteen, she was one of the finalists for Elite's Look of the Year in 1994, and she just didn't want to do it. She's an academic and an intellectual and wanted nothing to do with it. She gets scouted all the time in New York—every effing week, somebody comes up to her. It's like, if you are 6'6", everybody tells you to play basketball.

He went on to explain that she had been criticized for her decision to reject modeling:

Yeah, well people sometimes berate her and say, What's wrong with you? It's a challenge for her in her work, because she's beautiful and she's dealing with a lot of men, and they don't—I mean she's a summa cum laude from Wellesley, she's a brilliant girl, and it's a source of frustration in her life. And she doesn't like being objectified, and that was the whole turnoff about modeling. She said, I'm trotting myself out as if all I had to offer was the way I look. And for her that wasn't a compulsion, but for every ten girls, there's only one of them who doesn't want to do this.

These stories point toward a shift in attitude toward modeling in the course of the regime of the blink's rise. They contrast clearly with the story told at this chapter's outset, in which seeking employment as a model was something to be kept hush-hush. The sense of obligation is a key tool for recruitment to glamour labor. It appeals to the fear that you are not being all you can be, that if you don't reach for the ring, the world will pass you by, if you don't at least try for this one clear chance to reach your potential, you will forever miss out. Various scholars have touched on this trend, most notably in terms of the enterprise self, someone who is ready to be the "CEO of me," self-directed, and solely responsible for the outcome of their actions.[35]

The dawn of the regime of the blink changed the scouting business irrevocably. No longer a casual affair, the pressures to bioprospect to find new ways to profit from unpredictable mutations in the population that might result in the next big "look" intensified. While the paths for image distribution proliferated and our attention grew more fleeting, innovations in imaging techniques created new markets for bodily vitality. The gold rush prompted both the explosion in the number of scouting companies seeking modeling talent and the rise of interest in, and aspiration to, the worlds of modeling and fashion. For many, it seemed, being in a model search contest fulfilled "a kind of dream," as Carolyn the model agent put it, the culmination of many childhood imaginings. As the final section of this chapter illustrates, selling modeling as a fun dream has, in the last few decades, become a common form of entertainment. Infiltrating young girls' play, it sells the engagement with being fashionable as something worth striving or competing for, a risk worth taking.

The early 2000s saw the rise of "talent search" reality television shows. For the anthropologist Stephanie Sadre-Orafai, "TV/talent/job search reality shows in creative industries like music, fashion, and other performing arts use the seeming neutrality of 'the market' to advance 'tenets of new forms of neoliberal labor.' "[36] The consequence? *America's Next Top Model* and shows like it normalize placing the "burden of failure and success on the individual isolated from broader social dynamics." Citing the efflorescence of model search shows, Sadre-Orafai argues that

> shows like "America's Next Top Model" (UPN 2003), "Man Hunt: The Search for America's Most Gorgeous Male Model" (Bravo 2004) and "Sports Illustrated Swimsuit Model Search" (NBC 2004) . . . reframe the figure of the model. In fact, the rise of these shows marks a popular shift in interest from models as celebrity personalities to an interest in modeling as a quotidian and allegoric practice. Whereas previous programs highlighted the glamour and exclusivity of modeling and fashion professions, recent shows underscore the broad applicability of fashion work, chronicling unknowns' attempts at these practices.[37]

As Sadre-Orafai has pointed out, the work of modeling was recast by these shows, taken down from the lofty heights of exclusivity, and brought into the everyday, as something everyone could and should want to do. Glamorizing the labor of becoming a model, showing the audience step by step how to do it, demystified it, making it accessible to all. Once this move was made, the pressure to engage with glamour labor increased. Those who seem to have any kind of potential at all are feeling the pressure even more keenly to expose themselves, risk their time and energy, educate themselves about fashionable practices, and seek the fashionable lifestyle as an avenue to desired work and employment.

Glamour labor functions, in part, to make taking these risks, going on these ventures, seem attractive, fun, and something everyone should try. This aspect of models' glamour labor helps accrue the mystique of modeling to the brand of modeling, making it attractive, engaging, and accessible. The supermodels who became household names were a big part of this process, as was fashion's permeation of everyday life via the growth in the number and ubiquity of fashion weeks, the proliferation of fashion television programming, and the upswing in the sheer number of fashion images, resulting from the imperatives of the current imaging regime. A key element of evoking the "glamour" in glamour labor involves acting like you don't, as one of my respondents put it, "want it too much." In keeping with this attitude, most of my respondents seemed quite nonchalant about being discovered, as if it could happen to just about anyone.

While the aspiring model Brittany made savvy use of the fax machine, the regime of the blink's email and Internet capabilities have made it easier than ever to "scout yourself," so to speak. The growing density of communication networks consolidated and intensified this system, reducing travel time and producing an ever-finer net of connections between feeder markets and fashion centers, in the move from Polaroids sent through the mail, to faxed photographs, to the daily barrage of emailed and uploaded photos of model hopefuls seeking possible futures through the click of a mouse. The young model agent Cameron observed that since the transition to the Internet,

> wannabe models are much more educated about the industry and about the agencies. We get hundreds of emails every day with pictures attached. I mean, theoretically, it's rare, but it's certainly, if there's the right girl, and she took the right pictures, we would fly her to New York. It's part of scouting. Wannabe models read this site models.com relentlessly. Across the world, fourteen-year-olds who want to be models somehow find that site and educate themselves.

While agencies receive hundreds of images daily, a writer close to the industry described how, for the most part, these photos go no further than to provide a steady source of office entertainment at modeling agencies:

> Though diamonds do exist in the considerable rough of photos that pour into a top agency each week, unsolicited pictures often have another use: office entertainment. Scouts and bookers aren't above gathering round the more bizarre submissions for a good laugh.[38]

Why do so many think they should try for the chance? Biopolitical forces in the age of the blink prompted not only the quest for legitimacy through achieving "beauty" according to reigning standards but also the notion that fashion is a basic human right and should be available to all.

McFashion: Everyone Can Be a Fashion Superstar

The blink technologies of high-speed communication and transportation, combined with the globalized labor force and marketplace that has enabled fast-fashion retailers, such as Zara and H&M, to copy runway looks in a matter of weeks, provided new means for the general public to engage in the practice of being fashionable. Starting in the 1970s and accelerating after the 1990s, fashion's exclusivity shifted to a new form of "massclusivity"[39] spreading the democratic notion of "fashion for all." For young people, in developed countries especially, it became the norm to keep up with changing styles, invest in them, treat the street like a runway, and try to look "of the moment." In the course of blogging about these activities, clicking through to fashion websites, watching fashion television shows, and attending fashion-oriented publicity events, young people's glamour labor increasingly drove the fashion system and shows no signs of abating.

As fast fashion brought fashion to the masses, its widespread availability, combined with the mystique of being "discovered" and catapulted into modeling's glamorous world, pulled many into a regime of engaging with fashion's imperatives, which served to resource them as a population, as a set of raw materials from which new sources of profit might arise. Recently, the fashion studies scholar Minh-Ha T. Pham has discussed fashion blogs as sites of capital accumulation, where willing participants work to produce sites that provide free advertising and ready-made audiences for corporations that produce fashion.[40] This environment attracted audiences to participating in modeling culture. The public was given an all-access pass to what used to be behind closed doors, styling themselves and producing their own fashion shoots, displaying them for all to see on the Internet. These new levels of self-regulated participation can be linked to the way the technologies of the blink allow more interactivity, creating what the communication scholar Henry Jenkins calls "affective economics,"[41] in which viewers are allowed to (or, I would argue, are made to feel they ought to) participate in creating the brand culture—or in this case, fashion culture.

Consequently, in the regime of the blink, while the hunger for new faces became more widespread and keen, the public appetite for and acceptance of fashion intensified as well, stimulating an upsurge of interest in modeling, as well as promoting the notions that we should all be like fashion models, styling our everyday lives, promoting our image for all who care to see it, posting our outfits on "what I'm wearing today" blogs, or catering our "look" to try to capture the attention of street fashion photographers in stylish and hip neighborhoods such as New York's Soho, London's Brick Lane or Shoreditch, or Paris's Latin quarter or Le Marais.

Playing at Fashion

Since the dawn of the regime of the blink, learning to offer up one's creative energy, to freely spend it in pursuit of the fashionable life, has become a lesson that is reaching younger and younger audiences. While children don't necessarily play games in which they risk their life savings or their assets to land a paying job in the tech industry, as venture laborers commonly do, they do learn the kinds of risk-taking behavior required by these winner-take-all markets and learn to value the notion that one must "put yourself out there" in order to succeed in these settings.[42] Taking the chance may be enough for them because, in so doing, they register their legitimacy in a system designed to encourage risky behavior, encourage investing one's time and money for extremely uncertain odds, activities typical of glamour labor in the regime of the blink.

Although the Barbie doll started out as a fashion model before becoming, among other things, an astronaut and an architect,[43] her sideline as a model is no comparison to the extent and availability of fashion-themed toys and activities marketed to young people since the onset of the regime of the blink. Girls as young as three-years-old play "fashion show" with their Colorforms Magic Fashion Show toys[44] or their Barbie Fashion Show and Runway Case kits.[45] The Polly Pocket runway set has also been popular with younger consumers,[46] and if furry friends are more appealing, the Zhu Zhu Pets Fashion Catwalk might just do the job.[47]

Should the aspiring fashionista want a more hands-on experience, perhaps she can convince her parents to sign her up for one of the many "modeling" camps that have sprung up in recent years. One such camp advertises itself as giving attendees the scoop on the ins and outs of the industry while learning the "various types of modeling" and getting them informed about "all that's fashionably fabulous."[48] While the idea for this camp may see a far cry from catching frogs in the woods or doing macramé in the arts-and-crafts tent, it might seem quite attractive to the young girl who grew up watching the televised modeling competition reality show *America's Next Top Model* or making her Polly Pockets sashay down the catwalk.

This access in the United States to fashion "play" starts young and keeps going strong through the tweens and into adulthood. For girls ten and over, Nintendo's Wii has an *America's Next Top Model* game in which they can become one of ten contestants aspiring to be the next big supermodel by choosing a personality, styling a look, competing for very critical judges, and even picking the occasional catfight. When they are all grown up, those who want to live the fantasy of fashion in real life can take a five-day/four-night "Fashion Week Tour of Paris," which offers private shopping and "look" coaching on a chaperoned shopping tour, a visit with a fashion designer or famous fashion studio, tickets to a fashion show, a photo shoot, and—to cap it all off, as the website described it—invitations to "swanky parties in Paris."[49] For those who wanted the inside fashion scoop and were willing to pay for it, the bespoke travel tour operator Remote Lands has offered customizable trips to fashion weeks all over Asia. Prices started at a mere $15,000 and included prime seats, backstage passes, VIP party invites, and the chance to be escorted around town by local magazine editors.[50]

Playing at self-commodification from a young age, spending one's leisure time learning to be a better and more prolific fashion consumer in pursuit of the right look, or perfecting that "model" walk or body are activities that also feed into the process of self-branding.[51] The scouting system institutionalized its practices and intensified the scope and reach of its search nets and mining apparatus, making opportunities for self-branding more prevalent, as street scouting and the virtual scouting of fashion blogs upped the ante of street style and model search contests and modeling agency websites multiplied the opportunities for self-scouting in exponential ways.

While there are myriad reasons that young people might be willing to submit themselves for scrutiny by modeling experts in the hopes of being discovered—such as a lack of real work opportunities, or the influence of the gendered division of power in which girls see their looks as their only source of validation—the eagerness of these young women to participate also points to the growing influence of beauty as a biopower, which converts beauty into a "universal human need," thus conflating the pursuit of beauty and that of freedom in ways that serve to instrumentalize "beauty" as an index of worth.[52]

As she points out regarding the role of the Kabul Beauty School in Afghanistan, the fashion studies scholar Mimi Nguyen claims such organizations overtly offer beauty as a path to personhood for Afghan women while covertly operating on the hope that "beauty can engender a new world order" by connecting the "maximization of the feminine self to the instrumentalization of human existence."[53] Following this logic, the pursuit of beauty, the rising desire to enter into the fashion system, to follow its rules, supports various power interests, as it renders populations ready to be scouted in order to mine their potential. The mechanisms that pull these populations in are less targeted than the non-governmental organizations Nguyen discusses, in terms of converting populations to Western ways. Arguably, a model search contest in Siberia attracts aspirants who are already familiar with the world of international fashion. Yet the fact that international scouting and model search contests attract participants from countries all over the world speaks to the ways that the values of fashion and beauty are reaching further afield, spreading the values of self-regulation and enterprising to maximize one's potential, facilitating the growth of glamour labor.[54] Self-branding feeds willing participants into the biopolitical regime of beauty, offering up individuals to make up the mass in which agents and scouts might go bioprospecting for sources of future value. While Nguyen is concerned with the treatment of women in the global South, her point of view is useful for understanding how the pursuit of beauty and the pursuit of freedom are increasingly conflated in ways that enable beauty, as an "empowerment technology," to be used globally to advance neoliberal ends by telling subaltern women they need a makeover and by telling the men who live with them to get out of the way of these ideals.[55]

In this respect, however, beauty as a biopower becomes an organizing logic in which, as George Orwell might have put it, some pigs are more equal than others.[56] That is, while some portions of the population willingly engage with the tenets of being "fashionable" or "beautiful" as fashion defines it, for others, no amount of effort will break down the barriers to entry. Racism, in its most basic sense of exclusion on the basis of physical traits such as skin color, continues to be a well-documented problem in the fashion industry.[57] Understanding racism within the context of mining populations for genetic accidents is complicated, however. While, on the one hand, the dearth of models of color on runways speaks to their overt exclusion by fashion decision makers, at the same time, experts within the industry extol the virtues of the kinds of racial mixing that can produce a highly unusual and valuable "look." As the next chapter illustrates, race in modeling functions as both an effect of skin color and a set of signifiers to be manipulated in the service of creating a particular look, which, although dealing in the virtual, symbolic realms, nonetheless has real consequences.

8

Black-Black-Black

How Race Is Read

For Antoine, a commercial casting director, thinking about race in modeling was not a simple black/white proposition. He gave me an example. Instead of saying, "I want a black model," clients might request "a twenty-five-year-old model with native features and interesting hair." Since he works mostly with clients in the United States, "native" features might translate into "not too Caucasian looking," a notion that has its own meaning in the industry. Warming to his subject, Antoine explained, "'interesting' usually means dread locks, twists, even an afro" but "not your standard what we would think of as looking like African American hair, hence the label 'interesting.'" He went on to point out that, unlike editorial clients, who are willing to take bigger risks, commercial clients

> don't want someone whose skin is really black because it doesn't photograph as easily. Really dark skin is more editorial, it's more edgy looking; commercial clients prefer lighter skin because it's what the Midwest can relate to. These clients don't want someone who looks, for lack of a better way to say it, like a savage, or a person from the bush.[1]

This agent's casual use of the terms "savage" and "bush" for "lack of a better way to say it" indicates a high level of comfort with deeply stereotypical language that is quite common in the industry.[2] The gradations of skin tone he described, however, speak to subtleties affecting attitudes about race, couched in the language of aesthetics. The story of modeling's racial divides has shifted from one imaging regime to the next, from outright exclusion to a gradual acceptance, but only for those willing to do the glamour labor required by the fashion aesthetics ruling the day.

During the cinematic age, the work required for crafting the black model image was clearly laid out. The segregated universes of fomented desire aimed at parallel mid-century audiences needed unmistakably non-white stand-ins, used for creating duplicate ads for the newly emerging "Negro" market. In the transition from gaze to glance to blink, however, the lines were blurred. The script was tossed out, and more subtle forms of exclusion emerged in the whirling froth of constant newness. Race became one among many characteristics, a brand value to power up or down, an aesthetic choice that claimed it didn't truck with racism. The transition from outright exclusion to race as an aesthetic shifted the burden of this responsibility onto individual workers, ramping up their glamour labor, differentiating its demands depending on the workers' place in the market.

Racism in the Fashion Industry: By the Numbers

How can we know that this discrimination in fashion actually exists, beyond anecdotal testimony to the fact? Quantitative data regarding black models' versus white models' employment rates are scarce, and existing reports tend to be gleaned from journalistic sources or hearsay. The U.S. Bureau of Labor Statistics only began tracking the number of "demonstrators, product promoters, and models" as a category sometime in the early 1990s, and their statistics are not broken down by race or gender. According to the bureau's *Occupational Outlook Handbook*, models held about forty eight hundred jobs in 2012, and the occupation was expected to increase 15 percent compared to all occupations through 2022, with fewer job openings than job seekers.[3]

Despite media attention to the issue of racial discrimination in hiring models, the industry as a whole has not come forward with reliable statistics regarding the racial makeup of the modeling workforce. Even Bethann Hardison, the head of the first all-black modeling agency in the United States, and an outspoken critic of fashion industry racism, does not routinely cite government statistics in interviews.[4] To examine the widespread popular understanding that black models are employed less often than white models, in the absence of hard empirical data gathered by a government agency or industry analysts, media outlets as varied as *Essence*, *Ebony*, the *Wall Street Journal*, the *New York Times*,

Women's Wear Daily, the *Guardian*, the *Telegraph*, and the *Independent*, have counted the number of models of color on the runway during one season, or the number black models appearing in magazine pages, or relied on agencies' self-reported head counts of how many models of color are on their books.[5]

While not gathered by sanctioned government sources, evidence in media reports do seem to point toward a lower employment rate of black models and other models of color on the catwalks and in magazines. According to the fashion periodical *Women's Wear Daily*, in the fall of 2007, fully one-third of New York Fashion Week's fashion shows used no models of color at all. The next year, things improved slightly. The website *Jezebel* (jezebel.com), a popular fashion blog that began tracking these numbers in 2007, reported that, in 2008, the shows at New York Fashion Week gave 18 percent of runway spots to black models, which was 6 percent better than the year before. The slight improvement in the numbers of black models employed on fashion runways was fleeting, despite the now-famous issue of Italian *Vogue* devoted entirely to depicting black models, which was published in an effort to draw attention to the color imbalance in fashion representation.[6] *Jezebel* tallied a drop in the number of black models on the runway from 18 percent back to 16 percent in the Fall 2010 shows held in New York.[7]

Using similar counting techniques, scholars have demonstrated the paucity of jobs for non-European-looking or non-Caucasian-looking models. In 1997, researchers found that 10 percent of advertisements oriented toward white readers contained black models. Other research found more images of black people in magazines in recent years, but they were concentrated in specific areas, such as the sports section of the magazine.[8] In 2009, the sociologist Ashley Mears reported that, for the Spring/Summer 2007 collections, the fashion website *Style.com* (www.style.com) "recorded the shows for 172 fashion houses, yielding a total of 677 models." Of that 677, she counted 27 non-white models ($N = 15$ with dark skin, $N = 12$ with Asian features), totaling less than 4 percent representation of models of color on the catwalk, as compared to 13 percent of the total U.S. population.[9] This pattern reflects the broader pattern of minority employment in the United States, with black women disproportionately affected by unemployment.[10] In a 2013 article in the *New York Times*, Eric Wilson lamented that, even after all the brouhaha

caused by the 2008 all-black issue of Italian *Vogue* and industry promises to do better by the race issue, essentially nothing in the fashion
industry has changed.[11]

With regard to the race or ethnicity of modeling professionals—such
as model agents, editors, photographers, designers, and the hair and
makeup professionals who work with models—readily available statistics are also scarce. The outcry following the appointment of a white
fashion director to the staff of *Essence* magazine, in July 2010, however,
stemmed at least in part from the widespread understanding that the
fashion industry, as the magazine's editor, Angela Burt-Murray put it,
"is overwhelmingly white." She went on to point to the underrepresen-
tation of people of color on the mastheads of magazines, at the front
rows of fashion shows, and as designers and stylists of fashion lines.[12]
Overall, within the modeling industry, and in the professions that work
with models, levels of black employment appear to be far lower than the
representative numbers of the population.

The Typology of the Model "Look"

Models' glamour labor requires striving to approximate the fashion
ideal, commodifying one's "look" to match the ever-changing whims
of clients. Looks are not completely arbitrary, however. They are governed by a system of "types." According to the sociologist Ashley Mears,
model markets' volatility and uncertainty stem from the whims of fashion, leading modeling professionals to copy one another, hoping to
"tame uncertainty" and "lend coherence to an otherwise turbulent market."[13] Referring to Howard Becker's "shared ways of doing things" common to an "art world," including the modeling industry, Mears points to
the "type" as one of the "conventions" on which modeling professionals "rely . . . to coordinate their actions."[14] A "type" is a euphemism for
a combination of qualities, including a model's age, gender, ethnicity,
and appearance. Types are often racially defined without clearly saying so. A client who calls an agency looking for a model of an "exotic"
type, or an "all-American" preppy, uses language that veils a desire
for a model of color or a blue-eyed blond. Types shape and define the
various model markets, divided between young girls just starting out
(often referred to as "in development" or "new faces"), runway models,

commercial models, men, children, and what is often referred to as the "high board"—the high-level models who bring in the top fees. While black models in the United States may work in any one of these markets, historically the term "ethnic model" served as a catchall for any model that does not fit the standard white model "type."[15]

For one model, Shana, this system shapes the industry with assumptions that seem ridiculous from her perspective, like the idea that "black people don't drink Chardonnay," an observation she countered with "but, you know, we do drink wine." She wished for the opportunity to represent a wider range of products. In her experience, however, "it doesn't matter what you look like because the casting director already knows what they want. The underlying racism is not spoken, but it's understood, it's just the way it is." Corroboratively, the anthropologist Stephanie Sadre-Orafai found that casting personnel at an "ethnic" modeling agency used cues related to skin tones or types as a shorthand to quickly explain a model's "look":

> Casting requests were rife with elaborate color descriptions and national modifiers bound up in racial hierarchies. Whether it was "London beat," "brown-skinned Bollywood," or "black-black-black" these requests quickly indexed general facial features, skin tone, and hair type and color.[16]

Model agents, Sadre-Orafai explained, talk this way to save time when "communicating a model's look or feel." Ostensibly about national characteristics, in practice, "alternative images and ideas are smuggled into these descriptions," including "national reputations for certain sexual proclivities, attitudes, and behaviors."[17]

This racialized shorthand invokes a long history. In this country, the enslavement of Africans has left a bitter legacy of lynching, discrimination, segregation, and other racial violence that the general population actively seeks to forget. The catchphrase "Black Is Beautiful" has been used as a legitimate comeback to the attitudes that equated black physiognomy with ugliness, primitivism, and the potential for barbaric behavior. In the course of U.S. history, the struggle for fair representation has extended not only to legal rights but also to the reigning images of American blackness. Values projected by advertisements were shaped not only by the corporate "gaze"[18] but also shaped by the "white gaze," more generally.[19]

The white gaze has most famously been identified by Frantz Fanon as the process in which the "white man" weaves "the black man" out of "a thousand details, anecdotes and stories" in a dialectical relationship, where the black man must "be black in relation to the white man," the "other" to his whiteness. In this relation, the black man's image of his body is "solely negating." Fanon describes how, during an encounter on a train with a little girl who says, "Look, a Negro!" he feels this gaze for the first time, discovering his "blackness, my ethnic features: deafened by cannibalism, backwardness, fetishism, racial stigmas, slave traders . . ." In response, he feels he gives himself up "as an object" to that gaze, an experience very like what my respondents described.[20] Social activists and intellectuals such as bell hooks and Patricia Hill Collins have sought for many years to redress the damage done by pejorative images of black people constructed by this gaze and popularized in advertising and entertainment media, from the blackface minstrel shows premised on the assumed stupidity and laziness of the "Negro" character, to popular caricatures of the black buffoon, such as Stepin Fetchit, and Amos 'n' Andy, to the madonna/whore dichotomy epitomized by the black mammy character, Aunt Jemima, or the overtly sexual Jezebel.[21]

As the historian Elspeth Brown has documented, racist advertising from 1920 to 1950 in the United States contained only two roles for black men and women. The role of "Pullman porter, cook, or waiter" was exemplified by a smiling waiter appearing in the pages of the *New Yorker*, exclaiming "Yes, Suh, Boss, I's Got de Best!" while proffering a tray of Laird's Apple Jack Brandy.[22] The female role of "cook, laundress, and housekeeper," embodied by the comfortably plump mammy, boasted, "It's Helsey, honey!" as she held up a freshly polished crystal wine goblet to an admiring white child looking on.[23] According to Brown, it was this racist archive of advertising imagery "against which Negro modeling agencies sought to construct a counter-archive of bourgeois respectability."[24]

When "dominant agencies such as John Powers or Harry Conover barred blacks from bookings," Brown observed, "a duplicate Negro modeling industry emerged to provide models for duplicate advertising directed at black consumers."[25] The same year Eileen and Jerry Ford founded Ford Models, a talented team of African and European Americans founded Brandford Models, the first African American modeling agency in the United States.[26] Taking a page from John Robert Powers's book, founder Barbara Watson used the power of the press to carefully craft a consistent narrative about her models. Just as Powers sought to distant his long-stemmed roses from the louche image of the call girl, Watson struggled to distance her models from the timeworn bifurcation of the mammy or the jezebel. She recast her models as staunch upholders of bourgeois values, middle-class taste, and a sanitized sexuality. In early glimmerings of glamour labor, Brandford models engaged with fashion as a route to inclusion, challenging the dominant discourse that equated "beauty with whiteness."[27]

Battling the twin pillars of exoticism and exclusion, images of elegantly coiffed and clothed black models in the pages of postwar magazines such as *Ebony*, *Jet*, and *Our World* challenged the "lily-white standards" of the industry. Seeking to redraw biopolitically inflected lines of exclusion, Watson made sure her models were, like their white mid-century counterparts, tall and slender, with narrow waists (twenty-three inches being the ideal).[28] Watson saw her work as a contribution to "racial progress," using "beauty culture and model training as an innovative approach to race discrimination in the U.S.," as the historian Laila Haidarali observed.[29] Brandford models only appeared in public in elegant tenue, their clothes tailored, their grooming meticulous. Elspeth Brown saw this sanitization as a "politics of respectability" that shepherded "blacks toward middle class, assimilationist ideals" concerning the body and its comportment. The visual signs of respectability were "deportment, skin color, clothing, and (straightened) hair."[30] These polished beauties stood in stark contrast to the commonly accepted stereotypes depicting African American women as "unattractive, rural, and unkempt."[31] With whiteness and nationalism defining feminine beauty, the price for inclusion in a world of freedom and equality involved adhering to narrow dictates of racialized gender expectations.

Haidarali detailed a particularly pointed discourse common in many black-oriented mid-century magazines. Via training in proper use of cosmetics and clothing, "plain girls" were transformed into "glamour girls" in a popular series of articles that read like a glamour labor primer.

One such article in *Ebony*, set out quite simply to demonstrate that "Negro girls are beautiful too."[32] Magazine stories offering "instruction and testimony to the accessibility of beauty" sought to extend the means to achieving the "model look" as a path to at least a "superficial equality" for blacks.[33] These "plain-girl" transformations advanced assimilationist values that were eventually cemented into the public consciousness as *the* path to beauty. Despite expansion in advertising to "Negro markets" and the growth and institutionalization of black modeling by the organization of Brandford and other black model agencies in the 1940s and 1950s, however, even "the 'busiest Negro photo models'" could not quit their jobs as "receptionists, typists and secretaries."[34] Alluding to an aesthetic practice that would eventually dominate the industry, one model told the *New York Post* in 1955, "They always say we are too tall, or too short, or too fat or too skinny . . . but actually I'm sure it's because we're colored."[35] Claiming (and even believing) the "look" is not right masks the underlying racism, hiding it even from those perpetrating it.

By 1969, however, things had changed. As rising social consciousness loosened the tight strictures of mid-century conformity, the gradual shift to the regime of the glance elevated the natural, uncontrived look to a new dominance. While the "typical Anglo-Saxon type model with delicate features and the lightest of the black complexions" was still in demand, the former-model-become-manager Candy Jones noted that photographers and TV clients who began to call for "the Afro-look (featuring the tightly curled cropped hairdo of African women)" were especially concerned that the girls "look Negro," and so asked for models with the "darkest complexions."[36]

Thus, while black models starting to be used in the sixties, they were featured either as black versions of white girls or as "exotic" types. There was "no room for the average-looking girl. . . . If you were black you had to be beautiful and stunningly confident,"[37] as a professional model who researched the industry explained.

One such beauty was black model Donyale Luna, who stepped into the exotic role with an easy elegance worn loosely on her rangy, six-foot tall frame. A woman of extreme proportions, her otherworldly grace, wide mouth, and impossibly long neck were thoroughly unlike the more compact and delicate proportions of her 1950s predecessors. Although her influence was less widespread than Twiggy's, she, too, shocked the fashion system. The same year Twiggy was dubbed the face of 1966, Luna was the first black model to appear on the cover of British *Vogue*.[38]

In the regime of the glance, the new value of personality and spark translated into widening opportunity, particularly on the runway. Haidarali noted the long history of black models' participation in community fashion shows, organized by "civic clubs, sororities, women's organizations and charm schools" to raise money for charity.[39] Lacking corporate sponsorship, participants often modeled their own clothes, receiving accolades for their "savvy consumption and personal style."[40] Black models became experts in displaying personal flair, as epitomized by the post-war era model Dorothea Towles's fifteen-city tour in the early 1950s. Reportedly, Towles "brought six trunks of real show stoppers" from Europe at her own expense, modeling them anywhere from college campuses to New York ballrooms. Eunice Johnson's Ebony Fashion Fair had the same goal—to introduce black audiences to high fashion. This tradition left black models well positioned for their famous runway "coup" in the 1970s.[41] As a 1978 model manual plainly stated, "There is a market for black models," but it is "primarily in the fashion show area. There are certainly more black models working in this field than in photography."[42] During this time, black models seemed to have a lock on the "free and easy style" that brought "pizzazz" to the runway, as dancing with vibrant energy became the special domain of black fashion runway models.[43] Their celebrated verve reached a fetishized status, and it seemed that black models would soon be well represented in fashion, bearing out Candy Jones's radical 1969 prediction that "world conditions," such as "war, international politics, our domestic climate, civil rights, taxes, etc.," will have a "bearing on the model type and look of the 1970s. I predict we will have a Negro girl become world recognized as a model," a prediction she lumped in with the prospect of fashionable Soviet women, a market for older models, and the decline of one, single, fashionable type.[44]

It wasn't until the 1980s, with the first sparks of the regime of the blink, that black models gained a real toehold in the U.S. fashion modeling market. As Julia, a white model I interviewed pointed out, when she started modeling, being African American, "made a big difference at the time, they were not open to African American girls at all." She surmised that being black served to limit and finally stall the career of an African American model who seemed to be on the same trajectory as she. While she and her African American friend got the same types of bookings at first, her friend "never really made it to the big time—she only made it to the medium range," whereas Julia quickly ascended to international star status, appearing on the runways of top designers and the covers of magazines in both New York and Paris. As she recalled, opportunities were extremely limited in the late seventies and into the early eighties:

> Back then, there was only like two—Beverly Johnson and Iman. Oh, and Sheila Johnson. There were three that were big, for the ten years that the model I was talking about worked.

Rashumba, another black model popular in the 1980s and 1990s, noted the smaller number of jobs for "ethnic" models in the same time frame, saying, "For a long time, you could have eight white girls, and only one ethnic girl in an ad; magazines would put only one ethnic girl on the cover every year at best."[45] It was not until after the regime of the blink and the infiltration of fashion into everyday life that consistent work for black models became a possibility.[46]

The work involved in winning these coveted jobs, however, was heavily inflected by pressures borne of the blink regime. In the same way model figures in general attenuated within pressures to catch fleeting attention in a rising tide of images, the ideal for black models also became more extreme. Superexotic models such as Iman[47] and, later, inky-black-skinned Alek Wek[48] found work epitomizing the African type, while models with Caucasian features, such as Beverly Johnson, the first black model to appear on the cover of American *Vogue*, found success depicting a dark-skinned version of the all-American girl next door. By the late 1990s, although the barriers were still there, they took on a different tone within the affective economics of effervescent markets. Rather than ban black models outright, aesthetic factors took on a new weight. Clients who wanted an ethereal feel, or a creamy color scheme, sometimes didn't even realize that meant they didn't want a black model.

Managing Ethnicity under the White Gaze: Erasing Ethnicity

The look and feel of working to produce an "aesthetic" took on a new tone in the late 1990s. As producing the right image or brand became crucial for economic success, these concerns extended to employees' presentation of self at work in a far more codified manner. Some scholars identified new forms of working on the body and demeanor to achieve an image desired by clients as "aesthetic labor," a strand that weaves into models' glamour labor.[49] Specifically, aesthetic labor entails what the sociologists of work Chris Warhurst, Anne Witz, and Dennis Nickson have deemed work on one's inner and outer self to produce a certain attitude or demeanor for the workplace— to "'look good' and/or 'sound right' to customers."[50] While aesthetic labor is usually aimed at a achieving a top-down, corporately defined image, Joanne Entwistle and I found that, in the freelance work of modeling, the pressures for aesthetic labor are greater because what the client wants is "ill defined and can change on a whim," in keeping with what the sociologist Ashley Mears refers to as a set of "floating norms."[51] In reality, getting a lock on the requirements for success is like chasing a unicorn; everyone knows what one is, but no one can show it to you.

Part of the problem lies in the fact that aesthetics are often subjective. Denying any racism, gatekeepers such as model agents and designers blame aesthetics, saying that the choice of models for a particular job must fit a particular "color scheme," as one model agent put it. Using aesthetics to excuse racial exclusion in appearance-based professions nonetheless contributes to the social construction of racial stereotypes.[52] This social construction is mobilized both by the kinds of aesthetic labor my respondents felt they had to perform and by the choices made by decision makers in the industry when they recruit and style models in keeping with a particular "aesthetic." While the effects of race are real in the industry, in terms of how difficult it is for black models to get jobs, when black models' glamour labor is used to produce an agreed-upon "aesthetic" look, "race" takes on a somewhat performative tone, shaped according to client's fluctuating standards, under the ever watchful eye of the "corporate gaze."

Straightening kinky or curly hair in keeping with a white standard of beauty intensified black models' aesthetic labor, in effect calling for them to minimize their racial characteristics. The pressure to look more European American has been a theme in the beauty industry for quite some time,[53] and this erasure of ethnicity represents a specialized aspect of aesthetic labor. Black models more acutely experience these disparate aesthetic demands, sometimes calling for them to produce themselves in line with European ideals of beauty, while at other times, having to emphasize their "otherness," for their clients. In this sense, under the "white gaze," the look of the "other" becomes either a bodily resource or a liability in a stylized workplace performance.

As digitization made the inchoate forces that govern the imprecise realm of what's beautiful, hot, or cool move faster and farther, powering-up or powering-down various aspects of one's look by means of aesthetic labor made race into a brand that constructs the body's vital forces for the marketplace. The black models I interviewed reportedly minimized or maximized their racial characteristics strategically, to increase their marketability. Unless they were expressly highlighting their exoticism, many black models seeking success in the mainstream felt they needed to meet aesthetic standards that seemed monochromatically white. Several of the respondents interviewed for a documentary about race in modeling referred to the industry's desire for black models who look like white models, but "dipped in chocolate." One booker was quite explicit, saying that those who do make it look like

> white girls that were painted black. That's "beauty" to the industry's perspective. . . . When you come in with big eyes, big nose, big this, whatever, big lips, things that are common traits in African Americans, it doesn't work. For those lucky few girls who have white girl features. . . . It's kind of messed up, but that's just the way the industry is.[54]

As this documentary seemed to indicate, as long as a black model looked white, she had a chance to make it in the industry. Even if she had the face, however, her body might stand in her way. This film also depicted a sequence in which a casting agent for a fashion show observed, after auditioning the black model whose experiences this film documented, that "black models, they tend to be like, a little wider hips, and a little

The newest way to hyper shine.
New. Pure Color Lip Vinyl
Gloss Stick

ESTÉE LAUDER
Defining Beauty

Figure 8.1. Liya Kebede's first photo after being signed as a new face of Estée Lauder cosmetics. She represented the brand from 2003 to 2007. Estée Lauder ad campaign, Spring 2003.

more round. So sometimes, even though the face is amazing, she has a fit problem." Not surprisingly, despite her 34-24-35 measurements, this model was not cast for the show.

With very few exceptions, successful black models in the fashion industry have European American–looking hair and features. Like her predecessors Naomi Sims[55] and Beverly Johnson,[56] Liya Kebede, the first black model to sign an Estée Lauder cosmetics contract in its fifty-seven-year history, is a relatively light-skinned African woman with straight hair, a small nose, and narrow features.[57] Her ascent to being the face of Estée Lauder points to the preference for this look and style. When I asked Cody, a New York model agent, if it would be fair to say that she looks relatively Caucasian, he concurred:

> No, you wouldn't be off base, because it's I think something that is not said, but everyone knows. I think that that's, it's something that's true, it's more like, Oh, she doesn't look so African American. It's like saying, I want an Asian girl, but I want her to be more Eurasian because I want her to have, you know, I hate to say it, but Caucasian features. You know? No one would ever dare to say that. But it's the truth. It's what no one would ever dare to say, but everyone thinks.

Here, Cody is speaking to unspoken forces that shape modeling work. While the corporate gaze calls for a look at that is accessible, when overlaid by the white gaze, this look translates as Caucasian, pulling for more intense demands for black models' aesthetic labor to achieve this look. Black models are not always asked to erase their "otherness," however. Sometimes the "white gaze" pulls for an emphasis on ethnicity, to produce stereotypical images that feed into racial attitudes linking black people with "savages" from the "bush." In the age of the blink, these stereotypes have intensified. Consequently, black models' glamour labor sometimes involved having to "perform" their race, as defined by the white gaze, to meet their clients' expectations of what black should look like.

Performing Race for the White Gaze

When "types" are used to market products, ingrained attitudes take significance over whatever individual look or skills a black model might employ, and these have real consequences in terms of the opportunity structure. These ingrained attitudes can have the effect of creating what the industrial relations scholar Deborah Dean identified as "internally segmented labour markets," which she found in the field of acting but which exist in modeling as well.[58] These internal segmentations, in which jobs are available to some people and not others, according to varying characteristics, are defined not only by the black/white divide but also specific shades of skin.

For some, this means paying attention to fine gradations of skin color that determine whether they will be suitable for a commercial print job. Leo, a black male seventeen-year veteran of the business, detailed the criteria:

> They'd say black, not mixed, it depends on how precise they want. Because they are usually going for something, you know, dark skin or light skin. See, I'm not dark, nor am I light, I'm brown skin, and so I can go with both, but it depends on what they're asking for.

This self-awareness needed to market oneself as a "type" is required of all models, but the need for aesthetic knowledge about the semiotics of skin is particularly prevalent in the black modeling market and is a less common concern for Caucasian models. Understanding the subtle and not so subtle messages about acceptable racial types within the industry makes up some part of every black model's job.

The freelance nature of the modeling industry demands non-stop attention to constructing one's body according to the needs of the corporate gaze. Just as prostitutes market themselves in "culturally specific ways," creating "looks" and "types" that will appeal to a specific customer's expectations,[59] models sometimes are encouraged to treat their ethnicity as a resource for their "look." A widespread "look" is primitive, wildly sexual, or animalistic. The social commentator Jean Kilbourne's video analysis of how media shape gendered stereotypes depicted image after image of black models in advertisements with faces painted to look like tigers or other jungle creatures, wearing tropical prints or other exotic attire.[60] One researcher found that black models tend to be featured in "only four roles: musician, athlete, celebrity or object of pity."[61] J. Alexander, best known as a judge on the U.S. television show *America's Next Top Model*, identified this tendency, saying, "Some people are not interested in the vision of the black girl unless they're doing a jungle theme and they can put her in a grass skirt and diamonds and hand her a spear."[62] Shana, a commercial print model, found that she came up against this kind of "pigeonholing" shaped by the white gaze when she was pushed toward taking jobs for "black hair-care products, or sexy body shots for contraceptives, and other ads that didn't pay well." In her experience, minority models were often encouraged "to do nude modeling for album covers, or MTV, which play on the sexy African American association," in keeping with what the media researcher Marcia Littlefield called the "porno chick" image.[63]

What is entailed in ramping up one's "ethnicity" for a particular shoot? Laura, hired no doubt for her light-skinned beauty and ethnically ambiguous features, nonetheless found herself in a job modeling clothing designed expressly for black women filtered through a white person's idea of what a black person looks like. In an experience resonant with historic attitudes about black bodies, readily evident in the popularity of the bustled skirt that imitated the shape of the Hottentot Venus in the eighteenth century, Laura was asked to put on what she called a "booty." She and another model had been "doing the shows"— that is, walking designer's runways during the various fashion weeks— and so were "very skinny," a body type that did not fit with the client's idea of their customer. Laura explained:

> Because it was ethnic style geared toward the black community, the jeans were cut larger in the booty and larger in the thigh and tops were cut bigger in the breast. So they gave us booty pads. I'm not kidding . . . it looks like a girdle that has bits in it, and then maybe thigh stuff added too, some of them go all the way down to the thigh. Because all black women of course have big booties, you know, baby got back! And, you're just kinda like, Oh, give me a break.

She was also offended by the stereotyping that seemed evident in the style of the clothes, saying: "It was like some white person's idea that every black person went to Baptist church more than once a week and was goin' to a barbecue in the evening and wore a hat." As this example illustrates, whether hiding or emphasizing their "blackness" to serve client's needs, black models create images that reinforce existing stereotypes, either by idealizing Caucasian facial features and hair types or by playing into various types of bigoted imagery they may find distasteful, yet they feel they must accept it if they are to work in the industry at all. In so doing, their glamour labor feeds into a system that makes this kind of work attractive to others, selling the stereotype as the "look" that's hot, which should be emulated, at all costs.

In the late 2000s, the co-founder of a UK-based modeling agency, Premier Model Management, bluntly stated that

> sadly we are in the business where you stock your shelves with what sells.
> . . . Black models don't sell. People don't tend to talk about it, but black models have to be so beautiful and perfect because we can't have a lot of diversity with black models.[64]

This argument, while logical, appears to minimize the fact that, as one industry analyst reported, "black women in the United States spend more than \$20 billion on apparel each year, according to estimates by TargetMarketNews.com,"[65] fully one-tenth of the U.S. women and girl's apparel market overall, estimated at around \$200 billion in personal expenditures per year.[66]

Regardless of black women's apparel spending, the norm for the last several decades has been to have the token black model on the books or in the ad campaign. Work distribution is affected most acutely by gatekeeper's assumptions about what will sell, with the consequence that black models are given limited opportunities, within the kinds of "tokenism" my respondents describe.

Shifting the Burden of Risk

In this reconfiguration, race becomes one of many factors in what makes or breaks a look, which has the effect of apparently erasing traditional forms of racism, even though they are still in play. In this scenario, the dividing line is drawn not between those who look one way or another but, rather, between those who want it badly enough and those who are willing to work hard enough (and become savvy enough to decode the mixed messages about how to produce the right look, in the prescribed manner) in order to "bring it" on demand. In this scenario, only the black models who are willing to work the hardest, be the best, and be better than all the rest, are going to succeed.

Astou, a Senegalese fashion model, described the differential standards to which black models were held, saying:

They ask more things of black models than they do of white models, for sure, for instance, you can see a white model who is 5'6",[67] who just has an amazing face, maybe, and not a great body, but still . . . but for black girls you have to be like very tall, very skinny, amazing body, amazing butt, everything.

While height requirements might be relaxed for certain types of model, in her experience, black models get this kind of break less often. All models are required to be tall and slender. To be "very tall, very skinny," have an "amazing body," and an "amazing butt" represents the apotheosis of requirements typical of the modeling industry, an extreme that seems to be the *baseline* entry point for black models.

If black models have to be taller, thinner, and better looking than the average model, they also have to bring a higher level of aesthetic skills to their workplace by, for instance, knowing their best makeup colors or knowing the "looks" or "types" they represent to others. Most non-ethnic models can show up at a fashion show or photo shoot clean faced and ready for makeup, where professionals transform them into the look required for the day. Black models, however, may have to develop these skills for themselves, as some make up artists are either not adept at, or do not have the tools for, making up black skin. At fashion shows, the runway model Astou found out through trial and error that she should bring her own makeup after being avoided by makeup artists on shoots:

> When you arrive, they pretend they don't see you, because they are scared, since they don't know how to do black skin. So now I do it myself. I bring my own makeup and say, "It's here, if you want to use it." And they go, "Oh my God, thank you so much! I didn't have your color." I'm so dark, it's hard for them to get my color.

Similarly, she does her own hair, to protect it from the kinds of products that are routinely used at shoots and fashion shows:

> They will put anything to have their look for that day. They just don't care. So I have extensions, which is very expensive. I have to do it every three to four weeks. I could have it done every two to three months, but I like to have it fresh, so I like to have it done a lot.

While all models must invest time and money to look right for the various markets in modeling, black models have to go that much farther, supplying their own makeup and styling their own hair in order to do the same job as white models.

Even though these professionals are hired to help them produce the look on set, they do not have the right makeup colors or are inexperienced with styling black hair. Laura, a black model who appeared on the cover of *Sports Illustrated* and was a contract model for a major cosmetics company, expressed her frustration with what she saw as a double standard, in which she was required to provide tools for the makeup artist and hair stylists that other models were not. Most of the makeup artists she dealt with were white and routinely did not have the right shades to prevent her skin from looking "ashy" or "gray." She explained,

> If you know that I was black, why don't you have a makeup artist who shows up with the right makeup? They've been on the job for a week, and they know that I'm coming on like, the third day. They have ten different base colors for white models and you can't even have one for black models? And they say, you didn't bring your base? What do you mean you didn't bring your base, all the black models bring their base!

With regard to hair, Laura also found that, often, "the hairdresser doesn't really know how to do black hair and has been afraid do it." She frequently did it herself, explaining, "I'm not losing a client because you can't be bothered to do my hair, so I'm just going to do my own hair."

In general, she found that white hair stylists knew little to nothing about styling black hair, while Japanese and Hispanic stylists, when she was lucky enough to encounter one on set, knew somewhat more. Most of the freelance hairdressers with whom she worked did not know how to do black hair. She guessed that, owing to the paucity of black models working in fashion, "they don't get much opportunity."

For these black models, the job itself was quite different than it was for white models, and their aesthetic labor took on a different tone, requiring them to shoulder the burden of the extra investments of time and money to produce the right look while dealing with what they experienced as an unhelpful attitude from those professionals who had been hired to help them achieve the right look for the client. As Laura remarked,

> Sometimes, I bring my base just because it's a perfect match and I really can't be bothered. You know what I mean? But if I happen to forget it, it shouldn't be my problem. I mean, I'm not a makeup artist. I'm not getting paid to be a makeup artist. You're the makeup artist.

As this remark suggests, sometimes black models feel like they have to do someone else's job as well as their own.

Ingrained attitudes stemming from the semiotic significance of black skin, coupled with the subjective structure of hiring in the modeling industry, leads to limited opportunities for black models. This paucity of opportunity is met with an oversupply of applicants, creating a self-imposed effort to produce a "look" that exceeds perfection by industry standards on the workers' part and extreme selectivity on the part of employers. Further, the hiring structure's organization by means of "types" smuggles in stereotypical attitudes, in which models are hired or denied work depending on how close they are to the norm of what is considered fashionably acceptable at any given time.

The way models of color are treated on the reality show *America's Next Top Model* clearly evidences the idea that it is not the system but the individuals in it who are to blame for their success or failure. As contestants (and viewers) learn to groom themselves to look fashionable during the makeover segment of each cycle, accumulating self-presentation tips from the judges' critiques, Tyra Banks sums up this intangible aspect of the work, saying, "Your personality got you to this level, but it's not going to get you to the next level. What's gonna get you to the next level is that *unh*, that *je ne sais quoi* that you just can't put your finger on, okay?"[68]

Honing this *je ne sais quoi* demands a total devotion to beauty as an empowerment strategy and a willful ignorance of underlying structures that might influence how levels of effort are evaluated. Banks, a black model herself, acknowledges the industry's rampant racism. She puts the burden of success or failure, however, on the contestants. She admonishes them to be better, faster, and stronger to succeed in a very uneven playing field. While the scouting system seems to be driven by the search for the new and different to feed the voracious hunger for new faces, at the same time, what counts as fashionable is overlaid by attitudes limiting the opportunities for certain types to achieve legitimacy within that system.

While models may not, as a group, be "aesthetically challenged," they may still suffer from what the law professor William Corbett called "appearance-based discrimination."[69] Arguably, good looks are a "bona fide occupational qualification," as outlined by Title VII of the U.S. Civil Rights Act of 1964, for the job of modeling. Yet, where race is concerned, the parameters of this qualification become fuzzy. Decision makers in the industry routinely turned to "aesthetics" to blur the line between racial and appearance-based discrimination, or what some researchers refer to as "lookism."[70]

Conceivably, recent court cases pointing out the clearly racist overtones of basing hiring decisions on looks alone in retail and other semiskilled industries are a move toward uncovering the latent racism in "lookism."[71] Yet appeals to aesthetics can veil the connection between the system of "types" used in the industry and how it reinforces taken-for-granted practices. Professionals' microlevel everyday practices construct those types, and yet participants feel they can still treat race as a thing on the macro level, separate from what they do, making this structure of meaning hard to dismantle.

Appealing to aesthetics further masks the effect of race on black models' job prospects and on-the-job experiences, leaving those who experience it little recourse for identifying it. If race is just part of a color scheme, which shade of fuchsia will look good on which skin tone becomes more important than worrying about the dearth of black models on runways and in editorial work. Cody, the head of a New York modeling agency, was unsure, for instance, whether the absence of black models in the industry during the 1980s "had anything to do with the industry being bigoted." I asked what he meant by this; he explained,

I don't think race is really an issue regarding designers and clients. I think what happens is that they get creative and they don't see their products on darker-skinned girls, which I don't understand. They don't cater towards . . . they cater more toward what their creative flow is versus what should be in their minds as far as public awareness. They might say they don't like that color on a black or an Asian girl, I'd rather have it on a Caucasian girl. That's what been said to me by designers. So, it's a color scheme, so I don't think it has anything to do with being a race issue, I think it's a creative flow.

Designers catering to their "creative flow" tend not to select black models because they do not fit the "color scheme." Yet when some in the field make it a point to use black models—as was the case in the notorious black *Vogue Italia* issue, depicting only black models in its editorial pages,[72] or when Diane von Furstenburg routinely uses more black fashion models for runway shows than her peers—appeals to aesthetics are pushed aside by political concerns. When I asked Cody whether Diane von Furstenburg's choice to use black models might only have been governed by creativity, he allowed that "she *is* the president of the CFDA [Council of Fashion Designers of America]." So, "of course" it was also a "political statement."[73]

Treating race as a color scheme leaves workers little recourse to object to the situation, as typified by the veteran black model Leo's comment, "I have no control over it. I can't make comments because I'm grateful that I have the job." It seems dissociating race from racism also works as a marketing tool in the industry. Leo, for instance, typecast himself as having an "all- American look," saying he is "very conservative, not editorial or extremely exotic." In marketing himself as "all-American," Leo explained that he is "selling to the new America." This comment about "the new America" echoes the story the industry likes to tell about itself. While most of the models I interviewed were quite cognizant of how race shapes a model's potential earning power and experiences on the job, most of the agents either denied race was a problem or claimed that the industry is very forward thinking about it. Some agents believe this openness to cultural blending puts the modeling industry on the cutting edge. Jan, a male model agent, proudly explained that

one of the great joys of the modeling business is that you see what this country will look like in one hundred years. You're at the forefront of multicultural people mixing together. What they're producing is unbelievable—a whole new type of person is evolving, the genes are mixing. That's what's so fascinating.

This search for the perfect mix has become much more common in the last five to ten years. According to casting director Collette: "Clients have been asking specifically for mixed race, or 'ethnically ambiguous' talent. This expression has become de rigueur. They want 'what is he, I don't what he is.' So when you look at the person you question their ethnic origin. It's mutable, it's not clear, and it's intentional." In this ambiguous space of mutability, race takes on a different kind of significance, which highlights the slippery nature of aesthetics within a digitized, surface-oriented world where appearance is becoming increasingly paramount.

Examining black models' glamour labor highlights how producing the model "look" shifts the burden of responsibility for any interpreted racism onto notions of aesthetics and labor. This move feeds into biopolitical notions of which bodies are valuable, which are willing to try to fit the aesthetic, and which are not. While beauty as an "empowerment strategy" extended fashion's promise to more of the population by marking some "looks" as inherently desirable, others were marked as needing work, needing a makeover, needing to work harder than the rest to even gain a toehold in fashion's fold. In this evaluative calculus, those who are unwilling or unable to work in this direction are just so much refuse, cast aside, not part of the fashion story.

Thinking about race within beauty as a biopower demands taking not only the typical racist practices of exclusion based on physical traits into account; it also necessitates sorting out "race" within biopolitics. Within this logic, racism takes on new meaning, in which, as the French philosopher Michel Foucault has argued, it is " 'far removed' from the racism that takes the 'form of mutual contempt or hatred between races.' "[74] Rather, the social theorist Patricia Clough has told us, racism, in the context of biopolitics is "deployed as something like a crude evolutionism, it permits the healthy life of some populations to necessitate the death of others, marked as nature's degenerate or unhealthy ones."[75] The fashion system in which some populations have access to the constant cycle of the cheap and chic at the cost of others who work under inhuman conditions to produce those fashions is just one example of this type of biopolitical divide. The history of black beauty employed to advance racial progress in black modeling highlights how beauty as a biopower legitimates some populations' efforts to maximize their potential while devaluing those who don't get with the fashion program.

The ability to draw this line is a tastemaker's prerogative, and as such it is a hotly guarded position. Defining beauty has long been a means of drawing the line between the human, the civilized, the legitimate, and the rest. In her argument for the biopower of beauty's role in "geopolitical contexts of neoliberalism and human rights discourses," the fashion and gender studies scholar Mimi Nguyen reminded us that, since the Enlightenment, Kantian notions of aesthetics have linked the beautiful with the good, calling on "imperial disgust" in the discernment of the beautiful from the ugly.[76] For the philosopher Immanuel Kant, *only* a European had the adequate aesthetic sensibility to determine what is beautiful, since people from other parts of the world had "no concept of the morally beautiful."[77] Since the French philosopher Michel Foucault was no stranger to Kant's idea of beauty as arousing a "feeling of life being furthered,"[78] it is not much of a stretch to see, as Nguyen does, beauty as a biopolitical force by which to "make beautiful" is to "make live."[79]

This strand is evident in the history of black modeling, as the nature of that exclusion became more complex. The careful scripting of the black model image in the cinematic regime produced a parallel narrative of black beauty, which translated into valuable energy that seemed to break through to the fashion mainstream in the regime of the glance. This temporary acceptance of the natural black girl (hair and all) was not only a response to social pressure but also to imperatives inherent in the glance regime's pull for transparency and initial rejection of artifice.

The blink's need for shorthand imaging that could have a reliable impact, however, latched onto existing types, pushing them to the extreme. Consequently, from the first push against racist imagery through assimilation to white middle-class beauty, "looking white" became one of the few routes to success for black models in fashion modeling. At the same time, the fashion world reserved a special place in its heart for the exotic, such as Donyale Luna and Iman, presented as creatures not quite of this world, for shock value. Even superstar Naomi

Figure 8.2. Opening spread for the feature "Wild Things" from *Harper's Bazaar*, September 1999, featuring Naomi Campbell. Photo by Jean-Paul Goude.

Campbell has done her fair share of primitivism, her supple limbs and shining skin appearing to give a cheetah a run for his money in one memorable spread.[80] Between these two oscillating extremes, as race morphed from immutable quality to malleable brand within the newly valued changeability of the body in the blink regime, only those willing to glamour labor the hardest to capitalize on this mutability would be rewarded.

While Kant sought to legitimate exclusions and violence based on skin morphology, the rise of digitization and the biomediated body has enabled new forms of exclusion based on concepts of the body as organism giving way to the idea of bodily potentials, used to sort populations into probabilities of more or less vitality. By this logic, those who can't or won't subscribe to the pursuit of beauty as the pursuit of the good life must be excluded from its benefits, and the dividing lines of racism extend beyond mere skin color to notions of vitality. In this configuration, an individual's productive power is not measured in how many hours of work they can do but, rather, how much they can transform or modulate themselves to become "whatever" aesthetic is in demand at any time.

Cameron, a Caucasian model agent in his mid-twenties who has seven years of scouting experience and has worked at one of the top modeling agencies in New York City, noted this use of race as an aesthetic quality, saying:

> They mine different areas of the world. Eastern Europe, South America, now one of the biggest trends I see is multicultural, models who are from mixed ethnic backgrounds. That's one of the few ways you can find a unique girl.

His statement seems to imply that the modeling industry is interested in stretching racist assumptions, but there is another process at work behind the drive to "mine the world" for a unique girl. The quest for "ever-wilder" ethnic mixes is fed at least in part by the goal of capitalizing on finer gradations of racial division, and segmentation, into markets. Further, the fascination with mixed ethnic backgrounds is fed by an interest in exoticism, in which an ethnic mix is presented as an object to be admired. In this sense, race becomes something to work with, an aesthetic, a quality to be powered up or down, similar to the way fashion plays with gender via cross-dressing and the stylization of androgyny so common in fashion images.

Overall, race in modeling plays out in three specific ways. First, model markets' subjective structure, which exacerbates racist tendencies in hiring practices, causes two outcomes. On the one hand, with no objective criteria to measure ability, modeling industry gatekeepers, such as model agents and clients who hire models, subjectively rely on the social characteristics of race and gender, categorized into "types," to recruit and market models. This practice has played out in forms of "tokenism," in which only one black model would be required for a group shot, leaving six spots available to other types of models, narrowing the number of jobs available to black models as a result. On the other hand, in the face of this structural limitation, black models I spoke to reported feeling they were held to a stricter aesthetic standard regarding their height, weight, and overall appearance, making modeling jobs not only harder for them to get but also harder to perform. Second, within this tokenism and typing, black models' glamour labor sometimes took the specific form of managing the appearance of race, in keeping with the racial "types" limiting the number of jobs available to black models. Arguably, this glamour labor of maximizing or minimizing one's racial characteristics expands the concept to encompass the embodied work elicited by the watchful eye of not only the corporate "gaze" but also the "white gaze." Thus the intensely embodied aesthetic work of those in the free-lance sector becomes more acutely evident when race is taken into account. Finally, while demands on black models to manage their racial characteristics can function to solidify existing stereotypes, model industry gatekeepers' belief they are responding to "aesthetics," not race, shields them from their own contribution to this social construction.

9

Touch-Ups

Making the Model Better

The September 1994 issue of the now-defunct women's fashion magazine *Mirabella* depicted a close-up of a model's face, described by the gushing cover copy as "an extraordinary image of great America 'beauty.'" Lovely as she was, there was something distinctly odd about her. Her vacant stare seemed almost inhuman. In fact, it was. In a headline-making move, using an increasingly popular technology, the magazine showed a model with a face digitally cobbled together by the fashion photographer Hiro from the faces of six other models.[1]

Was this the end of modeling as we knew it? It certainly was the end of something. To come full circle, this chapter returns to the 1990s, when the supermodels' onslaught of branded beauty and personalities larger than life took a turn toward a more vulnerable, frail ideal. I conclude with a discussion of the supermodels and the waifs, two iconic figures who represented not only ideal bodies but also ideal workers in the digital age. Putting them in context will engage some of the issues surrounding the conceptual underpinnings of this book, as well some future implications regarding the entanglements of bodies, images, and technology I have described.

As some would have it, the 1990s backlash against gains in women's rights in previous decades contributed to the demise of the image of strong Amazonian supermodels.[2] In addition, as the recession of the early nineties made the exuberance of the go-go eighties a thing of the past, the supermodels became too expensive and too unwieldy to sustain themselves, according to some professionals in the industry. Whatever the case, in the early nineties, numerous journalistic accounts relayed the "death" of the supermodel.[3] Suddenly small was in, and no model was smaller or more vulnerable looking than Kate Moss. The anti-supermodel, Moss became the iconic figure of the age, with exactly

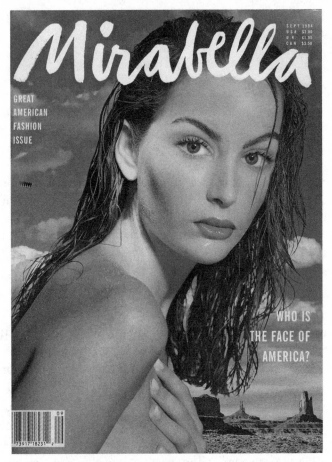

Figure 9.1. *Mirabella* cover, September 1994.

opposite proportions to the 1980s glamazonian queens, her blank, inscrutable expression, small stature, and refusal to speak a wholesale rejection by the fashion industry of the physicality and personality that had come before.[4]

There is more to the story, however, than tightening neoliberal constraints and a rejection of the femme fatale image. As the feminist scholars Donna Haraway, Elizabeth Grosz, and Judith Butler remind us, the body is a "material semiotic node," a nexus of various technologies, cultural and social, mediating and productive.[5] As the preceding examples have illustrated, thinking of the body this way requires linking imaging technology to whatever productive and scientific technologies hold sway, at whatever moment the fashionable body is considered. From the syncopated efficiency of the flapper, to the smoothly calibrated haughtiness of the mid-century swan, followed by the staccato rhythms of the 1960s "it" girl, the techno-utopian dreams of the cyborg followed through to the algorithmic morphing of today's fleeting ideal, a drive for visibility and exposure animated each successive regime.

Figure 9.2. Kate Moss for Calvin Klein, Spring 1994.

Changes in the nature of modeling work, overall, and especially since the 1990s, have altered how modeling engages with fashion and glamour labor and how fashion and modeling have created and pulled publics into a mediated system circulating bodily energies. Fashion modeling work attracts publics to glamour labor, hooking them to technologies that measure, seek to shape, and also enhance the ebbs and flows of moods, feelings, propensities, and vitality—components of our affectivity.[6] On a broader scale, modeling in the age of the blink serves as a metaphor for the merging of biomedia and social media at the site of the fashionable ideal, to illustrate how the "affective shimmer"[7] of this regime has pulled for a new logic of the body's value.

Pixels, Perfection, and the Fashionable Ideal

In 1982, Jane Fonda released a series of workout tapes that would soon become a cultural phenomenon.[8] Riding Jane's coattails, supermodel Cindy Crawford appeared in a series of "wildly successful" exercise tapes. Publicly declaring that she was "never going to be a size zero," Crawford, in a shapely red leotard, demonstrated how to achieve her supermodel physique. Despite the fact that achieving this physique might never come to pass for the average American couch potato, thousands bought the video and, so, bought into the idea that the glamour and beauty of being a model could be theirs as well, as long as they worked hard enough at it.[9]

In the late 1980s and early 1990s images of models became more toned (or "buff" in the contemporary parlance), exhibiting what one fashion history expert Harold Koda terms a "powerful physicality" visible in the "deep contours" of Linda Evangelista's strong back, for instance, or the tightly toned, muscular, yet refined silhouette presented by Christy Turlington's shoulders or Naomi Campbell's long dancer's legs.[10] Markets built around the care and tending of various body parts grew as gym culture boomed.

Both men and women jumped on the fitness bandwagon; as aerobics became a buzzword, Arnold Schwarzenegger made his ascent to a cultural icon in the aftermath of his late seventies *Pumping Iron* (1977) fame. The level of gym memberships rose from the 1980s onward.[11] As gym memberships rose, more and more bodies came under the logic of accumulation, which operated by plumbing the desire to get fit and look right as a new source of corporate profit.[12]

Much was made of the supermodels' new "look" in part because it revered a new way of being in the body. Midway through the 1990s, the famed fashion photographer Steven Meisel observed that

> women today are striving to be perfect, to be the ultimate Barbie doll. . . . I can't think back in history where women have been so plastic. I mean, how many women are going out to have face lifts and are having their teeth done and are dying their hair? Sociologically, it's definitely a modern thing.[13]

This trend toward a "plastic" or worked-over body originated in the early twentieth-century dream of the rationalized body. This dream evolved as cybernetics and biotechnology emerged as new productive forces within the United States's economy. In this transition, the dream of the ideal body morphed from mechanized syncopation to a machine body hybrid. It is now evolving again, toward the notion of a fully manipulatable, microdissectible body composed of units of information susceptible to calculation and optimization. Digitization facilitated thinking of the body as information, flattened out into a series of ones and zeros, easily divided into pixilated units open to configuration through connection to other dynamic systems, shifting the metaphor to a modular body, an open system that is easy to change. This growth of digital technologies incited a trend toward treating the body as an accumulation strategy, to be invested in not just as a worker but also as a productive resource, both in terms of its physicality and in terms of its social connectedness.

The informatization of the body had key effects on the fashionable ideal. The cyborg body, almost inhuman in its worked-out, plucked, polished, sculpted, and manufactured dimensions, became a cultural trademark of the 1980s and early 1990s. A cyborg is a body/machine hybrid, part organic, part technological. The figure of the cyborg moved into the popular imagination during the 1970s and 1980s. As the *Six Million Dollar Man*'s minor prostheses graduated to the *Terminator*'s full-body treatment, *Blade Runner*'s cyborgs seduced us as aerobicized, carefully sculpted bodies emerged from gyms across the country and slunk across the pages of fashion magazines.[14] While the 1920s lithe figure of the flapper translated the ideal of mechanized perfection into human form and warriors of the 1960s slimming culture such as Twiggy and Penelope Tree embodied television's idealized cybernetically controlled loops of inputs and outputs, the ideal of the biomechanically engineered body found expression in the sculpted muscles of the supermodels. The supermodel epitomized the cyborg, the body perfected beyond recognition, slimmed to the max while also being built up beyond "normal" proportions. Supermodel Christy Turlington described this "glamazon" ideal, saying, "You couldn't be too tall, the hair couldn't be too big and the boobs were pushed up and out."[15] Musician George Michael's 1992 video *Too Funky* clearly depicted the idealization of this look.[16] In the video, supermodels' bodies, transformed via elaborate breastplates and head dresses into the smooth metallic planes of a robot, or the swooping angles of a sports car, glided down a runway to an insistent beat.

This altogether-different body—born of the digitized, post-industrial regime of computerization, robotization, and miniaturization—represented a new ideal: the porous body, open to technology and, in fact, inseparable from it.[17] The digital technologies that gave rise to the Internet have capitalized on this porousness, affording unprecedented access to bodily affectivity, the in-excess of being, the energy and mutability that characterize living things. Harnessing or at least channeling that energy has been made possible by the kinds of entanglements with technology that have become normal and desirable, such as being totally wired, to hone and promote your brand whenever possible, to the point at which your every sleeping and waking moment is being tracked, systematized, and networked, in the process of doing your best glamour labor.

The turn toward understanding bodies in terms of affectivity can help explain why, for instance, fashion imaging moved from molding specific consumer desires toward creating a more diffuse attachment to, or feeling about, a brand, as evidenced in modeling work's move from being highly scripted to being more open to a model's vulnerability and ability to project a feeling or mood, a shift this book documents. Arguably, this changed goal in models' imaging work, from producing loyal customers to promoting a brand, represented an attempt to harness previously unexploited forms of human energy for productive ends, as modeling

Figure 9.3. Emma Sjöberg wears the ensemble "Super Star Diana
Ross" in the Theirry Mugler Prêt-à-Porter Collection, Spring–
Summer 1991. Emma Sjöberg wore the same outfit in the video,
directed by Thierry Mugler, for the song "Too Funky" by George
Michael (1992). Sjöberg also appeared wearing a bustier designed
to look like a motorcycle. The video included Sjöberg, Tyra Banks,
Nadia Auermann, Estelle Hallyday, and Linda Evangelista. The
video was intended as a follow-up to Michael's "Freedom '90"
video, which featured all the supermodels (Naomi Campbell,
Tatjana Patitz, Linda Evangelista, Christy Turlington, Cindy
Crawford). Photo by Patrice Stable.

shifted and molded itself toward channeling affective energy for profit. As microelectronics enabled the increased inroads of biotechnology and social technologies as dominant forces in our culture, optimization and enhancement of the physical and social body informed the fashionable ideal, making bio- and social analytics into a new stock-in-trade within the mechanisms of glamour labor. The fully enhanced or optimized body, as a cultural ideal, feeds a notion of the body as something to be dissected and manipulated, worked on as individual parts, each brought to its maximum level of enhancement or optimization.[18] Glamour labor operates within forms of capital accumulation that increases productivity through improved organization or invention, increasing quantification and measurement of potentials to become, to connect, to coalesce into publics that become markets. As technologies of health became technologies of life, the mood shifted from the pursuit of health through bodily intervention and biotechnology toward the pursuit of the body pushed beyond its limits, the supernormal, the human, but fully enhanced. Rather than motivation to make lifestyle changes by avoiding dangers—such as breast cancer, or heart disease, to which we are susceptible—the force of obligation shifted from prevention to prediction, in a move from avoidance to enhancement. Increasingly, bodies are valued as potentials, indexed to market dynamics, not in terms of labor time, but "lifetime."[19]

Thus the regime of the blink saw the ascendance of a new ideal body, made available to technological intervention and enhancement, in the form of the worked-on, worked-out, "working-it," fully connected body. The supermodel and the waif embodied two extremes, diametrically opposed ideals that the historian of beauty Lois Banner notes originated in the burgeoning consumer culture of the early 1900s. One ideal was "adolescent and childlike" while the other was "voluptuous and earthy."[20] Adding a class dimension to the analysis, Banner argues that the flapper idealized a lean line in part to avoid pornographic associations with the hourglass figure popular in the theater and the "working class culture from which it had emerged."[21] Later years saw fashion's gaunt mannequins evoking an "adolescent asexual model of beauty" juxtaposed with the "voluptuous earthy one," embodied quite clearly in the 1950s by the likes of actresses Jayne Mansfield and Marilyn Monroe, or again in the

1970s by model Lauren Hutton's rangy physique contrasting with actress Raquel Welch's lush curves.

In the 1990s, the feminist philosopher Susan Bordo noted the continued persistence of these two ideals of feminine attractiveness, although she described them as a muscular, athletic look and a "spare, 'minimalist' look."[22] For Bordo, these body types also represent two opposing developments in feminine beauty ideals, which sent a paradoxical, yet productive, message. Compulsive dieting to reduce the body, on the one hand, and body building to beef it up, on the other, both combated a form of cultural anxiety about "internal processes out of control—uncontained desire, unrestrained hunger, uncontrolled impulse."[23] Reducing to the bone or building muscles up represent a battle in the "struggle to manage desire in a system dedicated to the proliferation of desirable commodities."[24] Bordo sees this regulation of desire in consumer society as problematic. It pulls publics in opposite directions. First, the kind of self-restraint necessitated by a proper work ethic, which drives the economy, is highly admired and rewarded. At the same time, the availability of these rewards foments desire. The glittering attractions of consumer display stimulates our "hunger for constant and immediate satisfaction," which in turn also drives the economy.[25]

While Banner is interested in class divisions, Bordo's focus is on anxieties, in a form of cultural angst that drives consumer culture. What these two scholars do not see, or are less interested in exploring, is the productive capacity of the bodies themselves. The body's constant modulation, from built-up to pared down, organizes and drives the economy just as much as the anxiety Bordo identified. Further, while Banner's analysis correctly identified important class components of the dominant ideal, it misses the influence of scientific, imaging, and production technologies on how this bodily aesthetic first emerged and has been driven to extremes in the last several decades.

The regime of the blink seems to push all favored female silhouettes toward the nth degree, toward an outsized (or downsized, in the case of models) version of their origins. In the excess valued by the age of the blink, fashion models have grown more finely muscled or exceedingly thin, even as the fleshy curves so long ago popularized by silent-screen star Theda Bara's Venusian silhouette were later pushed to extremes

Figure 9.4. Image of Theda Bara from *Cleopatra* (1917).

by the likes of actress/model Pamela Anderson's epic proportions, the rounded orbs and convex valleys of her body created by the surgeon's knife. In this cultural moment, stars like Kim Kardashian and Beyoncé also display voluptuous silhouettes, their derrieres making news whenever they are on display.

Perhaps extremes in body styles in the last few decades have resulted from forces other than just the creation of consumer desire, patriarchy, or designers' status competition and aesthetics at work. Why isn't consumerism fully to blame? Fantasy may sell, but if skinny models are what every consumer wants to see and to be like, how does this explain the late 2000s backlash against this look?[26] Further, if clothes can be shown to their best advantage only on "tiny" models, why have successful models come in various proportions, from tall and rangy to short and voluptuous, for most of modeling's history, and why have they shrunken precipitously only in recent years? With regard to the fact that "fantasy" sells, my respondents used the word "aspirational" to describe the kinds of images that promote an impossible physique, one that rarely occurs in nature, as the ideal. The idea behind an impossible standard is to presumably keep the public striving (and buying products) to reach it. Of course, creating a sense of inadequacy in consumers has worked well as a sales strategy, with images that promise to confer the youth, sexiness, and glamour prospective buyers woefully lack if only they would buy the product.

If a slender model promotes a sense of inadequacy that drives consumers to buy products to try to be more like her, then an even-more slender model will produce a more extreme sense of lack and drive more intense consumer desire. This argument may go some way toward explaining the trend toward extreme model downsizing in recent years. Yet how can it explain the maintenance and, some argue, a worsening of these standards despite obvious public discomfort with the ever-shrinking ideal? While the model scholar Ashley Mears has compellingly argued that the model "look" at any given time can be tied quite clearly to status competition among elites in the industry, and so is essentially de-linked from any influence by public opinion, she is less interested in explaining how the model "look" has changed in recent years.

Can the powerfully repressive forces of patriarchy alone explain this idealization of slender or frail-looking women as a fashionable "look"? The idea that women's gains in power in the workplace and family life, which have allowed them to take up more social space and power, caused the image of the desirable woman to shrink, literally taking up less space and projecting an image of powerlessness, has its merits. It does not adequately account, however, for the most recent extreme attenuation of female models' bodies I am describing here. If the fashionable body is the slender, asexual one, then there is more to the picture than just patriarchal influences when it come to the look of fashionable bodies.

Are the designers to blame? Arguing, as the designers and agents do, that a slender model is a better clothes hanger does little to explain the recently intensified attenuation of the ideal, in which female models who stand 5'10" yet have twenty-three- inch waists have become more common, as evidenced by the measurements of the 2000s models Agyness Deyn and her 5'11", twenty-three- inch-waisted contemporary Caroline Trentini. Similarly, Lara Stone, who has had a reputation for being a more voluptuous model, while towering tall as Trentini, at times has had a twenty-two-inch waist. A survey of current models also reveals lesser-knowns such as Aleksandra Marczyk, who is 5'10" and measures 33-23-35,[27] and Anna Z., who measures a precise 5'11.5" yet has the diminutive measurements of 32.5-22.5-35.5.[28] If consumerism, fashion designer's aesthetics, or patriarchal forces do not adequately explain recent changes in the fashionable ideal over the last twenty or so years, what does? If these others forces could fully explain it, then the ideal would have remained the same for as long as patriarchy, consumerism, and fashion designer's desires have held sway.

Yet the ideal has changed more in the last few years than it has in the decades all the way from modeling's inception up until the 1990s, when these more rapid changes started to occur.[29] In findings comparing beauty pageant winners, Playboy Bunnies, and models, for instance, the break after the 1990s was evident across the board. While all groups became steadily slimmer for the several decades between the 1950s and the 1970s, after the 1990s, there was a pronounced turn around. While models still became slimmer, Playboy Bunnies actually gained weight.[30]

While designer's desires, patriarchal forces, and rampant consumerism have had some influence, the newfound ability to manipulate information, and bodies themselves, through medical intervention and digitization has profoundly affected the model ideal. The digital image is the fully manipulatable image. Digitizing the material into the virtual, and therefore the alterable, is an increasingly common practice of the digital age. The cultural interest in manipulating the body, starting from the 1970s fitness craze and continuing on through recent fascinations with surgical and pharmaceutical bodily modification, represents a shift to investing in the methods of extraction from the body itself as raw material, rather than, say, investing in coal mining or steel production. Beyond the patriarchal and consumerist ideologies some theorists blame for the intensified demand, especially on women, for engaging in slimming or bodily fitness management techniques, I point also to the idealization of a new form of productive body: the body merged with technology.

Arguing from this angle adds a new layer to understandings of culturally idealized bodies. Read this way, the lean lines that fashion models depict represent more than what the feminist Sharlene Nagy Hesse-Biber calls a "cult of thinness" that is tyrannizing women. When Hesse-Biber claims that, during the 1980s, women were pushed to resemble a "slender Amazon" whose "subcutaneous fat layer, which gives the softness to the female physique, has been rejected in favor of large, hard muscles," she is not only describing a cult-like thinness but also the cyborg ideal represented most readily by the physicality of the 1980s supermodels.[31] When the feminist sociologist Victoria Pitts-Taylor blames images of skinny models for the exponential rise in cosmetic surgeries, she is linking surgical work on the body to the idealization of the waif-like proportions best represented by Kate Moss in the 1990s. Certainly Pitts-Taylor is right to claim that the expansion in plastic surgery rates in the United States, which quadrupled between 1984 and 2005, reaching a new total of two million operations, is "astonishing," especially when combined with the over eight million non-surgical procedures, such as Botox and skin resurfacing performed in the same time frame, which brings the total to ten million.[32] The rise in rates of elective cosmetic surgery are not only evidence of women making themselves into the types of "docile bodies" the French theorist Michel Foucault describes, as Pitts-Taylor claims. The fact that so many have gone under the knife is also evidence of the rise of the kind of glamour labor that seeks to stimulate bodily modulation as a normalized practice.

This logic helps elucidate how the trend toward attenuation of the fashionable body now seems to be affecting male models' bodies as well. Some industry insiders have referred to the relatively recent attenuation of the male ideal as the "Slimanization" of male models, referencing the Dior Homme designer Hedi Slimane, who began presenting slim-cut suits on male models who were "thin to the point of resembling stick figures," as one fashion pundit put it, in the mid- 2000s.[33] Slimane seems to have started a trend with far-reaching consequences. As the *New York Times* fashion and lifestyle commentator Guy Trebay points out, "somebody shrunk the men," explaining that, "where the masculine ideal as recently as 2000 was a buff 6-footer with six-pack abs, the man of the moment is an urchin, a wraith or an underfed runt."[34] While body styles may come and go with the fashion seasons, even the market is betting on the long-term effect of this particular trend, translating it from high fashion to the more prosaic realm of men's underwear in the form of a corset of sorts: a waist-cinching, stomach-flattening T-shirt to be worn under a man's regular clothes. Demand for this constricting garment was surprisingly high. In the summer of 2009, Saks sold almost a third of its inventory in less than four weeks, which, according to the men's fashion director there, is "incredible."[35] In 2012, Spanx, the "body compression" shapewear line that has been extremely successful with women, introduced a menswear line, aptly called "Manx," which promised "precision targeted shaping power," as the Neiman Marcus website put it, for only $78.00 a T-shirt.[36] It seems perhaps that Susan Bordo is right to call the "starving white girls" the "forward guard, the miners' canaries warning of how poisonous the air was becoming for everyone."[37] Bordo couldn't have seen, however, the complexities that emerged with the new fluidities of "both/and" borne of the age of the blink.

Muscular to thin and back again, as long as the body is being manipulated, broken down into variable parts, it is playing a newly attractive role in the matrix of production. This trend exemplifies a tendency to take the fashionable body to the nth degree, super built up or super skinny, always in the process of moving from one end of the pendulum swing to the other, never arriving at either, in a new regime where good is never good enough and the work is never done. In other words, in the regime of the blink, it is not the imposition of a standard of thinness that matters, it is the activation of productive processes that regulate rates of weight loss or gain, body building or reduction, the transformation from one state to another. Driven to seek enhancement, always optimizing to try to reach a receding threshold, in the age of the blink, new populations are pulled into performing, or at least wanting to perform, glamour labor as modulated waves of affectivity resonate in and through bodies. Because the ideal model body is continually shaped by the whims of fashion, models are the perfect ambassadors for this kind of lifestyle, urging everyone to engage with it.

Supermodels, Waifs, and the Glamour Labor Lifestyle

The supermodels glamorized this total exposure, since they made the work of being "always on" look glamorous and fun, just like the fashion models I interviewed, who report it as a 24/7 job. Here, I am reminded of the model I interviewed in a model apartment who exclaimed, "It's like a lifestyle, it takes over you life. It's not like when you go work at the Gap and then come home and be normal." This trend began back in the 1970s and 1980s, when the demand for models to be "camera ready" expanded beyond their work in the studio to encompass every moment of their waking lives. Once producing one's "look" became part of the job, the 1980s supermodels embraced this new requirement. As Veronica Webb, one of the few successful black models in the 1980s,[38] remembers it, they performed the job of being camera ready to perfection, saying, "None of those girls are stupid. You would never catch them not looking fabulous, not dressed, not up-to-the-minute, not being that thing."[39]

By becoming "that thing," the supermodels were shaping both their bodily energies and interpersonal social connections to enhance and optimize them, to take them to the max, to use the lingo of the era in which they were a strong social force. As the previous chapters argue, models helped make publics see themselves as always already in need of a makeover, by glamorizing the willingness to engage in constant control over and efforts to improve their "look," as well as to project the right kind of personality, to increase their influence.[40] Consequently, as the malleable body became the new fashionable norm, models glamorized the goal of pushing the body toward being constantly made over, always already in the process of transformation.

While the worked-out and worked-up body of the cyborg came to epitomize the fashionable and productive ideal on one side, the emaciated proportions of the waif came to be the face of the other. These models exuded a kind of vulnerability that depicted the body in need of intervention, to be shored up by biotechnological solutions to strengthen and extend its life force, a force the waifs so obviously lacked. At the same time, they epitomized the ultra-attenuated fashion ideal—where the supermodels were sculpted warriors, the waifs, born of the age the blink, presented starved-looking bodies to time-starved eyeballs, too distracted to notice anything less than a body at the edge of its powers, seeking to exceed its conventional limits, standing in sheer opposition to the aesthetic that came before. The half-fed-looking waifs glamorized the notion of "heroin chic," beautiful bodies wasted by drugs at a time coinciding with the growing power of pharmaceutical companies, whose proficiency in producing biotechnology made profits by identifying and proposing treatments for diseased bodies, prosthetics for inadequate bodies, and drug therapies, such as Viagra, for those bodies that simply didn't perform.[41] In the image of the cyborg, the ideal of a body hybridized with machines in the robotization of modern production gave way to that of a body actually merging with the machine via biotechnologies in the compliant figure of the waif.[42]

The supermodels and the waifs idealized this body intermingled with technology, not only by depicting the human figure in a state of continual alteration and modulation, with an eye toward physical enhancement, but also in enhancing and optimizing the lifestyle they adopted in the course of their work. In this climate, enhancement technologies, both bodily and social, become very attractive as market and consumer culture shaped demands for intervention to produce not just healthy bodies but glamorous ones.

Placed as they were at the forefront of body culture, images of models became instrumental in pulling the general public into the matrix of bodily production, glamorizing not only the worked-on, worked-up, and "working-it" body but also the flexible risk-taking worker, willing to engage in forms of self-scrutiny, management, and manipulation, as I have discussed. Tentatively in the late 1970s and coming into full force in the 1980s onward, models were not only pressured to achieve a "photo-ready" look, both onstage and off, they were increasingly encouraged to model a lifestyle that encouraged everyone to do the same. This lifestyle involved keeping up with fashion, not only by following clothing trends but also by engaging wholeheartedly in the work of producing an appropriate image. Not only was the pursuit of the ever-shrinking waistline or the worked-out body sold to us by models who seemed to embody this ideal, the heightened level of public awareness of modeling helped to sell modeling itself as a desirable lifestyle that encompassed working out, looking good and being connected, in the know, and up on what's fashionable.

Figure 9.5. Stella Tennant from "Serious Fun" in *Mirabella*, September 1994, photographed by Glen Luchford in Las Vegas. Tennant was shot with an elongating lens to make her look even taller and thinner, and her pose deliberately apes Twiggy, her hip bones are jutting through her dress.

This malleable ideal can be more fully grasped by showing how the notion of what makes a "good" worker, for any given era, shaped modeling. In the 1920s, for instance, the qualities for the ideal worker were quite different than they are today. The best kinds of workers were up to standard, interchangeable, and as controlled and predictable as possible. Conformism was good; someone who could fall into lockstep to produce a rationalized, predictable product was ideal. Consequently, the models idealized in this era were presented as a matched set, pretty maids in a row, with identical smiles and outfits (recall John Robert Powers's "uniform" of the crinolined skirt and hatbox for his models). The conformist ideal held sway through to at least the middle of the last century, but with the forces of de-industrialization and the rise of the service and information economy, especially in the United States, a new ideal emerged. This ideal was the manic worker, someone who is always going to the extreme, ready to train herself, push herself to the limit, work 24/7, be unpredictable, a networked entrepreneur full of new ideas. As noted by the previous examples, the ideal model as glamour laborer sought to commodify her physicality, life, and leisure time, placing no limits, reserving nothing "outside" the market transaction, in an effort to fully commit to managing her being in the world to seek full optimization on all fronts, biological and social.[43] As the previous chapters have illustrated, this work epitomizes glamour labor in the affective mode, which seeks to capitalize on the body's tendency to exceed its boundaries. Pushing for this excess paradoxically resulted in models being both more tightly controlled yet also set loose to find their own way, with the hope that they might bring something unexpected to the table. While models "model" a willingness to submit to micro levels of measurement and management in the course of their daily work, they also are expected to bring something immeasurable to the work transaction (to "be a rat," for instance, or just "go with the flow"). In so doing, they epitomize the ideal worker, the one willing to submit to any means of manipulation and incitement to get the goal of hitting it big, living "the life," being on the inside of glamour.

My data also illustrate that fashion models—constantly on the move, traveling to follow the fashion calendar—epitomize the flexible, mobile worker, one that is up for constant re-skilling, ready to change from job to job at a moment's notice. In this sense, models epitomize the "manic" worker, the unpredictable "crazy" genius, the artist whose very inconsistency is a quality to be rewarded, as the anthropologist Emily Martin has described. While she is not interested in the concept of affect, Martin's words hint at the growing importance of affective flow between bodies, facilitated by new imaging and connective technologies. Models "model" the "manic" worker, driven by animal spirits, unpredictable, always on the go, always already in the process of making over, consistently engaging with body-modulating technologies—or giving the appearance of doing so—working for that element of surprise or delight in the process of glamorizing this engagement as fun or something desirable for all.

As models were encouraged to embrace these demands as part of the job, they inadvertently glamorized them, their youth and attractiveness making it seem fun to pick up stakes and travel to another country to seek work or to work around the clock without a break in the kind of "stop-go 'bulimic' patterns . . . in which periods with no work can give way to periods that require intense activity," which cultural labor scholars have described in other sectors of the creative industries.[44] Further, by constantly working on their body, to always be ready to change in keeping with fashion's whims, they glamorized the practice, making what once seemed optional into something everyone should want to do. By making it look fun and cool, being the perfect chameleons (for which Linda Evangelista, with her constantly changing look, was famous), models—and, more important, the modeling lifestyle projected to the public by the countless televisions shows, websites, and news coverage devoted to the subject—glamorized the constant need to transform one's body and persona to match a changing ideal and attracted publics to the kinds of social and visual technologies that regularize interactions in ways that are quantifiable and therefore subject to new forms of manipulation.[45]

Analogous to accumulating the body's vitality in terms of storing dead tissue to enliven the living, for instance, social media organize and store up information about community and connection that potentially could be mobilized as a source of profit if those connections can be made to push the energy of the population toward particular activities (of biotechnical enhancement, or consumption of other goods). The profit lies in exposing one's vital forces to quantification, organization, and intervention on both the biological and social fronts, in the form of glamour labor I have described.

While he does not use the term, the social theorist Jonathan Beller sees glamour labor's mining of the body, its feelings, its reactions, its potential for connection and action—that is, its vitality—as a kind of "burrowing into the flesh" in order to solve the capitalist problem of "expansion and the falling rate of profit."[46] Vitality, as a resource, is extracted by coupling the body with technologies that channel its life energies for profit—via the offer of a gym to manage a body's fitness; or drugs that play on the desire to grow hair, control an unruly child, or promote sexual potency; or screens to draw attention, as they play on the desire to be "in the know" and feel part of something; or communication channels that illustrate just how "in the know" you are.

As the philosopher Judith Butler reminds us, bodies are given via frames of intelligibility, and biology, imaging technologies, and fashion all frame the lived body.[47] The notion of the biomediated body, which dictates that biology is increasingly framed by technology to make it productive, is a central tenet in my conception of how glamour labor works.[48] My thinking about how affect and affective energy are bodily potential that can be harnessed to profit from its mutability uses a conception of affect informed by biology's capacity to mutate or create, whose expansion has recently been enabled via biomediation.

The gradual transition in the dominant imaging regimes in the United States is the story of frames. As I have argued throughout, from the body enframed by the photograph, to the narrative frame of the cinematic gaze, to television's staccato, frame-jumping glance, to the pixilated blink of digitization, each regime has pulled the body into a new frame of intelligibility. Martin Heidegger argues in his famous essay "The Question Concerning Technology" that "technology is a way of revealing," one of whose chief characteristics is regulating that which it reveals. Interestingly, he uses the notion of "enframing" to denote the process that takes place when humans and technology interact.[49] I take from this notion the idea that the development of photographic imaging technology not only literally enframed the human form but also brought with it a drive toward exposing that form, in a push toward an opening up of the body to this nascent technology. If technology's essence tends toward revealing, penetration, and a challenge to reveal all that comes within its purview, then it makes sense that photographic technology tended to pull for a body that was fully exposed, the opacity of the body penetrated and made transparent by exposure, moving it toward the ideal of the "flesh colored glaze" described by the philosopher Jeremy

Gilbert-Rolfe as characteristic of the surface lit from within, typical of the regime of the blink.[50]

The camera's "new way of seeing" also conferred reality on the body. The cultural theorist Susan Sontag, in her classic treatment of the genre, *On Photography*, explains, "We learn to see ourselves photographically; to regard oneself as attractive is, precisely, to judge that one would look good in a photograph."[51] This ideal's inexorable pull is intensified by the tendency, in industrial countries, for people to "seek to have their photographs taken" because they believe that they are "made real by photographs" in a social acknowledgement or recognition.[52] This tendency organizes populations via a biopolitics of beauty into glamour laborers who seek to be photographed as a value or a good and those who don't know how or don't want to. This process pits "real" people against "others," applying differential values to different parts of the population.

Within this biopolitical logic, those who seek to have their photograph taken are more real than those who end up in photographs because of tragedy in their lives. Those who become real via a representation of themselves are seen as more powerful as the image actually pulls the body into reality. As the visual theorist Kaja Silverman argues, our bodies and representations of them are far less distant than we like to believe. In fact, by identifying ourselves via culturally ratifying images, we experience a "corporeal assimilation of the image" that "collapses the distance between the body and the image which defines it."[53] Body ideals become bodies in the flesh in the moment of assimilating the image when a "transformation of actual muscles and flesh into a photographic representation" occurs. In this moment, according to the French theorist Roland Barthes, the photograph becomes "the corset of my imaginary essence."[54]

Thus corseted, the ideal body was the photographed body. The next frame of intelligibility, the cinematic regime, then shaped the ideal according to its peculiar nature. Film fragments images, and viewers suture them back together, producing a continuity where there was none. In the cinematic moment, advertising, by Liz Moor's sociological analysis, provided a mode of "suturing" citizens into a capitalist system of consumption, where consuming marketed products provided "the only means to achieve various social and personal ends."[55] The resulting "automation of perception," the theorist Jonathan Crary argues, made "synthesis . . . mandatory," an automation that "continues unabated along other lines today."[56] This process of suturing viewer to machine fostered an "'industrialization' of visual consumption."[57] This structuring experience made "the fragmentation of perception inherent in the apparatus" into a "mechanically produced continuum that 'naturalized' the disjunctions."[58]

When the cinematic gaze standardized vision, attaching it to the mechanized syncopation of the projector, model's bodies were standardized as well, trained and honed by the first model agency founder John Robert Powers's Long Stemmed American Beauties, their seeming disjunctions "naturalized" under Powers strict care. At the same time, internalizing the wire and bones of corsetry pulled this mechanical bodily practice into the realm of the biological. Rather than apply a piece of technology (the corset) to the body from without, the body itself absorbed the technology, becoming a resource to be optimized and enhanced, either disciplined or "cured" of the tendency to exceed the boundaries of acceptability or incited to push these boundaries into new productive terrains. Subsequent forms of imaging brought new ideas and called for new ways of being in the rhythms of enforced obsolescence, elevating the ephemeral nature of attention as a productive force. Within what Crary called a new economics of "attraction/distraction," fashion imagery promoted fashion seasons, trends, and images, entraining audiences into new forms of attentiveness, broadening the terrain of glamour labor.

After the move to television as a dominant norm, and especially since the onset of digitization, modularizing the body, separating it into discreet parts to be manipulated, for optimization and enhancement, began to dominate bodily practices and inform how models' bodies were managed to maximize their productivity in the age of the blink. This process is especially evident in what the French philosopher Gilles Deleuze identifies as "faciality," in which the body and face are translated into surfaces that mobilize signification in new ways. While Deleuze does not use this term to discuss models directly, this process arguably describes how the whole ensemble of the face, the hair, the look of the model's movements, the skin, and the details of the model image gradually usurped the body as the dominant object in the space of the photograph, a process that emerged as an important force in the 1960s. The pull by the shift in imaging regimes toward the pictorial order of television, then, contributed to an intensification of the glamour labor of models, insofar as the most intimate details of their appearance, especially the face, the key conveyor of affect, became a whole new focus of attention and investment.

In the shift from the narrative construction of the subject in the cinematic norm of imaging to the "auto affective circuit" of the televisual, images were no longer edited together seamlessly to construct a narrative with which the viewing subject identified, finding their subject position within the story.[59] In contrast, in the televisual regime, "neither narrative nor stories are necessarily or primarily the way in which the viewer and television are attached to each other."[60] With the televisual, in particular, comes the notion of automatic time, photographic time in which duration is conceived as instantaneous, moving faster than the subject, in which images are generated by imaging machines in an "autonomous series" that "requires no interval to pass through a subjective formation."[61] Rather, images affect viewers directly, making points of contact, leaving impulses, intensities, and perhaps actions in their wake.

When television's glow eventually animated many a living room, its cybernetic feedback loops quickened the pace of perception from the gaze to the glance, while a new attraction to surfaces lit from within idolized the dewy-faced glow of coltish girls such as Twiggy and Penelope Tree, a look later epitomized by the fresh-scrubbed beauties such as Christie Brinkley, and Cheryl Tiegs. This imaging regime's laws of transmission created a new sense of urgency. The television image's immediacy, what the television scholar Mary Ann Doane calls its "present-ness," created a new set of demands for image makers.[62] Suddenly, in the intimacy of the small screen, faces were brought to viewers up close and personal. Small details, like how much one sweats, took on new significance, as indicated by the 1960 presidential debate, in which some claim Nixon's pallor and profusely sweating brow lost him the election.

These trends pulled for a new way of interacting with the camera, making the face paramount. This new imaging mode pulled for work with what the social theorist Nigel Thrift calls the kinds of "deep-seated physiological change written involuntarily on the face."[63] Calling on semi-conscious resources of being, working to bring them to the surface, models were learning to mine "deep expressive habits" to hone a sort of "anticipatory readiness about the world," to be responsive for the camera.[64]

In the contemporary regime of the blink, imaging practices have morphed to accommodate shortened attention spans, as capitalism chases the productive power not only of the ability to work but also of bodily vitality itself. This is the era in which, as the feminist scholar Patricia Clough points out, the "function of media as a socializing/ ideological mechanism has become secondary to its continuous modulation, variation, and intensification of affective response in real time."[65] In this environment, we need to look not at "presumptions about the power of meaning" or the "deep structures of subjectivity," as the sociologists Don Slater and Joanne Entwistle remind us.[66] We need, instead, to track how technical apparatuses link us to brands, images, or models within social and bodily interactions sparked by packaging, advertising images, Twitter feeds, and other media. Looking at how the work of making these images has changed over time reveals significant changes in understandings about what a body is and what it is for.

Conclusion

The Affective Turn

While I do not claim that my findings from the modeling industry can resolve debates about mind/body dualism, my work engages with questions of how bodies are conceived to examine how those conceptions shape social action and affective systems of power and regulation. This chapter situates my findings about modeling, embodiment, and technology in the debates about affect stirred up in the age of the blink. Starting in the mid 2000s, as the blink regime pulled bodily forces of affect and affectivity into new networks of value, affect became an urgent concept to investigate within academic circles.[1] Pushing the notion of affect to include an interim space between body and mind, physiological arousal and conscious realization of it, dovetailed with the move toward exploring post-structuralist notions of the body. The "affective turn" in social theorizing built on post-structuralist feminist accounts of the self and the body (such as those found in the work of Elizabeth Grosz, Judith Butler, and Donna Haraway),[2] which sought to destabilize the notion of the rational, self-governed subject. The notorious post-modern "death of the subject" favored a conception of self, body, gender, and materiality that did not assume the existence of a subject residing in what the sociologist Erving Goffman refers to as an "epidermally bounded container."[3] Rather, it depicted the self as what the social theorist Donna Haraway has famously termed a "material semiotic node,"[4] existing through interaction, ineluctably entangled in shifting networks of culture, power, language, and images.

Affect can be a confusing concept, since, as the media scholars Melissa Gregg and Gregory Seigworth point out, "there is no single, generalizable theory of affect," in part because "affect emerges out of muddy, unmediated relatedness."[5] The muddiness of the concept may explain a common problem with critiques of affect studies, in which scholars conflate "affect," "affects," and emotion, even though they conceptualize different things. It's an easy mistake. These are slippery distinctions. Some affect theorists embrace the idea that there are fixed basic affects, or physical bodily states, that give rise to the emotions and exist cross-culturally. Others suggest that affect is a flow that is only individualized when it is stopped and named as an emotion.[6] This book falls in the latter camp.

Crucially, affect conceived as flow, rather than distinct states of response (e.g., affects and emotions), enables thinking about technological connections between and with bodies that facilitate excitement or engagement without necessarily requiring reflective thought, persuasion, or meaning. Affect is part of the mood or attitude in a crowd or the intake of breath at the sight of a striking image, moments that bypass meaning making and directly engage energy levels that flow through bodies.[7] Affect as flow explains why growing connectivity has pushed advertising away from informing about products or dictating a specific response to creating an amorphous mood across loosely affiliated groups, with the goal of going viral rather than targeting a specific consumer. The complexities of embodying an image in the froth of volatile, networked markets speaks to the ineffable things that happen when bodies interact and move beyond the contexts of those interactions, when what happens becomes more than the sum of the parts, in flows of affectivity. For these reasons, I have focused on the role of affect and affectivity to analyze modeling work, rather than look to affects and emotions.

The previous examples of models channeling the atmosphere in the room, the urgency of being there when the "it" dress swishes by, the call to get into the flow for a photo, and the glamour labor of constructing body and image within the flows of fashion may involve emotion, but emotion does not tell the whole story. Seeing bodies as regulated and enhanced by engagement with circuitries connecting them across swaths of space, while making their inner space more accessible, describes a notion of affect or affectivity, prior to meaning, cognition of emotion, or the identification of discrete affects, that is, bodily states. Affect, affects, and emotion are not the same thing, however, and assuming their interchangeability commits a critical error. To those who claim affect is simply emotion, I answer that affect delineates resonances that circulate among bodies when they come in contact with and have an impact on one another, a phenomenon quite different from those subjective responses we as individuals define as emotions.

While models do, of course, perform emotional labor, insofar as they work to manage their own emotions to produce a desired feeling in others, I conceptualize the glamour labor of modeling work in terms of affective labor to account for phenomena that the concept of emotional labor cannot fully explain. While emotional labor aims at producing a desired emotion within oneself to produce a corresponding emotion within a client, or recipient of service, affective labor exploits the body's tendency to exceed its boundaries, putting the body in relation to technologies that can measure and organize affective flows, flows that move through bodies as sensations before they are made sense of and named as emotions.

Certainly, when dealing with fashion, we must consider emotion pivotal. Most of us uncritically assume that advertisements make us feel certain emotions. Yet we live in an age in which images wash over us, creating sensations, which, as the performance studies theorist Maurya Wickstrom argues, form a sort of "somatic absorption . . . of the brand."[8] Further, affect conceptualizes more than just feeling; it also refers to the body's life energy itself, the spark of life in our very cells. Considering affect as only emotion completely misses the crucially embodied, physical aspects of this phenomenon.

Many of the models I interviewed for this study described having to sort out how to read the feel of a room or to sense how to move in the clothes, to become whatever the situation demanded in the moment for that client, entering into the "affective reconnaissance" that the scholar of affect studies Emma Dowling so usefully describes.[9] The demand for this sort of sixth sense highlights questions about where individual feelings and emotions end and communal bodily energies begin, as models work to hook into swirling flows of "imitation/suggestion," influencing us at the level of bodily experience.[10] Examining the way affect works, in its circuit from affect (the sensation) to affection as an emotion (making sense of it), is central to my analysis. This angle affords intense scrutiny of the processes through which media technologies measure and regulate affect, not on an interpersonal or emotional scale, but on the level of sheer contact.

In sum, emotional states are identifiable bodily states within people. Affect describes what happens when energies flow between beings, shaping proclivities and dispositions in their wake. It also describes the inherently unpredictable dynamics of the body.[11] Thus, while the cultural studies scholars Melissa Gregg and Gregory Seigworth describe it as "the vaporous evanescence of the incorporeal," affect, in fact, is also thoroughly embodied.[12] The concept of affect and affectivity is crucial for opening a space to reason and think about intensities or sensations that dispose the body to act in ways that, to use Spinoza's terminology, either augment or diminish a body's capacity to act, engage, or connect.[13] These embodied energy flows are registered prior to, and in excess of, cognition, a critical tenet in debates about the role of affect in social life.

The Snowman, Crying Children, and the Meaning of It All

While the idea that we sense or feel before we reason may seem intuitively obvious, from subliminal seduction to the most "out there" theories of emotion and affect studies, there is a great deal of debate about when, exactly, we cognize what we experience. The communication theorist Brian Massumi argues for the importance of the half-second delay between image perception and cognition of its meaning. His view of the "primacy of the affective in image reception" splits off an image's content from its effect.[14] By this he means that there is a split between the qualities of the image and the intensity of the image, since there is a space in time between when the image affects us and when we figure out what it means. Perfume ads are particularly adept at exploiting this phenomenon. While once aimed at telling the story of the sort of person who might wear this perfume or depicting scenarios in which to use the product, more recent advertisements have relied on the shock of naked bodies, or parts of bodies, with the perfume bottle either lying nearby or superimposed over the images of slick surfaces, geometric shapes, and bodily configurations, replete with sexual overtones evocative of any manner of ways to approach interacting with the product, without dictating any particular one. In other words, these kinds of images have an effect that does not necessarily correspond to their meaning. Similarly, the geographer Nigel Thrift advocates for this point of view in his contention that the media and mediated environments, such as promotional events or branded stores, actively work on and shape the space of pre-cognition, in the realm of affect where "intentions or decisions are made before the conscious self is even aware of them."[15]

While some have revered the scholars Brian Massumi and Nigel Thrift to almost guru status within the growing field of "affect studies," others have sharply critiqued their reliance on certain findings in brain science, science that claims there is a "half-second delay" between the onset of brain activity and our conscious awareness of the event.[16] Massumi and Thrift have been charged with misinterpreting the data from these studies, using them selectively or taking them at face value. In fact, their work *does* rely on theories of the brain and emotions that have been subject to "significant debate and contestation," which is important to note.[17] The humanities scholar Ruth Leys carefully studied the experimental results upon which Massumi, in particular, and Thrift, in part, relied for making claims about the role of affect and affectivity in perception. For Leys, Massumi's interpretation of the snowman experiment, a study that documented how children's responses to a sad film varied with different sound tracks, "willfully or otherwise misreads the data in order to create paradoxes where there were none."[18] Leys also takes Thrift to task for jumping from analysis of the brain research to politically untenable conclusions.[19] Leys also, however, points out that the researchers themselves, upon whose findings Thrift and Massumi relied, have acknowledged the high level of "complexity" of the results and the "difficulty of interpreting them," a status that helps explain the differing conclusions that can be drawn from them.[20]

Affect studies has gotten scholars so hot under the collar because the notion of affect taps into debates about whether we are creatures of reason or emotion, a dispute that has a long history and remains inconclusive.[21] Further, discussing affect demands taking a stand in debates about cognition and meaning with regard to how they interact with images, debates that feed directly into issues of the nature of emotion and the question of whether or not we cognize in order to have emotions, which in turn shape our ideas of politics and political will.[22] At stake is the age-old debate between nature and nurture, as well as efforts to resolve the problem of mind/body dualism inevitably aroused by discussions of how to understand the experience of the "lived" body. Some have argued categorically that social scientists have no business translating the findings of brain science into other domains, since they use different grammars and orders of meaning.[23] These critiques miss the point that neuroscience and, more generally, molecular biology and biomedicine not only are scientific domains but also function as authoritative discourses about the nature of reality, cultural forces that work to shape understandings of what a mind is and what a body can do.

Glamour Labor and the Body as Capital

In the cultural moment I've been describing, bodily and social vitality has become a resource for capital on a level different from what it had been thus far, not only in terms of the body's capacity to work, to convert physical and social energy into a resource for production, but also in terms of the body's life force itself, brought to market by the kind of glamour labor I have described. Emerging notions of the body as not just the holder of capital but *as* capital—that is, something that can be worked on to increase its value—kick-started the nascent fitness industry, resulting in a fitness boom that capitalized on bodily anxieties stirred by an increasingly image obsessed society. These anxieties, taken to the next level, sparked the explosion in plastic surgery rates and later spurred the use of pharmaceuticals and bodily and social tracking technologies to achieve the body beautiful. The burgeoning fitness, cosmetic surgery, pharmaceutical, and, ultimately, the personal-data industries, such as fitness and health trackers and apps, have provided a means for converting the body's unruliness, its tendency to soften to flab, or its varying ability to build muscle into productive resources.

Models engage in practices that idealize a way of being in the world that encourages opening up the body to technological exposure. Reading fashion blogs, following Twitter feeds, seeking to embody the optimally enhanced look of the day—all this makes collective energies available for tracking and manipulation. Further, as models advance various fashions in bodies while they themselves work to embody ever-changing bodily trends, the "model" body has come to personify an openly manipulated body, attracting publics to a way of being in the world that makes resourcing physical bodies and social connectivity, via making them available to technological mapping and manipulation, something everyone should want to do.

This book has treated how the model glamorizes this kind of engagement with technology, in pursuit of capitalizing on the body's malleability and changeability, which it is the model's job to make look attractive and fun. Fostering this changeability encourages the enhancement of bodies in the process of optimization. Optimization refers not only to human biology, however; my findings and analysis push the thought of technological enhancement outside of the biomedical paradigm and expand it to include the enhancement of our affective capacity by means of electronic media. In sum, one must be enterprising to achieve the kind of ageless body and happy soul now made possible for everyone by the newly available neutraceuticals, cosmetic procedures, gene therapies, and the selective serotonin re-uptake inhibitor (SSRI) families of drugs promoted by contemporary consumer culture. In obeying that imperative to engage with technology, you not only open up your body to technological intervention, you open up your likes and proclivities, your connections to others, the building blocks of your community, and your propensities to act and to be surveilled, monitored, and shaped in ways that are profitable to advertisers, brand managers, and corporations that want not only to sell you things but to sell you and your attention as units of value as well. Your bodily affectivity and vitality are resourced as potentials to connect, to get sick, to want to look good, to have the gene for breast cancer, to dye your hair or go to the gym, or to read a book and talk about it.

All of these activities are not separable. We are forced to think about the body as both biological and virtual when thinking about optimization and enhancement. By thinking through affectivity and how it connects people through social media, for instance, and how these connections are being capitalized on, we are forced to think about the body as thoroughly distributed through both modes of being. Glamour labor to look good or cool or "with it" is thus inseparable from the glamour labor aimed at extending the image far and wide, in the effort to put one's bodily potentials into the circuitry that make up one's "presence" physically and virtually. To put it succinctly, in the circuit of glamour labor, where the model/consumer/fashion/image/product nexus converges in the event of the model "look," models make the labor of enhancement attractive. Models glamorize a bodily variability that is not just about promoting diet pills or about getting consumers actively engaged in body projects but also about investing in your engagement with others. It is an investment in stimulating your interest, in varying not only your wardrobe according to fashion but also your body, your relationships, and your workstyles, as you make your feelings, proclivities, and moods available to electronic calibration and measurement.

Understanding how fashion modeling is situated in this larger apparatus that organizes and regulates bodies in general demands exploring how models, as glamour workers, "model" the body opened to access by technology. Modeling work involves being fashionable, embodying the dream of a fully optimized life, and therefore it contributes to the twenty-first-century trend toward making bodily potential and connectivity continuously available to metering and regulation, an availability that facilitates capital's constant expansion. Glamour labor encourages an embodied entanglement with technology that banks on possibilities inherent in both bodily vitality and the capacity for connection.

Tracking these patterns of glamour labor opens us up to questions regarding the relationships among bodily affectivity, optimization, and the incarnation of the social movement known as the quantified self. The newfound ability to track every moment of lived existence made possible by the digital age has animated the quantified self-movement, as its acolytes cheerfully log every possible aspect of their body's rhythms, outputs, and actions to reach their ideal goals, whether it is to have a body that is "model thin" or to be the kind of person who is firing on all fronts, pushed toward her maximum potential, always optimizing, improving, enhancing, a prime directive for living the fashionable life. At the same time, the klieg light of fashion's exposure has elevated not only people but also parts of people to star status, as audiences have became intimately familiar with Cindy Crawford's mole, Linda Evangelista's hair, or, more recently, Kate Upton's breasts and Cara Delavigne's eyebrows. Fostering fashions in bodies fans the flames of the desire for biomedical interventions for enhancement, fine-tuning it to manage bodies and parts of bodies, as well as for enhancing social connections, to build up the social viability of one's image.

As more bodily perceptions and resonances are tracked and possibly altered by technologies aimed at enhancing the body, to be in style, or have a "model" body, the confluence of forces I have described as glamour labor are moving into new realms of post-human enhancement with the line between bodies and technologies so obscure as to be impossible to draw at all. In the shift to the biopolitics of beauty, only those bodies open to the glamour labor of biomediation and social calibration are valued in the regime of the blink. As there is no one single optimum body, or top-of-the-heap style, there is no end in sight to the process.

While some publics pursue designer bodies and digital friends, others can only make it into fashion's fold as workers who produce the fashions in clothes or electronics that feed the passions of the more developed world. Fashion modeling has done its job so well that the fashionable life has become irresistibly attractive, making it difficult to give up glamour's pleasures, even in the face of tragedies such as the deaths of over a thousand underpaid and overworked factory workers in Bangladesh. These workers died in 2013 when Rana Plaza, a commercial building hastily constructed to make profits as quickly as possible, collapsed and crushed them as they labored to make "cheap and chic" clothes popular with retailers of "fast fashion."[24]

Similarly, amid growing concerns about the nature and use of what has come to be known as Big Data, huge sections of the populace don activity trackers like Fitbits, download health-enhancement apps, track their sleep habits, and log their nutrition practices and goals, ostensibly in pursuit of the body beautiful, while blogging, Facebooking, and tweeting about their accomplishments and watching their Klout scores all the while. Adding to these enticements to engage are the countless fashion blogging, commentary, and community websites, from the professionally polished *Sartorialist* (www.thesartorialist.com) to the "girlfriends just helping each other out" vibe of what-to-wear sites *Go Try It On* (www.gotryiton.com), which was acquired by and subsumed under *Rent the Runway* (www.renttherunway.com), a site designed specifically to profit from users sharing their experiences and opinions of how they look in the outfits offered by the site.

The attraction of these practices is hard to resist, and the nature of the system in which they seem to be not a choice but a necessity needs examining in detail, a project to which this book contributes. It is highly unrealistic to condemn these practices and say we all should stop. The question is moot as to whether people can avoid becoming glamour laborers; rather, we now need to ask how the process perhaps can be redirected, made more equitable, more humane. If the biopolitics of beauty is a driving force in drawing the lines between those willing to be glamorous and those who need to get with the program, then perhaps redefining glamour to be more inclusive, or altogether different, might be one path to this goal. At the same time, other industry changes that have been criticized for "greenwashing" away disreputable corporate practices do seem to be a response to a real concern, driven by social media's connectedness and the Internet's ability to expose such practices, to strive toward more sustainable fashion, conscious consumption, and a return to individual practices such as clothing repair, refashioning, and reselling that might help some, at least, slow fashion's ever-accelerating treadmill to a more manageable speed.

There are some glimmers of this process in the works. In this cultural turn I have described, no one shape seems to be dominant; size matters less than variability.[25] Rather than upholding one ideal as the most desirable, morphing bodies always make news. Perhaps there is some hope for a new aesthetic here? There are a wide variety of bodies highlighted by tabloid headlines, which breathlessly cover this or that starlet's weight gain, pregnancy, lip enhancement, or weight loss, documenting new diets, surgeries, and fitness regimes. "Makeover" television, a perennial favorite, also highlights bodies of all different sorts, pushing toward a relatively uniform ideal, but an ideal that has excluded far more in the past than it does today. Tabloid reporting, so often reprehensible, nonetheless strikes a hopeful chord when highlighting how the body, in all its permutations, makes news. Debates about whether the Kardashian girls are fat, or which starlet has lost too much weight, may resonate with a consistent ideal from which to judge, but they also imply an evolution away from categorical rejection, toward an ideal that includes more body types.

Other evidence of this morphing ideal can be seen in the glamour labor of fashion blogging, which has brought more types of bodies into the realm of the fashionable. In blogs such as *Gabi Fresh* (gabifresh.com), *Nicolette Mason* (www.nicolettemason.com), *The Curvy Fashionista* (http://thecurvyfashionista.com), and the like, in which traditionally plus sized women became fashion queens in their own right, bloggers use their fleshiness and generous curves to carve out a niche for their own kind of glamour, modeled on high-fashion ideals but set to their own tone.[26] The level of exchange afforded by technologies designed to profit from the drive for affective community, such as Facebook, Instagram, and Twitter, has also empowered models to speak up about the body-image practices common in the industry. A recent outburst in a news item exemplified the now two-way nature of the fashion image. A model who had borrowed Fella swimwear to pose for a photographer friend posted the images they made on Instagram, only to find out that Fella had reposted the image—but with a radically reduced version of her body, Photoshopped to look pounds thinner. In an increasingly common comeback, she Instagrammed the original alongside the altered images, claiming, "'My body is a size 8, not a size 4. That's my body! I refuse to stand by and allow ANY company or person to perpetuate the belief that "thinner is better". All women are beautiful, and we come in different shapes and sizes! It is NOT OKAY to alter a woman's body to make it look thinner. EVER!"[27]

Fashion's limit-pushing energies are also crossing racial and gender lines. The Fall 2014 campaign for luxury brand Balmain features six models, each of a different ethnicity. While the fashion scholar Minh-Ha T. Pham might dismiss this as "multicultural window dressing," it could be evidence of a move in a better direction.[28] While a white model is in the center of the group, the models of color are not simply her foil; they are all clothed in equally luxurious goods and occupy the same visual plane. Similarly, luxury goods store Barneys's use of transgendered models in their media ruckus–stirring Spring 2014 campaigns might also be guilty of transcultural tourism, using "otherness" to sell goods. I would argue, however, that the Barneys campaign takes body fashioning to the next level, presenting blurred gender lines as fashionably close to the cutting edge. Rather than being a drop in the bucket, campaigns like this might just be the tip of an iceberg.

In the age of the blink, beauty standards have become less rigid, more fluid, and less consistent. The rising importance of affectivity in the modeling transaction has influenced the current ideal of a changeable body, manipulated and modified in the name of optimization. Since the

1980s, especially, the ideal has become one of flux, of change, of always being ready to push harder, to go farther, to be something else. Despite what seemed at first glance to be a drive toward a relentlessly skinny look, in fact, new fashionable ideals have become less rigidly uniform than in decades past. This fluidity has stemmed in part from the way blink technologies of digitization have facilitated modification, capitalizing on the body's malleability. Starting in the 1980s and 1990s, modeling, rather than working toward a fixed and standardized image, moved toward an openness to transformation in pursuit of a fleeting ideal whose goal is to be constantly in flux, always in processs, on the way to something other than what one already is—a process modeling work glamorized to the general public, selling the idea that constant transformation is fun, cool, and something everyone should want to do.

For all of fashion's surface qualities, its stakes run surprisingly deep. Much of what's deemed "cool" or "hip" can be traced back to the forces of fashion. While the fashion world is notoriously elitist, closed, and difficult to penetrate, in the age of the blink, as the previous chapters illustrated, fashion has become increasingly diffused to the general population. From the rise of fast fashion, to live streaming fashion shows, blink technologies have facilitated unprecedented access to fashionable clothes, information about the latest styles, and advice and guidance about how to wear them. Highlighting the complex set of factors involved in glamorizing bodily and social enhancement may go some way toward understanding the inner workings of the glamour machine. The powerful mix of pleasure and exploitation at the heart of these processes make them hard to dismantle or even resist. It is my sincere hope that this book's provocations highlight a path toward a saner, more habitable direction, one that is fashion forward without leaving anyone behind.

APPENDIX

A Chronology of Modeling in the Media, 1980–2010

STYLE WITH ELSA KLENSCH: 1980–2000. Television program, CNN.

FORD SUPERMODEL OF THE WORLD: 1981–present. Contest (not held in 2003).

FASHION TELEVISION (FT): 1985–2012. Television channel, CTV.

HOUSE OF STYLE: 1989–2000. Television program, MTV. It was reported that MTV was rebooting the program in 2009, but only one episode aired, hosted by models Bar Rafaeli and Chanel Iman.

MODELS: THE FILM: 1991. Peter Lindbergh, director. Documentary about Naomi Campbell, Cindy Crawford, Linda Evangelista, Tatjana Patitz, and Stephanie Seymour.

SHAPE YOUR BODY WORKOUT: 1992. Cindy Crawford video.

NEXT CHALLENGE WORKOUT: 1993. Cindy Crawford video. The follow-up to the *Shape Your Body Workout*.

MODELS INC.: 1994–1995. Television program, Fox.

PRÊT-À-PORTER: 1994. Robert Altman, director. Film set in the modeling world.

SWAN: 1994. Book. Naomi Campbell's "novel" about the modeling industry (ghost-written by someone else). London: Heinemann.

ELLE TOP MODEL: 1994–1998. Magazine. The quarterly imprint of *Elle* focused exclusively on models, their lives, diets, workout plans, etc. The first magazine devoted entirely to models, published quarterly in twenty-three countries.

UNZIPPED: 1995. Douglas Keeve, director. Documentary film on Isaac Mizrahi featuring the supermodels.

VH1 (OR VH1/VOGUE) FASHION AWARDS: 1995–2002. Television awards program, VH1. Included Supermodel of the Year Award and Male Model of the Year Award.

MTV FASHIONABLY LOUD: 1999–2002. Television movie series, MTV. A *House of Style* tie-in that paired fashion shows with live musical performances.

JUERGEN TELLER GO-SEES: 1999. Book. Teller published a collection of candid portraits of famous models making casting visits to his studio with their books. Zurich and New York: Scalo.

STYLE.COM: 2000–present. Website. Initially the online home of *Vogue/W*. www.style.com.

MODELS.COM: 2000–present. Website. A site dedicated exclusively to models in the media, ranking of "top fifty" female and male models. http://models.com.

FULL FRONTAL FASHION: 2000–present. Television program, multiple television networks; website, Twitter feed, and documentary productions, Sundance TV. The first television program to air fashion week shows in their entirety, with an emphasis on designers rather than models and rubbernecking of celebrity and fashion editor attendees at shows. Relaunched in 2009 as a web presence (www.sundance.tv/blog/tag/full-frontal-fashion-1), with documentaries for Sundance without any of the original hosts, and as a Twitter feed (@fullfrontalfashion), which was current as of March 20, 2015. The web presence has designer profiles, but no model profiles, and all the linked films are about designers.

ZOOLANDER: 2001. Film. Ben Stiller, director. Parody of the modeling life, spin-off of interstitials that Ben Stiller created for the VH1/Vogue Fashion Awards. (A sequel had been announced as of 2014 with Justin Theroux as director.)

FASHION BLOGS: 2002–present.

- 2002. Fashion blogs first enter the blogosphere.
- 2004–2005. Street fashion blogs appear in 2004 with *The Sartorialist,* (www.thesartorialist.com) and in 2005 with Refinery29 (www.refinery29.com).
- 2008. Personal style blogs start. Tavi Gevinson's *Style Rookie* (www.thestylerookie.com, now defunct) quickly became one of the best known. Personal style blogs center on show reports and ad and editorial commentary, celebrate avant-garde designers like the designer Rei Kawakubo, the group threeASFOUR, the brand Rodarte, etc., and include photographs of the writer's own fashion endeavors. In effect, the writers have become their own models. In 2010, the fashion bloggers from *Style Rookie, Bryanboy* (www.bryanboy.com), *Racked* (www.racked.com), etc., were part of the nominating and voting process for the CFDA (Council of Fashion Designers of America) awards.

THE DEVIL WEARS PRADA: 2003. Book. Bitchy roman-à-clef by Lauren Weisberger about working as an assistant at *Vogue.* New York: Doubleday.

FASHION IN FOCUS: 2003–2005. Television program. Behind-the-scenes infotainment about the NYC fashion industry, with a focus on designers and fashion business.

AMERICA'S NEXT TOP MODEL: 2003–present. Television program, multiple networks. Arguably the *Tyra Banks Show* (2005–2010, mutliple networks), a television talk show, could function as an offshoot of this because she talked so much about her career and other models.

TOP MODEL (AMERICA'S NEXT TOP MODEL FRANCHISE): 2004–present. Television program. A reality tv show in forty-plus countries worldwide.

PROJECT RUNWAY: 2004–present. Television program, multiple networks. Fashion design contest show where models have a mostly silent role as they are real bodies for the designers to fit their clothes to.

T: THE NEW YORK TIMES STYLE MAGAZINE: 2004–present. Published fifteen times a year with web presence on NYtimes.com, with an emphasis on fashion media trends and designers (www.nytimes.com/pages/t-magazine/index.html).

MAKE ME A SUPERMODEL (UK): 2005–2006. Television program, Channel 5.

UGLY BETTY: 2006–2010. Television program, ABC. Comedy set at a fashion magazine office.

A MODEL LIFE: 2007. Television program, TLC. Reality modeling series hosted by Petra Nemcova, one season long.

FASHION TELEVISION CHANNEL: 2007–present. Television channel, multiple networks.

MAKE ME A SUPERMODEL (AUSTRALIA): 2008. Television program, Seven Network.

MAKE ME A SUPERMODEL (US): 2008–2009. Television program, Bravo.

THE CUT: 2008. Blog. This is part of the fashion blog subset of *New York* magazine (nymag.com), with coverage of fashion week and offside commentary from the bloggers of *Go Fug Yourself*, a comedic fashion gossip blog. Its existing database of models and designers are updated to be the largest collection on the Internet. Preliminary fashion week blog coverage began in September 2006.

MODELINIA: 2009. Blog. Devoted to model profiles and the modeling lifestyle, covering models in the media (www.modelinia.com/blog).

FASHION ONE: 2010–present. Television network, worldwide. A web and mobile TV site devoted to all things fashion (www.fashionone.com).

NOTES

PREFACE
1 Name changed to protect anonymity.

INTRODUCTION
1 I have quoted interviewees throughout; all names have been changed.
2 The idea that models have "sell-by" dates, like cartons of milk, is discussed at length with regard to a model's shelf life in Ashley Mears's sociological analysis of the industry, *Pricing Beauty: The Making of a Fashion Model* (Los Angeles: University of California Press, 2011).
3 The body of work that coined the term "aesthetic labour" is now referred to as the Strathclyde Group school of thought. See, e.g., Chris Warhurst, Dennis Nickson, Anne Witz, and Anne Marie Cullen, "Aesthetic Labour in Interactive Service Work: Some Case Study Evidence from the 'New' Glasgow," *Service Industries Journal* 20, no. 3 (2000): 1–18; Chris Warhurst and Dennis Nickson, *Looking Good, Sounding Right: Style Counselling in the New Economy* (London: Industrial Society, 2001), and "'Who's Got the Look?' Emotional, Aesthetic and Sexualized Labour in Interactive Services," *Gender, Work and Organization* 16, no. 3 (2009): 385–404.
4 Maurizio Lazzarato, "Immaterial Labour," in *Radical Thought in Italy: A Potential Politics*, ed. Michael Hardt, Paolo Virno, Sandra Buckley, and Brian Massumi (Minneapolis: University of Minnesota Press, 1996), 133–147. I discuss this concept in "Modeling a Way of Life: Immaterial and Affective Labor in the Fashion Modeling Industry," *ephemera: Theory and Politics in Organization* 7, no. 1 (2007): 250–269. The marxist scholars Michael Hardt and Antonio Negri further refined this concept into the "immaterial paradigm" of labor in *Multitude: War and Democracy in the Age of Empire* (New York: Penguin, 2004), whose overarching tendencies take three specific forms: the informatization of production (via computerization or robotics), the rise of "symbolic-analytical services" (management, problem solving, and routine symbol manipulation), and affective labor, performed either through actual or virtual human contact or interaction, which produces "intangible feelings of ease, excitement, or passion" (Michael Hardt and Antonio Negri, *Empire* [Cambridge, MA: Harvard University Press, 2000], 293).
5 Gina Neff, Elizabeth Wissinger, and Sharon Zukin, "Entrepreneurial Labor among Cultural Producers: 'Cool' Jobs in 'Hot' Industries," *Social Semiotics* 15, no. 3 (2005): 307–334; David Hesmondhalgh, *The Cultural Industries*, 3rd ed. (London: SAGE, 2012); David Hesmondhalgh and Sarah Baker, *Creative Labour: Media*

Work in Three Cultural Industries (Abingdon: Routledge, 2011); Angela McRobbie, *In the Culture Society: Art, Fashion, and Popular Music* (London: Psychology Press, 1999).

6 I am taking an angle on "the good life" inspired by the French philosopher Michel Foucault, who discussed the "technique for maximizing life" as a form of power and control in *The History of Sexuality* (New York: Vintage, 1990), 1:123.

7 Ultimately I am thinking about "affect" both in terms of the space of encounter and the space of enhancement by technologies that tap into bodily vitality to profit from their mutability.

8 Based on Nikolas Rose's discussion of the "ageless body" and "happy soul"—the goals of optimization and enhancement he described in "Molecular Biopolitics, Somatic Ethics and the Spirit of Biocapital," *Social Theory and Health* 5 (2007): 3–29.

9 Kathleen Barry, *Femininity in Flight: A History of Flight Attendants* (Durham, NC: Duke University Press, 2007), 37.

10 Ibid.

11 Mark Deuze, *Media Life* (London: Polity, 2012). The literature on cultural labor is extensive. In addition to Neff et al., "Entrepreneurial Labor"; Hesmondhalgh, *Cultural Industries*; and McRobbie, *In the Culture Society*, see, e.g., Terry Flew, *The Creative Industries: Culture and Policy* (London: SAGE, 2012).

12 Angela McRobbie, "Reflections on Feminism, Immaterial Labour and the Post-Fordist Regime," *New Formations* 70, no. 4 (2010): 60–76. See also Gina Neff, *Venture Labor: Work and the Burden of Risk in Innovative Industries* (Cambridge, MA: MIT Press, 2012); and Andrew Ross, *Nice Work If You Can Get It: Life and Labor in Precarious Times* (New York: NYU Press, 2009).

13 Not direct quotes, but an overview of the sentiments expressed by my respondents and the model "how-to" books I consulted.

14 As I have done with Gina Neff and Sharon Zukin in our paper, "Entrepreneurial Labor." See also Neff, *Venture Labor*; and Ross, *Nice Work*.

15 Emily Martin, *Bipolar Expeditions: Mania and Depression in American Culture* (Princeton, NJ: Princeton University Press, 2007), 42.

16 Ibid.

17 "Medicalization" refers to the process by which normal human physical functioning is increasingly seen as a medical condition that needs treatment (e.g., in the medicalization of childbirth, pregnancy is recoded as an illness in need of medical treatment). I use it here to explain the process by which the healthy body is increasingly seen as something in need of intervention and treatment, converting its regular function into a source of market value. "Mediatization" refers to the process whereby media technologies change social relations, identity, and conceptions of the body. I use this concept to explain the process by which the body is increasingly treated as an image and information, and this image/data/body becomes the self across various platforms. This distributed self includes the

physical presence of the body, all the mediated images of that body, and all the data generated by that body.

18 These are activities that the French theorist Michel Foucault has famously claimed typify the kind of "enterprise society" that we now inhabit. See Michel Foucault, *The Birth of Biopolitics: Lectures at the Collège de France, 1978–1979*, trans. G. Burchell (New York: Palgrave, 2008), 241. For an excellent treatment of "medicalization," see Nikolas Rose, *The Politics of Life Itself: Biomedicine, Power, and Subjectivity in the 21ˢᵗ Century* (Princeton, NJ: Princeton University Press, 2006). With regard to mediatization, there is a large literature, including Knut Lundby, *Mediatization: Concepts, Changes, Consequences* (New York: Peter Lang, 2009).

19 Rose, in "Molecular Biopolitics," 13, quoting Michel Callon and Vololona Rabeharisoa, "Gino's Lesson on Humanity: Genetics, Mutual Entanglement and the Sociologist's Role," *Economy and Society* 33 (2004): 1–27.

20 This organizing has the goal of optimizing the population, bringing out its potential, pulling as many as possible into practices of "the good life." The feminist scholar Mimi Thi Nguyen has usefully elaborated this notion by describing "beauty as a form of 'right living' " in "The Biopower of Beauty: Humanitarian Imperialisms and Global Feminisms in an Age of Terror," *Signs* 36, no. 2 (Winter 2011): 359–383. These aspects of glamour labor illustrate the differences between biopower and biopolitics. While discipline is a biopower that works on individuals at the level of the self, biopolitics is a politics of regulation, as Foucault has argued, institutionalizing techniques aimed at controlling "the series of random events that can occur in a living mass" and managing them to promote the survival of the species. To be exact, as Foucault has explained, biopolitics "does not exclude disciplinary technology, but it does dovetail into it, integrate it, modify it to some extent, and above all, use it by sort of infiltrating it, embedding itself in existing disciplinary techniques. . . . Unlike discipline, which is addressed to bodies, the new non-disciplinary power is applied not to man-as-body but to the living man, to man-as-living-being; ultimately, if you like, to man-as-species" (Michel Foucault, *"Society Must Be Defended": Lectures at the Collège de France, 1975–1976*, trans. David Macey [1997; reprint, New York: Picador, 2003], 242). The goal of this form of power is a "regularizing" of biological processes, to achieve a certain state in the population, rather than achieve control over any particular individual. Biopolitical control seeks to optimize birthrates, diminish death rates, and "optimize the state of life" through regularizing it (ibid., 249, 246).

21 The phrase "biopolitics of beauty" was inspired by Joanna Zylinska's article, "Of Swans and Ugly Ducklings: Bioethics between Humans, Animals, and Machines," *Configurations* 15, no. 2 (2007): 125–150, in which she found that television makeover culture was organized according to a "biopolitical logic of modernity, which sees the bodies and lives of others—fat women with crooked teeth, not-yet-democratic-enough Iraqis—as always already in need of a makeover" (142). While Zylinska aligns the viewers with the species to be saved, comforted

as these isolated and contained others who are sacrificed to keep them safe from the ills the others represent, since her publication, the message has shifted; arguably, all of us are now in need of a makeover, in need of schooling in the values fashion models embody, constructing all viewers as "always already in need of a makeover."

22 Alice Marwick, "Big Data, Data-Mining, and the Social Web," talk given at the *New York Review of Books* event "Privacy, Power and the Internet" (New York, October 30, 2013), *Tiara.org: A Feminist Technology Blog*, www.tiara.org/blog/new-talk-big-data-data-mining-and-the-social-web, accessed August 25, 2014. In this talk she outlines how online and offline behavior is "combined, analyzed, and sold" by private data companies to "marketers, corporations, governments, and even criminals." See also Tiziana Terranova, "Free Labor: Producing Culture for the Digital Economy," *Social Text* 18, no. 2 (2000): 33–28.

23 Conversations about brands and branding often revolve around their frustratingly elusive nature and the difficulty of pinning them down. This kind of thinking is exemplified by talk overheard in the coffee shop where I was writing one morning. In what appeared to be a marketing meeting at the next table, the leader of the discussion said, "The brand side is harder because it's not logical, and that's like, super uncomfortable for a lot of people" (at the Upright Brew House, West Village, New York City, July 2, 2014). The sociologist Liz Moor has explored how brand managers define their brand, not as an object or sign, but rather as a "social presence" trying "to catalogue the total social presence of the brand, to register every context and process in which it plays a part, every practice in which it is mobilized," as discussed in Don Slater and Joanne Entwistle's essay, "Models as Brands: Critical Thinking about Bodies and Images," in *Fashioning Models: Image, Text and Industry*, ed. Joanne Entwistle and Elizabeth Wissinger (London: Berg, 2012), 28. Similarly, Melissa Aronczyk and Devon Pager refer to the "unquantifiable social values" contained in brands, which organizations nonetheless try to capture in numbers (in *Blowing Up the Brand: Critical Perspectives on Promotional Culture* [New York: Peter Lang Publishing, 2010], 8). The communication scholar Sarah Banet-Weiser has called them "the essence of what will be experienced" (in *Authentic*^{TM} [New York: NYU Press, 2012], 4), while the media studies scholar Alison Hearn lays out how the brand is valued not for "what 'it says, but what it does'" (in "Meat, Mask, Burden: Probing the Contours of the Branded Self," *Journal of Consumer Culture* 8 [2008]: 197–217, quoting Andrew Wernick, *Promotional Culture: Advertising, Ideology, and Symbolic Expression* [London: SAGE, 1991], 190).

24 Analyzing the myriad ways consumers interact with models, the sociologists Don Slater and Joanne Entwistle in fact describe a large portion of how glamour labor organizes model/consumer interactions: "The stereotypical young woman as potential victim of size zero imagery is not simply engaging with specific represented bodies in reiterated texts; she is engaging with body values through

everyday dress practices; social networks and peer relationships and competitions; regulatory structures (e.g., school or workplace dress codes, formal and informal); leisure spaces, practices, and regulations; complementary commodities and aesthetic forms (e.g. the relationship between music cultures and fashion); domestic and familial dynamics; retail structures; aesthetic genres such as modeling competitions and reality TV formats, and on and on and on" (Slater and Entwistle, "Models as Brands," 29).

25 *Visionaire* is a magazine known for its unusual formats and approach to fashion. One limited-edition issue entitled "Larger than Life" was three feet by four feet and provided images that were almost true to scale; another entitled "Forever" was printed on stainless steel and aluminum.

26 As documented in Brooke Duffy's cogent treatment of the effect of digital technologies on traditional magazines, *Remake/Remodel: Women's Magazines in the Digital Age* (Urbana: University of Illinois Press, 2013).

27 As per the character Miranda's famous response in the film *The Devil Wears Prada* about the blue sweater that the main character Andy wears:

"This . . . stuff"? Oh. Okay. I see. You think this has nothing to do with you. You go to your closet and you select . . . I don't know . . . that lumpy blue sweater, for instance because you're trying to tell the world that you take yourself too seriously to care about what you put on your back. But what you don't know is that that sweater is not just blue, it's not turquoise. It's not lapis. It's actually cerulean. And you're also blithely unaware of the fact that in 2002, Oscar de la Renta did a collection of cerulean gowns. And then I think it was Yves Saint Laurent . . . wasn't it who showed cerulean military jackets? I think we need a jacket here. And then cerulean quickly showed up in the collections of eight different designers. And then it, uh, filtered down through the department stores and then trickled on down into some tragic Casual Corner where you, no doubt, fished it out of some clearance bin. However, that blue represents millions of dollars and countless jobs and it's sort of comical how you think that you've made a choice that exempts you from the fashion industry when, in fact, you're wearing the sweater that was selected for you by the people in this room from a pile of stuff.

(Quote taken from *The Devil Wears Prada* at IMDb, n.d., www.imdb.com/title/tt0458352/quotes, accessed August 14, 2014).

28 This concept of engaging both the physical and the virtual aspect of a prospective employee is also reflected by recent practices in which potential employers search for and examine an applicant's online presence, including their Facebook page, Twitter feed, and Klout score; the latter is an agglomeration of one's impact within social networks such as LinkedIn, Twitter, Instagram, Facebook, Google+, etc.

29 Nigel Thrift, "Understanding the Material Practices of Glamour," in *The Affect Theory Reader*, ed. Melissa Gregg and Gregory Seigworth (Durham, NC: Duke University Press, 2010), 299.

30 Virginia Postrel, *The Power of Glamour: Longing and the Art of Visual Persuasion* (New York: Simon & Schuster, 2013), 8. Postrel's definition is useful despite her denial that celebrity is associated with glamour, a claim with which I do not agree.

31 Mears, *Pricing Beauty*, 6.

32 Slater and Entwistle, "Models as Brands," 24.

33 Ibid., 25.

34 Ibid. It is helpful to conceive of the model look as part of a complex system in which nothing is either a brute material object or merely a sign but rather dissolved into the "networks that format and sustain" both, as Slater and Entwistle have discussed. They use Actor Network Theory (ANT) to decipher how "*no* object is 'simply' an object in the sense of a thing-in-itself with intrinsic properties or qualities, or in the sense of a brute materiality as opposed to a sign. ANT has been (in)famous for dissolving all objects into the networks that format and sustain them" (ibid., 23).

35 All of whom define and shape "an assemblage of qualities" that make up the look (ibid., 25).

36 A "go-see" is like an interview or audition, in which a model goes to see a potential client to try out for a job.

37 Teresa Brennan, *The Transmission of Affect* (Ithaca, NY: Cornell University Press, 2004), 1–3.

38 Deborah Gould, citing the founding father of sociology Émile Durkheim, who coined the term, in *Moving Politics: Emotion and ACT-UP's Fight against AIDS* (Chicago: University of Chicago Press, 2009), 244.

39 Brian Massumi, *Parables for the Virtual: Movement, Affect, Sensation* (Durham, NC: Duke University Press, 2002), 25.

40 Anna Gibbs, "Disaffected," *Continuum: Journal of Media and Cultural Studies* 16 (2002): 335–341.

41 Mears, *Pricing Beauty*, in which she discussed "vibrant exchanges," 250.

42 Herbert Blumer, "Fashion: From Class Differentiation to Collective Selection," *Sociological Quarterly*, 10, no. 3 (1969): 275–291.

43 Ibid., 280.

44 Nigel Thrift, *Non-representational Theory: Space, Politics, Affect* (New York: Routledge, 2007), 65; also, regarding media susceptibility, see Gibbs, "Disaffected."

45 See, e.g., where the sociologist Joanne Entwistle has referred to the aesthetic markets of modeling as "effervescent," in which the speed at which fashions come and go affects the value of commodities within fashion markets (Joanne Entwistle, *The Aesthetic Economy of Fashion: Markets and Value in Clothing and Modeling* [London: Bloomsbury, 2009], 19, 55).

46 As discussed in Celia Lury, *Brands: The Logos of the Global Economy* (London: Routledge, 2004), and "Brand as Assemblage: Assembling Culture," *Journal of Cultural Economy* 2, no. 1 (2013): 67–82; Slater and Entwistle, "Models as Brands"; Elizabeth Moor, "Branded Spaces: The Scope of 'New Marketing,'" *Journal of*

Consumer Culture 3, no. 1 (2003): 39–60, and *The Rise of Brands* (Oxford: Berg, 2007). See also Adam Arvidsson, "Brands: A Critical Perspective," *Journal of Consumer Culture* 5, no. 2 (2005): 325–358.

47 To quote Michael Gross, a chronicler of the modeling industry, it was a "a sleepy backwater business run by a dowager empress." Michael Gross, *Model: The Ugly Business of Beautiful Women* (New York: Morrow, 1995), 348.

48 Creating an "enormous gain in speed and flexibility over earlier forms of electronic communication," as the media scholar Vincent Mosco has pointed out in *The Digital Sublime: Myth, Power, and Cyberspace* (Cambridge, MA: MIT Press, 2005), 155.

49 From 1985 to April 1994 the Internet grew from some 200 networks to well over 30,000. During the same period, the number of people wired into the Internet worldwide grew from roughly 1,000 to over 25 million. In mid-1994 the number of Internet users and traffic flow over the network were each growing from 10 to 15 percent per month (Robert Frank and Philip Cook, *The Winner Take All Society: Why the Few at the Top Get So Much More than the Rest of Us* [New York: Penguin, 1995], 52).

50 Susannah Fox and Lee Rainie, "The Web at 25 in the U.S.," pt. 1: "How the Internet Has Woven Itself into American Life," Pew Research report, February 27, 2014, www.pewinternet.org/2014/02/27/part-1-how-the-internet-has-woven-itself-into -american-life, accessed March 17, 2015.

51 Sanjay Acharya, "ITU Releases 2014 ICT Figures," press release, International Telecommunications Union, Geneva, May 5, 2014, www.itu.int/net/pressoffice/ press_releases/2014/23.aspx#.VQhU82TF_e0, accessed March 18, 2015.

52 One YouTube video was in fact called "Model Falling Funny" (www.youtube.com/ watch?v=qO1WXziEtz4&index=2&list=PL1F4F9B90927B61D, accessed March 11, 2015); it has received over 480,000 hits, while another, called "Beautiful Models Falling Down," generated more than 15 million views as of 2015 (www.youtube .com/watch?v=L1kwNojDwNo/, accessed March 10, 2015).

53 Malcolm Gladwell, *Blink: The Power of Thinking without Thinking* (New York: Penguin, 2006), quoting Simon, 1971, 40–41.

54 Here Thrift plays on Raymond Williams's famous idea of the "structure of feeling" in *Non-representational Theory*, 186.

55 A reigning regime or "pictorial order" is composed of commonly accepted modes of perception and styles or norms of image presentation and imaging techniques (Jeremy Gilbert-Rolfe, *Beauty and the Contemporary Sublime* [New York: Allworth Press, 1999], 179). See also the poststructuralist feminist Patricia Clough's notion that the dominant mode of imaging and the dominant forms of power are connected within a specific "regime of representation" that enforces particular social and cultural practices, as discussed in Patricia Clough and Jean Halley, eds., *The Affective Turn: Theorizing the Social* (Durham, NC: Duke University Press, 2007), 16. Within what David Harvey has famously called a "time-space compression" of the digital age, we find "processes that so revolutionize the objective

qualities of space and time that we are forced to alter, sometimes in quite radical ways, how we represent the world to ourselves" (David Harvey, *The Condition of Postmodernity* [New York; Wiley, 1992], 240). For further discussion, see Paul Virilio, *The Vision Machine* (Bloomington: Indiana University Press, 1994), 63, regarding the "logistics of the image" that "have evolved through different periods of propagation," from the formal logic of painting that ended in the eighteenth century, to the dialectical logic of photography and film, the "frame of the 19th century," to the paradoxical logic that begins with video recording and continues into today's computer graphics and technology, moving through a shift from representation, to presentation, to virtualities.

56 Thrift, *Non-representational Theory*, 243.

57 Brian Massumi, "Fear (the Spectrum Said)," *Positions: East Asia Cultures Critique* 13, no. 1 (2005): 31–48.

58 Ibid., 32.

59 We need, instead, to track how we are "attached or detached to this or that brand/image/model through socio-cognitive processes that, in part are determined by technical apparatuses—packaging, imagery, advertising, and a host of other newer media" (Slater and Entwistle, "Models as Brands," 31).

60 Susie Orbach, *Fat Is a Feminist Issue: The Anti-diet Guide to Permanent Weight Loss* (New York: Berkley Books, 1978), front matter.

61 Michel Foucault, *Discipline and Punish: The Birth of the Prison*, 2nd ed. (New York: Vintage, 1995), 138.

62 Sandra Lee Bartky, "Foucault, Femininity, and the Modernization of Patriarchal Power," in *The Politics of Women's Bodies*, ed. Rose Weitz (Oxford: Oxford University Press, 2010), 65.

63 Ibid., 27. Further, Bartky found fashion's bodily ideal to be a prime culprit for the discipline of dieting, saying, "The current body of fashion is taut, small-breasted, narrow-hipped, and of a slimness bordering on emaciation; it is a silhouette that seems more appropriate to an adolescent boy or a newly pubescent girl than to an adult woman. Since ordinary women have normally quite different dimensions, they must, of course diet" (28).

64 See Susan Bordo, *Unbearable Weight: Feminism, Western Culture, and the Body* (Berkeley: University of California Press, 1993).

65 Susan Faludi, *Backlash: The Undeclared War against American Women* (New York: Crown, 1991), 203–204; and Naomi Wolf, *The Beauty Myth: How Images of Beauty Are Used against Women* (New York: Morrow, 1991), 9–12. I would add that the 1990s waifs were a backlash to the strong, shoulder-padded women who tried to "have it all" in the 1980s.

66 Quoted in the article by Judith Stone, "He's Just Big, She's Fat," *Health Magazine*, May/June, 67–70; see also Stone, "He's Just Big: She's Fat—Sexual Differences on Body and Self Image," *Vibrant Life*, January–February 1994. This idea was graphically illustrated in both Jean Kilbourne's video *Killing Us Softly 3*, dir. Sut Jhally (documentary; Northampton, MA: Media Education Foundation, 2000),

and Jackson Katz's treatment of masculine and feminine gender roles in the video *Tough Guise: Violence, Media, and the Crisis in Masculinity*, dir. Sut Jhally (documentary; Northampton, MA: Media Education Foundation, 2002).

67 Taking this broad purview seems to demand analysis of both men and women's bodily ideals and the ways they have changed over time. While analyzing how men's bodily ideals are affected by changes in the dominant mode of imaging and of production is an interesting question, to study this effect in detail not only goes beyond the scope of this book, it also misses the point that, historically, it is women's bodies on display that are most deeply affected by technological developments in imaging. As John Berger succinctly states, within visual culture as we've come to know it, "men *act* and women *appear*" (John Berger, *Ways of Seeing: A Book* [London, Penguin, 1972], 47). He also says on the same page that "she turns herself into an object—and most particularly an object of vision: a sight." The woman must treat herself as a "sight." That is to say, it is women's role to appear, to present themselves to be looked at. The feminist film theorist Laura Mulvey has famously argued along similar lines, claiming the woman exists in film solely in terms of her "to-be-looked-at-ness," since, in a world ordered by sexual imbalance, pleasure in looking has been split between active/male and passive/female. The determining male gaze projects its fantasy onto the female figure, which is styled accordingly (Laura Mulvey, "Visual Pleasure in Narrative Cinema," in her *Visual and Other Pleasures* [New York: Palgrave, 1989], 25).

68 Mulvey, "Visual Pleasure in Narrative Cinema," 25.

69 Bartky, "Foucault, Femininity," 35.

70 The "soul sucked out" comment is from Brigid Keenan's *Women We Wanted to Look Like* (New York: St. Martin's Press, 1977), 133, from an interview with a high-fashion model who became a spokesmodel for a large cosmetics firm. Cindy Crawford's comment is from footage in Ann Alvergue and Michael Isabel's 2002 documentary, *And Again* (Brooklyn: Eye Spy Films, 2002).

71 Zylinska, "Of Swans and Ugly Ducklings." These phrases are referencing Foucault's notion of biopolitics and Martin Heidegger's notion of *Gestell*, the enframing of human existence by technology, as a mode of being in the world, which challenges it forth or renders it a standing reserve revealed by technology.

72 Hearn, "Meat, Mask, Burden," 201.

73 Ibid.

74 Ibid., 427.

75 The Fashion Insitute of Technology (FIT) and the New York Public Library in Manhattan, as well as the Pratt Institute in Brooklyn.

76 Mears describes a typical scenario, detailing the anger and dejection a model felt after lining up in a hallway with about eighty other girls to go inside for a casting, only to have a casting director come out and bark "stay" or "leave" to each girl as he swept by (Mears, *Pricing Beauty*, 87).

77 U.S. Bureau of Labor Statistics, "Labor Force Statistics from the Current Population Survey: Women in the Labor Force: A Databook," table 3: "Employment

Status by Race, Age, Sex, and Hispanic or Latino Ethnicity, 2008 Annual Averages," www.bls.gov/cps/wlftable3.htm, accessed March 1, 2015.

78 Models are also a transient population, living for a few weeks to a month in any given city in the fashion circuit of New York–Paris–Milan–London. There might be four hundred or fewer working models in New York City at any given time, precluding the construction of a large data set.

79 There are specialized models who do parts and hair modeling and those who do specific ages, such as child models, but they fall beyond the scope of this book.

80 Howard S. Becker, Art Worlds (Berkeley: University of California Press, 1982).

81 Jordan Sales, So You Want to Be a Model? Find Out What the Agents and Scouts Are Really Looking For (Victoria, BC: Trafford, 2002).

82 Georg Simmel, The Sociology of Georg Simmel, trans. Kurt Wolff (Glencoe, IL: Free Press, 1950), 404.

CHAPTER 1. SUPERMODELS OF THE WORLD

1 Alex Kuczynski, "Trading on Hollywood Magic: Celebrities Push Models off Women's Magazine Covers," New York Times, January 30, 1999.

2 As quoted by Bob Colacello in "A League of Their Own," Vanity Fair 50, no. 9 (September 2008): 354. The quote refers to the fact that Naomi Campbell is black and the other two models are white.

3 Ibid., 395.

4 Michael Gross, Model: The Ugly Business of Beautiful Women (New York: Morrow, 1995), 492.

5 Paraphrased from Colacello, "A League of Their Own."

6 Cindy Crawford, Shape Your Body Workout (New York: Goodtimes Home Video, 1992); Naomi Campbell, Swan (London: Heinemann, 1994); Robert Altman, dir., Ready to Wear (Prêt-à-Porter) (New York: Miramax Films, 1994); Douglas Keeve, dir., and Isaac Mizrachi, Unzipped (documentary; New York: Miramax Films, 1995).

7 Harriet Quick, Catwalking: A History of the Fashion Model (Minneapolis: Wellfleet Press, 1997).

8 Kristin Tillotson, "Supersaturated: Supermodels—They Strike a Pose and America Can't Resist," Minneapolis Star Tribune, June 7, 1995.

9 Marcus Schenkenberg, Marcus Schenkenberg: New Rules (New York: Universe, 1997); Veronica Webb Sight, Adventures in the Big City (New York: Hyperion, 1998).

10 Jay McInerney, Model Behavior (New York: Vintage, 2000); Bret Easton Ellis, Glamorama (New York: Vintage, 2000); Lisa Simon, Picture Me Famous (New York: Pocket Books, 1995); and Francine Pascal, Sweet Valley High: Model Flirt (New York: Bantam, 1997).

11 Quick, Catwalking, 142.

12 David Harvey, *The Condition of Postmodernity* (New York; Wiley, 1992); Sharon Zukin, *The Cultures of Cities* (Oxford: Blackwell, 1995). Using the carmaker Henry Ford's factory-centered production of the Model T as a metaphor, "Fordism" refers to the industrial age, when the assembly line was the main force of production in developed countries, such as Europe and the United States. As industrial production moved toward outsourcing and mechanization in the 1970s, a trend that came into full flower in the 1980s, communication and coordination grew in importance and became central to the flexible and just-in-time methods of production that have been characterized as post-Fordist.

13 Teri Agins, *The End of Fashion* (New York: Morrow, 1999), 51.

14 Ibid., 279.

15 Ibid., 277, quoting Thomas Kamm, "War of the Handbags Escalates as LVMH Revives Gucci Quest," *Wall Street Journal,* June 10, 1999.

16 Ibid., 41.

17 Harold Koda and Kohle Yohannan, *The Model as Muse*: *Embodying Fashion* (New Haven, CT: Yale University Press, 2009), 102.

18 Daniel Harris, *Cute, Quaint, Hungry, and Romantic: the Aesthetics of Consumerism* (New York: Basic Books, 2000), 223.

19 Lois Banner, *American Beauty* (New York: Knopf, 1983), 287. The Bill Blass quote is from Charles Gandee, "1950s: Designer Bill Blass Remembers the Years of Cocktails, Café Society and the Cool American Chic (an Interview with Bill Blass)," *Vogue* 470 (November 1999): 537–538.

20 Agins, *End of Fashion*, 30.

21 Bill Blass quote is from Gandee, "1950s." Norma Rantisi, "How New York Stole Modern Fashion," in *Fashion's World Cities*, ed. Christopher Breward and David Gilbert (London: Berg, 2006), 119.

22 Ruth La Ferla, "Front Row," *New York Times*, June 3, 2003, www.nytimes.com/2003/06/03/nyregion/front-row.html?pagewanted=print, accessed June 18, 2009.

23 Lauren Hutton's and Margaux Hemingway's contracts are described in Koda and Yohannan, *Model as Muse*, 101.

24 The first cover was on *Time* magazine, March 6, 1978. Her activities are described in Gross, *Model*, 368.

25 Koda and Yohannan, *Model as Muse*, 134.

26 Eileen Ford, as described in Gross, *Model*, 348.

27 Ibid.

28 Ibid.

29 Ibid., plate 515.

30 "The Story of Elite," April 11, 2011, www.elitemodellook.com/thefinal/cover/2011-11-04.html, accessed March 1, 2015.

31 Hugh Sebag-Montefiore, "Dogfight on the Catwalk: Mark McCormack Is Shaking Up the Management of the World's Supermodels and the Fur Is Flying," *Sunday Telegraph* (London), 1996, 6.

32 Ibid.

33 Gross, *Model*, 345.

34 Joanne Entwistle and Elizabeth Wissinger, eds., *Fashioning Models: Image, Text and Industry* (London: Berg, 2012), 175.

35 Colacello, "A League of Their Own," 358.

36 Gross, *Model*, 490–491.

37 Robert Frank and Philip Cook, *The Winner Take All Society: Why the Few at the Top Get So Much More than the Rest of Us* (New York: Penguin, 1995), 38.

38 Ibid., 50.

39 Eric Bean and Jenni Bidner, *Complete Guide for Models: Inside Advice from Industry Pros* (New York, Lark Books, 2004), 10.

40 Koda and Yohannan, *Model as Muse*, 134.

41 Gross, *Model*, 463.

42 Colacello, "A League of Their Own," 358.

43 The quote and the following are from Gross, *Model*, 492.

44 Ibid., 463.

45 This is often misquoted as "We won't get out of bed for less than $10,000."

46 David Bailey, *Models, Close Up* (New York: Universe, 1999), 139.

47 Tillotson, "Supersaturated."

48 Scott Woolley, "High-Class Lookers," *Forbes*, March 22, 1999.

49 Debbie Press, *Your Modeling Career: You Don't Have to Be a Superstar to Succeed* (New York: Allworth Press, 2004).

50 Bailey, *Models, Close Up*, 50.

51 Quick, *Catwalking*, 154.

52 Notably, the age of television focused on the power of the close-up and the importance of the affectivity of the face, a strong influence that developed through the 1970s and came into full flower in the 1980s and onward. This effect was being felt not only in modeling but in other arenas as well. It was in the 1980s that Michael Jordan became a sports superstar. Prior to his rise to stardom, sports marketing had focused on the team, rather than on individual players. Jordan's stardom was a new phenomenon, which personified his team, representing a new marketing technique. Soon players, rather than teams, were being pitted against one another in the media, affording the opportunity for close-up shots of player's faces and a concentration on their personalities. Jordan's endorsements represented a new form of celebrity for sports stars and, I argue, stemmed from the same forces that created the supermodels.

53 David F. Prindle, *Risky Business* (Boulder, CO: Westview Press, 1993), 39.

54 Manuel Castells, *The Rise of the Network Society*, vol. 1 of *The Information Age: Economy, Society and Culture* (Oxford: Blackwell, 1996); see also Walter LaFeber, *Michael Jordan and the New Global Capitalism* (New York: Norton, 2002), 70.

55 LaFeber, *Michael Jordan*, 70.

56 Regarding the growing audience for fashion, a 2009 report cited a "record month" for NYmag.com, among others: "Not all the numbers have been tallied, but it

looks like New York's Fashion Week helped deliver a significant traffic punch for number of magazine Web sites." Jason Fell, "New York Fashion Week a Traffic Boon for Fashion Magazine Sites," *Folio*, February 27, 2009, www.foliomag.com/ 2009/new-york-fashion-week-traffic-boon-fashion-magazine-sites, accessed March 2, 2015. See also the Appendix.

57 Guy Trebay, "Fashion Diary: All Fashion All the Time: It's a Global Show Now," *New York Times*, February 11, 2002. The Fashion Channel is available in some, but not all, cable markets in the United States, Europe, and Asia.

58 New Media Age (NMA) Staff, "A Fashion Channel for Every Season," July 31, 2001, https://econsultancy.com/nma-archive/12194-a-fashion-channel-for-every -season, accessed March 12, 2015.

59 According to Trebay, a fashion reporter, "Outside of Europe, India and China have become the largest consumers of fashion content in the world." Guy Trebay, "Fashion Diary: All Fashion, All the Time: It's a Global Show Now," *New York Times*, February 11, 2002.

60 Laura Mulvey, *Visual and Other Pleasures* (Bloomington: Indiana University Press, 1989).

61 John Ellis, *Visible Fictions: Cinema, Television, Video*, 2nd ed. (London: Rout- ledge, 1992), 24. See also Gilles Deleuze's work on the movement image and time image in his two volumes on *Cinema*, especially in terms of the sensory motor link that makes up the subjective space of cinema's movement image and how that link breaks down in the televisual space of the time image (Gilles Deleuze, *Cinema 1: The Movement Image*, trans. Hugh Tomlinson and Barbara Habber- jam [Minneapolis: University of Minnesota Press, 1986], and *Cinema 2: The Time-Image*, trans. Hugh Tomlinson and Robert Galeta [Minneapolis: University of Minnesota Press, 1989]). Richard Dienst works from this periodization to think through the difference between the cinematic narrative presentation and television's non-narrative presentation of image streams. Richard Dienst, *Still Life in Real Time: Theory after Television* (Durham, NC: Duke University Press, 1994). Patricia Clough uses this formulation to situate ethnographic writing against the backdrop of mass communication technologies within analyses of narrativity and post-structuralism (Patricia Clough, *The End(s) of Ethnography: From Realism to Social Criticism (Sociological Observations)* [Beverly Hills, CA: SAGE, 1992]).

62 The French philosopher Gilles Deleuze, in his work on cinema, differentiated the two moments of the "gaze" and the "glance" as the "movement image" and the "time image." The movement image worked according to a "sensory motor schema" tied to the organic rhythms of perception, in which images make sense, following a logical sequence through space and time reflected most clearly by the text-heavy, clearly explanatory advertisements popular before the emergence of television. In the "time image," any point in time can meet any other point in time, the real mixes with the imaginary, and images follow no particular sequence, which make them particularly susceptible to affective forces (Deleuze,

Cinema 2, regarding "movement image," 2–3, and for the "time image," and its mixing of present and past, see 98–99).

63 Joseph Turow, *Breaking Up America: Advertisers and the New Media World* (Chicago: University of Chicago Press, 1997), 5.

64 Stuart Ewen, *PR! A Social History of Spin* (New York: Basic Books, 1996), 199; and Prindle, *Risky Business*, 38.

65 Nigel Thrift, *Non-representational Theory: Space, Politics, Affect* (London: Routledge, 2007), 97.

66 Brian Winston, *Media Technology and Society: A History from the Telegraph to the Internet* (London: Routledge, 1998), 318.

67 For the phrase "feeling-cum-behavior," see Thrift, *Non-representational Theory*.

68 Patricia Clough, *Autoaffection: Unconscious Thought in the Age of Teletechnology* (Minneapolis: University of Minnesota Press, 2000), 70–71.

69 While couch potatoes still exist, aimless surfing has migrated to the Internet, and concentrated bursts of narrative form have re-emerged on television in the form of the extended drama, in television shows, with *The Sopranos* (1999–2007) being one well-known example. This resurgence of the narrative form on television arguably represents a response to the inherent fragmentation of attention that started with television but has climaxed to new levels in the form of the Internet. Simultaneous with the long form narrative's re-emergence on television, has come the rise of devices that continue to fragment attention, that are often employed while viewing, in the form of checking the show's website for details about what is being watched or engaging with others while watching via social media.

70 Mimi Thi Nguyen, "The Biopower of Beauty: Humanitarian Imperialisms and Global Feminisms in an Age of Terror," *Signs* 36, no. 2 (Winter 2011): 364.

71 As Nguyen has pointed out, "If, as Michel Foucault notes, biopower is concerned with the management of life, with 'an intensification of the body, a problematization of health and its operational terms,' then the attachment to beauty . . . would have us expand Foucault's original conception of biopower to include beauty as 'a question of techniques for maximizing life.'" Consequently, "beauty, as a discourse and concern about the vitality of the body but also the soul, can and does become an important site of signification, power and knowledge about how to live . . . as such, beauty becomes a form of 'right living'" (ibid., 360).

72 Nguyen's main concern in "The Biopower of Beauty."

CHAPTER 2. THE RUNWAY

1 Caroline Evans, "The Enchanted Spectacle," *Fashion Theory: The Journal of Dress, Body and Culture* 5, no. 3 (August 2001): 271–310; see specifically 274–275.

2 Marshall McLuhan, *Understanding Media* (1964; reprint, Cambridge, MA: MIT Press, 1995), 195.

3 As in a "tea dance," a dance in the early afternoon or evening. This performance was "derided by many contemporaries" but was in a format that has come to

be an integral part of the contemporary fashion show, as discussed in Evans, "Enchanted Spectacle," 275–278.

4 Ibid., 299.

5 Kaja Silverman, *The Threshold of the Visible World* (New York: Routledge, 1996); and Laura Mulvey, "Visual Pleasure and Narrative Cinema," *Screen* 16, no. 3 (1975): 6–18.

6 Fashion marketing professionals and some brand marketers do stress the idea of the "story" of a brand. I argue, however, that this story is part and parcel of the brand image, created in part by the immediate impact of the fashion show.

7 Caroline Evans, "Jean Patou's American Mannequins: Early Fashion Shows and Modernism," *Modernism/Modernity* 15, no. 2 (2008): 243–263, and "Enchanted Spectacle"; and Elizabeth Wilson, *Adorned in Dreams: Fashion and Modernity* (1987; reprint, London: I. B. Tauris, 2013).

8 Caroline Evans, "Enchanted Spectacle," and "The Walkies: Early French Fashion Shows as a Cinema of Attractions," in *Fashion in Film*, ed. Adrienne Munich (Bloomington: Indiana University Press, 2011), 110–134; Charlotte Herzog, "'Powder Puff' Promotion: The Fashion Show-in-the-Film," in *Fabrications: Costume and the Female Body*, ed. Jane Gaines and Charlotte Herzog (London: Routledge, 1990).

9 Edith Saunders, *The Age of Worth, Couturier to the Empress Eugénie* (Bloomington: Indiana University Press, 1955), 89.

10 Ibid., 90.

11 Ibid., 110.

12 Ibid. Caroline Evans suggests that many fashion books contain the "erroneous claim . . . that Worth was the first to use live mannequins," tracing this error of fact to a statement in Paul Poiret's autobiography, where he says, "The living mannequin . . . was invented by the great Worth, the first of the name, the pioneer of the industry of *la grande couture*" (see Paul Poiret, *King of Fashion: the Autobiography of Paul Poiret* [Philadelphia and London: J. P. Lippincott Co., 1931], 149). According to Evans, Diana de Marly argued that "Worth merely increased the number of house mannequins used by many Parisian dressmakers" and drew attention instead to the mercer Gagelin's mannequin parades (see Diana de Marly, *The History of Haute Couture, 1850–1950* [London: B. T. Batsford, 1980], 103–104).

13 Evans, "Enchanted Spectacle."

14 Gillis MacGil, *Your Future as a Model* (New York: Richards Rosen Press, 1964), 32.

15 *Demimondaine*, literally French for "half world," refers to underworld associations. Originally referring to behaviors violating bourgeois values, it later became a euphemism for "prostitute"; see de Marly, *The History of Haute Couture*, 140. *Demimondaines* were "the 'half-worldly' courtesans with whom French gentlemen could engage in sensual and other worldly pleasures, unknown to their wives" (Stuart Ewen and Elizabeth Ewen, *Channels of Desire: Mass Images and the Shaping of American Consciousness* [Minneapolis: University of Minnesota Press,

1992]). As such, chorus girls were viewed along the same lines as prostitutes and other ladies with disreputable social status. The model-turned-scholar Patricia Soley-Beltran observed, similarly, that, in spite of their fame, models were not received in polite society since mannequins were considered menials (Patricia Soley-Beltran, "Charming Power: Models as Ideal Embodiments of Normative Identity," *Trípodos: Llenguatge, Pensament, Comunicació* 18 [2006]: 27). To make ends meet, most of them were "looked after" by men (according to 1920s model Vera Ashby, better known as the legendary "Sumurun," quoted in Brigid Keenan, *The Women We Wanted to Look Like* [New York: St. Martin's Press, 1977], 113).

16 De Marly, *The History of Haute Couture*, 140.

17 Evans, "Enchanted Spectacle," 273.

18 Harriet Quick, *Catwalking: A History of the Fashion Model* (Minneapolis: Wellfleet Press, 1997), 27.

19 Nick Lee, "Becoming Mass: Glamour, Authority, and Human Presence," in *The Consumption of Mass*, ed. Nick Lee and Rolland Munro (Oxford: Blackwell, 2001), 174–188, esp. 183.

20 Charles Castle, *Model Girl* (Secaucus, NJ: Chartwell Books, 1977), 14.

21 Evans, "Enchanted Spectacle," 275.

22 Ashley Mears, *Pricing Beauty: The Making of a Fashion Model* (Los Angeles: University of California Press, 2011), 92.

23 Evans, "Enchanted Spectacle," 280.

24 Herzog, " 'Powder Puff' Promotion," 150.

25 Evans, "Enchanted Spectacle," 283.

26 Keenan, *The Women We Wanted to Look Like*, 111.

27 Herzog, " 'Powder Puff' Promotion," 138.

28 Evans, "Enchanted Spectacle," 283.

29 *New York Times*, "Balancing the Books of a Season at Coney Island; 20,000,000 People Visited the Resort Last Summer and They Spent There Something Like $45,000,000," October 24, 1909, 45, http://timesmachine.nytimes.com/timesmachine/1909/10/24/106777761.html, accessed August 15, 2014.

30 Stuart Ewen, *PR! A Social History of Spin* (New York: Basic Books, 1996); and Larry Tye, *The Father of Spin: Edward L. Bernays and the Birth of Public Relations* (New York: Picador, 2002).

31 Ewen and Ewen, *Channels of Desire*, 139.

32 William Leach, *Land of Desire: Merchants, Power, and the Rise of a New American Culture* (New York: Pantheon, 1993), 93.

33 Evans, "Enchanted Spectacle," 285.

34 Leach, *Land of Desire*, 274.

35 Ewen and Ewen, *Channels of Desire*, 149.

36 The discussion of "editing out waste" appears in Elspeth H. Brown, *The Corporate Eye: Photography and the Rationalization of American Commercial Culture, 1884–1929* (Baltimore: Johns Hopkins University Press, 2008), 77. "Visible mechanics" appears in Jean-Louis Comolli, "Machines of the Visible," in *The Cinematic*

Apparatus, ed. Teresa de Laurentis and Stephen Heath (London: Macmillan Press, 1980), 123.

37 Evans, "Enchanted Spectacle," 287.

38 Siegfried Kracauer, as quoted in Evans, "Jean Patou's American Mannequins," 249 (see Siegfried Kracauer, *The Mass Ornament: Weimar Essays*, trans. Thomas Y. Levin [Cambridge, MA, and London: Harvard University Press, 1995]).

39 Evans, "Enchanted Spectacle," 287.

40 Ibid., 281–282.

41 Michael Gross, *Model: The Ugly Business of Beautiful Women* (New York: Morrow, 1995), 49. This may not have been the first catwalk; it was the "first recorded instance of a catwalk" (ibid.).

42 Ibid.

43 Evans, "Jean Patou's American Mannequins," 243.

44 Marlis Schweitzer, *When Broadway Was the Runway: Theater, Fashion, and American Culture* (Philadelphia: University of Pennsylvania Press, 2009), 180.

45 Herzog, "'Powder Puff' Promotion," 134–159.

46 Charles Eckert, "The Carole Lombard in Macy's Window," in Gaines and Herzog, *Fabrications*, 120.

47 Evans, "Jean Patou's American Mannequins," 260.

48 Jean-Noël Liaut, *Cover Girls and Supermodels, 1945–1965* (New York: Marion Boyars, 1996), 119.

49 Evans, "Enchanted Spectacle," 293.

50 Liaut, *Cover Girls*, 119.

51 Quick, *Catwalking*, 75.

52 Liaut, *Cover Girls*, 14.

53 Evans, "*Enchanted Spectacle*," 293.

54 Ibid., 300.

55 Keenan, *The Women We Wanted to Look Like*, 111.

56 Ibid.

57 Castle, *Model Girl*, 33.

58 Mary Quant, *Quant by Quant* (New York: G. P. Putnam's Sons, 1966), 95.

59 Ibid., 94.

60 Ibid., 95.

61 Evans, "*Enchanted Spectacle*," 297.

62 Ibid.

63 Quant, *Quant by Quant*, 94.

64 Ibid., 128.

65 Evans, "*Enchanted Spectacle*," 300.

66 Ibid.

67 As designated by Evans; see ibid., 301.

68 Ibid., 301.

69 Ibid.

70 Teri Agins, *The End of Fashion* (New York: Morrow, 1999), 37.

71 Evans, "*Enchanted Spectacle*," 301.

72 Ibid., 303.

73 Castle, *Model Girl*, 29.

CHAPTER 3. THE PHOTO SHOOT

1 Ann Alvergue and Michael Isabel, *And Again* (Brooklyn: Eye Spy Films, 2002).

2 Nigel Thrift, "Understanding the Material Practices of Glamour," in *The Affect Reader*, ed. Melissa Gregg and Gregory J. Seigworth (Durham, NC: Duke University Press, 2010), 307.

3 David Slater, "The Fount of Inspiration: Minnie Clark, the Art Workers' Club for Women, and Performances of American Girlhood," *Winterthur Portfolio* 39, no. 4 (Winter 2004): 235.

4 Hillel Schwartz, *The Culture of the Copy: Striking Likenesses, Unreasonable Facsimiles* (New York: Zone Books, 1996), 326.

5 Michael Gross, *Model: The Ugly Business of Beautiful Women* (New York: Morrow, 1995), 47.

6 Richard Ohmann, *Selling Culture: Magazines, Markets and Class at the Turn of the Century* (New York: Verso, 1996), 234.

7 Carolyn Kitch, *The Girl on the Magazine Cover: The Origins of Visual Stereotypes in American Mass Media* (Chapel Hill: University of North Carolina Press, 2001), 5.

8 Ibid.

9 Robert A. Sobieszek, *The Art of Persuasion: A History of Advertising Photography* (New York: Abrams, 1988), 19–20.

10 Schwartz, *Culture of the Copy*, 326.

11 Daniel J. Kornstein, "The Roberson Privacy Controversy," *Historical Society of the Courts of the State of New York*, no. 4 (2006): 3–7, 13, www.nycourts.gov/history/programs-events/images/Judicial-Notice-Newsletter-04.pdf, accessed August 18, 2014; Kornstein sources the Roberson quote as coming from the *Rochester Democrat and Chronicle*, January 15, 1967, 3A, col. 3.

12 Ibid.

13 This legislation has lived on to the present day in the "release" form that contemporary models use to govern the use of their likeness, which codifies the length and number of times an image can be used. Without a release, a photographer is not allowed to sell an image of model as there is no way to verify the model's consent.

14 Schwartz, *Culture of the Copy*, 327.

15 William Leach, *Land of Desire: Merchants, Power, and the Rise of a New American Culture* (New York: Pantheon, 1993), 93.

16 Kitch, *The Girl on the Magazine Cover*, 4.

17 Jean-Louis Comolli, "Machines of the Visible," in *The Cinematic Apparatus*, ed. Teresa de Lauretis and Stephen Heath [London: Macmillan Press, 1980], 123. Coomolli further stated, "Coupled with the geographical extension of the

field of the visible and the representable, by journies, explorations, colonisations, the whole world becomes visible at the same time it becomes appropriatable" (ibid.).

18 Sandra Morris, *Catwalk: Inside the World of Supermodels* (New York: Weidenfeld & Nicolson, 1996), 87.

19 Gross, *Model*, 149.

20 Harold Koda and Kohle Yohannan, *The Model as Muse: Embodying Fashion* (New Haven, CT: Yale University Press, 2009), 18–19.

21 Ohmann, *Selling Culture*, 233. Society ladies' are named in Koda and Yohannan, *Model as Muse*, 10.

22 Harriet Quick, *Catwalking: A History of the Fashion Model* (Minneapolis: Wellfleet Press, 1997), 54.

23 Ibid.

24 William Leiss, Stephen Kline, and Sut Jhally, *Social Communication in Advertising: Persons, Products and Images of Well-Being* (New York: Routledge, 1997), 281.

25 Ibid.

26 Brigid Keenan, *The Women We Wanted to Look Like* (New York: St. Martin's Press, 1977), 134.

27 Jane Gaines and Charlotte Herzog, eds., *Fabrications: Costume and the Female Body* (London: Routledge, 1990), 16.

28 Sobieszek, *Art of Persuasion*, 32.

29 Morris, *Catwalk*, 87; James Sherwood and David Bailey, *Models, Close Up* (London: Universe, 1999), 6.

30 The quote is from Quick, *Catwalking*, 54. The latter point is from Jackson Lears, *Fables of Abundance: A Cultural History of Advertising in America* (New York: Basic Books, 1994), 329.

31 Charles Castle, *Model Girl* (Secaucus, NJ: Chartwell Books, 1977), 26.

32 Ibid.

33 John B. Kennedy, "Model Maids," *Collier's*, February 8, 1930, 9.

34 Castle, *Model Girl*, 77.

35 Ibid.

36 Ibid., 29.

37 Keenan, *The Women We Wanted to Look Like*, 140. The rest of this quote is ". . . and a new kind of girl had to be found to model the utility frocks, someone ordinary, cheerful, smiling through."

38 See under 1946 at "Timeline: A History of Magazines," part of "Magnificent Magforum—University of Westminster Journalism Website," n.d., www.magforum .com/time.htm#bbc, accessed August 18, 2014.

39 Keenan, *The Women We Wanted to Look Like*, 140.

40 Antony Beevor and Artemis Cooper, *Paris after the Liberation, 1944–1949* (London: Hamish Hamilton, 1994), as quoted in Patricia Soley-Beltran, "Charming Power: Models as Ideal Embodiments of Normative Identity," *Trípodos: Llenguatge, Pensament, Comunicació* 18 (2006): 27.

41 Nigel Cawthorne, *The New Look: The Dior Revolution* (Edison NJ: Wellfleet Press, 1996), 106.

42 Ibid.

43 Keenan, *The Women We Wanted to Look Like*, 117–118.

44 Liz Moor, *The Rise of Brands* (Oxford: Berg, 2007), 2.

45 Castle, *Model Girl*, 33.

46 The quote is from Quick, *Catwalking*, 69.

47 Koda and Yohannan, *Model as Muse*, 29.

48 Sherwood and Bailey, *Models, Close Up*, 12.

49 Koda and Yohannan, *Model as Muse*, 29–30.

50 Ibid.

51 Castle, *Model Girl*, 92.

52 Ibid.

53 Soley-Beltran, "Charming Power," 28.

54 Jean Shrimpton, quoted in Jennifer Craik, *The Face of Fashion: Cultural Studies in Fashion* (London: Routledge, 1994), 105.

55 Jeremy Gilbert-Rolfe, *Beauty and the Contemporary Sublime* (New York: Allworth Press, 1999); Gilles Deleuze, *Cinema 2: The Time-Image* (Minneapolis: University of Minnesota Press, 1989).

56 Daniel Harris, *Cute, Quaint, Hungry, and Romantic: The Aesthetics of Consumerism* (New York: Basic Books, 2000), 214.

57 Ibid. Interestingly, Harris surmised that "conventions of rigidity and blankness that arose from the association of fashion with graphically imprecise drawings linger on as a remnant of this older tradition, tending to foster a look of vacancy" still seen in many fashion photographs (215). The philosopher Nick Lee also said that contemporary models "are valued for their mastery of glamour, maximizing the amount they are looked at, while minimizing any awareness that they are looked at" (Nick Lee, "Becoming Mass: Glamour, Authority, and Human Presence," in *The Consumption of Mass*, ed. Nick Lee and Rolland Munro [Oxford: Blackwell, 2001], 184–185, esp. 183).

58 Harris, *Cute, Quaint*, 216 .

59 Sherwood and Bailey, *Models, Close Up*, 12.

60 Castle, *Model Girl*, 74.

61 Gilbert-Rolfe, *Beauty*, 15.

62 Ibid.

63 Up until the framing of the photographic age, "paint" was not yet socially acceptable. The growth of interest in fashion, linked with the struggle for woman suffrage, created a more permissive climate for consumption and adornment, paving the way for paint's social acceptance. See Kathy Peiss, *Hope in a Jar: The Making of America's Beauty Culture* (New York: Metropolitan Books, 1998).

64 Harris, *Cute, Quaint*, 222.

65 Ibid.

66 Ibid., 223.

67 Bee Shyuan-Chang, "Foundations Made for a High Definition Era," *New York Times*, April 3, 2012.

68 Ibid.

69 Susan Wood Gearhart, *Opportunities in Modeling Careers* (Lincolnwood, IL: VGM Career Horizons, NTC/Contemporary Publishing Group, 1999), 23.

70 A well-known model at the time, Carmen Dell'Orefice started out at thirteen, but her photos made her look thirty-six. The youth ideal was not confirmed as fashionable until the 1960s youth quake. Within this historic conjunction, the demand to look as if one were covered in a flesh-covered glaze, which depended on a dewy complexion to fulfill the ideal of the translucence, was met, not with makeup, but by using younger girls.

71 Models' starting ages were noted in the *Model as Muse* exhibit at the Metropolitan Museum of Art, May 6–August 9, 2009, www.metmuseum.org/exhibitions/listings/2009/model-as-muse, accessed January 29, 2015; the Gisele Bündchen story is from Koda and Yohannan, *Model as Muse*, 205.

72 Ashley Mears discussed the phenomenon of the "sell-by" date, in terms of a model's "shelf life," in *Pricing Beauty: The Making of a Fashion Model* (Los Angeles: University of California Press, 2011), 95.

73 Gearhart, *Opportunties*, 23.

74 Ibid., 24.

75 Castle, *Model Girl*, 158.

76 Ibid.

77 Keenan, *The Women We Wanted to Look Like*, 133.

78 Ibid.

79 Ibid., 128.

80 Craik, *Face of Fashion*, 107.

81 Castle, *Model Girl*, 64.

82 Diana Vreeland, *D.V.*, ed. George Plimpton and Christopher Hemphill (New York: Knopf, 1984), as quoted by Gross, *Model*, 249.

83 Maurya Wickstrom, *Performing Consumers: Global Capital and Its Theatrical Seductions* (New York: Routledge, 2006).

CHAPTER 4. COVER GIRL

1 Michael Gross, *Model: The Ugly Business of Beautiful Women* (New York: Morrow, 1995), 462. He is discussing Elaine Irwin, Tatiana Patz, and Karen Mulder, along with supermodels Christy Turlington, Naomi Campbell, Cindy Crawford, and Linda Evangelista.

2 "Question: What Are the Requirements for Being a Model?" *Models.com*, n.d., http://models.com/help/005-what_are_requirements.html, accessed January 29, 2015. See also Mears, "Discipline of the Catwalk: Gender, Power, and Uncertainty in Fashion Modeling," *Ethnography* 9, no. 4 (2008): 429–456. Mears points out that, while many models publicly lie about their measurements, they can only realistically get away with fudging their stats by an inch or two at the most.

3 The average American woman, in contrast, is 5'5" and weighs 142 pounds. *Allure* magazine reports that the dress size of the average American woman is a U.S. size 14, yet the dress size at which a model qualifies as being *plus*-size is a size 12; see Sarah Susan Van Boven, "Models," *Allure* 17, no. 7 (July 2007): 36.

4 Gross, *Model*, 272.

5 Paul Poiret, *King of Fashion: The Autobiography of Paul Poiret* (Philadelphia and London: J. P. Lippincott Co., 1931), 151.

6 According to my respondents, the general rules for height and weight are that women should be a minimum of 5'9" and men at least 5'11". Women should weigh less than 115 pounds with measurements no larger than 34" bust, 24" waist, and 34" hips. Men should wear a suit size of 40 regular.

7 Charles Castle, *Model Girl* (Secaucus, NJ: Chartwell Books, 1977), 22.

8 JoAnne Olian, *The House of Worth: The Gilded Age, 1860–1918* (New York: Museum of the City of New York, 1982), 3.

9 Nancy Green, *Ready to Wear and Ready to Work: A Century of Industry and Immigrants in Paris and New York* (Durham, NC: Duke University Press, 1997), 33.

10 "The chests and heights of over one million military conscripts were measured during the American Civil War. (Large numbers of women were measured at women's schools, starting with Vassar College in 1884) . . . the idea that garments could be made en masse—for anonymous bodies, according to a limited set of predetermined sizes—began to take hold" (ibid., 30).

11 These corsets were worn in a configuration "which meant they couldn't sit down all day" (Brigid Keenan, *The Women We Wanted to Look Like* [New York: St. Martin's Press, 1977], 111).

12 Ibid.

13 Edith Saunders, *The Age of Worth, Couturier to the Empress Eugénie* (Bloomington: Indiana University Press, 1955), 110.

14 Valerie Steele, *The Corset: A Cultural History* (New Haven, CT: Yale University Press, 2001), 143.

15 This happened in the 1920s, according to Caroline Evans, "The Enchanted Spectacle," *Fashion Theory: The Journal of Dress, Body and Culture* 5, no. 3 (August 2001): 287.

16 Lois Banner, *American Beauty* (New York: Knopf, 1983), 287.

17 Harold Koda, *Extreme Beauty: The Body Transformed* (New York: Metropolitan Museum of Art, 2001), 73.

18 In her eponymous 1991 book, Naomi Wolf defines the "beauty myth" as "a violent backlash against feminism that uses images of female beauty as a political weapon against women's advancement" (Naomi Wolf, *The Beauty Myth: How Images of Beauty Are Used against Women* [New York: Morrow, 1991], 9). The beauty myth ties a woman's value and power to how attractive she is and promises that, if she can just attain "beauty," then she will be happy. For Wolf, this promise is patently false, a political weapon used against women to keep them in their place. While

this myth is as old as patriarchy, Wolf traces its most recent incarnation to the 1830s, when the cult of domesticity was born of the industrial revolution, built on the male breadwinner/submissive female helpmate dyad, supporting new capitalist work arrangements. Since then, the myth has flourished whenever "material constraints on women are dangerously loosened" (11). With each surge in women's public power, each victory in the battle over female bodily control, has come a corresponding backlash of idealized images that have become slimmer with every decade. Thus, winning the vote in the early 1900s gave rise to a new ideal embodied by the boyish figure of the 1920s flapper. The stick-thin model Twiggy rose to fame in the wake of new freedom wrought by the Pill in the 1960s. In this view, women's increased corporate and political leadership in the 1990s inversely reflects the "waif" and size 0 fashion models' shrinking dimensions, currently in fashion. See also Susan Faludi, *Backlash: The Undeclared War against American Women* (New York: Crown, 1991), 203–204; and Wolf, *The Beauty Myth*, 9–12.

19 Elizabeth Wilson, *Adorned in Dreams: Fashion and Modernity* (1987; reprint, London: I. B. Tauris, 2013), 114. See also Gail Corrington, "Anorexia, Asceticism, and Autonomy: Self-Control as Liberation and Transcendence," *Journal of Feminist Studies in Religion* 2, no. 2 (1986): 51–61.

20 Wilson, *Adorned*, 115. The historian Elspeth Brown also noted this new emphasis on regimentation and control of the body for work in *The Corporate Eye*.

21 Stuart Ewen and Elizabeth Ewen, *Channels of Desire: Mass Images and the Shaping of American Consciousness* (Minneapolis: University of Minnesota Press, 1992), 152.

22 Ibid., 151, quoting Ingrid Brenninkmeyer, "The Sociology of Fashion" (Ph.D. diss., University of Fribourg, 1962), 163.

23 Ewen and Ewen, 151.

24 Eugenia Paulicelli, *Fashion under Fascism: Beyond the Black Skirt* (Oxford: Berg, 2004), 20.

25 Ibid.

26 Ibid.

27 Valerie Steele, *Paris Fashion: A Cultural History* (New York: Oxford University Press, 1988), 252.

28 "The yankee menace" (ibid., 257).

29 Ibid., 256.

30 Brown, *The Corporate Eye*, 6.

31 Wilson, *Adorned*, 158. Arguing this appealingly simple point runs the risk of fetishizing one influence, photography, within a field of different influences and tendencies. Even within photography, other influences were at work. The aesthetic of pictorialism, e.g., an influence the historian Elspeth Brown found in the advertising photography of this era, rejected photography's realism in favor of a more emotional expression, using the camera "like a brush" rather than a recording device (Elspeth Brown, *The Corporate Eye: Photography and the*

Rationalization of American Commercial Culture, 1884–1929 [Baltimore: Johns Hopkins University Press, 2008], 187). The fact that both the pictorialist aesthetic and the black-and-white realist aesthetic Elizabeth Wilson described co-existed seems to throw Wilson's argument into question. Wilson, however, discussed only fashion photography. The pictorialist style was popular in general advertising photographs and was not as evident or influential in the domain of fashion. Discussing influences beyond the realm of photography, Wilson also specifically tied the slim aesthetic to the artistic movements of modernism and futurism whose look shaped the clothes becoming popular when fashion photography really began to hit its stride in the later twenties. Thus, although pictorialism was also a photographic practice of the day, clearly, the modernist photographic aesthetic of fashion shaped the fashionable body toward a cleaned, lined, mechanistic look.

32 Wilson, *Adorned*, 116, citing Anne Hollander, *Seeing through Clothes* (1975; reprint, New York: Avon Books, 1993).

33 Elizabeth Wilson, "All the Rage," in *Fabrications: Costume and the Female Body*, ed. Jane Gaines and Charlotte Herzog (London: Routledge, 1990), 34. The cultural studies scholar Jennifer Craik alluded to this idea as well, saying, "The modernist influences of the 1920s and 1930s contributed to representational techniques that emphasized form over content" (Jennifer Craik, *The Face of Fashion: Cultural Studies in Fashion* [London: Routledge, 1994], 100).

34 Wilson, *Adorned*, 116.

35 "In 1918, total gross advertising revenues in general and farm magazines was $58.5 million. By 1920 the gross had reached $129.5 million; and by 1929, $196.3 million. . . . In the period 1900–1930, national advertising revenues multiplied thirteen fold (from $200 million to $2.6 billion)" (Stuart Ewen, *Captains of Consciousness: Advertising and the Social Roots of the Consumer Culture* [New York: McGraw-Hill, 1976], 32, 62).

36 Kathy Peiss, *Hope in a Jar: The Making of America's Beauty Culture* (New York: Metropolitan Books, 1998), 103.

37 As the journalist Larry Tye noted in his biography of Edward Bernays, the 1920s were a time when propaganda became a powerful tool used to "reshape reality" (Larry Tye, *The Father of Spin: Edward L. Bernays and the Birth of Public Relations* [New York: Picador, 2002], 52).

38 John Robert Powers, *The Powers Girls: The Story of Models and Modeling and the Natural Steps by Which Attractive Girls Are Created*, 1st ed. (New York: E. P. Dutton & Co., 1941), 21.

39 Ibid.

40 Gross, *Model*, 15; William Leach, *Land of Desire: Merchants, Power, and the Rise of a New American Culture* (New York: Pantheon, 1993), 309.

41 According to my survey of the business listings in the *Manhattan Yellow Pages* at the New York Public Library, the number of modeling agencies has grown every year, since the first firm was incorporated in the 1920s. The number of agencies

listed in the Manhattan Yellow Pages increased from 8 to 143 between 1935 and 2002. The number of models has grown as well. The *2010 Occupational Outlook Handbook* said that, in 2004, models held about 2,200 jobs; the profession was expected to grow about as fast as average for all occupations throughout 2014 (U.S. Bureau of Labor Statistics, *2010 Occupational Outlook Handbook*, www.bls .gov/cps/wlftable3.htm, accessed May 2010). In a climate in which businesses have sought tighter control over unpredictable workers and markets, other countries have followed suit: "The first model agency was opened in London [The Lucie Clayton Agency, in] 1928. It was the brain child of [the former model] Sylvia Gollidge, a brown-eyed girl from Blackpool who stood five feet eleven inches tall and had insured her long blonde hair for a thousand pounds" (Keenan, *The Women We Wanted to Look Like*, 114); Dorian Leigh opened the first modeling agency in Paris in the 1950s, according to Gross, *Model*, 158. This wave of professionalization swept the fashion industry, as well. It got better organized as retailers, cosmetics firms, and advertisers joined forces with garment manufacturers, merchandising stylists, and women's magazines via tie-ins and other promotions to regulate and codify the vagaries of fashion for more predictable profits (Peiss, *Hope in a Jar*, 129).

42 Powers, *The Powers Girls*, 45.

43 John B. Kennedy, "Model Maids," *Collier's*, February 8, 1930, 9–10.

44 Ibid., 10.

45 Ibid.

46 Ibid.

47 Gross, *Model*, 44.

48 Powers, *The Powers Girls*, 21.

49 Leach, *Land of Desire*, 309.

50 Powers, *The Powers Girls*, 24.

51 Leach, *Land of Desire*, 310.

52 Powers, *The Powers Girls*, 27.

53 Ibid.

54 Gross, *Model*, 44. With regard to naming his models, see also Powers, *The Powers Girls*, 32.

55 Gross, *Model*, 48.

56 Ibid.

57 Don Slater and Joanne Entwistle, "Models as Brands: Critical Thinking about Bodies and Images" in *Fashioning Models: Image Text and Industry*, ed. Joanne Entwistle and Elizabeth Wissinger (London: Berg, 2012).

58 Castle, *Model Girl*, 183.

59 Leach, *Land of Desire*, 309; see also Gross, *Model*, 1995.

60 Powers, *The Powers Girls*, 21–22.

61 Johnathan Crary, *Suspensions of Perception* (Cambridge, MA: MIT Press, 2001), 138.

62 Jonathan Beller, *The Cinematic Mode of Production: Attention Economy and the Society of the Spectacle* (Hanover, NH: Dartmouth College Press, 2006), 38. Vertov discussed these terms widely and treated them in *Kino-Eye: The Writings of Dziga Vertov*, ed. Annette Michelson, trans. Kevin O'Brien (Berkeley and Los Angeles: University of California Press, 1984).

63 Powers, *The Powers Girls*, 49.

64 Castle, *Model Girl*, 134.

65 The cost of producing these books was always charged to the models. When asked about having to pay for these books each year out of her earnings, Jamie explained, "We were not given a choice in the matter."

66 Elizabeth M. Matelski, "The Color(s) of Perfection: The Feminine Body, Beauty Ideals, and Identity in Postwar America, 1945–1970" (Ph.D. diss., Loyola University of Chicago, 2011), 26, citing Hillel Schwartz, *Never Satisfied: A Cultural History of Diets, Fantasies, and Fat* (New York: Free Press, 1986), 231.

67 Ibid.

68 Kennedy, "Model Maids."

69 Castle, *Model Girl*, 29.

70 Gross, *Model*, 59.

71 Maureen Daly, "The Trouble with Women . . ." in *Ladies Home Journal*, August 1946, 8, as cited in Elizabeth Matelski, "'Build Ups' and 'Slim Downs,' Re-shaping America, 1945–1970," *Skepsi Journal* 5, no. 1 (2012): 46.

72 Matelski, "The Color(s) of Perfection," 26.

73 His models, known as Conover Cover Girls, were so popular and well known, they inspired the 1945 movie, *Cover Girl*.

74 Matelski, "The Color(s) of Perfection," 27.

75 Carole Conover, *Cover Girls: The Story of Harry Conover* (Englewood Cliffs, NJ: Prentice Hall, 1978), 48.

76 Gross, *Model*, 66.

77 Carole Conover, *Cover Girls*, 48.

78 Harry Conover, *Who Is She?* (New York: Harry Conover Publications, 1945).

79 Matelski, "The Color(s) of Perfection," 101–102. Also, as Matelski has pointed out, "although Audrey Hepburn and Marilyn Monroe represented two very different types of popular actresses in the 1950s, both women's figures were the same variation on the classic hourglass figure. Monroe's 36-24-34 figure to Hepburn's 31.5-22-31 is the same waist-to-hip ratio of .70" (ibid., 33).

80 For example, an article entitled "Physical Perfection, the Old Hollywood Way" carried the deck "Flesh Sculptors: Screen Players Find It's Fun to Keep Healthy—Here's How." The article's diet and exercise advice was punctuated with photographs of screen stars Ginger Rogers, Fred Astaire, and Marlene Dietrich (*Literary Digest*, March 6, 1937, 18–19, www.oldmagazinearticles.com, accessed March 22, 2014).

81 As per the "rocket bra" discussed by Wendy A. Burns-Ardolino in *Jiggle: (Re)Shaping American Women* (Lanham, MD: Lexington Books, 2007), 29.

82 "Flesh Sculptors: Keeping Healthy in Tinseltown," *Literary Digest*, March 6, 1937, 18–19, quote on 18, www.oldmagazinearticles.com, accessed March 22, 2014.

83 John Robert Powers and Mary Sue Miller, *The Secrets of Charm* (Philadelphia: John C. Winston Co., 1954).

84 Maurice Zolotow, "The Hatbox Brigade," *Coronet*, February 1944, 98, www .oldmagazinearticles.com, accessed March 14, 2015.

85 Ibid., 97.

86 These pressures may have affected more specialized forms of bodily display, such as dance. My main concern here, however, is bodies that were deployed to display fashion, which were, consequently, governed by fashions in bodies.

87 Green, *Ready to Wear*, 42.

88 Keenan, *The Women We Wanted to Look Like*, 144; this was only in England.

89 Matelski, "The Color(s) of Perfection," 20.

90 Ibid., 20–21.

91 Ibid., 35.

92 Ibid.

93 "Thus, beginning in the 1950s, Americans, particularly women, dieted and exercised their way towards skinnier, more firm and trim figures as a consequence of a tightened relationship between fashion, foreign policy, insurance figures, and medical opinion. A new, all-consuming discourse in prescriptive literature, namely women's magazines, demanded thinness above all" (Matelski, "'Build Ups' and 'Slim Downs,'" 43).

94 Ibid.

95 Castle, *Model Girl*, 91.

96 Harold Koda in *Model as Muse* has the founding date as 1947 (30).

97 Gross, *Model*, 103.

98 Magazines were extremely influential during this period. According to the historian Elizabeth Matelski, "When *Seventeen* magazine debuted in September 1944, the first run of 400,000 copies sold out in six days. By February 1947, circulation exceeded 1 million and by July 1949, over 2.5 million girls were reading the magazine" ("The Color(s) of Perfection," 44). Fashion magazines' growing influence were part of an increase in magazine consumption more generally, as Matelski points out: "During the 1950s, in fact, five out of six women read at least one magazine every week" (ibid., 24).

99 Clyde Matthew Dessner, *So You Want to Be a Model!* (Garden City, NY: Halcyon House, 1948), xv.

100 Gross, *Model*, 103.

101 Keenan, *The Women We Wanted to Look Like*, 147.

102 Castle, *Model Girl*, 91.

103 Gross, *Model*, 71.

104 Powers, *The Powers Girls*, 29.

105 Ibid., 30.

106 Keenan, *The Women We Wanted to Look Like*, 147.

CHAPTER 5. THE FASHIONABLE IDEAL

1 Mary Quant, *Quant by Quant* (New York: G. P. Putnam's Sons, 1966), 182.

2 Ibid.

3 Ibid., 186.

4 Ibid., 187–188.

5 Ibid., 188.

6 Ibid., 184.

7 Ibid., 199.

8 David Bailey, *Models, Close Up* (New York: Universe, 1999), 15.

9 Cited as a desirable role model in Daphne du Maurier's *Rebecca* (1938; reprint, New York: Doubleday, 2002), 37.

10 Michael Gross, *Model: The Ugly Business of Beautiful Women* (New York: Morrow, 1995), 203; Brigid Keenan, *The Women We Wanted to Look Like* (New York: St. Martin's Press, 1977), 150.

11 Harriet Quick, *Catwalking: A History of the Fashion Model* (Minneapolis: Wellfleet Press, 1997), 96–97. As a child I remember seeing her appear on a few television variety shows, but she seemed more a sad relic of a former age than the scene-stealing superstar she once had been.

12 Roberta Pollack Seid, *Never Too Thin: Why Women Are at War with Their Bodies* (New York: Prentice Hall, 1989), 64.

13 Keenan, *The Women We Wanted to Look Like*, 150.

14 Gross, *Model*, 205.

15 The hard-won freedom from restrictive stays and boning in women's undergarments wrought by the women's movement of the 1960s and 1970s was smuggled back as restrictions to the natural waistline, under the guise of the fashionably lean body.

16 Gillis MacGil, *Your Future as a Model* (New York: Richards Rosen Press, 1964), 14.

17 Viju Krem, *How to Become a Successful Model* (New York: Arco Publishing Co., 1975), 27.

18 Eve Matheson, *The Modeling Handbook: The Complete Guide to Breaking into Local, Regional, and International Modeling* (New York: Henry Holt & Co., 1995), 205.

19 The popular catchphrase was associated with the ad campaign of the Barbizon School of Modeling, which appeared, for instance, in *Co-Ed* 19, no. 1 (September 1973), and in many publications of this sort during the 1970s and 1980s. The Barbizon School also published a how-to book by Francine Marlowe, *Your Career Opportunities in Modeling* (New York: Barbizon Int'l, 1983), although Marlowe declined to use the popular tagline in this collection of advice.

20 Donna Rubinstein, *The Modeling Life* (New York: Berkley, 1998), 160.

21 Susan Wood Gearhart, *Opportunities in Modeling Careers* (Lincolnwood, IL: VGM Career Horizons, NTC/Contemporary Publishing Group, 1999), 24.

22 Eileen Ford, *Eileen Ford's Book of Model Beauty* (New York: Simon & Schuster, 1968), 16.

23 Eileen Ford, *Secrets of the Model's World* (New York: Trident Press, 1970), 36.

24 Candy Jones, *Modeling and Other Glamour Careers: The First Complete Guide to Professional Modeling* (New York: Harper & Row, 1969), 47.

25 Ibid.

26 Ibid., 49.

27 Ibid., 3.

28 Krem, *How to Become a Successful Model*, 21.

29 Ibid., 27.

30 Ibid., 109.

31 Hal Greene, *Professional Modeling* (Redondo Beach, CA: Killy-Moon Press, 1975), 15.

32 Ibid., 55. This practice echoes the coercive weigh-ins that dominated the airhostess industry in the 1960s and 1970s, a group under similar surveillance to ensure their bodies fit a standard, in this case for creating the airlines' brand, as discussed in Drew Whitelegg's *Working the Skies* (New York: NYU Press, 2007), 142–143; and Kathleen Barry's *Femininity in Flight: A History of Flight Attendants* (Durham, NC: Duke University Press, 2007), 48.

33 Krem, *How to Become a Successful Model*, 21.

34 Cecily Hunt, *How to Get Work and Make Money in Commercials and Modeling* (New York: Van Nostrand Reinhold, 1982), 25. It should be noted that, with vanity sizing popularized in the 1980s, a woman's size 6 became a size 2.

35 Ibid.

36 Kyle Roderick, *The Model's Handbook: For Every Woman Who Wants to Be a Model or Look Like One* (New York: Morrow, 1984), 110. This book was first published in Great Britain, so the sizes listed are UK sizes.

37 Marie Philomene Anderson, *Model: The Complete Guide to Becoming a Professional Model* (New York: Doubleday, 1988), 16.

38 Ibid., 18.

39 Gearhart, *Opportunities*, 23.

40 Ibid., 24.

41 Ibid.

42 Ibid., 117.

43 Nina Blanchard, *How to Break into Motion Pictures, Television, Commercials and Modeling* (New York: Doubleday, 1978), 195.

44 Ibid., 205.

45 Marlowe, *Your Career Opportunities*, 53.

46 Ibid.

47 Eric Perkins, *The Insider's Guide to Modeling: The Pros Tell You How* (New York: Nautilus Books, 1985), 65.

48 Ibid., 23. Emphasis in original.

49 Ibid., 29.

50 Matheson, *The Modeling Handbook*, 26.

51 Ibid. "Energy" or "personality" or "projection" are mentioned on 5, 86, 92, 123, 129, and 130 as a quality deemed necessary for success.

52 Rubinstein, *Modeling Life*, 160.

53 Ibid.

54 Ibid., 162.

55 Ibid.

56 Eric Bean and Jenni Bidner, *Complete Guide for Models: Inside Advice from Industry Pros* (New York: Lark Books, 2004), 58.

57 Ibid., 61.

58 Ibid., 74, 77.

59 Kendall Herbst, "The Cut: CFDA Panel on Skinny Models: Coco Rocha Admits to Using Diuretics," *New York Magazine*, June 11, 2008.

60 Tiziana Terranova, "Futurepublic: On Information Warfare, Bio-racism and Hegemony as Noopolitics," *Theory, Culture and Society* 24, no. 3 (May 2007): 125–145, quote at 137.

61 Ibid., 138.

62 Bean and Bidner, *Complete Guide*, 61.

63 Roderick, *The Model's Handbook*, 110.

64 "Christian Zamora: Hair, Makeup and Lash Stylist," n.d., www.christianzamora .com, accessed July 6, 2014.

65 David Serlin, *Replaceable You: Engineering the Body in Postwar America* (Chicago: University of Chicago Press, 2004).

66 Elizabeth Grosz, *Space, Time, and Perversion: Essays on the Politics of Bodies* (New York: Routledge, 1995), 33–38.

67 Patricia Clough, "The Affective Turn: Political Economy, Biomedia and Bodies," *Theory, Culture and Society* 25, no. 1 (2008): 2.

68 French for "I don't know what."

69 Patricia Ticineto Clough and Craig Willse, "Human Security / National Security," *Beyond Biopolitics: Essays on the Governance of Life and Death*, ed. Patricia Clough and Craig Willse (Durham, NC: Duke University Press, 2011), 59.

CHAPTER 6. THE JOB

1 New York State, Department of Labor, "Unemployment Insurance: Title 2 Definitions," n.d., www.labor.ny.gov/ui/dande/title2.shtm, accessed June 19, 2012.

2 Ibid.

3 Chapter 668s, 7505-A of the New York Labor and Compensation Law (1992).

4 A term prostitutes are also known for using. In both cases, referring to their job as "the life" suggests the all-encompassing nature of doing the job.

5 Maurizio Lazzarato, "Immaterial Labour," in *Radical Thought in Italy: A Potential Politics*, ed. Michael Hardt, Paolo Virno, Sandra Buckley, and Brian Massumi (Minneapolis: University of Minnesota Press, 1996), 133–147, quote at 133. The

marxist scholars Antonio Negri and Michael Hardt further refined this concept into the "immaterial paradigm" of labor, whose overarching tendencies take three specific forms: the informatization of production (via computerization or robotics), the rise of "symbolic-analytical services" (management, problem-solving and routine symbol manipulation), and affective labor, performed either through actual or virtual human contact or interaction, which produce "intangible feelings of ease, excitement, or passion" (Michael Hardt and Antonio Negri, *Multitude: War and Democracy in the Age of Empire* [New York: Penguin, 2004]). See also Michael Hardt and Antonio Negri, *Empire* (Cambridge, MA: Harvard University Press, 2000), 293. Health services and the entertainment industry, e.g., both depend on outputs of affective labor such as caring and emoting. These types of services are usually in-person services, but the production and manipulation of affect or feeling can also be achieved through human contact that is virtual (such as the work of an actor appearing in a movie, or the work of a model appearing in a photograph).

6 Lazzarato, "Immaterial Labour."

7 Brigid Keenan, *Women We Wanted to Look Like* (New York: St. Martin's Press, 1977), 133.

8 While Michael Arthur and Denise Rousseau discussed the notion of boundaryless career trajectories, they acknowledge the dissolving lines between off time and on time engendered by this economic trend (Michael B. Arthur and Denise M. Rousseau, *The Boundaryless Career: A New Employment Principle for a New Organizational Era* [New York: Oxford University Press, 1996]).

9 Virginia Postrel, *The Substance of Style: How the Rise of Aesthetic Value Is Remaking Commerce, Culture, and Consciousness* (New York: Harper Collins, 2003), 6.

10 Michael Hardt, "Affective Labor," *Boundary 2* 26, no. 2 (1999): 89–100; Hardt and Negri, *Empire* and *Multitude*; Brian Massumi, *The Politics of Everyday Fear* (Minneapolis: University of Minnesota Press, 1993), and *Parables for the Virtual: Movement, Affect, Sensation* (Durham, NC: Duke University Press, 2002); Patricia Clough, *Autoaffection: Unconscious Thought in the Age of Teletechnology* (Minneapolis: University of Minnesota Press, 2000); and Patricia Clough and Jean Halley, eds., *The Affective Turn: Theorizing the Social* (Durham, NC: Duke University Press, 2007). See also Henry Jenkins regarding "affective economics," which describes the shift toward open-ended relations between consumers and products (Henry Jenkins, *Convergence Culture: Where Old and New Media Collide* [New York: NYU Press, 2006]).

11 Liz Moor, *The Rise of Brands* (Oxford: Berg, 2007), 3.

12 Nigel Thrift, "Reinventing Invention: New Tendencies in Capitalist Commodification," *Economy and Society* 35, no. 2 (May 2006): 279–306, quote at 285–286.

13 Sarah Banet-Weiser, *Authentic™: The Politics of Ambivalence in Brand Culture* (New York: NYU Press, 2012), 42.

14 Ibid., 43.

15 Emma Dowling, "The Waitress: On Affect, Method, and (Re)Presentation," *Cultural Studies—Critical Methodologies* 12, no. 2 (April 2012): 109–117. In a similar vein, as the psychologist Teresa Brennan posed the question, to explain how affect is transmitted, "is there anyone who has not, at least once, walked into a room and 'felt the atmosphere'?" (Teresa Brennan, *The Transmission of Affect* [Ithaca, NY: Cornell University Press, 2004], 1).

16 Models at this level usually work for the high-fashion magazines, such as *Vogue, Elle,* or *L'Officiel.* They often model couture clothes and work for highly esteemed clients selling luxury goods, such as Hermes, Chanel, or Louis Vuitton.

17 Arlie Hochschild, *The Managed Heart: The Commercialization of Human Feeling* (Berkeley: University of California Press, 1983).

18 Eric Perkins, *The Insider's Guide to Modeling: The Pros Tell You How* (New York: Nautilus Books, 1985), 50; emphasis added.

19 Anna Gibbs, "Disaffected," *Continuum: Journal of Media and Cultural Studies* 16 (2002): 335–341.

20 Benedict de Spinoza, *Ethics*, trans. Edwin Curley (1994; reprint, New York: Penguin Books, 1996), 70.

21 Richard Doyle, "LSDNA: Rhetoric, Consciousness Expansion, and the Emergence of Biotechnology," *Philosophy and Rhetoric* 35, no. 2 (2002): 153–174.

22 As the social geographer Nigel Thrift has described it, "affect" is a force that "generates sensory and emotional gratification" and "produces shared capacity and commonality" (Nigel Thrift, "Understanding the Material Practices of Glamour," in *The Affect Theory Reader*, ed. Melissa Gregg and Gregory Seigworth [Durham, NC: Duke University Press, 2010], 291.

23 Patrik Aspers, *Markets in Fashion: A Phenomenological Approach*, 2nd ed. (2001; reprint, London: Routledge, 2006), 44.

24 This value in relationships explains why, in part, models will do a high-status job for well- known magazines such as *Vogue* for very little money; an editorial shoot for such a magazine often pays as little as $100–$150 for the day, whereas the same amount of time spent for a commercial client could be valued at several thousand dollars.

25 This production of relationships as one of the core activities of modeling work also speaks to Hardt and Negri's definition of affective labor as that which "always directly constructs a relationship" (Hardt and Negri, *Multitude*, 147).

26 Michael Gross, *Model: The Ugly Business of Beautiful Women* (New York: Morrow, 1995), 506.

27 Rosalind C. Gill, "Technobohemians or the New Cybertariat? New Media Work in Amsterdam a Decade after the Web" (Amsterdam: Institute of Network Cultures, 2007).

28 Such markets tend toward young workers, between the ages of sixteen and twenty-four, who are slightly more likely to be women or blacks (A. Plovinka, "A Profile of Contingent Workers," *Monthly Labor Review* 119 [1996]: 10–21; Isik

Zeytinoglu, *Changing Work Relationships in Industrial Countries* [Amsterdam: John Benjamins Publishing, 1999]).

29 Robert Frank and Philip Cook, *The Winner Take All Society: Why the Few at the Top Get So Much More than the Rest of Us* (New York: Penguin Books, 1995).

30 See, e.g., Angela McRobbie, "Reflections on Feminism, Immaterial Labour, and the Post-Fordist Regime," *New Formations* 70, no. 17 (Winter 2011): 60–76.

31 "While women have almost always done 'immaterial and affective labour, often with little recognition in both fields,' precariousness was only discussed 'at the moment when the Western male worker began feeling the negative effects of the new post-industrial flexible job market'" (Gill and Pratt, "In the Social Factory?" 11, citing Laura Fantone, "Precarious Changes: Gender and Generational Politics in Contemporary Italy," *Feminist Review* 87 [2007]: 5–20, at 7).

32 To Gill and Pratt's tentative question posed in 2008, I say, Yes, indeed!: "Might the growth of precarization also be connected to the growth and development of the worldwide web and the huge expansion of the cultural industries and cultural production—both areas which are characterized by the degree to which they presume precarious labour?" (Gill and Pratt, "In the Social Factory?" 11).

33 Ashley Mears, *Pricing Beauty: The Making of a Fashion Model* (Los Angeles: University of California Press, 2011), 41, 49, 60.

34 Heidi Klum says this on each episode of the reality television show *Project Runway*.

35 In September 2005, Kate Moss experienced a "professional free fall, following publication by a London tabloid of a grainy video image said to depict her snorting cocaine at a London recording studio" (Guy Trebay, "Taking the Fall for Fashion," *New York Times*, September 29, 2005), after which several of her high-profile clients yanked their campaigns. Less than a year later, however, she seemed to be in even more demand than ever, appearing in several high end campaigns (according to an informal accounting as of September 2006, in American *Vogue* she was featured in at least five campaigns, including such well-known marks as Dior, Louis Vuitton, and Versace), as if the notoriety had boosted her career.

36 Plum Sykes, "View from the Top," *Vogue*, August 2008, 185.

37 Alice Marwick, *Status Update: Celebrity, Publicity, and Branding In the Social Media Age* (New Haven, CT: Yale University Press, 2013), 15.

38 Immaterial labor is typified by moments in which it seems "life becomes inseparable from work" (Lazzarato, "Immaterial Labour," 138).

39 For a full breakdown of how modeling work is actually a form of entrepreneurial labor that plays into the current needs of capitalism for workers willing to assume more than their fair share of risk, see Gina Neff, Elizabeth Wissinger, and Sharon Zukin, "Entrepreneurial Labor among Cultural Producers: 'Cool' Jobs in 'Hot' Industries," *Social Semiotics* 15, no. 3 (2005): 307–334.

40 David Grazian, *On the Make: The Hustle of Urban Nightlife* (Chicago: University of Chicago Press, 2008), 77, 86.

41 Ibid., 86.

42 Ibid., 78.

43 Ibid., 79–80.

44 Ibid., 83.

45 Allen Salkin, "Hard at Work: The Model Whisperer," *New York Times*, February 10, 2008.

46 Ashley Mears, "Who Runs the Girls?" *New York Times*, September 20, 2014.

47 Elizabeth Currid, *The Warhol Economy: How Fashion, Art, and Music Drive New York City* (Princeton, NJ: Princeton University Press, 2007), 87.

48 Ibid., 89.

49 Ibid., 95.

50 Neff et al., "Entrepreneurial Labor."

51 David Grazian, "Book Review of *The Warhol Economy: How Fashion, Art, and Music Drive New York City*, by Elizabeth Currid," *Journal of Planning Education and Research* 28 (2008): 116, esp. 117, referring to Neff et al., "Entrepreneurial Labor."

52 Currid, *The Warhol Economy*, 6.

53 Adam Arvidsson, "Brands: A Critical Perspective," *Journal of Consumer Culture* 5, no. 2 (2005): 235–258, quote at 245.

54 Ibid., 245, citing A. Barry, *Political Machines: Governing a Technological Society* (London: Athlone, 2001); and S. Zizek, "You May!" *London Review of Books*, March 18, 1999, 3–6.

55 Arvidsson, "Brands," 248.

56 Ibid., 246.

57 Ibid., 248; see also Banet-Weiser, *Authentic*, 84.

58 Renata Espinosa, "Ford Names New Supermodel of the World," *Fashion Wire Daily*, January 17, 2008, http://fashionwiredaily.com, accessed August 30, 2014.

59 Mel Fabrikant, "Ford Supermodel Finalists Invade Westfield Garden State Plaza Shopping Center," *Paramus (NJ) Post*, January 15, 2008, www.paramuspost.com/article.php/20080115121232740, accessed August 30, 2014.

60 Eric Wilson, "Waiting to Show Model Behavior," *New York Times*, March 26, 2007.

61 Markets at that time were confirmed by the former *America's Next Top Model* judge, Nigel Barker, in conversation on August 14, 2007. See also the *America's Next Top Model: International Versions*, 2008, http://americantopmodels.blogspot .com/2008/02/international-versions.html, accessed January 30, 2015, for con-current data, as well CWPress, "About *America's Next Top Model*," n.d., www .cwtvpr.com/the-cw/shows/americas-next-top-model/about, accessed March 31, 2015, for more recent data.

62 The website *Tyra*, at Tyra.com, accessed August 5, 2014.

63 Performing, Mark Andrejevic has called it, "the work of watching" as well as the work of being watched (Mark Andrejevic, *iSpy: Surveillance and Power in the Interactive Era* [Lawrence: University Press of Kansas, 2007], 13–14). Tyra

ringtones were found at *America's Next Top Model* website, www.cwtv.com/shows/americas-next-top-model/about, n.d., accessed January 2010.

64 Timothy Greenfield-Sanders, *About Face: Supermodels Then and Now* (New York: HBO, 2012), is a documentary about models aging in a business that demands they try to stay forever young; it aired July 30, 2012, on HBO's cable network.

CHAPTER 7. SCOUTING

1 Caroline Evans, "Jean Patou's American Mannequins: Early Fashion Shows and Modernism," *Modernism/Modernity* 15, no. 2 (2008): 243–263; John Robert Powers, *The Powers Girls: The Story of Models and Modeling and the Natural Steps by Which Attractive Girls Are Created*, 1st ed. (New York: E. P. Dutton & Co., 1941), 43.

2 These quotes are from a *New York Times* human interest piece on a freelance casting director who scouts models for a living; see Ginia Bellafonte, "Believe Her If She Asks You, 'Would You Like to Be a Model?'" *New York Times*, May 8, 2001, B11. Kate Upton, American supermodel, was discovered on YouTube (David Gardner, "From Cutie to £50Million Beauty: How YouTube Sensation Kate Upton Became Most In-Demand Supermodel and Her 20 Best Pictures," *Mirror Online*, July 22, 2012, www.mirror.co.uk/news/world-news/kate-upton-the-youtube-sensation-whos-1153874, accessed June 10, 2014.

3 Eric Bean and Jenni Bidner, *Complete Guide for Models: Inside Advice from Industry Pros* (New York, Lark Books, 2004), 10.

4 Kristin Peterson, "Benefit Sharing for All? Bioprospecting NGOs, Intellectual Property Rights, New Governmentalities," *PoLAR* 25, no. 1 (2001): 78–91.

5 See also Eugene Thacker, *Biomedia* (Cambridge, MA: MIT Press, 2004).

6 Peterson, "Benefit Sharing for All?" 78.

7 As Sarah Banet-Weiser has pointed out, the "quest for visibility" has become a normative practice for twenty-first-century empowerment (Sarah Banet-Weiser, *Authentic™: The Politics of Ambivalence in Brand Culture* [New York: NYU Press, 2012]).

8 Mimi Thi Nguyen, "The Biopower of Beauty: Humanitarian Imperialisms and Global Feminisms in an Age of Terror," *Signs* 36, no. 2 (Winter 2011): 374.

9 *IMTA: International Models and Talent*, http://imta.com website, accessed January 11, 2013.

10 *ProScout, Inc.*, at proscout.com, accessed January 11, 2013; this website has since gone dark.

11 *Model Scouts*, www.modelscouts.com, accessed January 11, 2013.

12 Marc Lacey, "In Remotest Kenya, a Supermodel Is Hard to Find," *New York Times*, April 22, 2003.

13 Ashley Mears, *Pricing Beauty: The Making of a Fashion Model* (Los Angeles: University of California Press, 2011), 167.

14 A French term that roughly translates as "beautiful-ugly."

15 Mears, *Pricing Beauty*, 124.

16 Ibid.

17 Ibid., 157.

18 Joanne Entwistle, *The Aesthetic Economy of Fashion: Markets and Value in Clothing and Modeling* (London: Bloomsbury, 2009), 3.

19 Mears, *Pricing Beauty*, 250.

20 Ibid.

21 Herbert Blumer, "Fashion: From Class Differentiation to Collective Selection," *Sociological Quarterly* 10, no. 3 (1969): 278–279.

22 Pierre Bourdieu, *Distinction: A Social Critique of the Judgement of Taste* (Cambridge, MA: Harvard University Press, 1984).

23 Mears, *Pricing Beauty*, 127.

24 See the Elite World website at www.elitemodelworld.com, accessed February 12, 2008, and January 11, 2013.

25 *PR Newswire*, "Ford Models Kicks Off Its 22nd Annual SUPERMODEL OF THE WORLD World Finals in Punta Cana, Dominican Republic," press release, December 2, 2002. The 2012–2013 iteration incorporated a Myspace.com access to the competition. The 2014 competition is described at the Ford Models website at *V Magazine*, "Model Search," n.d., www.fordmodelsblog.com/featured/the-2014-ford-vvman-model-search-is-here/#slide-2, accessed March 18, 2015.

26 The winner had been selected the day before, from the thousands of hopefuls who had competed that week, and then "declared" the winner that night.

27 Ashley Sabin and David Redmon, *Girl Model* (documentary; United States: Carnivalesque Films, 2012).

28 Anthony Slide, *Inside the Hollywood Fan Magazine: A History of Star Makers, Fabricators, and Gossip Mongers* (Jackson: University Press of Mississippi, 2010), 15.

29 Modelnews.com, at modelnews.com, accessed June 2012. While this particular comment has since been taken down, many modeling websites include warnings about scams, such as the Model Mayhem "Newbie Forum" section devoted to teaching new models about scams; see "Newbie Forum: New Models: Learn about Scams," *Model Mayhem*, n.d., www.modelmayhem.com/forums/post/575330, accessed March 18, 2015. For a complete listing of similar complaints, see "John Casablancas Modeling: Consumer Complaints and Reviews," n.d., *Consumer Affairs*, www.consumeraffairs.com/modeling/john_casablancas.html, accessed March 19, 2015.

30 Les Henderson, *Under Investigation: The Inside Story of the Florida Attorney General's Investigation of Wilhelmina Scouting Network, the Largest Model and Talent Scam in America* (Azilda, ON: Coyote Ridge Publishing, 2006), 28.

31 Mears, *Pricing Beauty*, 74.

32 Gina Neff, *Venture Labor: Work and the Burden of Risk in Innovative Industries* (Cambridge, MA: MIT Press, 2012); see also Gina Neff, Elizabeth Wissinger, and Sharon Zukin, "Entrepreneurial Labor among Cultural Producers: 'Cool' Jobs in 'Hot' Industries," *Social Semiotics* 15, no. 3 (2005): 307–334.

33 The term "comp card" is short for "composite card," a model's business card and resume rolled into one. The comp card is usually on card stock or a page online with photos of the model showing the various "looks" the model can produce and usually includes a full-body shot and a close-up. The comp card lists the model's stats, including her measurements and agency contact information. Models usually pay out of pocket to have these cards produced.

34 Although my sample does not profess to be scientific, eleven out of the thirty-two I interviewed came into the business via entering a modeling contest or being scouted, with three being men and eight being women.

35 These attitudes resonate with values put forth by the self-help and business management literature that preaches that one must "play to your strengths" and "leverage your assets," unquestioned adages for the post-industrial "gig" worker. See Ruth Milkman and Ed Ott's *New Labour in New York: Precarious Workers and the Future of the Labour Movement* (New York: ILR Press, 2014), 154, regarding the "gig economy"; or Paul Mladjenovic, *Micro Entrepreneurship for Dummies* (Hoboken, NJ: Wiley, 2013), regarding gig work. The message: You fit the model type, so you should monetize this! Or you have no work ethic! Regardless of what other talents and interests you have, your look is the most valuable thing about you in our image economy. (I thank the sociologist Pamela Donovan for pointing out this connection.)

36 Stephanie Sadre-Orafai, "The Figure of the Model and Reality TV," in *Fashioning Models: Image, Text, and Industry*, ed. Joanne Entwistle and Elizabeth Wissinger (London: Berg, 2012), 119–133, quote at 120. Here she is referring to analysis by communication scholars Laurie Ouellette and James Hay.

37 Ibid., 120.

38 Nathan Ellis, "Exit the Supermodel, Enter the Superagency: Synergy and Diversification, Not First-Name Fame and Fabulousness, are the New Priorities of the Model Business," *Tearsheet.com*, 2001. This text is no longer on the *Tearsheet.com* website, but is in the author's archives.

39 Nebahat Tokatli, "Global Sourcing: Insights from the Global Clothing Industry— the Case of Zara, a Fast Fashion Retailer," *Journal of Economic Geography* 8 (2008): 21–38, regarding "massclusivity," see 23.

40 Minh-Ha T. Pham, forthcoming book planned on shifting technologies and structures of Asian fashion labor in the twenty-first century, discussed at her faculty page, Minh-Ha Pham, Cornell University, Asian American Studies Program, http://asianamericanstudies.cornell.edu/people/Pham.cfm, accessed January 30, 2015.

41 Henry Jenkins, *Convergence Culture: Where Old and New Media Collide* (New York: NYU Press, 2006), 20.

42 The need to, as the saying goes, to "put yourself out there," is characteristic of the "creative risk taking" and the "proactive" values held dear by the venture laborers Neff describes; see Neff, *Venture Labor*, 66, 81.

43 Barbie's recent career moves include not only spaceflight and architecture but also computer engineering and paleontology (see, e.g., www.amazon.com/

Astronaut-Barbie/dp/B004ICRE78, www.amazon.com/Barbie-Can-Architect
-Doll-Playset/dp/B0043WAP56/ref=pd_bxgy_t_text_y, www.amazon.com/
Barbie-Can-Computer-Engineer-Doll/dp/B0042ESG9W/ref=sr_1_3?ie=UTF8&
qid=1359061239&sr=8-3&keywords=architect+barbie, and www.amazon.com/
Barbie-Can-Be-Paleontologist-Doll/dp/B006403UK8/ref=pd_bxgy_t_text_z, all
accessed January 30, 2015).

44 Colorforms Products, "Magic Fashion Show," n.d., www.colorforms.com/magic
-fashion-show.htm, accessed August 31, 2014.

45 Mattel's Barbie Fashion Show, at www.amazon.com/Neat-Oh-Barbie-Fashion
-Dressing-Runway/dp/B006ZAU85Q, n.d., accessed March 20, 2015.

46 Polly Pocket Fashion Frenzy Superset, n.d., http://www.amazon.com/Polly
-Pocket-Fashion-Frenzy-Superset/dp/B0017UXNNS, accessed September 14, 2014.

47 Zhu Zhu Pets Fashion Catwalk, n.d., www.amazon.co.uk/Zhu-Pets-Fashion
-Catwalk-Pet/dp/B004TJ10T8, accessed January 30, 2015.

48 The Cre8Institute Modeling Camp, www.cre8tinstitute.com/modeling.html,
accessed June 12, 2012.

49 See "Fashion Week Tour," n.d., www.fashionweektour.com. Brochures are available in English and Chinese.

50 A recent visit to the Remote Lands website (www.remotelands.com) revealed that
this tour is no longer offered, perhaps a casualty of the global financial crisis that
started in 2008.

51 As Banet-Weiser has noted, processes of self-branding directed at girls play
especially on the notion of consumerism as empowerment, that one can become
what Anita Harris calls a "can-do" girl, the queen of self-determination (*Future
Girl: Young Women in the Twenty-First Century* [New York: Routledge, 2004]).
Banet-Weiser's riff off of Anita Harris's analysis of American girlhood dovetails
with Rosalind Gill's astute observation that, in the post-feminist culture prevalent
in Web 2.0, a young girl's body is construed as both a source of power and "as
always already unruly and requiring constant monitoring, surveillance, discipline
and remodeling (and consumer spending) in order to conform to ever narrower
judgments of female attractiveness" ("Postfeminist Media Culture: Elements
of Sensibility," *European Journal of Cultural Studies* 10, no. 2 (2007): 147–166),
quoted in Banet-Weiser, *Authentic™*, 62). Similarly, Alice Marwick notes that in
the age of Web 2.0, participatory culture's promise to confer new liberties har-
nesses individuals instead into endless cycles of self-branding and other forms of
status seeking in order to become legitimate actors on the public scene. See Alice
Marwick, *Status Update: Celebrity, Publicity, and Branding in the Social Media Age*
(New Haven, CT: Yale University Press, 2013).

52 Nguyen, "Biopower," 374.

53 Ibid., 360, 374.

54 In a similar vein, Minh-Ha T. Pham calls out authorities linking fashion to freedom in post-9/11 politics in "The Right to Fashion in the Age of Terrorism," *Signs:
Journal of Women in Culture and Society* 36, no. 2 (Winter 2011): 385–410.

55 Nguyen, "Biopower," 374.

56 As famously stated in George Orwell's *Animal Farm: A Fairy Story* (London: Secker & Warburg, 1945).

57 See, e.g., diversity in the modeling advocate Ben Barry's work, "Selling Whose Dream? A Taxonomy of Aspiration in Fashion Imagery," *Fashion, Style, and Popular Culture* 1, no. 2 (2014): 175–192; or the Canadian documentary *The Colour of Beauty*, dir. Elizabeth St. Philip (Toronto: National Film Board of Canada, 2010). See also Brent Huff, dir., *Chasing Beauty: The Ugly Side of Being Pretty* (documentary; New York: Viacom, Logo TV, 2013).

CHAPTER 8. BLACK-BLACK-BLACK

1 Within modeling, there are two distinct markets: one for fashion and runway modeling, and one for commercial modeling. Fashion models tend to cultivate an "edgy" or editorial look, i.e., extremely thin, sexually remote, with a kind of beauty or attractiveness that does not tend to appeal to a mainstream public, instead appealing to the fringe or edges. Editorial models' work appears most often in the non-advertising pages of a fashion magazine. Editorial models are hired by fashion editors to depict the latest trends to a relatively narrow market. In contrast, commercial models work for advertisers to sell products, from clothing to laundry detergent, and therefore need mass demographic appeal. This distinction in modeling resembles the divide between avant-garde and commercial art (Ashley Mears, "Size Zero High-End Ethnic: Cultural Production and the Reproduction of Culture in Fashion Modeling," *Poetics* 38, no. 1 [2010]: 21–46; and Joanne Entwistle, "The Aesthetic Economy: The Production of Value in the Field of Fashion Modeling," *Journal of Consumer Culture* 2, no. 3 [2002]: 317–339).

2 Antoine also may have been comfortable saying these things to me because my own background as a Caucasian woman. My appearance facilitated asking about race in most of the interviews, as my respondents seemed to assume I had no agenda regarding the issue, and they therefore spoke relatively freely about it. I also found that the black models and the Latin model agent I interviewed appreciated having the forum to talk about issues that they usually kept to themselves; one model made it very clear the importance of seeing these ideas get into print, grabbing the recorder enthusiastically and saying "Are you listening, people?"

3 See the statistics at the U.S. Bureau of Labor Statistics's *Occupational Outlook Handbook* page on "Models," January 8, 2014, www.bls.gov/ooh/sales/models.htm, accessed March 17, 2015. In 2008, the U.S. Bureau of Labor Statistics's *Occupational Outlook Handbook* (www.bls.gov/ooh) included at that time a somewhat telling descriptive photo illustration of two working models, both of whom were slender, female, and white. Corresponding illustrative photos of "top executives" depicted two portly, older, white gentlemen, while the entry for "security guard" depicted a burly African American man (www.bls.gov/oco/ocos337.htm, www.bls.gov/oco/ocos012.htm, and www.bls.gov/oco/ocos159.htm, accessed January 25, 2008. Since then, the webpage has been updated and shows a black female model, as well as a

male model, on the "Models" page, and the "top executive" and "security guard" pages prominently feature women and people of color.

4 See, e.g., Louise France, "Black. Beautiful. Barely Seen," *Guardian*, November 1, 2008, www.guardian.co.uk/lifeandstyle/2008/nov/02/bethann-hardison-black -models, accessed August 28, 2014.

5 Constance C. R. White, "Blackout: What Has Happened to the Black Models?" *Ebony*, September 2008, http://books.google.com/books?id=OdMDAAAAMBAJ &lpg=PA98&ots=buaPUL2ZIP&dq=The%20black%20girls%20coalition&pg= PA100#v=onepage&q=Balenciaga&f=false, accessed August 28, 2013, is a typical example of how the story is told and the kinds of data that are used.

6 Sarah Mower, "Fashion World Stunned by Vogue for Black," *Guardian*, July 26, 2008, www.theguardian.com/lifeandstyle/2008/jul/27/fashion.pressandpublishing, accessed February 3, 2015.

7 Anna Holmes, "Where Are All the Black Models? Let's Start by Asking Anna Wintour," *Jezebel*, October 15, 2007, http://jezebel.com/310667, accessed October 20, 2009.

8 Scott Plous and Dominic Neptune, "Racial and Gender Bias in Magazine Advertising," *Psychology of Women Quarterly* 21 (1997): 627–644. These researchers found that black models appeared in approximately 10 percent of the advertisements in magazines that were oriented toward white readers, a proportion that more closely represents the proportion of black people in the population of the United States. Other research has shown that there have been more images of black people in magazine photographs in recent years but that these may be concentrated in specific areas, such as the sports section of the magazine (Tara-Nicholle Beasley Delouth, Brigitte Person, Daryl Hitchcock, And Beth Menees Rienzi, "Gender and Ethnic Role Portrayals: Photographic Images in Three California Newspapers," *Psychological Reports* 76 (1995): 493–494.

9 Mears, "Size Zero," 23.

10 Minority women in particular are disproportionately affected by unemployment: "The unemployment rate for all women was 8.1 percent and 10.3 percent for men in 2009. For Asian women it was 6.6 percent; white women, 7.3 percent; Hispanic women, 11.5 percent; and black women, 12.4 percent. Black women and men exhibited the lowest employment rates of all workers in 2009 (57.3 and 59.1 percent of all eligible workers respectively, as compared to 62.8 percent for white women and 69.7 for white men)" (U.S. Bureau of Labor Statistics, "Labor Force Statistics from the Current Population Survey: Women in the Labor Force: A Databook [2009 Edition], Table 3. Employment Status by Race, Age, Sex, and Hispanic or Latino ethnicity, 2008 Annual Averages," www.bls.gov/cps/wlftable3 .htm, accessed May 2015).

11 Eric Wilson, "Fashion's Blind Spot," *New York Times*, August 8, 2013.

12 Zandile Blay, "The *Essence* Controversy Is More than Skin-Deep," http://nymag .com/thecut/2010/08/the_essence_controversy.html, accessed September 16, 2014.

13 Mears, "Size Zero," 25.

14 Ibid.

15 In her *Complete Idiot's Guide to Becoming a Model* (New York: Alpha Books, 1999), 292, the former model Roshumba Williams defined an "ethnic" model as "anyone who isn't considered Caucasian, meaning anyone of Spanish, Asian, or African descent."

16 Stephanie Neda Sadre-Orafai, "Developing Images: Race, Language and Perception in Fashion Model Casting," in *Fashion as Photograph: Viewing and Reviewing Fashion Images*, ed. Eugénie Shinkle (London: I. B. Taurus, 2008): 141–153, esp. 150.

17 Ibid., 149.

18 The idea of the corporate gaze is based on Laura Mulvey's conception of the "male gaze" in film, in which the spectator is pulled into line with male desire, as the one who is looking, whereas females become objects rather than actors in the narrative, presented in their "to-be-looked-at-ness"; see Laura Mulvey, *Visual and Other Pleasures* (1989; reprint: New York: Palgrave, 2009), 19. The corporate gaze shapes employees to the corporation's desire, delineating how they should appear, in line with corporate needs, and the spectators take on the corporation's desire as their own.

19 Frantz Fanon, *Black Skin, White Masks* (1952; reprint, New York: Grove Press, 2008); S. Elizabeth Bird, "Gendered Construction of the American Indian in Popular Media," *Journal of Communication* 49, no. 3 (1999): 61–83.

20 Fanon, *Black Skin*, 92.

21 Donald Bogle, *Primetime Blues: African Americans on Network Television* (New York: Farrar, Straus & Giroux, 2001); bell hooks, *Black Looks: Race and Representation* (Boston: South End Press, 1992); Patricia Hill Collins, *Black Sexual Politics: African Americans, Gender, and the New Racism* (New York: Routledge, 2004); and Marci Bounds Littlefield, "The Media as a System of Racialization Exploring Images of African American Women and the New Racism," *American Behavioral Scientist* 51, no. 5 (2008): 675–685.

22 Elspeth Brown, "Black Models and the Invention of the Negro Market: 1945–1960," in *Inside Marketing: Practices, Ideologies, Devices*, ed. Detlev Zwick and Julien Cayla (Oxford: Oxford University Press, 2011), 189–190.

23 Ibid., 192.

24 Ibid., 189.

25 Ibid., 195.

26 Ibid.; Laila Haidarali, " 'Giving Coloured Sisters a Superficial Equality': Remodelling African American Womanhood in Early Post-war America," in *Fashioning Models: Image, Text and Industry*, ed. Joanne Entwistle and Elizabeth Wissinger (London: Berg, 2012), 56.

27 Haidarali, "Giving Colored Sisters," 62.

28 Ibid.,70.

29 Ibid.,59.

30 Brown, "Black Models," 202.

31 Haidarali, "Giving Coloured Sisters," 60.

32 Ibid.,71.

33 Ibid.,72.

34 Ibid.,76–77.

35 Ibid.,76.

36 Candy Jones, *Modeling and Other Glamour Careers* (New York: Parker & Row, 1969), 83.

37 Patricia Soley-Beltran, "Charming Power: Models as Ideal Embodiments of Normative Identity," *Trípodos: Llenguatge, Pensament, Comunicació* 18 (2006): 29.

38 Although she hailed from Detroit, Donyale Luna worked predominantly in Europe, and the different history of racial tensions there coded her unique look as "mixed" rather than "black."

39 Haidarali, "Giving Colored Sisters," 78.

40 Ibid.

41 The 1970s runway "coup" was most recently documented by Deborah Riley Draper in her documentary *Versailles '73: American Runway Revolution* (2012), showing the Battle of Versailles, a fashion face-off including five American and five French designers. The Americans' thirty-five-minute fashion show used eight black models of the eleven who walked, including Pat Cleveland, and shocked even the French into realizing that American fashion had arrived.

42 Nina Blanchard, *How to Break into Motion Pictures, Television, Commercials and Modeling* (New York: Doubleday, 1978), 194.

43 Francine Marlowe, *Your Career Opportunities in Modeling* (New York: Barbizon Int'l, 1983), 19.

44 Jones, *Modeling*, 69.

45 Williams, *Complete Idiot's Guide*, 292.

46 Notably, after the late 1970s, the model "how-to" books I consulted ceased to differentiate between black and white models. Discussions of "Negro" modeling were gone, and separate mentions of "ethnic" or "black" modeling disappeared. Several 1980s treatments did not mention or depict black models at all. A 1998 book, however, discussed briefly how the "color line" in modeling still existed (see Donna Rubinstein, *The Modeling Life* [New York: Berkley, 1998], 74). Despite efforts to counteract its influence, it has not fully disappeared. A flurry of articles in the late 2000s seems to have made no difference (see, e.g., Jenna Sauers, "Fewer Models of Color Work New York's Fashion Runways," *Jezebel*, February 22, 2010, jezebel.com/5476920/fewer-models-of-color-work-new-yorks-fashion-runways, accessed February 3, 2015; Guy Trebay, "Ignoring Diversity, Runways Fade to White," *New York Times*, 14 October 2007, www.nytimes.com/2007/10/14/fashion/shows/14race.html?pagewanted=all, accessed February 3, 2015). Telling almost the same story half a decade later, the color line in fashion once again made headlines in 2013 (see, e.g., Allison P. Davis, "The Cut: What Prada's New Black Model Means for Fashion," *New York Magazine*, July 2, 2013).

47 Iman is the iconic Somali model of the 1970s and 1980s, who is currently married to David Bowie.

48 Alek Wek is a Sudanese model who started modeling in 1995 after being discovered in an outdoor market in London.

49 Anne Witz, Chris Warhurst, and Dennis Nickson, "The Labour of Aesthetics and the Aesthetics of Organization," *Organization* 10, no. 1 (2003): 33–54; see also Chris Warhurst, Dennis Nickson, Anne Witz, and Anne Marie Cullen, "Aesthetic Labour in Interactive Service Work: Some Case Study Evidence from the 'New' Glasgow," *Service Industries Journal* 20, no. 3 (2000): 1–18; Chris Warhurst and Dennis Nickson, "'Who's Got the Look?' Emotional, Aesthetic and Sexualized Labour in Interactive Services," *Gender, Work and Organization* 16, no. 3 (2009): 385–404; Dennis P. Nickson, Christopher Warhurst, Anne Witz, and Anne Marie Cullen, "The Importance of Being Aesthetic: Work, Employment and Service Organization," in *Customer Service: Empowerment and Entrapment*, ed. Andrew Sturdy, Irena Grugulis, and Hugh Willmott (Basingstoke: Palgrave, 2001), 170–190; Dennis Nickson, Chris Warhurst, Anne Marie Cullen, and Allan Watt, "Bringing in the Excluded? Aesthetic Labour, Skills and Training in the 'New' Economy," *Journal of Education and Work* 16, no. 2 (2003): 185–203; Lynne Pettinger, "Brand Culture and Branded Workers: Service Work and Aesthetic Labour in Fashion Retail," *Consumption Markets and Culture* 7, no. 2 (2004): 165–184; Leslee Spiess and Peter Waring, "Aesthetic Labour, Cost Minimisation and the Labour Process in the Asia Pacific Airline Industry," *Employee Relations* 27, no. 2 (2005): 193–207; Deborah Dean, "Recruiting a Self: Women Performers and Aesthetic Labour," *Work, Employment and Society* 19, no. 4 (2005): 761–774; Chris Warhurst and Dennis Nickson, "A New Labour Aristocracy? Aesthetic Labour and Routine Interactive Service," *Work, Employment and Society* 21, no. 4 (2007): 785–798, and "Employee Experience of Aesthetic Labour in Retail and Hospitality," *Work, Employment and Society* 21, no. 1 (2007): 103–120. When aesthetic labor was first identified, researchers found that workers were aligning their look and demeanor with clear-cut corporate codes, in which details of personal behavior—such as how to address superiors—and details of appearance—such as whether or not to wear a suit, how to wear one's hairstyle, and for women, the appropriate makeup—were dictated by one's employer.

50 Witz et al., "The Labour of Aesthetics," 33. See also Warhurst et al., "Aesthetic Labour"; Nickson et al., "The Importance of Being Aesthetic" and "Bringing in the Excluded?"; Pettinger, "Brand Culture"; Speiss and Waring, "Aesthetic Labour, Cost Minimization"; Dean, "Recruiting a Self,"; and Warhurst and Nickson, "A New Labour Aristocracy?" "Employee Experience," and "'Who's Got the Look?'"

51 Joanne Entwistle and Elizabeth Wissinger, "Keeping Up Appearances: Aesthetic Labour in the Fashion Modelling Industries of London and New York," *Sociological Review* 54, no. 4 (2006): 774–794; Ashley Mears, *Pricing Beauty: The Making of a Fashion Model* (Los Angeles: University of California Press, 2011), 88.

52 A finding corroborated by both Dean, "Recruiting a Self"; and Mears, "Size Zero."

53 See Susan Bordo, *Unbearable Weight: Feminism, Western Culture, and the Body* (Berkeley: University of California Press, 1993), for a fascinating discussion of "whitening" ethnic features through surgery or colored contacts (in the chapters "Whose Body Is This?" and "Material Girl").

54 Elizabeth St. Philip, dir., *The Colour of Beauty* (Toronto: National Film Board of Canada, 2010).

55 Naomi Sims is famous for being the first black model to appear on the cover of *Ladies Home Journal* in 1968.

56 Beverly Johnson was the first African American model to appear on the cover of the American *Vogue* magazine in 1974.

57 Guy Trebay, "A Black Model Reaches the Top, a Lonely Spot," *New York Times*, April 8, 2003.

58 Deborah Dean, "No Human Resource Is an Island: Gendered, Racialized Access to Work as a Performer," *Gender, Work and Organization* 15 (2008): 161–181, esp. 176.

59 J. T. Parsons, *Contemporary Research on Sex Work* (Binghamton, NY: Hawthorne Press, 2005).

60 Sut Jhally, dir., and Jean Kilbourne, *Killing Us Softly 3* (documentary; Northampton, MA: Media Education Foundation, 2000).

61 Soley-Beltran, "Charming Power," 30.

62 Trebay, "Ignoring Diversity."

63 Littlefield, "The Media as a System," 678.

64 Rob Sharp, "Fashion Is Racist: Insider Lifts Lid on Ethnic Exclusion," *Independent*, February 16, 2008, www.independent.co.uk/news/uk/home-news/fashion-is-racist-insider-lifts-lid-on-ethnic-exclusion-782974.html, accessed September 9, 2014.

65 Trebay, "Ignoring Diversity," 2008.

66 American Apparel and Footwear Association, *Trends: An Annual Statistical Analysis of the Apparel and Footwear Industries*, 2007 annual ed. (Arlington, VA: American Apparel and Footwear Association, 2008).

67 Five foot six is one to two inches shorter than the minimum desired height in the industry.

68 *America's Next Top Model*, cycle 9: The show's third season on the CW network. The first episode aired September 19, 2007.

69 William R. Corbett, "The Ugly Truth about Appearance Discrimination and the Beauty of Our Employment Discrimination Law," *Duke Journal of Gender, Law, and Policy* 14, no. 153 (2007): 157–158.

70 Chris Warhurst, Diane van den Broek, Richard Hall, and Dennis Nickson, "Lookism: The New Frontier of Employment Discrimination?" *Journal of Industrial Relations* 51, no. 1 (2008): 131–136.

71 A lawsuit filed against Abercrombie & Fitch, a nationwide retailer of clothes popular with teens and young people, highlighted the potential for unfairness

when companies seek to hire workers who subjectively "look good and sound right" over those who might bring a more complete suite of skills to the workplace. The lawsuit argued that the clothing chain discriminated against "blacks, Hispanics and Asians, by enforcing a nationwide corporate policy of preferring white employees for sales positions, desirable job assignments, and favorable work schedules" and encouraged recruitment from white fraternities and sororities (Associated Press, "Abercrombie & Fitch Faces Discrimination Lawsuit," *USA Today*, June 17, 2003). Similarly, in a case concerning the "hip" Mondrian Hotel in Los Angeles, several employees were fired for being "too ethnic" and were replaced by "15 new employees, whom the *Los Angeles Times* later described as 'cool looking white guys'" (Milford Prewitt, "Critics Say 'Good Looks' Win Job Advantages While Others Shut Out, EEOC: Many Believe 'Face Value' More Important than Skill," *Nation's Restaurant News*, May 12, 2003).

72 *Vogue Italia*, "The Black Issue," July 2009. Notably, this issue is selling for about $100 on eBay as of this writing.

73 The *Washington Post*'s Robin Givhan claimed von Furstenburg's choice was a mixture of both aesthetics and politics. The show seemed less about a politically charged "ethnocentric aesthetic" than von Furstenburg's palette, which seemed custom-made to be especially flattering to people of color (Robin Givhan, "In New York, 'Black Style' Spins the Color Wheel," *Washington Post*, September 12, 2006). More recently, von Furstenberg has been praised for being one of the "few designers who used more than one model of color in her Fall 2013" show (Laura Mallonee, "'The Result Is Racism': Former Supermodel Condemns New York Fashion Week's Lack of Diversity," *Observer*, September 6, 2013, http://observer.com/2013/09/bethann-hardison-letters-condemning-fashion-week-racism-models, accessed September 5, 2014).

74 Michel Foucault, quoted by Patricia Clough, "The Affective Turn: Political Economy, Biomedia and Bodies," *Theory, Culture and Society* 25, no. 1 (2008): 18.

75 Ibid.

76 Mimi Thi Nguyen, "The Biopower of Beauty: Humanitarian Imperialisms and Global Feminisms in an Age of Terror," *Signs* 36, no. 2 (Winter 2011): 360, 366.

77 Immanuel Kant, *Critique of Judgement*, trans. Werner S. Pluhar (1790; reprint, Indianapolis, IN: Hackett Publishing Co., 1987), 112; Nguyen, "Biopower," 360.

78 Kant, *Critique* of Judgement, 98, Nguyen, "Biopower" 362.

79 Nguyen, "Biopower," 363.

80 See the opening spread for the feature "Wild Things" in *Harper's Bazaar*, September 1999, featuring Naomi Campbell, photo by Jean-Paul Goude.

CHAPTER 9. TOUCH-UPS

1 This experiment resembles the "Golden Mean," the *Vanity Fair* November 1933 cover that merged the faces of Marlene Dietrich, Greta Garbo, Joan Crawford, and other stars into a "blandly pretty face," but achieving such an effect was far more difficult, and less widespread, in the 1930s than it would become sixty years later.

2 "The appearance of the waif in a patriarchal culture that has been significantly challenged by multiple feminisms was interpreted as a rebuke to feminists" (Thomas Shevory, *Body Politics: Studies in Reproduction, Production and (Re)Construction* [Westport, CT: Praeger, 2000], 186). It is notable that the waifs and Susan Faludi's *Backlash: The Undeclared War against American Women* (New York: Crown, 1991) became best-sellers around the same time.

3 Leisa Barnett, "Death of the Supermodel," *Vogue*, September 4, 2007, www.vogue.co.uk/news/2007/09/04/death-of-the-supermodel, accessed July 3, 2014; also see Harold Koda and Kohle Yohannan, *The Model as Muse: Embodying Fashion* (New Haven, CT: Yale University Press, 2009), 191.

4 See A. A. Gil, "The Silent Beauty," *Vanity Fair*, no. 553 (September 2006): 344–351, which discusses how Kate Moss made a habit of not speaking in public at the time. The cult of personality lived on in the actresses who usurped the models on the covers of magazines. Industry insiders attribute this shift to a new cautiousness on the part of clients due to the consolidation of small fashion houses into larger corporations and the growth of celebrity magazines and the culture of celebrity worship that resurged during the 1980s. Some argued that the supermodels had become so expensive it was the same price to get an actress, which some clients found more "relatable," in industry parlance. Interestingly, this phenomenon seems to be more American than anything else, as fashion models were not kicked off the covers of fashion magazines in other countries. While American *Vogue* has not had a model on the cover in years, *Vogue Italia*, Spanish *Vogue*, and Chinese *Vogue* routinely featured models on their covers, as they do currently.

5 The concept of "node" is found in Donna Jeanne Haraway, *Simians, Cyborgs, and Women: The Reinvention of Nature* (New York: Routledge, 1991), 200.

6 The social theorist Patricia Clough, citing the critical theorist Mark Hansen's work, has referred to affectivity as "the body's internal sense of its movement, its tendencies or incipiencies," which, Clough adds, gives access to the sense of the body's own indeterminacy (Patricia Clough, introduction to *The Affective Turn: Theorizing the Social*, ed. Patricia Clough and Jean Halley [Durham, NC: Duke University Press, 2007], 5, 6, in reference to Mark Hansen, *New Philosophy for New Media* [Cambridge, MA: MIT Press, 2004], 7). See also Hansen, quoting the philosopher of the body Simondon: "Affectivity . . . appears to bring something from the exterior, indicating to the individualized being that it is not a complete and closed set [*ensemble*] of reality" (Gilbert Simondon, *L'individuation Psychique et Collective* (Paris: Aubier, 1989), 108, cited in Mark Hansen, *Bodies in Code* [New York: Routledge, 2006], 170–171, where Hansen points out that "it is, in short, affectivity that calls into being commonality beyond identity . . . affectivity, in sum, furnished the possibility for a 'resonance' beyond or beneath the category of the individual identity," an aspect of the concept that ties into the biopolitical organization of affective forces).

7 Melissa Gregg and Gregory Seigworth, eds., *The Affect Theory Reader* (Durham, NC: Duke University Press, 2010).

8 *Workout Starring Jane Fonda* (Karl-Lorimar Home Video, 1982). That same year, Reebok introduced the first aerobics shoe for women, and female office workers, their high heels stowed in shoulder bags, confidently strode to work in skirt suits and sneakers, breaking fashion's rules.

9 Koda and Yohannan, *Model as Muse*, 138.

10 Ibid., image of Naomi Campbell on 155, Christy Turlington on 165, and Linda Evangelista on 174.

11 Industry reports trace how the fitness industry grew from a "sport-specific enterprise appealing to a select few in the 1960s, to an industry of the 21st century targeted to the masses who have adopted fitness activities as a regular part of their daily routine," evidenced by these numbers:

> From 1987 to 1996, the number of Americans who were health club members increased from 13.8 million in 1987 to a high of 20.8 million in 1996. By 1993, nearly 43.9 million people in the United States reported they were involved in sport or fitness activities at least 100 days per year. (Matthew Robinson, *Profiles of Sport Industry Professionals: The People Who Make the Games Happen* [Boston: Jones & Bartlett Publishers, 2001], 309)

12 Under this logic, attacking excess flab and fat once again became a cultural obsession, but this time on a far grander scale. As the sociologist of sport Jennifer Smith Maguire has argued, the twentieth-century shift from linking fitness to social improvement of the population to the more narrow goals of self-improvement and self-actualization proved highly beneficial to the burgeoning consumer and service industries that catered to an ever-more appearance-driven culture. Although physical fitness was always an American concern, as Maguire argued, linking it to the notion of the body as a form of capital fueled an acceleration of the commercialization of fitness from the 1970s onward (Jennifer Smith Maguire, *Fit for Consumption: Sociology and the Business of Fitness* [New York: Routledge, 2007], 2, 24).

13 Michael Gross, *Model: The Ugly Business of Beautiful Women* (New York: Morrow, 1995), Gross, 495.

14 *Six Million Dollar Man* (television series; 1973–1978), *Terminator* (film; 1984), *Blade Runner* (film; 1982).

15 Bob Colacello, "A League of Their Own," *Vanity Fair* 50, no. 9 (September 2008): 358.

16 This aesthetic influence was contemporaneous with the mainstreaming of gay culture's body cult, which looked back to the idealization of the male physique in ancient Greece and Renaissance Italy (as my colleague, the literary theorist Ashley Dawson, has helpfully pointed out).

17 As the sociologist Carol Wolkowitz explained, workers became "humanware" when humans were "adapted to the capacities of microelectronics, rather than

vice versa," resulting in "an increasingly porous boundary between human beings and technology," since the "use of prostheses that extend human reach and precision adapt the human being and begin to dissolve the distinction between human and non-human" (*Bodies at Work* [London: Sage, 2006], 59).

18 Per the social theorist Nikolas Rose, in recent decades technical intervention on the body is no longer seen only in terms of "health and illness" but is rather aimed at "optimization," in which the goal is not to eradicate abnormality but to create a supernormal body, using technologies that make it possible to "refigure—or hope to refigure—vital processes themselves in order to maximize their functioning and enhance their outcomes" (Nikolas Rose, *The Politics of Life Itself: Biomedicine, Power, and Subjectivity in the 21st Century* [Princeton, NJ: Princeton University Press, 2006], 6, 18).

19 Tiziana Terranova, "Futurepublic: On Information Warfare, Bio-racism and Hegemony as Noopolitics," *Theory, Culture and Society* 24, no. 3 (May 2007): 125–145, quoting Brian Massumi on 137.

20 Lois Banner, *American Beauty* (New York: Knopf, 1983), 283.

21 Ibid., 129.

22 Susan Bordo, *Unbearable Weight: Feminism, Western Culture, and the Body* (Berkeley: University of California Press, 1993), 191.

23 Ibid., 189.

24 Ibid., 198–199.

25 Ibid.

26 In 2008 a controversy arose surrounding "too skinny" models after two models died within eighteen months. First, a Uruguayan model died, reportedly from anorexia with the complication of heart failure, moments after stepping off a runway during Fashion Week in Montevideo. Soon after, a Brazilian model, who some said had been living on apples and tomatoes, died of an anorexia nervosa–related infection. These deaths made international news, and in response, the organizers of Madrid Fashion Week placed a ban on "skinny" models walking in shows. This outcry echoed sentiments that have surfaced periodically. Echoing the bumper sticker reading "Forget OXFAM, feed Twiggy," Kate Moss's "so-thin-she's-practically-translucent" image prompted retaliatory graffiti saying "FEED ME" across her stomach: "Costumed in a white string bikini, her pale skin fading into the stark background, Moss gazes softly at passers-by from Calvin Klein posters all over Manhattan. Graffiti scrawled on her image loudly accuse Klein of promoting bulimia and anorexia. Feed me. Please send breadcrumbs c/o Calvin Klein. Calvin Klein wants to make you vomit. The offending words are often covered by fresh, anger-free posters overnight" (*New York Times*, "SUNDAY, May 22, 1994; Hitching a Ride," May 22, 1994, www.nytimes.com/1994/05/22/magazine/sunday-may-22-1994-hitching-a-ride.html, accessed September 14, 2014; "so thin" comment courtesy of sociologist Kristin Miller).

27 "Aleksandra Marczyk," *Traffic Models*, n.d., www.trafficmodels.com/women/964/aleksandra-marczyk, accessed March 10, 2015.

28 Measurements are taken from the following: "8 Naked Supermodels and Their 'Very Different' Measurements in *Love* Magazine," *Skinny vs Curvy*, February 3, 2010, www.skinnyvscurvy.com/kate-moss/8-naked-supermodels-very-different -measurements-love-magazine.html, accessed February 4, 2015; Anna Z.'s measurements are at http://wilhelmina.com/new-york/models/image/women/586216/ anna-z, accessed March 18, 2015.

29 See, e.g., Giselinde Kuipers's fascinating study of global beauty, "Towards a Comparative Sociology of Beauty," n.d., www.sociologyofbeauty.nl/about/info, accessed February 4, 2014.

30 Carol Byrd-Bredbenner and Jessica Murray, "A Comparison of the Anthropometric Measurements of Idealized Female Body Images in Media Directed to Men, Women, and Mixed Gender Audiences," *Topics in Clinical Nutrition* 18, no. 2 (2003): 117–129, esp. 123.

31 Sharlene Nagy Hesse-Biber, *The Cult of Thinness* (New York: Oxford University Press, 2007), 92. Hesse-Biber cites how gym memberships and sales of exercise videos have been on the rise since the 1980s: "Twenty years ago, there were 300 diet books in print, while in 2004, 'Amazon.com listed 439 books concerning weight loss' in that year alone!" In fact, "the number of diet books seems to have doubled consistently every four years since 1992" (4).

32 Vicki Pitts-Taylor, *Surgery Junkies: Wellness and Pathology in Cosmetic Culture* (New York: Rutgers University Press, 2007), 3.

33 Guy Trebay, "Fashion Diary: The Vanishing Point," *New York Times*, February 7, 2008.

34 Ibid.

35 Eric Wilson, "Front Row: Men, Breathe in and Hold It," *New York Times*, July 15, 2009.

36 Website for date Manx introduced: *Business World Online*, "Going Undercover," www.bworldonline.com/content.php?section=Arts&Leisure&title= Going-undercover&id=54762, accessed July 19, 2012; Neiman Marcus, "Spanx Zoned Compression Tees and Tanks" (webpage offering Spanx for men), www .neimanmarcus.com/p/Spanx-Zoned-Compression-Tees-Tanks-Personal-Furnishings/prod121560066/?ecid=NMCIGoogleProductAds&ci_sku= prod113900010skuWHITE&ci_gpa=pla&ci_kw={keyword}, accessed July 19, 2012.

37 Susan Bordo, *Unbearable Weight: Feminism, Western Culture, and the Body*, 10th anniversary ed. (Berkeley: University of California Press, 2003), xx.

38 See Chapter 8, in this volume, for a full discussion of race and modeling.

39 Gross, *Model*, 505.

40 A prime example of a model who seems to be playing this system to her great advantage is the model Cara Delevigne, who not only fronts numerous high-fashion campaigns, and has the most famous eyebrows in the business, but also boasts 2.2 million Twitter followers, and counting.

41 For an excellent treatment of how biotech began to amass biocapital, see Kaushik Sunder Rajan's *Biocapital: The Constitution of Postgenomic Life* (Durham, NC:

Duke University Press, 2006). See also Meika Loe, *The Rise of Viagra: How the Little Blue Pill Changed Sex in America* (New York: NYU Press, 2006).

42 The sociologist of science Nikolas Rose explains that biomedical technologies and developing sciences of molecular manipulation that were coming to prominence in the era of the blink were unlike "robotics and computing." While robotics and the like have made the body into a cyborg, "the new molecular enhancement technologies do not attempt to hybridize the body with mechanical equipment but to transform it at the organic level, to reshape vitality from the inside (Rose, *Politics of Life Itself*, 20).

43 While this depiction resembles the "enterprising" worker made well known by the social theorist Nikolas Rose, it differs in that the enterprising worker is not necessarily tasked with optimizing their body's health and productive potential in the same way as a glamour worker feels the need to do.

44 Rosalind Gill and Andy Pratt, "In the Social Factory? Immaterial Labour, Precariousness and Cultural Work," *Theory, Culture, and Society* 25, nos. 7–8 (2008): 1–30, referring to work by Rosalind Gill, "Technobohemians or the New Cybertariat? New Media Work in Amsterdam a Decade after the Web," report, Network Notebooks no. 1 (Amsterdam: Institute of Network Cultures, 2007); Angela McRobbie, "Top Girls? Young Women and the Post-feminist Sexual Contract," *Cultural Studies* 21, no. 4 (2007): 718–737; D. Perrons, "Living and Working Patterns in the New Knowledge Economy: New Opportunities and Old Social Divisions in the Case of New Media and Care Work," in *Gender Divisions in the New Economy: Changing Patterns of Work, Care and Public Policy in Europe and North America*, ed. C. Fagan, L. McDowell, D. Perrons, K. Ray, and K. Ward (London: Edward Elgar, 2007); and Andy Pratt, "New Media, the New Economy and New Spaces," *Geoforum* 31, no. 4 (2000): 425–436.

45 Joanna Zylinska, "Of Swans and Ugly Ducklings: Bioethics between Humans, Animals, and Machines," *Configurations* 15, no. 2 (2007): 125–150, esp. 142.

46 Jonathan Beller, "Capital/Cinema," in *Deleuze and Guattari: New Mappings in Politics, Philosophy, and Culture*, ed. Eleanor Kauffman and Kevin Jon Heller (Minneapolis: University of Minnesota Press, 1998), 92.

47 Judith P. Butler, *Bodies That Matter: On the Discursive Limits of "Sex"* (New York: Routledge, 1993).

48 The sociologist Patricia Clough's concept of the "biomediated body" delineated a body that is not informationally closed but, rather, a body in formation, one that exceeds its boundaries and, in fact, only exists within the networked capacities of mediation, both in terms of biology become media (as in the case of genetic science) and the blurring of spaces between bodies by new media, with all the time-space compression and radical connectivity it affords (Patricia Clough, "The Affective Turn: Political Economy, Biomedia and Bodies," *Theory, Culture and Society* 25, no. 1 [2008]: 2; see also Clough and Halley, *The Affective Turn*, 207).

49 Martin Heidegger, *Basic Writings*, ed. David Farrell Krell (1977; reprint, New York: Harper Collins, 1993), 309, 324.

50 Jeremy Gilbert-Rolfe, *Beauty and the Contemporary Sublime* (New York: Allworth Press, 1999), 15. It should be noted that the "lit from within" tendencies started in the glance regime of television, but were amplified by the regime of the blink.

51 Susan Sontag, *On Photography* (New York: Farrar, Straus & Giroux, 1977), 85, as quoted in Kaja Silverman, *The Threshold of the Visible World* (New York: Routledge, 1996), 197.

52 Sontag, ibid., 199.

53 Silverman, *The Threshold of the Visible World*, 201–202.

54 Ibid., 198, quoting Roland Barthes, *Camera Lucida: Reflections on Photography*, trans. Richard Howard (New York: Hill & Wang, 1981), 12.

55 Liz Moor, *The Rise of Brands* (Oxford: Berg, 2007), 3.

56 Johnathan Crary, *Suspensions of Perception* (Cambridge, MA: MIT Press, 2001), 138.

57 Ibid.

58 Ibid. With regard to the Kaiserpanorama, a "precinematic" device popular in the 1880s, which was used for viewing three-dimensional still images, usually of historic or geographically interesting scenes, Crary asked, "By what logic of temporal sequence and spatial continuity does one move from the interior of the papal apartments in Rome to the Great Wall of China to the Italian Alps at 120 second intervals?" (ibid.).

59 Silverman, *The Threshold of the Visible World*; Laura Mulvey, *Visual and Other Pleasures* (Bloomington: Indiana University Press, 1989).

60 See Patricia Clough, *Autoaffection: Unconscious Thought in the Age of Teletechnology* (Minneapolis: University of Minnesota Press, 2000), 99.

61 Richard Dienst, *Still Life in Real Time: Theory after Television* (Durham, NC: Duke University Press, 1994), 160.

62 Mary Ann Doane, "Information, Image, Catastrophe," in *Logics of Television*, ed. Patricia Mellencamp (Bloomington: Indiana University Press, 1990), 222–239, esp. 222.

63 Nigel Thrift, "Intensities of Feeling: Towards a Spatial Politics of Affect," *Geografiska Annaler*, 86 B (1): 62.

64 Nigel Thrift, *Non-representational Theory: Space, Politics, Affect* (New York: Routledge, 2007), 38.

65 Clough, "The Affective Turn."

66 Don Slater and Joanne Entwistle, "Models as Brands: Critical Thinking about Bodies and Images," in *Fashioning Models: Image, Text and Industry*, ed. Joanne Entwistle and Elizabeth Wissinger (London: Berg, 2012), 31.

CONCLUSION

1 The mainstreaming of affect as a concept in academia took place starting in the early 2000s, from the publication of Michael Hardt and Antonio Negri's *Empire* (Cambridge, MA: Harvard University Press, 2000) and Brian Massumi's *Parables for the Virtual: Movement, Affect, Sensation* (Durham, NC: Duke University Press,

2002) to Patricia Clough and Jean Halley, eds., *The Affective Turn: Theorizing the Social* (Durham, NC: Duke University Press, 2007) and Melissa Gregg and Gregory Seigworth, eds., *The Affect Theory Reader* (Durham, NC: Duke University Press, 2010), with the bulk of publications coming out in the latter half of that decade.

2 Clough and Halley, *The Affective Turn*; Elizabeth Grosz, *Space, Time, and Perversion: Essays on the Politics of Bodies* (New York: Routledge, 1995); Judith P. Butler, *Gender Trouble: Feminism and the Subversion of Identity* (New York: Routledge, 1990), and *Bodies That Matter: On the Discursive Limits of "Sex"* (New York: Routledge, 1993); and Donna Jeanne Haraway, *Simians, Cyborgs, and Women: The Reinvention of Nature* (New York: Routledge, 1991).

3 Erving Goffman, *Frame Analysis: An Essay on the Organization of Experience* (1974; reprint, Boston: Northeastern University Press, 1986), 572.

4 Haraway, *Simians, Cyborgs*.

5 Gregg and Seigworth, *The Affect Theory Reader*, 4.

6 Affects—e.g., the nexus between various emotional and bodily states—and bodily affect—e.g., the ability to be affected or moved by flows of bodily energy—are not the same thing. The first school of thought is the fixed-state position that stems from the work of the psychologist Silvan Tomkins, who posited nine basic affects corresponding to specific facial and bodily configurations, occurring when the body experiences a particular affective syndrome in response to stimulus. These states are called "affects" rather than "emotions" because they refer to syndromes the body may experience whether the subject is conscious of these phenomena (e.g., calling them emotions) or not. These states are interest-excitement, enjoyment-joy, surprise-startle, distress-anguish, shame-humiliation, contempt-disgust, anger-rage, fear-terror, and dismell (a form of contempt). See Silvan Tomkins, *The Negative Affects*, vol. 2 of *Affect, Imagery, Consciousness*, 4 vols. (London: Tavistock; New York: Springer, 1962–1992), as quoted in Anna Gibbs, "Disaffected," *Continuum: Journal of Media and Cultural Studies* 16 (2002): 335–341, esp. 338. The second school of thought approaches affect from a Deleuzian, Spinozist, Bergsonian bent, in which "affect" is posited as an impersonal flow that does not belong to any "body." This approach is exemplified by Brian Massumi's work (*Parables for the Virtual* and "Fear (the Spectrum Said)," *Positions: East Asia Cultures Critique* 13, no. 1 [2005]: 31–48), but it is also taken up by Mark Hansen (*Bodies in Code* [New York: Routledge, 2006]) and Patricia Clough (in Patricia Clough and Jean Halley, eds., *The Affective Turn: Theorizing the Social* [Durham, NC: Duke University Press, 2007]) and is treated in part by Melissa Gregg and Gregory Seigworth (*The Affect Theory Reader*).

7 The conscious experience of an affective syndrome of anger-rage, e.g., may range from total unawareness, if this reaction is too dangerous to be admitted to consciousness, to a sense of slight irritation, to a rapid escalation to overwhelming feeling, depending on how subjects have been socialized to feel or not to feel their affective responses—that is to say, how wide the subjects' "band of intensity"

within their "affect profile" is (Gibbs, "Disaffected," 338). This position has been heavily criticized by Ruth Leys owing to her claim that the delineation of these affective states was based on faulty data, particularly with regard to Paul Ekman's work on facial expressions. See Ruth Leys, "The Turn to Affect: A Critique," *Critical Inquiry* 37, no. 3 (2011): 434–472, in which she criticizes what she calls the "Tomkins-Ekman paradigm." For Tomkins, see Tomkins, *Affect, Imagery, Consciousness*, vols. 1–4; for Ekman, see, e.g., Paul Ekman, "Universal and Cultural Differences in Facial Expression of Emotion," in *Nebraska Symposium on Motivation*, ed. J. R. Cole (Lincoln: University of Nebraska Press, 1972), 207–283.

8 Maurya Wickstrom, *Performing Consumers: Global Capital and Its Theatrical Seductions* (New York: Routledge, 2006), 27.

9 As Emma Dowling explains, affective reconnaissance refers to the sense of the room one must employ in order to figure out what to do next. See Emma Dowling, "The Waitress: On Affect, Method, and (Re)Presentation," *Cultural Studies—Critical Methodologies* 12, no. 2 (April 2012): 109–117. The "sense of the room" riffs off of Teresa Brennan's notion of feeling "the atmosphere" in a room, as described in *The Transmission of Affect* (Ithaca, NY: Cornell University Press, 2004), 1.

10 Nigel Thrift, *Non-representational Theory: Space, Politics, Affect* (New York: Routledge, 2007), 243.

11 I use this definition because I think it is important to distinguish affect from the biological notion of unconscious, automatic reaction (in response to stimuli), and to avoid biological reductionism. Thus I consider the body a center of action and reaction, as per Henri Bergson's notion of the body as an image that is affecting and affected by contact with its surroundings as a center of indeterminacy. See Henri Bergson, *Matter and Memory*, trans. Nancy M. Paul and W. Scott Palmer (1912; reprint, New York: Dover Philosophical Classics, 2004). The moment of indetermination before a body acts involves an infolding of outside data.

12 Gregg and Seigworth, *The Affect Theory Reader*, 3.

13 Benedict de Spinoza, *Ethics*, trans. Edwin Curley (1994; reprint, New York: Penguin Books, 1996), 70.

14 Massumi, *Parables for the Virtual*, 24 (emphasis in the original).

15 Thrift, *Non-representational Theory*, 7.

16 Massumi, *Parables for the Virtual*, 195.

17 Massumi, *Parables for the Virtual*, and Thrift, *Non-representational Theory*, argue that emotions have a non-cognitive component and therefore are indeterminate in ways that allow for the logic of chance to govern affective processes. Constantina Papoulias and Felicity Callard argue this is selective use of the data (in "Biology's Gift: Interrogating the Turn to Affect," *Body and Society* 16, no. 1 [2010]: 29–56). Where Massumi sees evidence that affect is pre-cognitive and therefore implies an inherently unpredictable dynamism of the body that is not limited by language or reason, Joseph Ledoux, e.g., sees evidence of a deeply entrenched evolutionary basis for emotional scripts that shape what we think in response to these non-cognitive emotions; see Joseph E. Ledoux, *The Emotional Brain:*

The Mysterious Underpinnings of Emotional Life (New York: Simon & Schuster, 1996), as cited in Papoulias and Callard in "Biology's Gift," 41. In other words, this indetermination is clamped down into habits that are evolutionarily adaptive, and therefore the freedom of interpretation of affect is closed off before it can begin. Since making this argument, however, Ledoux, at least, has adjusted his position to allow for more flexibility in the functioning of these scripts in mental processes; see Joseph LeDoux, "Rethinking the Emotional Brain," *Neuron* 73, no. 5 (2012): 653–676.

18 Leys, "The Turn to Affect," 467.

19 Ibid., 452.

20 Ibid., 467.

21 See, e.g., Jesse Prinz's work on the non-intentionalist paradigm in philosophy, *Gut Reactions* (New York: Oxford University Press, 2006), or the ongoing debates in the history of emotions (as exemplified by William Reddy's efforts to find a middle ground by means of conceptualizing the "emotive" in *The Navigation of Feeling: A Framework for the History of Emotions* [New York: Cambridge University Press, 2001] or cognitivist ideas such as those found in David Konstan's *Pity Transformed* [London: Duckworth, 2001]).

22 For those who take an "intentionalist" stance, or what is sometimes referred to as the "cognitivist theory of the emotions," the idea that there could be any emotional feeling without knowing about its meaning is anathema (see Andrea Scarantino, "Insights and Blindspots of the Cognitivist Theory of Emotions," *British Journal for the Philosophy of Science* 61 [2010]: 729–768, for an informative discussion of these debates and how they are related to neuroscientific findings about the role of cognition in the production of fear). In contrast, the philosopher Jesse Prinz, in *Gut Reactions*, has convincingly argued the other side, associated with Williams James's theory of emotions, which claims that emotions are not judgments but physiological changes that bring about judgments. The James-Lange hypothesis is opposed to the claim that emotions are cognitive and the result of reasoning. It is a theory developed independently by two scholars, William James, in "The Physical Basis of Emotion," *Psychological Review* 1 (1894): 516–529, and Carl Lange, in "The Emotions: A Psychophysiological Study," trans. Istar A. Haupt from the authorized German translation of H. Kurella, in Carl G. Lange and William James, *The Emotions* (Baltimore: Williams & Wilkins, 1922). The sociologist Deborah Gould's findings also support James-Lange, with regard to the politics of affect. As she argued in her book, *Moving Politics*: "The non-conscious, noncognitive, nonlinguistic components of our feelings affect our sense of political possibilities and in other ways both incite and hinder political action. A focus on affect reminds us to take the visceral and bodily components of politics seriously, preserving for the concept of 'experience' some of its *felt* quality, some of the sense of being moved by the world around us" (emphasis in original; see Deborah Gould, *Moving Politics: Emotion and ACT-UP's Fight against AIDS* [Chicago: University of Chicago Press, 2009], 441). For reasons I elucidate

throughout the book, I come down on the James-Lange side of the debate, examining the non-cognitive aspects of glamour labor in the affective mode, especially in terms of how this approach better explains the changes in modeling over time that I observed.

23 See, e.g., John Cromby's arguments ("Integrating Social Science with Neuroscience: Potentials and Problems," *BioSocieties* 2 [2007]: 149–169), outlined in Papoulias and Callard, "Biology's Gift," 49.

24 For one of many reports on the Bangladesh factory collapse, see Saeed Ahmed and Leone Lakhani, "Bangladesh Building Collapse: An End to Recovery Efforts, a Promise of a New Start," *CNN*, June 14, 2013, www.cnn.com/2013/05/14/world/asia/bangladesh-building-collapse-aftermath, accessed August 2013.

25 As, in fact, Pamela Anderson's growing and shrinking breasts could attest, when she had her implants removed, and then put back in again.

26 For an excellent analysis of this phenomenon in plus-size modeling, see Amanda M. Czerniawski, *Fashioning Fat: Inside Plus-Size Modeling* (New York: NYU Press, 2015).

27 Kate Lyons, "'It Is NOT OKAY to Alter a Woman's Body': Australian Model Meaghan Kausman Shames Swimwear Label for 'Drastically' Photoshopping Her Features after Underwater Fashion Shoot" *Daily Mail*, August 26, 2014, www.dailymail.co.uk/news/article-2734400/Australian-model-calls-swimwear-label-drastically-photoshopping-photos-underwater-shoot.html, accessed September 14, 2014.

28 Minh-Ha T. Pham, "Why Fashion Should Stop Trying to Be Diverse," *Threadbared*, September 30, 2013, https://iheartthreadbared.wordpress.com/2013/09/30/just-stop, accessed February 5, 2015, reprinted as "'Diversity' in Fashion Will Never Be Enough," *Salon*, October 2, 3013, www.salon.com/2013/10/02/diversity_in_fashion_will_never_be_enough_partner, accessed August 23, 2014.

INDEX

Abercrombie & Fitch, 30
advertising: changing strategy of, 16, 23, 40, 42, 54–55, 161, 165, 268 (*see also* brands and branding); and display as uncovering (Gilbert-Rolfe), 97–98; duplicate advertising for black consumers, 217, 221–222; early print, 84–85; ethnic style, 231; historical expansion of, 117; increased use of models, 86, 117; the "pseudo-event" as "reality marketing" (Grazian), 177, 178; racial stereotypes and, 221, 232
aesthetic considerations, 62, 112, 114, 115; and model size, 124–125, 126; and race, 216, 225, 236, 241–242
"aesthetic markets" (Entwistle), 195
affect economy, 143, 145, 147, 155, 165, 184, 211, 225. *See also* labor: affective
"affective reconnaissance" (Dowling), 167, 269
affective turn (in scholarship), 267
affectivity, 5, 12–13, 16, 60, 142, 246, 248, 262, 266, 268, 270, 277; and advertising, 42, 58; and attachment, 19, 63, 75, 248; contagion of, in fashion, 14, 15, 26, 167, 260; interpersonal, 269, 270, 273; and media expansion, 44; and models' work, 80, 105, 106, 166, 170; and need for "quirkiness," 147; and television, 56, 63; volatility of, 142, 156, 168, 170, 188, 262
affect studies, 15, 267, 271–272
agencies, modeling, 25, 44, 45, 117, 170, 217; all-black, 217; "annuals" of, 27, 125,

126, 131; black agencies and respectability politics, 221–222; control over and treatment of models, 141–142; expanding number of, 117; expenditures, 190; "mother agency" system, 191; part-time work and black modeling through, 223; "poaching" of models, 45; professionalization of models, 117–119; startup expenses for models, 204; and stylists, 169. *See also* models, personal lives of
The Agency (television show), 182
agency "annuals," 27, 125, 126, 131
aging of models, 2, 100–101. *See also* models: age appearance of
Agins, Teri, 41
Albert, Prince of Monaco, 36
Alexander, J., 230
Alt, Carol, 167
Altman, Robert, 36
Amazonian. *See* glamazon/glamazonian
America's Next Top Model (television reality show), 182, 213, 230, 235; Nintendo's Wii version, 213
Amos 'n' Andy, 221
Anderson, Pamela, 252
André J. (drag queen), 197
Anna Z., 254
anorexic (look), 20, 157, 194
Antoine (casting director), 216
apartments, temporary, for models, 32, 257
Armani, Giorgio, 42
Arnault, Bernard ("Wolf in Cashmere"), 41

ABOUT THE AUTHOR

Elizabeth A. Wissinger is Associate Professor of Sociology at the Borough of Manhattan Community College and Associate Professor of Fashion Studies at the City University of New York Graduate Center. She is the co-editor of Fashioning Models: Image, Text, and Industry (2012) and has published on fashion, bodies, and technologies in academic journals and blogs. She lives in Manhattan with her husband, daughter, and beloved dog, Lucky .